Artists Citizens Philosophers

SEEKING THE PEACE OF THE CITY

An Anabaptist Theology of Culture

DUANE K. FRIESEN

Foreword by Glen Stassen

Herald Press

Scottdale, Pennsylvania
Waterloo, Ontario

Library of Congress Cataloguing-in-Publication Data
Friesen, Duane K.
    Artists, citizens, philosophers: seeking the peace of the city: an Anabaptist
theology of culture / Duane K. Friesen
        p.cm.
    Includes bibliographic references (p.) and index.
    ISBN 0-8361-9139-0 (alk. paper)
        1. Christianity and culture. 2. Anabaptists. 3. Peace—Religious aspects—
Christianity. I. Title.
BR115.C8 .F68 2000
261'.088'243—dc21   00-039587

The paper used in this publication is recycled and meets the minimum require-
ments of American National Standard for Information Sciences—Permanence
of Paper for Printed Library Materials, ANSI Z39.48-1984.

Grateful acknowledgment is made for permission to quote from the following
copyrighted sources, all rights reserved: in ch. 5, from Phil Stoltzfus, "How to
Stop Constructing Things: Kaufman, Wittgenstein, and the Pragmatic End of
Constructivism," *Mennonite Life* (March 1997), 37-43; in ch. 6, from the song,
"Little Boxes," words and music by Malvina Reynolds. 01962 Schroder Music
Co. (ASCAP) Renewed 1990; in ch. 6, excerpt from "Song (4)" from *Collected
Poems 1957-1982* by Wendell Berry. Copyright 1985 by Wendell Berry.
Reprinted by permission of North Point Press, a division of Farrar, Straus and
Giroux, LLC; in ch. 8 from Alain Epp Weaver, "We All Drink from the Same
Stream," *Mennonite Life* (March 1997), 10-18.

ARTISTS, CITIZENS, PHILOSOPHERS
Copyright © 2000 by Herald Press, Scottdale, Pa. 15683
    Published simultaneously in Canada by Herald Press,
    Waterloo, Ont. N2L 6H7. All rights reserved
Library of Congress Catalog Number: 00-39587
International Standard Book Number: 0-8361-9139-0
Printed in the United States of America
Book design by Michael A. King, Pandora Press U.S., in consultation
with Gwen M. Stamm, Herald Press
Cover design by Gwen M. Stamm, Herald Press

10 09 08 07 06 05 04 03 02 01 00   10 9 8 7 6 5 4 3 2 1

To order or request information, please call
1-800-759-4447 (individuals); 1-800-245-7894 (trade).
Website: www.mph.org

Artists
Citizens
Philosophers

By the rivers of Babylon—
there we sat down and there we wept
when we remembered Zion.
On the willows there
we hung up our harps.
For there our captors
asked us for songs,
and our tormentors asked for mirth, saying,
"Sing us one of the songs of Zion!"
How could we sing the Lord's song
in a foreign land?
—Psalm 137:1-4

These are the words of the letter that the prophet Jeremiah sent from
Jerusalem to the remaining elders among the exiles, and to the priests, the
prophets, and all the people, whom Nebuchadnezzar had taken into exile from
Jerusalem to Babylon. . . . It said: "Thus says the Lord of hosts, the God of
Israel, to all the exiles whom I have sent into exile from Jerusalem to Babylon:
Build houses and live in them; plant gardens and eat what they produce. Take
wives and have sons and daughters; take wives for your sons, and give your
daughters in marriage, that they may bear sons and daughters; multiply there,
and do not decrease. But seek the welfare [shalom] of the city where I have
sent you into exile, and pray to the Lord on its behalf, for in its welfare you
will find your welfare."
—Jeremiah 29:1-7

For Christians are not distinguished from the rest of humankind by country,
or by speech, or by dress. For they do not dwell in cities of their own, or use
a different language, or practice a peculiar life. This knowledge of theirs has
not been proclaimed by the thought and effort of restless people; they are not
champions of a human doctrine, as some people are. But while they dwell
in Greek or barbarian cities according as each person's lot has been cast,
and follow the customs of the land in clothing and food, and other matters
of daily life, yet the condition of citizenship which they exhibit is wonderful,
and admittedly strange. They live in countries of their own, but simply as
sojourners; they share the life of citizens, they endure the lot of foreigners;
every foreign land is to them a homeland ["fatherland" in the original],
and every homeland ["fatherland" in the original] a foreign land. . . . They
spend their existence upon the earth, but their citizenship is in heaven.
—The Epistle of Diognetus V:1-16 (second century)

"Do not be conformed to this world, but be transformed by the renewing
of your minds, so that you may discern what is the will of God—what is good
and acceptable and perfect."
—Romans 12:2

Contents

Foreword

IN CHRIST AND CULTURE, the usually fair and respectful H. Richard Niebuhr wrote the only chapter in all his publications that is unfair to its subject. He wrote that Anabaptists theoretically reject culture, while in fact having their own culture. (Niebuhr did praise Anabaptists for having influence far beyond their numbers because they do live the Christian life.) Duane Friesen not only gives the lie to the claim that Anabaptists reject culture in theory but develops a consistent, Trinitarian and Christologically embodied theology of culture. He is thoroughly Trinitarian. And he has an embodied Christology. He emphasizes Jesus' embodiment in his Jewish culture and the church's embodiment of the way of Jesus in our artistic, political, and pluralistic culture. And he tags the tradition of evasion of the way of Jesus that is so widespread in much of church history.

The central and guiding metaphor throughout the book is Jeremiah's admonition to Jews in exile in Babylon: "Seek the peace (shalom) of the city where you dwell" (Jer. 29:7). This was the motto of the East German churches under the rule of the especially dictatorial and harsh communist, Eric Honecker. Faced with policies they could not approve, discriminated against systematically by the government, and cut off from their sister and brother Christians in West Germany, they had three possibilities. They could compromise their faith and become apologists for the regime in hopes of currying favor and advantage. They could withdraw as much as possible and not accept that they were dwelling in a communist society. Or they could follow the advice of Jeremiah (and Karl Barth) and work honestly, come to the aid of those in need, and do what they could to seek the justice and peace that shalom entails, while being clear that this was by no means a Christian society. The East Germans chose the latter option, and they were a remarkably faithful church in a hard time.

I traveled, taught, preached, and dialogued in East Germany. I learned much and loved the Christians I got to know for the warmth of their hospitality, the spirit of their Christian commitment, the fervor of their praying, and the genuineness of their solidarity and community. I saw the motto, "seek the peace of the city where you dwell," in churches north and south, east and west, in East Germany. This is an admonition not to withdraw behind the church walls, dwelling on your homesickness for a Jerusalem or a Germany closed to you, but to seek the shalom of the society where God gives you your calling.

This is also a parable for us in the "free" West. Ours too is by no means a Christian society: it is a pluralistic, tolerant, individualistic, self-congratulatory, capitalistic, money-valuing society. Friesen tells of six black children who burned to death in Elkhart because of economic injustice. "I raise the issue of deep injustice in the context of our experience of undeserved privilege because we will be empowered to respond to the needs of others with a generous spirit only if our response flows out of gratitude and thanksgiving for the grace and giftedness of our lives. . . . It is disconcerting and shameful how many in our culture believe that they deserve what they have."

Duane Friesen believes we, like the people of God in exile in Babylon and in East Germany, are called not to become an inward-turned ghetto but to seek to do God's will in the city where we dwell. "Jesus' challenge to hunger and thirst for justice conflicts with the values and practices of the dominant culture. But this conflict of values should not lead the church to shrink from responsibility for the public sphere by withdrawing into a separate enclave, or by privatizing or spiritualizing the Christian faith. Exile is a call to proclaim God's rule which is breaking into history, and to live by practices that can make life flourish in the cosmos."

Friesen was set on the course of this book by lectures he heard John Howard Yoder give, in which Yoder made Jeremiah 29:7 central. Some of those Yoder lectures have since been published in his *For the Nations*, a title distinguishing Yoder's understanding of God's will for the church from Stanley Hauerwas's *Against the Nations*. Friesen identifies with Jeremiah and Yoder and criticizes Hauerwas and Willimon (authors of *Resident Aliens*), as well as Ernst Troeltsch and H. R. Niebuhr, for setting up false dualisms. This book has spice in it.

Throughout Friesen shows he has learned well from John Howard Yoder. Intriguingly, he has also learned from Gordon Kaufman. He prefers Kaufman's existential wrestling with faith and doubt and with how to validate Christian faith in the pluralistic cities where we dwell. Many see Kaufman and Yoder as divergent and irreconcilable thinkers; for Friesen to witness to his having learned from both perks up one's ears and raises one's eyebrows. His own learning from both Kaufman and Yoder, as well as Troeltsch and Barth, shows that he does practice the seven steps for dialogue and learning from diverse others laid out in the book's concluding chapter. Moreover, he brings it off successfully. He develops criteria and a method for validating faith within the limits of historical particularity, as Kaufman would want him to. But he follows Yoder in rejecting Kantian dualisms, Kantian rationalisms and universalisms, and Kantian agnosticism about the content of revelation. This makes Friesen a highly attractive alternative between Kaufman and Yoder, as well as also between Hauerwas and Gustafson, whose debate he argues is misplaced: we do not have to choose between being the church and connecting with the larger culture.

The key question, Friesen says, is moral formation that is faithful to the way of Jesus, and Kantianism and utilitarianism do not help us with that. Consumer capitalism, the power of large corporations and a globalized economy, technologies that reduce intimate contacts, impersonal forces of large nation-states, urbanization, mobility, specialization, and separation of work spaces from living spaces erode the communities essential to moral formation—family, neighborhood, and church. Therefore we need to emphasize "focal practices" that are faithful to Christ and form moral character. Friesen draws his definition of focal practices from Larry Rasmussen and John Yoder. Their definitions are more clearly grounded in Christ and in New Testament church practices than Alasdair MacIntyre's oft-cited non-Hebraic, Aristotelian, "neutral" definition. The whole argument of Friesen's book gives us good reasons to prefer his historically engaged definition.

In chapter five, Friesen outlines twenty focal practices of the Christian community that define our identity, shape our character, and provide norms for our living. They give us criteria for how to seek the peace of the pluralistic city where we dwell while being clear about our identity and loyalty as followers of Jesus. I urge readers to notice how these practices are deeply rooted in Jesus Christ as the disclosure of the Trinitarian God.

Also worth noting is how these practices in turn provide the criteria for the concluding chapters on artistic imagination, dual citizenship, and human wisdom. The practice of the Sabbath, with its attention to God's presence in the darkness, the practice of the Lord's Supper, with its attention to suffering love and solidarity with others, and the practice of advocacy for the poor and powerless, guide Friesen's interpretation of artistic imagination. Almost all twenty focal practices undergird the ten guidelines for dual citizenship. And the practices of repenting, reconciliation, peacemaking, mutual aid, voluntary decision to become a follower of Christ, the dialogical process of discernment, and the Lord's Supper with its solidarity and love, all undergird Friesen's discussion of Christian faith and human wisdom.

When readers pay close attention to the Christological and Trinitarian roots of the twenty Christian practices, and to the way these practices in turn provide the guidance for artistic imagination, dual citizenship, and relating Christian faith to human wisdom, the striking unity of Friesen's overall argument shines forth brightly. Then we have particular-narrative theological grounding, concrete community practices, and ethical guidelines for dealing with a pluralistic, public world. A major accomplishment! Friesen is indeed a third way in addition to Gustafson and Hauerwas.

—*Glen Stassen, Lewis Smedes Professor of Christian Ethics*
Fuller Theological Seminary
Pasadena, California

Author's Preface

THIS BOOK WAS BORN out of my experience of a double historical consciousness. I am aware of how our specific cultural and autobiographical experiences shape our views of life. I am also convinced that we are most faithful to the Christian faith when we affirm its concrete historical roots in the Jew, Jesus of Nazareth, whose life, teachings, death, and resurrection are the orienting center of Christian life.

I write from the premise that theological reflection can be of most help and relevance to others when it begins by acknowledging and affirming the concreteness of historical context rather than when it abstracts itself from or denies its historic location. The ecumenical conversation that has enriched my work the most over the years has been dialogue with partners who have been willing to share from their own historical experiences and theological traditions. Though we all see "through a glass darkly," nevertheless it is through sharing our particular insights that we gain a fuller and richer vision of the Christian life.

The words *tension, ambiguity*, and *polarity* describe my "double" sense of Christian historical consciousness. I experienced this first in growing up as a Mennonite Christian in the farming community of Fairview near American Falls, Idaho. I had a strong sense of Christian identity as a member of First Mennonite Church of Aberdeen, Idaho. We did not live in a homogeneous Mennonite community like other Mennonites I knew in rural ethnic enclaves in Kansas and Pennsylvania. Our neighbors were of diverse religious backgrounds. I attended a public school. My parents were active in civic affairs in the community.

In so many ways we were like those around us. Yet we were also profoundly different. Being in the world but not of the world was an issue that pervaded our lives. That issue made us, in a fundamental sense, contemporaries of the Apostle Paul. Though we did not struggle with whether to eat meat offered to idols, or whether women should cover their heads, we too lived with the tension of being "in" the world, but not "of" the world.

11

My friends represented a rich variety of religious backgrounds. Some were Mennonites, several were members of the Church of Jesus Christ of Latter Day Saints, and others from various Protestant traditions. Though many of my school friends did not go to church, we shared much in common: our farm experience, 4-H projects, music, sports, the adventure of exploring the lava beds and the environments along the Snake River and around the American Falls Reservoir, and a passion for hunting. My brother and I learned Bible stories from my mother, who read to us regularly. My family had regular devotions before bedtime and always prayed before meals, but many of my friends did not. Almost all our neighbors worked on Sunday. We were strict observers of the Sabbath, except for caring for our animals, milking our cows, and irrigating our crops in summer.

In high school I was in a speech class with six other male students where I remember we had vigorous discussions about pacifism. When I turned 18 and registered at the local post office, I, unlike all my American Falls high school friends, registered as a conscientious objector to war. At American Falls High School I was active in student government, music, and basketball. I helped plan the senior ball as class president, but I did not attend it, since most Mennonites—as well as a few other conservative Protestants in the high school—did not dance.

Many of my high school friends went to the local movies every weekend. Movies were not actually forbidden in our home; we just did not go very often. To sum up my high school experience, I shared much in common with my friends. We enjoyed each other's company. Yet there was something profoundly different about the worlds that shaped our lives.

In many areas I experienced the tension between the larger culture and Christian faith as it had been passed on through my Mennonite tradition and family. The most severe tension was between the dominant belief that loyalty to country required military service and our conviction as Mennonites that following Christ entailed a life of absolute nonviolence. But we did not withdraw from politics. We believed deeply in democracy. Pacifism and politics belonged together in our family and in the Mennonite community of Aberdeen. My parents voted. My father, usually absorbed full-time with farm work, would find the time, even during summer daylight hours, to listen to the radio during the political conventions. My father was active on the Soil Conservation Service and the local hospital board. An uncle was a member of the school board in American Falls—a quite pluralistic community of Protestants, Catholics, and Latter Day Saints (LDS).

Aberdeen was not as pluralistic. The two largest groups in Aberdeen were the Mennonites and the LDS. The Aberdeen school board election was a most important issue as the Mennonites sought to resist the control of the local schools by the LDS. We believed in public education, but in a public education that was tolerant of religious pluralism.

In 1958 I left Idaho to become a student at Bethel College in Kansas. As I developed a strong interest in philosophy and literature, Christian pacifism and politics continued to "belong" together for me as a college student. As a freshman I attended meetings of the Intercollegiate Peace Fellowship of Mennonite Colleges at the United Nations in New York City. I remember the visit of Martin Luther King Jr. to our campus in 1959. I began to relate pacifism to issues of justice and to international issues of war and peace. I became acquainted with Charles Wells's newsletter, *Between the Lines*, and with the pacifism of John Swomley and his analysis of current issues under the auspices of the Fellowship of Reconciliation. Many students were intensely interested in the presidential debates between Nixon and Kennedy. Later, when Kennedy was trying to decide whether to resume the testing of nuclear weapons in the atmosphere, I became active along with other Bethel College students in a nationwide movement of students who went to Washington, D.C., to support Kennedy in his reluctance to resume nuclear testing in the atmosphere.

In the midst of these political concerns, a growing number of students became interested in the beginnings of the Anabaptist movement. We met together in small fellowship groups both to learn more about the underlying theology and ethic of the Anabaptist tradition as well as to express in our own lives and community life these convictions. In the context of this growing interest in Anabaptist theology and growing social and political concerns I made the decision to undertake graduate study in theology and ethics. This road led me first to Mennonite Biblical Seminary in Elkhart, Indiana, then to Berlin, Germany, and finally to Harvard Divinity School.

In the fall of 1963 an article in the *Christian Century*, "The Peace Churches as Communities of Discernment" by J. L. Burkholder, then a Mennonite professor of pastoral theology at Harvard Divinity School, caught the interest of a number of students. This article had a profound effect on my thinking, particularly his model of the church as a community of discernment as the basis for mission to the larger society. On the one hand, Burkholder sought to describe a model of the church, committed to the Lordship of Christ, and engaged in a process of discernment of what faithful obedience means in a culture tempted toward either individualistic pietism or pragmatic secularism. On the other hand, Burkholder called for a creative or pioneering mission to the larger society, determined by the needs of the world and the gifts of the church. Burkholder called particularly for the church to engage in projects to arouse public responsibility. The seminary students were concerned about racism in Elkhart, Indiana. And by 1965, there was a growing concern about the war developing in Vietnam. I saw both of these concerns as extensions of Burkholder's point of view—a biblical pacifism aimed at arousing public responsibility.[1]

After I graduated from seminary, our family went to Berlin, Germany, where the relationship of pacifism and politics was again of concern to me, particularly the question of how a church can be faithful in a Marxist society. There I learned how East German Christians (under the influence of Karl Barth) were applying Jeremiah's advice for people in exile to "seek the shalom of the city where they dwell."[2]

In graduate school I continued to struggle with the relationship of Christ and culture, particularly the relationship of pacifism and politics. I read Guy Hershberger's *War, Peace, and Nonresistance*, H. Richard Niebuhr's *Christ and Culture*, Ernst Troeltsch's *The Social Teaching of the Christian Churches*, and the writings of Reinhold Niebuhr. These scholars all basically agreed that pacifism and politics do not mix, and this created in me a deep sense of dissonance with my passionate commitment to both Christian pacifism and to political involvement. Their views did not fit what I had experienced growing up in Idaho. We were pacifists who were politically involved. We were Mennonites who had an identity that "marked" us off from others, yet we also participated in the culture around us. The paradigm of these thinkers did not fit my experience, my own sense of Christian responsibility, my reading of the Bible, my understanding of Anabaptist-Mennonite history, or of the history of other so-called "sect" types like the socially active Baptists and Quakers I knew.

So I began the search for a new paradigm to understand and describe the relationship of the Christian and culture. That task began in earnest with my dissertation on Troeltsch's *The Social Teaching of the Christian Churches*. I concluded that Troeltsch did not adequately portray the creative and transformative role of "sect-type" Christianity to which I belonged. This was because Troeltsch began with "Constantinian" assumptions in which he could envision a politically responsible ethic only if the church is closely aligned with the dominant political and economic institutions of society.

I owe my orientation in this book and my deep gratitude to that "cloud of witnesses" that has gone before me. Bethel College, where I have taught since 1970, belongs within the Dutch-Russian tradition in the General Conference Mennonite Church in the United States and Canada of "culturally engaged pacifism."[3] Culturally engaged pacifism is the belief that Mennonites should participate vigorously in the culture and offer their peace witness as a contribution to society. It has its roots in the work of C. H. Wedel, the first president of Bethel College, who believed that Mennonites should engage culture eagerly and embrace the issues posed by modern learning.

This tradition of engagement of the Christian faith with modern culture was continued by Edmund G. Kaufman, who was president of Bethel College from 1932 to 1952, and by his son, Bethel graduate and contemporary theologian, Gordon Kaufman.[4] In Canada this tradition is reflected in Frank Epp, also a Bethel College graduate, who throughout his life sought to address modern issues of contemporary politics and culture from the point of view of Christian pacifism.[5]

My work in helping begin a Peace Studies major at Bethel College in the early seventies sought to link the tradition of Christian pacifism and the insights of the social sciences. In the context of this work I wrote my book *Christian Peacemaking and International Conflict: A Realist Pacifist Perspective.*

The deliberations of the committees on which I have worked have contributed to my perspective on a theology of culture. I serve on the Mennonite Central Committee (MCC) Peace Committee, an advisory committee to the International Peace Office of MCC. We have struggled with such issues as how we should respond to "humanitarian" military intervention in Somalia and Bosnia, and what policy we should have on the sanctions in Iraq. Earlier I served on a committee of the historic peace churches and the Fellowship of Reconciliation that is interested in how Mennonites should relate to the ecumenical dialogue on peace and justice issues in the National Council of Churches, the World Council of Churches, and other Christian groups. From 1993 to 1998 I participated with an ecumenical group of scholars and activists in developing a "just peacemaking theory," the results of which have been recently published.[6]

In this book I continue in the tradition of culturally engaged pacifism, though I go much beyond issues of political ethics to address more broadly a theology of culture in its multi-faceted dimensions. The book is divided into two parts. Part One focuses on the church's identity: the foundation of a Christian theological orientation for an alternative cultural vision to the dominant culture. Part Two focuses on how the church engages the larger culture.

The central thesis of chapter one is that Jeremiah's letter to the exiles and the Epistle to Diognetus suggest a model of the church for the North American context today. Christians live with the tension of being citizens and aliens who are called to live by an alternative cultural vision. A brief survey of church history describes how an alternative cultural vision was undermined by a disembodied Christology influenced by Neoplatonism and by the imperialization of the church after Constantine. The free church or believers church tradition offers rich resources for a church that now lives in a post-Christendom age. The church's calling is not to withdraw from culture, but to seek the shalom, the peace and well-being, of the city where we dwell.

Chapter two begins with a descriptive analysis of Ernst Troeltsch's *The Social Teaching of the Christian Churches* and H. Richard Niebuhr's *Christ and Culture*. This chapter appears near the beginning of the book for the benefit of teachers of ethics and theology, since the Troeltsch/Niebuhr paradigm has been so powerful in defining the method for how ethicists and theologians have addressed the relationship of Christ and culture. Lay readers may wish to skip this chapter and go on to chapter three. After a descriptive analysis of Troeltsch and Niebuhr, the strengths and the weaknesses of their methodologies are then assessed. A more incarnational or embodied Christology and a more fluid and complex definition of culture is needed in order to develop a more discriminating analysis of the relationship of the church to culture as an alternative to totalistic conceptions like "against" or "in agreement" with culture.

Chapter three lays out a framework for theological reflection. I argue that it must be done with postmodern awareness of our historical particularity and the relativity of all knowing. The function of theology is twofold: to interpret what "is" in the most comprehensive sense and to tell us what we need to know to act, to live in the world. In a Christian theology of culture, Christ is the orienting center for our view of God, interpretation of the "human," and understanding of the cosmos within which human action unfolds. An adequate theology must dialectically relate two norms: faithfulness to a vision of God in Christ and the interpretive capacity of a theological view to make sense of God-talk for our time and place. The chapter concludes by showing how Martin Luther King Jr.'s theological vision satisfies these norms.

Chapter four shows how a Trinitarian model can provide a normative framework for a theology of culture. Postmodern philosophical categories of process and ecological wholeness are useful for developing a Trinitarian model that can provide a more complete and balanced normative model for the church. Using the image of a patchwork "story quilt," this chapter is built around nine themes or motifs. God as transcendent power calls into question our idolatry, as persuasive power challenges our preconceptions about domination and control, and as creative power awakens us to wonder. Christ inaugurates God's kingdom of righteousness and justice that demands our repentance, models nonviolent love through his life and death on the cross, and appears as a living reality to form a new community of diverse gifts and identities. The Holy Spirit liberates us from bondage to powers and authorities, renews us through the experience of grace and forgiveness, and is a reconciling presence to restore wholeness to the cosmos.

Chapter five describes the church as a community that embodies "focal practices," such as rituals of moral formation (baptism, the Lord's Supper, Sabbath, prayer) and process practices (the dialogical process of discernment, reconciliation, recognition of gifts). These are not abstract ideals or wishes, but visible, concrete ways of living that can be observed and evaluated by those outside the circle of faith as well as those within it.

Part two of the book provides the groundwork for how Christians engage the larger culture. The central thesis is that Christians engage culture through the process of transcultural, analogical imagination in which the gospel is translated into our time and place. Christians are called to engage the culture as artists (to seek aesthetic excellence), as citizens (to shape the common good), and as philosophers (to search for wisdom).

In chapter six, I argue that aesthetic experience is an integral part of our response to God, the Creator of the cosmos. Aesthetic delight is central to an embodied, incarnational vision of life that embraces the full range of sensual experience. Christians are called to be artists, to honor God and express the life of the Spirit through material culture that is aesthetically excellent and ecologically responsible. In planning cities, building and decorating our homes, and designing our places of worship, we should surround ourselves with a material culture that is excellent and contributes to the peace of the city where we dwell. And Christians must learn to make discriminating judgments about what is "good, acceptable, and perfect" as we relate to the power of music and visual image in our culture—both in the "high" and popular culture.

In chapter seven I examine several classic ways Christians have understood social responsibility (Augustine, classic Roman Catholic natural law theory, Luther, Calvinism and Puritanism). I argue for a believers church model founded on two principles. The first is a vision or model of the good society that grows out of the church's vision of the kingdom of God that it is called to embody. The second is a commitment to a process of analogical thinking that draws from that vision norms for other institutions beyond the church. For example, based on the church's vision of a nonviolent process of confronting an erring brother or sister (Matt. 18:15-18) the church by analogy will search for and model nonviolent methods for confronting evil in the larger society.

In chapter eight I develop the idea that in seeking the peace of the city, Christians incorporate human wisdom from a variety of sources into their vision for the city. The particular confession of Jesus Christ illuminates and includes all human wisdom, whatever its source. A dialectical understanding of the relationship between faith and reason is developed as we interact with people of other religious faiths and as we incorporate scientific knowledge in our ethical discernment. Faith seeks understanding, while understanding challenges and enriches faith.

In summary, in this book I attempt to "make theological sense" of the opportunities I have had the last thirty years to work in a small church-related liberal arts college where my dialogue partners have been colleagues from many different academic disciplines, not primarily persons in my own discipline. This interdisciplinary dialogue is one of the great advantages of the liberal arts college context. I am deeply grateful for the many conversations I have had with colleagues who are committed to exploring the intersection of theological discourse with the arts, sciences, and the professions. This book would not be possible without them.

I am also grateful to Bethel College for four sabbaticals, all of which have contributed to this book. In 1990–91 I was able to write a draft of the current work. Three sabbaticals in particular provided wonderful opportunities for ecumenical dialogue. The Institute of Ecumenical and Cultural Research at the Benedictine community of St. John's University and Abbey, at Collegeville, Minnesota, the Ecumenical Institute for Advanced Theological Research at Tantur, Jerusalem, and most recently a 1997–98 sabbatical helped me complete this manuscript. I owe special thanks to Lydia Harder of the Toronto Mennonite Theological Center, who arranged for me to teach the course "Peacemaking: The Church and Culture" at the Toronto School of Theology, Toronto, Ontario, where I tested the ideas in this book with a wonderful group of graduate students. I thank Willard Swartley, dean of the Associated Mennonite Biblical Seminary in Elkhart, Indiana, for inviting me to teach during Interterm in 1998. I thank the seminary community for their wonderful hospitality during the spring of 1998, when I did the bulk of the writing. I also want to thank Alan Kreider of Regent's Park College, Oxford University, England, for arranging a lecture at Oxford in May of 1998 and for the stimulating dialogue with the Regent's Park faculty.

So many people have contributed to the writing of this book, a process that has extended over about ten years. To those many unnamed persons whose names I have not listed, I express my thanks and offer my apology. I want to express thanks to my colleagues at Bethel College who may recognize ideas we have discussed in lunch conversations and faculty seminars. Thanks to the *Mennonite Quarterly Review* and the *Conrad Grebel Review,* which published my early thoughts on a theology of culture to provide an opportunity to test my ideas in the scholarly community.

I have learned much from many outstanding students I have been privileged to teach at Bethel College, as well as the graduate students I learned to know on my recent sabbatical at the Toronto School of Theology and the Associated Mennonite Biblical Seminary. Thanks to Elizabeth Schmidt, who gave considerable time in helping with an earlier draft and probably wonders some years later whatever became of that manuscript. I am deeply grateful to Glen Stassen, who invested significant time in his busy schedule to offer invaluable wisdom on both editorial matters and substantive issues.

Thanks also to the following persons who read either the final draft of the whole manuscript or particular chapters: Gayle Gerber Koontz, Lydia Neufeld Harder, Gordon Kaufman, Robert Regier, James Juhnke, Ted Koontz, and Timothy Madison. Phil Stoltzfus, my colleague in the Bible and Religion Department at Bethel College has been an insightful conversation partner the last several years, and I think him for his contributions to the chapter on the arts.

I am grateful to Herald Press, which over the years has published works of Christian scholarship that have been so important to the life and growth of the church. I would especially like to thank Loren Johns for his editing work and Michael A. King, of Pandora Press U.S., for guiding the manuscript through the publication process. Our children, who are active in the professions of art education, business, social work, and ecological restoration have gifted us with many conversations that have contributed to my thinking about a theology of culture.

And finally, I thank especially my wife, Elizabeth, for many conversations about the philosophy and practice of teaching and learning. She put up with me when I became too absorbed in this project, stood by me and encouraged me during the long process of research and writing, and was always ready to listen to ideas I tested out first on her. As we participate in our grandchildren's growth and development, we are reminded not to take our own projects too seriously, but rather to simply experience the joy and wonder of life. And at the end of this process we thank God for the gift of companions, family, friends, and colleagues, and for the church, the "great cloud of witnesses" that has endured over time and surrounds us in our work and in our play.

—*Duane Friesen* ·
North Newton, Kansas

Part 1

Orienting Ourselves:

Being
the
Church

Christians as
Citizens and Aliens

Christians are not distinguished from the rest of humankind by country, or by speech, or by dress. . . . They do not dwell in cities of their own, or use a different language, or practice a peculiar life. . . . They live in countries of their own, but simply as sojourners; they share the life of citizens, they endure the lot of foreigners; every foreign land is to them a homeland ["fatherland" in the original], and every homeland a foreign land. —The Epistle to Diognetus

CITIZENS IN A FOREIGN LAND

The Epistle to Diognetus expresses a profound tension at the heart of being a Christian in the world. The second-century writer to Diognetus describes Christians who share the language, customs, dress, and place of residence with their fellow citizens, while living in a way that makes them seem like strangers or aliens within their own country.

Like those of the second century, Christians today share a common cultural identity with other people wherever we live. Yet we are called to be distinctive by virtue of the stories and values that have shaped our lives. Christian existence is like being citizens and aliens at the same time. Sometimes others treat our particular language, beliefs, and practices as strange and foreign. Because we have internalized the different languages and practices that orient our lives, we cannot abandon our identity as citizens for the sake of our identity as aliens, nor can we cease to be aliens by being citizens. We live with both identities at the same time. We are in the world to the core. We are earthy creatures who belong to families, cities, and countries. We share the language, the mores, and customs of the culture into which we are born.

I share much with the culture into which I was born. It is like the air I breathe. I speak and think in the English language, a language that has been in the process of development for centuries. My particular use of the English language is colored by features I learned while growing up a Mennonite on a farm in Idaho as a "Friesen" (with family roots in the Ukraine). I studied in several academic communities, where I learned the academic jargon distinctive to places like Mennonite Biblical Seminary and Harvard Divinity School. And I have lived in Kansas for over thirty years and teach at Bethel College.

I used a computer to write this book, a technological development that presupposes a long tradition of scientific research and the development over several centuries of an institution, the corporation. This corporation invested resources to apply this scientific knowledge to technology and then marketed and sold this computer to me through a small business in Newton, Kansas. That transaction presupposes an economic system I take for granted every day as I buy groceries, gas, electricity, and much more—not only to survive, but to live a meaningful and productive life.

This economic system shapes my thinking, my actions, and the effects of my actions on everyone else in ways I am not even aware. We live in a world dominated by free-market thinking and acting. We think that worldviews and value systems are a matter of consumer choice. We choose the church we attend according to what satisfies our needs as we might choose a consumer product that best meets our needs. We enter and leave marriages based on felt needs, as if marriage were another consumer choice.

At a deeper level, Christians belong to the cosmos, like all human beings. We share the web of relationships that makes life in this cosmos possible. The cells that make our bodies work came to birth in processes that began billions of years ago. We are united in God with all humanity and with all being, from the stars of the heavens to the earth, the air, the trees, and the tiniest particles of the universe.

Many in the wider culture do not share the stories and metaphors that shape us as Christians. Our Christian lives are lived on the border between the world into which we were born and another country, another city. The church is shaped by a vision of God's kingdom, the ordering of human life by an alternative vision. Christians belong to the church, the body of Christ, a community that confesses loyalty to Jesus Christ, who calls it to live a way of life that places Christians in profound tension with many of the fundamental values of the larger culture. Christians belong to an alternative culture—the people of God—a society not identical with family or citizenship. It is a specific community within the larger cosmic community of all being. Though Christians share a universal identity with all beings in the larger cosmic community of the heavens and the earth, and though they share many of the cultural identities with their fellow North Americans, their existence as citizens also makes them "aliens" in their own country.

To put it another way, Christian existence involves polarities that pull us in opposite directions and sometimes seem like contradictions, yet must be held together in creative tension. Many of the debates in contemporary theology and ethics revolve around these tensions. For example, on the one side Stanley Hauerwas and William Willimon are calling the church to be an alternative community alien from the world.[1] Their writings identify the gulf between a Christian orientation to life and the larger dominant culture. We see this emphasis in Hauerwas's book, *After Christendom? How the Church is to Behave if Freedom, Justice, and Christian Nature are Bad Ideas.* George Lindbeck emphasizes the church's mandate to follow its "own rules of grammar" in explicating doctrine, rather than accepting the alien presuppositions of the larger culture.[2] Postmodern theologies critique the Enlightenment, with its attempt to subsume the Christian faith under universal reason. Such postmodern theologies stress Christian particularity, the confession that we are who we are because of a particular history and story in which the church responded to the concrete, historical witness embodied in Jesus' call to discipleship.

On the other side, James Gustafson labels this approach pejoratively as "sectarian." He emphasizes instead the connections or "intersections" between Christian theological reflection and the larger culture.[3] In his book *Intersections,* Gustafson says,

> This book is about intersections. It is about the points at which common interests in moral and policy proposals and in intellectual and academic life meet and cross each other, about the paths or roads that intersect at particular points, and about the kinds of disciplinary or perspectival traffic that meet.[4]

David Tracy believes that theology must move beyond the church to connect with the academy and the larger society in order to speak to larger public issues.[5] Gordon Kaufman stresses the historical and cultural relativity of all theological construction. He seeks to "make sense" of God language—not just for the church, but in dialogue with the wider culture.[6]

I believe that in important respects this debate is misplaced. We do not have to choose between "being" the church and "connecting" with the larger culture. Rather, we must do both. Glen Stassen, Larry Rasmussen, Diane Yeager, and John H. Yoder all demonstrate how one can emphasize the distinctiveness of the church while linking the church's vision positively with the larger culture.[7] But *how* we do both is the critical question and is what this book will explore in the chapters that follow.

I hope to develop a theology of culture that enables us to discriminate, to make choices about how we relate to the wider culture as a people with an alternative vision. We cannot make monolithic responses "against" culture or "in agreement" with culture. Rather, as the text from Romans 12 suggests, we must develop a theology and an ethic that will enable us to "discern what is the will of God—what is good, acceptable and perfect."

A CASE FOR "EXILE" AS A
METAPHOR FOR THE NORTH AMERICAN CHURCH

The texts from Psalm 137, Jeremiah 29, the Letter to Diognetus, and Romans 12 illuminate a vision for the church in North America at the turn of the millennium. These texts express in powerful metaphors a normative model for the church's relationship to its cultural context. Psalm 137 and Jeremiah's letter call for faithful response to the good news of God's commitment to restore the cosmos to the wholeness God intended.

Insofar as the church in North America is faithful to God's intention, the church now is in a state of exile similar to the Jews who were carried off into captivity in Babylon. If I am right, the church's central question will be, "How do we sing God's song in a foreign land!"

This may seem like an odd claim for the church in North America. Of course, our situation is quite different from the Jews in Babylon. I use the word *metaphor* to say that the church's relationship to its North American context is both like and unlike the situation of the Jews in the exile. Both United States and Canadian citizens live in societies quite different from the ancient Babylon of Nebuchadnezzar. In contrast to a totalitarian, repressive system of government, Christians here enjoy democracies where people participate in shaping the common good. We benefit from a legal system that protects basic human rights and that respects religious and political pluralism, and from an economic system that sustains individual ingenuity and initiative and provides for a high standard of living for many. We live in a culture rich in its variety of literature, the arts, and music, reflecting a diversity of values. There are good reasons for the church to embrace many of these values in our cultural context.[8] We benefit from science and technology that enable us to do everything from developing antibodies to cure disease and computers to communicate, to finding out how our ecosystem works in order to live responsibly on the earth. We are *not* "in" Babylon in any literal sense.

Most North American Christians do not understand themselves to be living in a state of exile. If anything, many Christians experience the church as particularly "at home" in North America. Many Christians in North America assume they are still living in something like holy Jerusalem, not in pagan Babylon. Like the people of Israel, for whom Jerusalem symbolized the City of David chosen by God, most North American Christians are "at home" in our cultural context. We see and experience little tension between the Christian faith and the dominant values of our culture. The church in North America is primarily like H. Richard Niebuhr's "Christ of culture" type because of its fundamental accommodation to the values of our cultural context. We do not see ourselves in Babylon, that symbol of idolatry and alienation from God.

The purpose of this book is not simply to give an "empirical" description of the view of the church held by many North American Christians. This exercise in Christian theological ethics is an argument for a particular vision of the church. This vision suggests that there are parallels between our situation and the Jewish exile that are theologically and ethically significant. I first turn to a brief overview of the Bible and church history to support my claim that the metaphor of exile fits the situation of the church in our time.

In the history of the church, we see a movement back and forth between periods when the church legitimated the dominant "Christian" civilization and periods when the church represented an alternative vision within the dominant culture. This tension is reflected in the Old Testament. The Jewish world into which the Christian faith was born was conscious of itself as an alternative to the dominant culture. From the time of the Babylonian exile, Jews have for most of their history lived as a minority culture within other dominant cultures. Jews lived as a minority within other dominant political systems, except for about a hundred years under the Maccabees until Pompey took political control of Jerusalem in 63 BCE, and since the establishment of the State of Israel in 1948.

However, the period prior to the monarchy under David also served as a powerful model for Jewish identity. The monarchical vision of the unity of religious faith and political power expressed in the yearning for a messiah conflicts with Jeremiah's exilic vision. In his letter to those exiled in Babylon, Jeremiah prescribes a strategy for living in a world where another culture is dominant and in political control. Jeremiah's vision for a life of faithfulness in exile and the Davidic monarchical vision are two competing paradigms in the Old Testament.

Jeremiah's vision "to seek the shalom of the city where we dwell" furthermore prescribes a way to respond to the feeling of anguish and rage some Christians experience in exile. Some Christians feel like the Jews who not only were aliens, but also had been "kicked out" forcibly from their own homeland. The question is, How do we respond to the feeling of exile? For the Israelites in Jeremiah's time, exile created anguish and rage, which we see reflected in Psalm 137. They wept by the waters of Babylon as they remembered Zion and were tormented by their captors to "sing one of the songs of Zion." How could they sing God's song in a foreign land? Their rage is expressed vividly in the last verse of the Psalm: "Happy shall they be who take your little ones and dash them against the rock!" (Psalm 137:9).

Many Christians in North America feel like "exiles." The church has lost the privileged position it once held in the days of Christendom. The church no longer enjoys the dominance it once had in the Puritan colonies of New England or the centrality it had for Canadians when *Canadian* meant Protestant and British. Many in the United States who once identified America as a "Christian" nation now feel like exiles in their own land. And many lament the loss. Some are outraged by the loss of central symbols in the dominant culture, such as prayer in the public schools, or manger scenes in the public square. They are tempted to search out the "enemy" in order to "dash them against the rock" with the hope of restoring a lost golden age equivalent to "return to Zion" in Jeremiah's time.

Jeremiah's timely advice in his letter admonishes the exiles not to pout, not to yearn for a lost golden age, and not to rage against their enemies. Instead he urges them to take responsibility for the city in which they live. In his words, "seek the welfare [shalom or peace] of the city where I have sent you into exile and pray to the Lord on its behalf, for in its welfare [shalom] you will find your welfare [shalom]" (Jer. 29:7).

Walter Brueggemann suggests that we can rethink models of the church by dividing the Old Testament into three basic time periods. The first period, Israel before the Monarchy, is analogous to a "new church start." Israel was dominated by "the Exodus liturgy that confessed that God called for moral, urgent, concrete disengagement from the power structures and perceptual patterns of the day (i.e., Pharaoh, and later the Canaanite city-states)."[9] Israel lived as "a community that was socioeconomically marginal," that had none of the features it later had as a stable political and economic establishment under Solomon. The second period—the Israelite monarchy, the convergence of "state and church"—is characteristic of only a small part of the Old Testament, yet Brueggemann argues that reading the Old Testament from this perspective has served well

> an established, culturally legitimated church. ... This pattern of stable religious institution, sympathetic civic leadership, secularizing intelligentsia and passionate prophecy all come to us as a cultural package. (I dare suggest that this is, *mutatis mutandis*, the governing model of modern, established Christianity in the West.)[10]

Brueggemann argues that the third period—post-exilic Israel—is especially appropriate for a vision of the North American church today. Israel developed strategies for survival as a distinctive minority faithful to God to avoid accommodation to the dominant culture around it. It developed a theology of hope to counter the tendency to escapism and despair. "This community, in the face of socio-political marginality, worked at the recovery of memory and rootage and connectedness." Brueggeman argues that "when we read the pre-David texts, if we pay attention, many of those texts are post-exilic and show not only the needs but also the faith of the later community."[11] Thus the stories of Genesis and Exodus, which describe times when the Hebrew people earlier lived within alien cultures, first under the Egyptians and then among the pagan Canaanites, are remembered in order to give guidance for a people in exile. Much of the Old Testament was put together to give guidance to a people living as a minority culture with various alien cultures.

Brueggemann notes the relevance of several sample texts. In the creation story of Genesis 1:1–2:4a, Sabbath serves as a mark of Jewishness. In Genesis 17 (and its parallels to Christian baptism), circumcision provides a way of marking a distinctive community. In Exodus 16, manna in the wilderness helps exiles live from the gifts of God in a culture where they are marginal and do not have an abundance of resources. And in Exodus 26, the design of the portable tabernacle enables pilgrimage with God prior to settlement in the land.[12] I highly recommend Brueggemann's entire book, in which he makes a case for why the metaphor of exile is especially appropriate for the contemporary church. Brueggeman's analysis has confirmed many of the conclusions I have reached in my reflection about these issues over the last ten years.

Within the world of exilic Judaism, a Judaism yearning for a messiah in the Davidic monarchical tradition, the Christian faith was born. Jesus grew up a Jew, learned the language and stories of his Jewish tradition, and participated in Jewish rituals and institutions. He understood God and taught about God's will for his people in the context of his particular time and place, quoting the Scriptures in Hebrew and teaching in Aramaic. According to the synoptic Gospels, the disciples of Jesus initially hoped that Jesus would be a messiah in the tradition of the Davidic monarchy. After Jesus' crucifixion and resurrection, however, his followers became convinced they were called to be a minority servant community after the pattern of their servant leader, Jesus. The "politics of Jesus" of the early church was a vision of a way of being in the world that rejected Davidic monarchical establishment, resisted withdrawal into quietistic Essene enclaves in the desert like the Qumran Community, and opposed collaboration with the dominating power (the Sadducean option).

After the destruction of the temple by the Romans in 70 CE, both rabbinic Judaism (in continuity with the tradition of the Pharisees with "Torah" as its orienting center) and the early church (with Christ as its orienting center) continued in the tradition of the exile. That is, they continued in faithfulness to God as minority communities within a culture dominated by alien political and cultural forces. Over a period of several centuries both communities developed a vision of what it means to be faithful. For the Rabbis, this vision culminates in the Mishnah and later the Talmud. For the followers of Jesus, the New Testament writings reflect a particular cultural vision or interpretation of life for a minority people with Jesus as their Lord—a people with a mission in the world of Roman imperial and Hellenistic cultural values. Both communities seek to discern what it means to be faithful—not through monolithic responses to culture as a whole, but by making discriminating judgments about which elements of the surrounding culture they can accept and which they must oppose to be faithful.

Paul's letters show the struggle to define the identity of this minority as it defined its cultural vision in concrete and specific ways—on sexuality, marriage, the role of women, ecstatic utterance, food offered to idols, circumcision—in relationship to the Jewish and Greco-Roman cultures around it. We see how Paul approached his own Jewish cultural context in a discriminating way. He neither rejected nor affirmed his cultural world through monolithic responses to culture as a whole.

Rather, through a complex process of reasoning, he affirmed his kinship with his Jewish roots, as in Romans 9, while also "relativizing" the rules of circumcision for Gentiles, as in Galatians. The Epistle to Diognetus, written about a century later, when the early church still lived as a minority within other dominant cultures, also reflects this discriminating process of reasoning. The author identifies what makes Christians distinctive and what Christians share with the larger culture.

Two fundamental shifts in orientation eroded the commitment of the church to an alternative cultural vision. The first was in the realm of ideas, when theologians like Justin Martyr (died c. 165 CE) translated the gospel into the categories of Neoplatonic metaphysics. His emphasis on the divine logos, at the expense of the historical Jesus, diminished the teaching of Jesus and the prophets about justice. The shift of emphasis to a realm of reality beyond historical time led to the neglect of the gift of God's good creation. The casting of theology into the categories of Neoplatonic metaphysics diminished the significance of the teachings of the prophets and Jesus about how the economically powerful hoard treasures and neglect God's rule and God's justice (Matt. 6:31), which was breaking into history. Larry Rasmussen summarizes the process begun by Justin.

> The disabling and ultimately tragic development is that the focus soon shifts from Jesus and the peculiar way he incarnated with his community, the way of his God, to the metaphysical relationship of the individual figure, Jesus, to the church's God, now become also the empire's God. In the most un-Jewish of all possible moves, the Jew Jesus became a "detached" Jesus at the hands of the great ecumenical councils. He was detached from his own historic community and the way, and found himself metaphysically fused to God alone. So one searches in vain in the classic creeds, those pure distillations of the faith, for anything at all about Jesus as the way in any moral sense, or of his community's way.[13]

A second fundamental shift in orientation occurred in the fourth to the fifth centuries. It is symbolized by the church's subservience to the Emperor Constantine when he became a Christian. The empire was gradually Christianized, the church imperialized, and the gospel compromised.

Now no longer a minority culture within other cultures, Christianity became the dominant culture. By the time of Ambrose and Augustine (around 400 CE) wars were fought by Christians to protect the Christian empire against "the barbarians." To meet this new challenge, the church borrowed the language of just war from pagan thought.

This process of "Christianization" culminated in the culture of the high Middle Ages. The practice of infant baptism symbolizes most clearly this cultural unity. To be baptized meant to be born into the only possible world of meaning. It was a symbol of social and cultural solidarity. So all infants in the empire were baptized without their being taught, their coming to faith, or their becoming disciples following Jesus (Matt. 28:19). Alternative worlds of meaning were a threat to Christendom. Jews were gradually "marked" as alien and expelled from many territories within Christendom. The "holy land" had to be wrested from the "Infidel." Islam posed an external threat in the sixteenth century as the Turks knocked at the doors of Vienna. Within the church itself, beginning particularly in the fourteenth and fifteenth centuries, reform movements posed a threat to a unified Christian culture. When infant baptism, the fundamental ritual of cultural solidarity, was challenged in the sixteenth century, all of Christendom (both its Catholic and Protestant forms) engaged in a massive effort to repress all dissent.

Since the sixteenth century, Europe and North America have become increasingly pluralistic. The secularization process brought two major types of changes. Social institutions gradually developed independently from the interpretive symbols and control of religious institutions. The split between the secular public world and the private church world,[14] the autonomous pursuit of technological or economic development, and the rise of the university and educational systems at all levels no longer under the tutelage of the church are obvious examples of this process. The secularization process is also a way of thinking as the pursuit of knowledge operates independent of any theological framework. This is particularly evident in the sciences, where explanations of the world are made without reference to "transcendent" or religious symbols. In the medieval university, theology was the queen of the sciences and provided the focus for knowledge. At the center of the modern university, autonomous reason, an Enlightenment concept, provides the focus for knowledge.[15]

Although Christians responded to this process in a variety of ways, two fundamental responses underlie the variety. Despite the process of pluralization and secularization, the dominant response presupposed a Christendom model. In a variety of ways, many Christians searched for that common glue that would unite them with their fellow human beings and the central political, economic, and cultural institutions of the dominant culture. In the early twentieth century, Ernst Troeltsch believed that the church could develop a social ethic for his time only if it rediscovered the great synthesis of the church with the wider culture that it produced in the Middle Ages and later in ascetic Protestantism (e.g., free church Puritanism). This hoped-for synthesis was the presupposition for his entire work. On this basis he argued for the more adequate "church" type because of its ability to synthesize with the dominant culture, and against the less adequate "sect" type,[16] defined as standing in opposition to the culture and thus unable to produce an adequate synthesis for a social ethic.[17]

The present book is an effort to define a different model, to show how one can develop a positive social ethic and theology of culture by drawing upon the "alternative culture" tradition of the Bible and of church history. In the history of the church, this tradition is known by a variety of names such as the Radical Reformation, the "free church," or the "believers church" tradition. John H. Yoder describes this type not as a

> specific denomination, but rather a perennial position taken, sometimes quite without coordination, in fact often without any knowledge of one another, by scores of renewal communities— including a dozen major, independently viable ones—across the centuries, and by renewal movements within established denominations as well.[18]

James McClendon Jr. calls it the "small b baptist tradition," meaning to include basically the same believers church groups that I name below.[19] This exile or alternative culture model has been rediscovered again and again in the history of the church. It was rediscovered by St. Francis in the thirteenth century, the Waldensians in the fourteenth, the Czech Brethren in fifteenth-century Bohemia, the Anabaptists of sixteenth-century Europe, the Quakers in seventeenth-century England, and the Church of the Brethren in eighteenth-century Germany. The Wesleyan renewal within Anglicanism in eighteenth-century England rediscovered it, as did Negro slaves who preserved their identity by singing the spirituals through several centuries of oppression in America. The Disciples on the frontier in nineteenth-century America, the black church and Martin L. King Jr. during the civil rights struggle, Oscar Romero, who died a martyr because he championed the poor in El Salvador, Desmond Tutu, who championed a just peace in South Africa, and Christians in Eastern Europe—all of these played key roles in nonviolent revolutions to transform their societies.

In short, the context for the church today is more like the situation of Jeremiah's time and the Epistle to Diognetus, than it was in the period of Christendom. Thus, a theology of culture for our North American context will seek to develop a vision of the church that is an alternative to Christendom models, which assume that the church is and should be integrally connected with the dominant institutions of society. A Christendom model assumes that the church is in a position to shape the entire social order by virtue of these linkages. With the breakup of Christendom, the church now faces the reality of secularization and the church's minority status in a world of religious pluralism.

Though particular streams in the history of the church can be of special help to us today, a Christian theology of culture today is broadly ecumenical. Even within the "Constantinian" stream of church history there are rich resources to use in constructing an alternative cultural vision. Though I believe a model of the church for our post-Constantinian age is best articulated by a "believers church" form of Christianity, we can only construct a vision of the Christian life from the resources of the whole church catholic.

Such a vision comes from church leaders like Augustine and Luther and is inspired by the great spiritual and artistic creations of Christendom, such as Gregorian Chant, the Gothic cathedral, and Bach's cantatas. All genuine Christian believers throughout the history of the church believed that to be a follower of Christ requires cultural discernment—sometimes putting them at odds with the dominant culture, sometimes affirming or "Christianizing" elements of their culture. At other times Christians will take a particular cultural form or practice and transform it by the gospel.

Any ecumenical vision must be clear about the identity of the church. Though we share much in common with our fellow humans, being a follower of Christ places us at odds with many of the dominant values of our culture (e.g., rampant consumerism, a culture of violence, ecological destruction, and radical disparities between the rich and the poor). We *are* "in" Babylon. How can the church sing God's song in the midst of the dominant music of our culture when it sings songs of triumphant nationalism, of racial and ethnic supremacy and hatred, songs glorifying and trusting in the power of technology for deliverance? Society's songs worship material well-being and self-indulgence. They portray sex and partnership as individualistic self-fulfilling free-market consumerism rather than covenant. A church that sings the Lord's song in the twenty-first century weeps as the Hebrews did in Babylon. This church weeps for the good earth increasingly raped and exploited for human ends, the air and water polluted to satisfy short-sighted selfish goals. It laments the rapid loss of animal and plant species as a consequence of anthropocentric values and interests. God's people weep for children who never had the chance to live full and productive lives as God intended, who die unnecessarily from war, poverty, disease, and hunger in the midst of wealth and self-indulgence.

The United States leads the world in military expenditures. The percentage of our citizens in prison is one of the highest in the world. We are one of the world's leaders in the number of persons executed through capital punishment. The gap between the wealthy and the poor is vast and continues to grow. A devastating number of children grow up without the presence of responsible adults to nurture them so they can flourish. Thousands of babies are aborted every year, and not, as some would argue, for justifiable reasons (threat to the mother's life, rape, or incest) but from sheer sexual indulgence without responsibility for the consequences of pregnancy.

How would the vision of Jeremiah and Diognetus apply to the church today? It is distressing that churches so often fail to live as if they were a transnational community with loyalties and commitments transcending their own nation states. In times of war Christians often kill each other in the name of their own nation, putting the lie to their oneness in the body of Christ and making a sham of holy communion. What difference would it make to the attitudes and actions of North American Christians if they kept in mind their solidarity with the Christians in the churches of Cuba and the Palestinian West Bank? How are we expressing our "oneness" with Iraqi Christians who survived the Persian Gulf War but whose children are dying as a result of sanctions imposed with the church's complicity? What does it mean to share the bread of Christ in holy communion if the church supports a foreign policy that wreaks havoc on brothers and sisters in Christ?

A CASE FOR A DISCERNING PROCESS AMID AMBIGUITY AND COMPLEXITY

North American Christians do not agree about what should be included in the litany of issues that defines whether the church is "in" Babylon or "at home" in Jerusalem. James Davison Hunter's book, *Culture Wars: The Struggle to Define America*, says we are fighting a culture war with one another over what the real issues are.[20] My point in this book, however, is not simply to take sides in "the culture wars." The purpose of this book is to help the church think carefully and critically from a solid biblical and theological foundation about how to discern its relationship to culture, not simply to respond from the political preference of either the left or the right. The basic problem is that both sides in the culture wars make Constantinian assumptions, each trying to control or shape the entire society according to its cultural vision. We need rather to think in terms of an alternative cultural vision that is different from both these positions. From this alternative perspective, the church is called to discern how it relates to its cultural context as suggested in Paul's letter to the Romans. "Do not be conformed to this world, but be transformed by the renewing of your minds, that you may discern what is the will of God—what is good, acceptable and perfect."

This discerning process is complex. There is no simple formula. The musical metaphors of dissonance and harmony describe the situation of the church in the late twentieth century. Tension, ambiguity, suspense—these words describe the dynamics of the Christian church's relationship to culture. Our language and conceptual thought frequently mask these ambiguities. To name is often to divide and distinguish, to think in categories of either/or: spirit or matter, good or evil, truth or falsehood, God or history, church or world, Christ or culture, life or death, order or chaos, freedom or determinism, form or novelty. As the church seeks to sing God's song, it will need to listen and discern carefully. What is that song? In what way can the church join in singing the songs of the culture in which it lives? Where will it sing another song—a song that will grate upon the ears of those who sing the songs of the dominant culture? And most importantly, what is the process by which people will come together in community, in a context of dialogue, to discern what is "good, acceptable and perfect"?

The Epistle to Diognetus reminds us of the complexity and ambiguity of the church's relationship to culture. On the one hand, the church is deeply rooted in its particular cultural contexts and it shares many of the values and practices of the culture in which it lives. At the same time its loyalty to Jesus Christ leads it to embody an alternative vision of life that conflicts with its surrounding culture. The description of a second-century alternative vision of life in the Epistle to Diognetus is striking. Christians do not speak a different language, dress differently, live in separate cities, eat different foods, or practice different customs. Yet they practice an ethic of love and respect to all even when they are treated with disrespect and persecuted. They are generous to others despite the fact that they are poor, and they treat their children differently from those around them.

The Epistle challenges us especially in identifying the church as a transnational body, a global community existing among the nations.

Every particular land where Christians live is the location of its responsibility to God and an occasion for it to seek the welfare of the city where it dwells. In that sense every land is home to the church, even where the church lives under hostile conditions. The church does not depend for its life on a particular form of government or economic system. It seeks to be obedient to God and seek the welfare of the city even in totalitarian and repressive systems. But every land is also a foreign land. Christians have an allegiance to another city. They belong to Jesus Christ. Thus, their loyalties and commitments transcend narrow national identities.

So why do I limit this theology of culture to the North American context? I do insist that we should be aware of the larger global context. We must do our thinking in the light of our existence as human beings who belong to the earth and to the larger cosmos. We also must be aware of how our lives in North America affect and are affected by human beings around the globe. Above all, we must not cut ourselves off from the suffering of others, no matter how distant from us.

Nevertheless, I think it is a mistake theologically to try to think about a theology of culture in general. Cultural analysis requires specificity if it is to have any substance and go beyond mere platitudes. Furthermore, it is presumptuous and arrogant to define how the church relates to culture in general. Only specific people in specific contexts—on location—can work out these issues.

The Epistle to Diognetus and Paul's letter to the Romans suggest a mode or style of discriminating thinking done in specific contexts on specific issues that is essential for the church today. What marks off the Christian community from the surrounding culture? The church is not simply "against" culture, nor does it simply adapt to the culture around it. It shares the language and the customs of the surrounding culture, yet it lives by another standard of goodness and truth. So it must discriminate between those elements of culture that are neutral in value, those that can be positively affirmed, and those that must be criticized and rejected, as Paul puts it, "that we may discern the will of God—what is good acceptable and perfect."

In sum, the church is in exile like the Jews in Jeremiah's time because it is a minority community that cannot and should not attempt to dominate or control the world like it did after Constantine. It is in exile, not because it feels alienated from creation or from other fellow human beings, but because Jesus' challenge to "hunger and thirst for justice" conflicts with the values and practices of the dominant culture. But this conflict of values should not lead the church to shrink from re-

sponsibility for the public sphere by withdrawing into a separate enclave, or by privatizing or spiritualizing the Christian faith. Exile is a
call to proclaim God's rule, which is breaking into history, and to live
by practices that can make life flourish in the cosmos.

A CASE FOR CITIZENS
WHO SEEK THE PEACE OF THE CITY

If the church sees itself in a state of exile, this does not mean, however, that it is "against" the culture in which it lives. An appropriate
stance is suggested by Jeremiah's letter to the exiles: "to seek the
shalom of the city where you dwell."

I first became aware of the significance of Jeremiah's letter when I
was in Berlin in 1965–1966. The question confronting East German
Christians was how a church can be faithful in the context of a Marxist society. While some North American theologians simply accepted
the cold war rhetoric, which called for deliverance of East Germany
from Communism by force of arms if necessary, the Swiss theologian,
Karl Barth, took a different position. He urged East German Christians
not to listen to the false prophets, like Hananiah of Jeremiah's time,
who looked for a quick restoration of the people and their institutions
in Jerusalem. He urged the Christians in East Germany to "build
houses" (to plan to stay awhile) and "to seek the shalom of the city
where they dwell." That is, he encouraged them to seek the welfare of
East Germany, in spite of it being Marxist.[21]

The Christians of East Germany were clear that the Marxist and
atheist society of East Germany was not a Christian society and that
they were in exile. But East Germany was where they were and they
were called by God to seek God's peace where they were. Just so, the
Christians of North America need to become clear that the materialis-
tic-capitalistic society where we live is not a Christian society and we
are in exile. But this is where we are and we are called by God to seek
God's peace where we live.

In one sense, Jeremiah's letter is also addressed to us in North
America. Jeremiah called for the Hebrews to plant gardens, to take
wives and have children, and to seek the welfare of the city where they
live. Behind the English word *welfare* is the Hebrew word *shalom*—a
word that means wholeness, the restoration of the cosmos as God intended it. Shalom means to bring healing to the earth, peace between
humans and the non-human world, healing to the human body and
spirit in its psychosomatic unity, and righteousness and justice to the
social order. "God's acts of salvation/liberation are channels for shalom

justice because they transform the situation of oppression to one of freedom and liberation for the oppressed."[22]

In other words, exile does not suggest withdrawal into a special enclave separate from the world. It refers to a community of people in the world who sing the Lord's song by seeking the well-being of the city where they dwell. It was important for the Hebrews to know who they were—God's people in Babylon, a foreign land—people who worshiped God, not the gods of Babylon and who remembered Zion and what God had done for them. It is important, too, for the church of the late twentieth century to know who it is—the body of Christ in a culture oriented to values that often destroy life rather than bring wholeness. It is important for the church to remember Jesus Christ, to recall what God has done for it through his life, suffering, death, and resurrection. The constant reminder of who the church is in the sacrament of the Lord's Supper is crucial to the church's identity. So the church must *be* the church. It must sing God's song.

But that song is not for itself; it is for the world. The church is God's body in the world. It is present to bring about the well-being (shalom) of the city where it dwells. The advice of Jeremiah to pray to the Lord on behalf of the city in which it lives is not a call for passivity—to let God act while the church watches and waits. Genuine prayer requires becoming intoxicated, consumed by God—becoming so filled with the Spirit of God that the church can become an agent of God's action in the world.

The prophet Jeremiah is a model for the church. He describes how the Spirit of God was like a fire that burned within his bones so that he could not keep God's message within him even though it brought him trouble and conflict with his people. To pray genuinely to God for the welfare of the city is to yearn with all one's heart for its well-being. To pray means to weep with God when the city chooses the way of death, to pronounce judgment, to yearn for, urge, and then act with the compassion of God that the city may choose the way of life.

It may seem that the model I am developing resembles that of William Willimon and Stanley Hauerwas in their book, *Resident Aliens*. Indeed I have learned much from them. Essential to the "Jeremiah and Diognetus Model," as Hauerwas and Willimon have so eloquently stated, is that the church must be the church. Christian people must know who they are, witness to that truth, and live that truth in their daily lives. But I find missing from their position a positive vision for the church's public witness of seeking the peace of the city. Their views are reflected in the following statement: "We argue that the political task of Christians is to be the church *rather than* to transform the world."[23] This statement reflects an either/or thinking that limits the power and significance of the church. The good news of the Christian faith *engages* the "powers and authorities," the corporate structures that oppress and rob the poor and destroy the environment. The stories of transformation in their book are limited to individual people in the context of the church. They do not adequately illuminate the dynamics of social transformation that are also powerful witnesses to the gospel.

If as they say, "Jesus Christ is the supreme act of divine intrusion into the world's settled arrangements,"[24] then the church is especially the church when its members scatter in their various places of employment and practice the professions within the institutions of our society, within political and economic life. The church is the church as members work with others in voluntary associations that seek to bring about change in society. It is the church when Christians propose policies to meet basic needs of human beings, as well as when they seek to write laws and administer laws to meet these needs.

I am concerned that *Resident Aliens* could legitimate the church's quiet complacency rather than spur it to a more radical faithfulness, as the authors intend. I prefer the balance reflected in Douglas John Hall's statement: "Intentional disengagement from the dominant culture, with which the older Protestant denominations of this continent have been bound up in the past, is the necessary precondition for a meaningful engagement of that same dominant culture."[25] The church is not simply *"against* the nations," as the title of Stanley Hauerwas's book has it. Rather, it is primarily *"for* the nations," the title of John H. Yoder's 1997 book.[26]

The position developed here is not "sectarian" in Troeltsch's sense (the church as withdrawing from society) or "Christ against culture." Based on the model of Christ, the church is to embody an alternative cultural vision that then becomes a basis for its mission and involvement in the cultural setting wherever it is, as a creative pioneering community.

We see this mission to the larger society evident in the writings of John H. Yoder, which are full of suggestions of how the church has been and can be culturally creative in contributing to the "shalom of the city where it dwells." The church is creative through alternative models of nonviolent conflict resolution, in the development of hospitals and schools, and through alternative models of restorative justice. By developing models of decision-making within the church, it has contributed to the development and growth of religious liberty and democracy, which predate the Enlightenment.[27]

Because it is out of step with the dominating culture, the church may appear irrelevant to the immediate decisions of power-holders in the dominant culture. But it has patience and hope because God is Lord of the nations. The church can learn from the Jews who first put into practice Jeremiah's model and lived out that model more faithfully than the church through hundreds of years of diaspora within dominant Islamic or Christian civilizations. About a millennium after Jeremiah's letter to the exiles, the Jews of Babylon brought into being the *Talmud*, that great body of Jewish wisdom that reflects the vitality of a minority community, often amid hostile conditions. What endures in history? Long after Nebuchadnezzar and ancient Babylon had ceased to be, long after Hananiah and prophets who advocated a dominant culture solution had disappeared, a faithful Jewish community continued to flower and contribute to the welfare of the cities where they dwelt century after century. They did this not by helping Nebuchadnezzar run Babylon more humanely. They contributed to the peace of Babylon by their own style of faithful, patient, and hopeful witness.[28]

The Epistle to Diognetus, then, particularly fits a church that lives as a minority in the world, a church that is in a "missionary" context. It fits a church that experiences the good news of the gospel in conflict with the surrounding culture. It is a church with a message, a sense of mission that calls for the renewal and transformation of the surrounding culture. It looks back to the loss of Hebraic roots in Neoplatonic metaphysics in the second and third centuries and Constantinian synthesis of church and culture in the fourth and fifth centuries as an era that must come to an end. The twentieth-century church of the exile calls for an end to a Constantinian church as the dominating institution of the culture, an ally of the controlling political and economic powers.

Many Christians, particularly in the United States still think about Christian responsibility within the framework of "Constantinian" assumptions. For many, the church legitimates and supports U.S. economic and political power in the world. Many Christians cannot distinguish between the good news of the gospel and what is good for the U.S. economy or its political interests around the world. Most Christians in the United States simply joined with their fellow Americans in supporting the Persian Gulf War. In the United States the church has become almost completely identified with the dominating culture of American imperial and technological power. I contend there is a better way to seek the peace of the city where we dwell.

This book is a call to rethink the nature of the church and its mission in the world. It is a call to rediscover the model of resident aliens who hunger and thirst after peace and well-being in Jeremiah, largely lived by the early church in its first three hundred years and renewed again and again in the history of the church. At the same time I call on Christians to participate fully as citizens, to seek the well-being of the cities where they dwell. We live in the midst of tension—as aliens *and* as citizens. Living with this tension is both a challenge and an opportunity, a venture of faith like Abraham's, who "was called to set out for a place that he was to receive as an inheritance; and he set out, not knowing where he was going" (Heb. 11:8).

We are empowered to set out in such a venture of faith because a great cloud of witnesses who have gone before us surrounds us.

> Therefore, since we are surrounded by so great a cloud of witnesses, let us also lay aside every weight and the sin that clings so closely, and let us run with perseverance the race that is set before us, looking to Jesus the pioneer and perfecter of our faith, who for the sake of the joy that was set before him endured the cross, disregarding its shame, and has taken his seat at the right hand of the throne of God. (Heb. 12:1-2)

A Method for Relating
Church and Culture:

A Dialogue with Ernst Troeltsch
and H. Richard Niebuhr

*[The Christian ethos] is an ideal which requires a new world if it is
to be fully realized; it was this new world-order that Jesus proclaimed
in His Message of the Kingdom of God. But it is an ideal which cannot
be realized within this world apart from compromise. Therefore the
history of the Christian Ethos becomes the story of a constantly
renewed search for this compromise, and of fresh opposition to this
spirit of compromise.* —Ernst Troeltsch[1]

ANYONE WHO CONSIDERS THE TOPIC of the relationship of church
and culture must take into account two groundbreaking works in the
field of Christian social ethics, Ernst Troeltsch's *The Social Teaching of
the Christian Churches* (1911) and H. Richard Niebuhr's *Christ and
Culture* (1951). One of my goals in this chapter is to make these works
accessible to the nonspecialist. Troeltsch and Niebuhr were creative
thinkers whose ideas can broaden and enrich all of us. Knowledge of
their work should not be limited to scholars.

These two thinkers were integrally linked to each other. Niebuhr
wrote his dissertation on Troeltsch's philosophy of religion and was
deeply influenced, as we shall see, by Troeltsch's typology of religious
association. Today these two books still fundamentally shape the discipline of Christian ethical reflection.

My objectives in this chapter are threefold. First, I want to describe
as sympathetically and objectively as I can Troeltsch's and Niebuhr's
method of thinking. My goal is to describe how they reason about the
relationship of the church and culture. Second, I will raise critical issues about their method of thinking, identifying both strengths and

43

weaknesses. Third, I will contrast the way we should approach the problem with how they do it.

DESCRIPTION OF TROELTSCH'S POSITION[2]

The Problem

Troeltsch's *The Social Teaching of the Christian Churches* (hereafter abbreviated ST) is not primarily descriptive sociology. Through his historical analysis he was responding to the modern social crisis.[3] Troeltsch wrote as a theologian and ethicist searching for a normative solution to the crisis of modernity. Troeltsch perceived an immense gap between the modern world and the social teachings of the New Testament. In the conclusion Troeltsch says,

> This social problem is vast and complicated. It includes the problem of the capitalist economic period and of the industrial proletariat created by it; and of the growth of militaristic and bureaucratic giant states; of the enormous increase in population, which affects colonial and world policy, of the mechanical technique, which produces enormous masses of material and links up and mobilizes the whole world for purposes of trade, but which also treats men and labour like machines.[4]

Since Troeltsch wrote nearly 100 years ago, this gap between a Christian vision of life and the modern situation has only grown wider. The power of modern science with its ability to isolate discrete areas of knowledge and harness that knowledge in modern technology continues to change the world profoundly. Bureaucratic management, especially through large corporations, has great power to accomplish aims that contrast starkly with the transcendent values of the kingdom of God. Even more than in Troeltsch's time, we have seen the globalization of a bureaucratic technological culture and the global impact of market capitalism. For Troeltsch the question is whether the Christian faith has the capacity to deal with this situation. As he concludes,

> Under these circumstances our inquiry leads to the conclusion that all Christian-Social work is in a problematic condition. It is problematic in general because the power of thought to overcome brutal reality is always an obscure and difficult question; it is problematic in particular because the main historic forms of the Christian doctrine of society and of social development are today, for various reasons, impotent in face of the tasks by which they are confronted.[5]

His thousand-page study of the history of the churches' social teachings was a Herculean effort—duplicated by no one before or since—to search in history for clues of how the church should respond to this crisis. For Troeltsch the answer was to find some way to synthesize the church's vision with the larger culture. Troeltsch had identified two examples of such a synthesis in the history of the church—in medieval Catholicism and in ascetic Protestantism. Ascetic Protestantism (developed especially in the seventeenth and eighteenth centuries) is a combination of Calvinism, the free church tradition, and pietism.

This mix of groups emphasized diligence in one's calling, hard work, frugality, a taboo on self-indulgence and pleasure, freedom of the individual, and a commitment to political democracy and liberalism. Max Weber had argued that it was this spirit that contributed to the rise of capitalism. Troeltsch argued that both medieval Catholicism and ascetic Protestantism had worked out a Christian social philosophy that could be combined with the main forces of the culture to produce a "unity of civilization." The crisis is that he sees no such prospect on the horizon for the modern world. He says we will need new ideas that we have not thought of previously in church history. The assumption that the church needs to fit in with society's values in a synthesis with modern culture is what I will later criticize as a "Constantinian" assumption.

The Typology of Religious Association

Troeltsch's distinctive contribution to historical analysis was his attention to the interaction of types of religious association and ethical thought. Christology and ethical norms are understood best not as abstract ideas divorced from context, but as embodiments of religious associations or churches. Troeltsch corrected the traditional view of history as primarily the history of ideas, or of church history as primarily the history of dogma. Troeltsch's legacy for Christian social ethics is his emphasis on the necessity of embodying ethical thought within institutions if these ideas are going to have a lasting impact upon history. Curiously, H. Richard Niebuhr's *Christ and Culture* departs from this basic Troeltschian insight by focusing again primarily on "thought" as the key to interpreting the relationship of Christ and culture.

Troeltsch is known especially for his church/sect, mystic typology of religious association as the interpretive key to the history of Christian social thought. He distinguished these types by analyzing the relationship of four variables: the type of religious association, the Christology of each of the types, the resultant ethic, and the implications of all this for the relationship of the church to other social institutions like the family, the state, and the economy. He believes that all three types were in some sense present from the beginning of Christianity, and have coexisted throughout the history of the church.

The church type is a large institution that is able to appeal to the masses. It emphasizes Christ as the redeemer, the one who brings grace and salvation to sinners. It adjusts the Christian ethic to fit the conditions of the world (which Troeltsch refers to as the "relative natural law"). So it develops a compromise or synthesis with the basic institutions of society to achieve a unity of civilization, as medieval Catholicism and ascetic Protestantism did.

The sect, by contrast, is a voluntary society. One becomes a member by one's own voluntary decision. The sect does not appeal to the masses, but to a minority of persons who have experienced the new birth and are willing to commit themselves to a radical ethic. For the sect, Christ is the lawgiver, the model of a radical ethic the adherents of the sect are called to follow. The sect refuses to compromise its ethic, adhering to what Troeltsch calls the "absolute natural law," the law of God of the Golden Age prior to the fall. The sect relates to the world either by withdrawing from the dominant social institutions of society or by seeking to revolutionize these institutions radically.

The mystic, in contrast to both the church and the sect, is more individualistic. It is less institutionalized and forms groups on a more personal basis. It views Christ primarily as the divine Spirit present in all reality. Mysticism emphasizes the world of ideas and personal religious experience, and is not hardened by doctrine and formal worship. It is able to relate positively to many of the developments in modern thought, though it is impotent in addressing the great social issues because it has no specific ethical content or institutional embodiment. It is too individualistic.

Troeltsch's Theological and Philosophical Dualism

The way Troeltsch set up the problem was fundamentally shaped by his own theological and philosophical dualism. His dualism is visible in several polarities that define his reasoning. Troeltsch searches for a normative framework that is not subject to the vicissitudes of history. In his earlier neo-Kantian period, still present in the ST, he argues for a normative "religious *a priori.*" This is a religious idea whose source is the Divine Life "beyond" history and beyond the sociocultural process, though it is always expressed within the relativities of history. Thus he treats religion from two perspectives. On the one hand, religion is a non-mediated *a priori* idea, an expression of the Divine Spirit which stands in sharp opposition to culture, and on the other hand, it is an "idea" that is synthesized with culture and expressed within the historical process in various institutional forms.

One of the functions of this idea is to counter Marxist reductionism of religion to economic and class factors. Religion is an independent causal power. In his conclusion Troeltsch says:

> The whole of this survey has shown that all that is specifically religious, and above all, the great central points of religious development, are an independent expression of the religious life. Jesus, Paul, Origin, Augustine, Thomas Aquinas, Francis of Assisi, Bonaventura, Luther, Calvin: as we study their thought and feeling we realize it is impossible to regard them as the product of class struggles and economic factors.[6]

Thus, when Troeltsch describes Jesus in the ST, he refers to the "Christian idea" expressed through the charismatic personality of Jesus. This idea is a highly spiritualized and idealized vision of an eschatological utopia. It points to an objective value "beyond" the world. The kingdom of God is no program of social reform. It has no concern with the state, with society, or even with the family. Though Jesus promises the poor and the suffering that they "shall have their tears wiped away and all their desires satisfied ... after all this is only natural in a message addressed to the poor; it is not the chief point. The center of His message was the glory of God's final victory, and the conquest of demons."[7]

Consequently, Jesus' radical religious ethic, with its indifference to the world and its transcendence of distinctions within the world, is the basis in church history for either radical revolution or withdrawal from the world. Because of the gap between God's kingdom and other institutions, such an ethic proved attractive especially among the sects who sought to follow Jesus. Only the church type, which is willing to "compromise" this radical otherworldly ethic of Jesus, can enter into a positive relationship with culture. The church type expresses the other side of religion—its capacity to enter into a synthesis with culture.

Throughout the entire ST Troeltsch worked, in a Hegelian way, with opposites that need to be synthesized. The "absolute" and the "relative" must be brought together in history. The religious idea must be expressed in the world. Jesus' radical ethic of the kingdom of God must be brought into relationship with the realities of culture. The sect type tends to emphasize one side of these antinomies: an ethic of law at the expense of grace—a radical, absolute natural law at the expense of its relative expression in history. Small disciplined minorities serve God at the expense of an ethic for the masses. They withdraw from the world in order not to make necessary compromises with the world. By contrast, the church type can best synthesize these opposites. It holds to an ethic of redemption that can generate an ethic of responsibility for the social order and adjust Jesus' radical ethic to the necessary compromises of a sinful world order while adjusting to the world in order to develop a synthesis with culture.

DESCRIPTION OF NIEBUHR'S POSITION[8]

Culture

Niebuhr defined culture in the broadest possible way as everything humans do that is not determined by strictly biological forces. He accepted Bronislaw Malinowski's definition from the *Encyclopedia of the Social Sciences*. Culture is "the 'artificial secondary environment' that man superimposes on the natural. It comprises language, habits, ideas, beliefs, customs, social organization, inherited artifacts, technical processes, and values."[9]

He said this is what the New Testament writers had in mind when they spoke of "the world." Culture is social, a human achievement that is intended to be "good for man." It is concerned with how to achieve a plurality of this-worldly values, ranging from economic wellbeing to an appreciation of the arts and literature.

Christ

Niebuhr began by considering various ways to define Christ. One of the possibilities was to use Troeltsch's typology. Troeltsch used a plurality of definitions of Christ. The sect sees Jesus as the giver of the new law, the mystic sees Christ as the living presence of the revelation of God, and the church sees Christ as the redeemer who mediates God's grace through word and sacrament. Though the church is diverse, Niebuhr sought in his initial definition a unity that underlies the diversity. He argued that "however great the variations among Christians in experiencing and describing the authority Jesus Christ has over them, they have this in common: that Jesus Christ is their authority, and that the one who exercises these various kinds of authority is the same Christ."[10] He acknowledged the difficulty of defining the "essence" of Christ, both because concepts cannot adequately capture the essence of a person and because every description is an interpretation and is thus relative to the particular standpoint one has in the church. Neverthe-less, as an ethicist, Niebuhr chose the admittedly "somewhat arbitrary device" of defining Jesus Christ in term of his "virtues" or "excellences of character."

He summarized these virtues as love, hope, obedience, and faith and humility (which Niebuhr said amount to the same thing). In every case, these ideal virtues or excellences of Christ are oriented to a God beyond the world of culture. "As the Son of God he points away from the many values of man's social life to the One who alone is good."[11] For example, "the virtue of love in Jesus' character and demand is the virtue of the love of God and of the neighbor in God. ... The unity of this person lies in the simplicity and completeness of his direction to-ward God."[12] Jesus' hope was not oriented to history, but his "hope was in God and for God. ... He was not dealing with history at all in the first place, but with God, the Lord of time and space."[13] Niebuhr concludes:

> Thus any one of the virtues of Jesus may be taken as the key to the understanding of his character and teaching; but each is intelligi-ble in its apparent radicalism only as a relation to God. ... The strangeness, the heroic stature, the extremism and sublimity of this person, considered morally, is due to that unique devotion to God and to that single-hearted trust in Him which can be sym-bolized by no other figure of speech so well as by the one which calls him Son of God. ... As Son of God he points away from the many values of man's social life to the One who alone is good; to the One who alone is powerful; from the many times and seasons of history with their hopes and fears to the One who is Lord of all times and is alone to be feared and hoped for; he points away from all that is conditioned to the Unconditioned. He does not di-rect attention away from this world to another; but from all worlds, present and future, material and spiritual, to the One who creates all worlds who is the Other of all worlds.[14]

Charles Scriven summarizes Niebuhr's position well: "'Christ' in the phrase 'Christ and culture' is thus the one who points us away from finite values to the Maker of all things."[15]

Niebuhr concluded his section on Christ by stating that this was only half the story. From this orientation to God, Jesus became the moral mediator to humans of God's love, hope, faith, obedience, and humility. "It involves the double movement—with men toward God, with God toward men; from the world to the Other, from the Other to the world; from work to Grace, from Grace to work; from time to the

Eternal and from the Eternal to the temporal."[16] Though Niebuhr used different terminology, the structure of his thought was quite similar to Troeltsch. Religion orients humans in its purest form beyond the world, then moves back into relationship with the world through various syntheses with culture.

The Types: Christ and Culture in Interaction

Niebuhr thus set up the problem with a sharp dualism: defining Christ (oriented to a God beyond culture) in opposition to culture (the world of human values and achievements). Nevertheless, Christ directs us, as mediator of God, back to the world to practice the virtues of love, hope, faith, obedience, and humility. So the church answers the question of how Christ and culture are related, not in just one way, but in a variety of ways.

This leads Niebuhr to set out his five ideal types—typical ways the church has responded to the relationship of Christ and culture. Two extreme types emphasize the poles in Niebuhr's dualism. The first type, oriented to the radical claims of a Christ oriented to God, is *against culture* and is similar to Troeltsch's sect type. The second type emphasizes the other pole in Niebuhr's duality, *accommodation to culture*, the continuity of Christ with culture, and is similar to Troeltsch's mystic type. The remaining three types, which are similar to Troeltsch's church type, all seek some kind of synthesis between the two poles. *Christ above culture* affirms some continuity with human culture, but not completely. So it views Christ as still above culture. *Christ and culture in paradox* emphasizes that Christians live in the tension between two worlds, two cities, two moralities. The last type views Christ as the *transformer of culture* by identifying dimensions of fallen human culture and converting them to serve God's purposes.

Niebuhr acknowledged that these types were a construct, partly artificial, and that no particular, historical reality fits any of the types. Thus he warned his readers not to employ the typology rigidly, but rather to use it to identify recurring "great motifs that appear and reappear in the long wrestling of Christians with their enduring problem."[17]

ANALYSIS AND EVALUATION OF TROELTSCH AND NIEBUHR

Strengths

Realistic social and cultural analysis. An adequate theology of culture must do the kind of realistic cultural and social analysis that we find in Troeltsch. Troeltsch faced squarely the serious challenges to the church posed by modernity. He identified both the sociological forces of a modern bureaucratic and technological culture that challenge the church's traditional social philosophies, as well as the intellectual forces of historicism and relativism that undermine the certainties of the church's theological foundations. Troeltsch recognized the new situation of the modern world and he refused to skirt these issues or simply to go to the past to find answers that addressed different problems in a different time and place.

A sociological/contextual understanding of history. We can learn much from Troeltsch's approach to history. Without reducing historical analysis to sociological forces, Troeltsch understood that history cannot be understood as simply the history of ideas or doctrines. Historical analysis must take into account how ideas are integrally connected with economic, political, and technological forces.

The significance of social organization for a Christian ethic. A Christian social ethic must be embodied socially. It can be sustained only if it is rooted in an organizational structure that keeps that ethic alive, disciplined, and active in the face of difficult issues posed by the larger culture. Troeltsch's method in the ST was in this one important respect stronger than Niebuhr's in *Christ and Culture*. He analyzed the problems as the relationship of the *church* to culture, not *Christ* and culture, as Niebuhr defined the problem, even though Niebuhr's theology has a strong social view of the person overall. Troeltsch wrote his history of the types by showing how the Christian ethic, and the Christian relationship to culture, is integrally connected to a view of the church. He was also aware that although the mystic type seems to be the most able to relate to the intellectual forces of the modern world, it is impotent in developing a social philosophy because of its lack of a sociology of religious organization.

The need for a theological/ethical plumb line. We need a deeply grounded theology and ethic in order for the church to be able to discern how it will relate to culture. Niebuhr was much stronger than Troeltsch in bringing to bear his own theological analysis as he evaluated each of the types. Troeltsch's own theology was thin and fuzzy. In contrast, Niebuhr asked a series of critical questions as he considered each of the types—except, surprisingly, for the type he preferred, Christ the transformer of culture.

The following are samples from *Christ and Culture* of the criteria Niebuhr brought to bear in his evaluation of each type: How balanced is each perspective in the light of Trinitarian theology? How does each address the problem of sin? How adequately does a type maintain its commitment and loyalty to Christ or too easily accommodate to culture? How does a position balance grace and ethics? Can a position provide for cooperation between Christians and persons of other religions and worldviews? Does a position fall into idolatry by absolutizing for all time a response that may have been faithful for only a particular cultural context? Later I will seek to build on Niebuhr's Trinitarian framework, a theological and ethical plumb line that can empower the church to be faithful as it confronts contemporary culture.

Importance of humility. I agree with Niebuhr's emphasis on openness to learning from all positions. He rightly advocated humility in face of the variety and complexity of the ways in which the relationship of Christ and culture have been understood in the history of the church. John H. Yoder criticized Niebuhr for appearing to be writing in a "tone of lofty and widely informed objectivity, [whereas] his position is clearly partisan, clothed in and carried by the pluralism of his presentation."[18] It is true that Niebuhr's clear preference was for "Christ the transformer of culture," the only position he did not criticize. We could say that he was not humble enough about his own preferences. Furthermore, he set up the argument in such a way as to lead the reader to the conclusion the last position is the preferred one and that the first two positions ("Christ against culture" and "Christ accommodating to culture") are particularly flawed.

However, the problem is not with the virtue of humility as such. The problem is rather with the instrument or model Niebuhr used. His typology fails to illuminate fairly and accurately the first two types, which Niebuhr criticized most strongly. Contrary to Yoder, however, his argument for humility as a central virtue in this endeavor is still valid in view of the complexity of these issues and the variety of answers that have been given.

Alternatives to Weaknesses in Niebuhr and Troeltsch

An incarnational/embodied Christology as an alternative to Troeltsch's and Niebuhr's dualism. Like Troeltsch before him, Niebuhr defined Christ in such a way that if one were to have a "pure" relationship to this Christ, one would by definition stand in opposition to culture. By treating culture as a monolithic entity to which Christ is related, Niebuhr set up a dichotomy between Christ and culture. Thus Niebuhr defined the problem as a tension between Christ *and* culture, as if the problem were an opposition between two monolithic entities separate from each other.

This definition of the problem determined the structure of the rest of *Christ and Culture*. Such an opposition is, of course, impossible, and he frequently criticized this type (represented by 1 John, Tertullian, Tolstoy, and the Mennonites) in his book for not being consistent. The "Christ of culture" type is even more problematic for Niebuhr because it represents those who accommodate completely to culture. Niebuhr thus set up the problem such that the only viable options are the remaining three types. These types are better because they seek to relate both poles, Christ and culture. But all three of these types assume the Christendom model that developed after Constantine, when the church became integrally linked with the dominant institutions of society and lost its prophetic alternative cultural vision.[19]

The problem is with definition. How should one begin? Instead of beginning with a definition of "Christ" as an ideal in opposition to culture, I believe we must begin with a definition of an embodied Christology, one that places Christ in the context of his Jewish culture in first-century Palestine. The problem here is analogous to the pre-Constantinian turn from a more Hebraic historicity to the metaphysics of Neoplatonism, which I described in chapter one.[20] Rather than beginning with a Christ abstracted from his time and place and defined in terms of a religious idea (Troeltsch's language), as an ideal of agape love (Reinhold Niebuhr's language), or virtues or excellences (H. Richard Niebuhr's language), we must begin with a view of Christ as the concrete presence of God *in the world of culture*.[21] Rather than defining Christ over against culture, Christ represents a cultural vision.

The tension, then, is not between Christ and culture, but between different cultural visions. There is no form or "essence" of Christianity (as Harnack sought to develop it) "outside" of or against culture. Rather, in the New Testament, different *cultural* visions come into conflict with each other. That Jesus Christ was *sarx* (fully flesh, and therefore culturally embodied) provides a norm for a discriminating ethic *within* culture. This also means that culture cannot be viewed as a monolithic entity, but rather relates in a discriminating way to the light of Christ.

Toward a more fluid and complex definition of culture instead of viewing culture as a monolith distinct from nature. This critique of Niebuhr and Troeltsch requires that we make two points: first, that we define *culture* in more fluid and complex ways, and second, that we rethink our language about how we see the relationship of culture and nature. Therefore, I need to digress for a few pages to reflect on the meaning of *culture*.

What is culture? I am interested here in an empirical definition, a definition largely dependent upon the work of modern anthropologists. Other more normative definitions are rooted in an earlier history of agriculture and husbandry and are still reflected in our language when we refer to a "cultivated" or "cultured" person, or to the high culture of a society.[22] We have already noticed Niebuhr's comprehensive definition as "everything which man superimposes on the natural."[23] Clifford Geertz gives more precision and specificity with his "semiotic" definition of culture. *Culture*

> denotes an historically transmitted pattern of meanings embodied in symbols, a system of inherited conceptions expressed in symbolic forms by means of which men [sic] communicate, perpetuate, and develop their knowledge about and attitudes toward life.[24]

A cultural system is a system of meaning (as differentiated from the social system and the personality system) that gives us direction for how to live. As Geertz puts it, "Between what our body tells us and what we have to know in order to function, there is a vacuum we must fill ourselves, and we fill it with information (or misinformation) provided by our culture."[25]

Geertz contrasts the blink of the eye and a wink. Both are complex physical reactions that can be understood in all their complexity from a physiological point of view. But a "wink" has symbolic meaning and significance as part of a complex psychosocial interaction between two lovers. We live by both blinks and winks. Our eyes would not continue to function in a physiological sense if we could not blink. But neither could we survive as human beings without "winks"—means of communicating our intentions and interests with other human beings.[26]

We can illustrate the significance of culture and its integral connection to our embodiedness as earth creatures by reflecting on the ordinary and common act of eating. Like all living organisms, humans are dependent on the physical and biological structure of the universe for life. As humans, we share with all living beings the physical limits or conditions that determine whether we live or die. My capacity even to think at this moment is dependent upon the existence of a brain. This complex organ is an integral part of a complex organism of systems that must function together harmoniously for my brain to work. My physical body develops from the interaction with the information built into the genetic code I inherited from my parents. This genetic code passed on to me is the result of millions of years of evolution. Human life has emerged within a physical universe and a biosphere that has evolved over billions of years. Thus when we make the "simple" observation of the universal condition of humans—that we must eat like all animals in order to live—we are presupposing what is anything but "simple" from a biological point of view.

Understanding the human behavior of eating is even more complex when we ask about the meaning of eating as a cultural phenomenon. The what, who, why, and how of eating is complex and varied among human beings. For Chinese, pork is a staple of the diet. For orthodox Jews and Muslims, eating pork is taboo. I grew up in an environment where my grandmother and mother had the special role of hosting guests by preparing a beautiful table and being present to serve them. As guests in a Muslim home on the West Bank, my wife and I ate with only the father and his male friends, while the women and children were absent from the table. In some Christian celebrations of the Lord's Supper, all persons who have confessed Christ are invited to share in the meal. In others, only those who have been baptized into a particular fellowship are welcome.

It is striking how important the proper eating of meals is in the Bible: with whom should one eat, what foods should be eaten, how one should eat. These concerns were important to the rabbis who were contemporaries of Jesus. They continued to be important to the church as well. One of the major conflicts in the early church concerned who may eat the Lord's Supper.

During one of my sabbatical leaves in 1984 at the Ecumenical Institute for Advanced Theological Research in Jerusalem there was a controversy about whether Roman Catholics and Protestants could participate together in the Eucharist in our special ecumenical setting. On a more trivial level, we know that a hot dog eaten at the Dairy Queen on the run during a brief lunch break does not have the same meaning as eating a hot dog while one enjoys a baseball game at Royals Stadium in Kansas City. Eating or not eating (feasts and fasts) are frequently the occasion for expressing fundamental beliefs and values. From the Passover and Sabbath meal in the Jewish tradition to the tea ceremony in Zen Buddhism, people express who they are and what they value. In our own culture, our attitude to food sometimes reflects an underlying alienation from our human identity as we struggle with anorexia, obesity, and various forms of addiction.

These examples of eating rituals among human beings reflect a wide range of human behavior and suggest a definition of culture. Culture is the world of meanings created by humans within the matrices of biological existence. What makes culture possible is human language—our capacity to interpret the meaning of human life through symbolic systems. Culture is that collection of symbolic systems or forms through which human beings express the meaning and significance of their lives in a way quite unlike other animal species, even though humans, like all animals, interact with and are dependent upon a physical and biological universe that sustains life.[27]

Understanding a particular culture involves attempting to understand and interpret its system of meaning. That involves the interpretation not only of language narrowly understood—what a culture expresses in its oral and written communication—but also of the meaning and significance of a people's behavior, artifacts, and institutions. *Language* in this broader sense means gesture and ritual, the structured bodily movement of dance, visual representations in sculpture and painting, organized sounds in music, architectural constructions of space, normative patterns of social life, and the institutional patterns that support and control those patterns.[28]

Our relationship to the earth and the larger cosmos is a critical element in a *cultural* perspective. For too long we have thought in terms of human/nature, soul/body, and mind/body dualisms. These dualisms have had disastrous consequences for our ecological understanding of reality, of how we humans are integrally related to the earth and to our own bodies. So while we see that culture is something we humans create and is not given as such by our genetic inheritance as earthy creatures, the *view* we have of our relationship to the earth is an integral component of an adequate cultural vision. This point is made well by Larry Rasmussen.

> Earth's distress is a crisis of culture. More precisely, the crisis is that a now-globalizing culture in nature and wholly of nature runs full grain against it. A virile, comprehensive, and attractive way of life is destructive of nature and human community together—this is the crisis. ... What we call "the environmental crisis" is a sign of cultural failure.[29]

He says we must learn a new language, and learning to speak this language is a function of our culture.

> We could learn to speak, for example, not of humanity *and* nature, but of humans *in* and *as* nature. Not of culture *and* nature, or history and nature, but of culture and history *in* and *as* nature. Not of society *and* nature, but of society and culture *in* and *as* nature humanly construed. After all, what we call society and cul-

ture are dramatic episodes of what earth does through us as part of earth itself, in the form nature called us.[30]

Niebuhr treats culture as if it were a monolithic whole—something with which one could be "in agreement" or "against." In fact, culture is diverse, fluid, and complex. To be human is to be fundamentally cultural, whether one is an Amish person in rural eastern Pennsylvania or a Harvard professor in urban Cambridge, Massachusetts. It makes no sense to describe an Amish person as "against" culture and a Harvard professor as "in agreement" with culture. Even Amish people share much in common with Harvard professors: they learn the common language of a culture; they communicate in English and follow the conventions of human interaction; and they share with the Harvard professors a basic understanding of the cosmos and of modern technology that makes the world work for both of them. In short, for both of them culture is the "air they breathe."

On the other hand, the Amish person in rural eastern Pennsylvania and the Harvard professor in urban Cambridge, Massachusetts, are worlds apart. That does not mean one is "against" and the other "for" culture. In their resistance to modern technology or rejection of participation in democratic politics, the Amish are not being anti-cultural. Rather, they have a different *cultural* vision than the Harvard professor. Even for Amish people, culture is complex and fluid. They both share and do not share the cultural world of Harvard professors.

Kathryn Tanner suggests that one of the problems in the interpretation of culture is rooted in the mistaken notion of much modern anthropology, that culture is "an internally consistent whole." This is a danger with a "semiotic" definition of culture; we seek to find the "meaning" of a culture, as if everything in the culture could be explained as one coherent and consistent reality. She says that

> interrelations among cultural elements tend to be far messier in fact than they appear to be in abstract theory. ... In contrast to the tight connections found in a machine or a deductive system, cultural elements in the form in which they are mobilized in practice have the partly integrated, partly discontinuous character of an octopus, its "tentacles" in large part separately integrated, [and] neurally quite poorly connected with one another ... who nevertheless manages both to get around and to preserve himself for a while anyway, as a viable if ungainly entity.[31]

This suggests also some limits of the "typological" method as used by Niebuhr. A type is admittedly an artificial construction of what the theorist who constructs the types thinks "belongs" together. So when Niebuhr criticizes the "against" culture type, he charges it with inconsistency. Tertullian and Tolstoy cannot be consistent in their rejection of culture.

> Man not only speaks but thinks with the aid of the language of culture. Not only has the objective world about him been modified by human achievement; but the forms and attitudes of his mind which allow him to make sense out of the objective world have been given him by culture. He cannot dismiss the philosophy and science of this society as though they were external to him; they are in him—though in different forms from those in which they appear in the leaders of culture.[32]

The problem is not with Tolstoy or Tertullian, but with Niebuhr's definition. A discerning cultural analysis would look at the ways in which Tolstoy or Tertullian discerns the complex and varied dimensions of culture—what they affirm and why, what they reject in the dominant culture, and what they take for granted as the "air they breathe."

Finally, there is also a fundamental flaw in Niebuhr's understanding of the word *world* in the New Testament. Niebuhr equates *world* in the New Testament with culture as a whole.[33] Walter Wink points out that the Greek word *kosmos* can mean world, universe, creation, humanity, the planet earth, and the theater of history. "But alongside them, there is in the New Testament another usage that is quite unique in that period. It refers to the human sociological realm that exists in estrangement from God."[34] In the Gospel of John, therefore, the followers of Jesus are to resist allegiance to the "world" as estranged from God, not necessarily to oppose culture in general. When Jesus says his kingdom is "not of this world," he does not mean "otherworldly" in the sense that his kingdom belongs to another sphere of reality outside the universe or outside of culture. Rather, Jesus is calling us to live in the world in faithfulness to God, rather than to follow the patterns of estrangement. If Wink is right, then the Christian approach to culture requires careful discrimination. One must ask which elements of the culture can be affirmed and which need to be resisted. Monolithic responses to culture as a totality are inappropriate and invalid.

The perennial issue confronting the church is the relationship between cultural visions, not between Christ and culture. Every expression of Christianity is embodied in cultural form. The foundation of the Christian faith in Jesus Christ comes to us in an embodied form, in the Jewish Jesus, whom the early church believed as sarx (flesh) to be the "Christ," the revelation of the God of the cosmos.

This picture of Jesus as the Christ comes to us in a cultural form in the concrete documents of the New Testament. The New Testament conveys a cultural vision through language: stories, letters to churches, metaphors, symbols, lists of virtues, and ethical exhortation. From this variety of linguistic forms we come to know a vision of life. This vision is understood not in one monolithic way, but is complex and varied, depending on the particular community to which the text is addressed and the particular context of that community. As we read these texts we see evidence of conflict with other cultural visions in their milieu and myriads of ways the New Testament documents are integrally connected with the cultural forms surrounding them.

A Christian vision is never noncultural. Thus, we should not define the issue as how we relate Christ *and* culture. Nor should we state the issue as a conflict between the church *and* culture. The church itself is embodied culturally. As an institution of culture, the church has a worldview and vision of life.

What then is the perennial issue that confronts the church? It is the question of how a cultural vision of life, referred to in the New Testament as the "good news of the gospel," can be brought into relationship with other cultural visions. How does it connect in positive ways? Where does it conflict? In what respects does that cultural vision modify or transform another cultural worldview or practice? The vision of the early church for us in North America, then, is not a noncultural reality "outside" of culture. Rather it represents an *alternative* vision of life that requires us to engage the culture around us in a discerning way.

A discriminating analysis rather than totalistic conceptions like "against" or "in agreement" with culture. No relationship to culture can be portrayed in totalistic language like "against" or "in agreement." The church has always approached culture in a discriminating way. The church has understood Christ in many different ways throughout history and these Christologies have served as plumb lines for determining how to relate to the surrounding culture.[35]

Furthermore, since culture is not a monolithic entity, but is fluid and represents a complexity of values, it must be related to in a discriminating way. Instead of monolithic response to culture, as an "embodiment" of Christ in the world, the church's position will vary— sometimes in sharp conflict with the dominant culture around it, sometimes in harmony with it, other times simply neutral, or sometimes seeking to transform the culture. The same individual person or group may express all of these positions, depending on what dimension of culture it is responding to.

So it is not inconsistent for Tolstoy as a Christian to oppose the use of violent force in the dominant culture, while using the Russian language to write great novels. John H. Yoder, referring to the analysis of Tertullian by George Forrell, notes that Tertullian discriminated about various dimensions of culture very concretely.

> Tertullian was very critical of idolatry and of the sword and the violence of war. Yet he was very affirmative about human intelligence, despite the fallenness of human nature. He was even positive about the moral and orderly qualities of the Roman empire as an intelligent organization, which when not taken in by idolatry is sober about its own finitude, and committed to doing justice.[36]

To illustrate this "discriminating" approach, the following is a quick list of possible relationships between the church and its surrounding culture. I can imagine the same person or church group holding to all of these positions simultaneously. This illustrates why totalistic portrayals of positions are misleading.

1. Opposition. An example of "opposition" would be refusal to participate in war. Yet Christians who oppose war can relate positively to the dominant culture by influencing public policy or participating in processes in the culture that are more likely to lead to peace.

2. Agreement. The support of public policies that protect religious liberty would be an example of "agreement." Such support is possible for Christians even if it means protecting the religious liberty of those with whom they profoundly disagree.

3. Neutrality toward a dimension of culture. An example here would be using the languages of many different cultures as vehicles for the translation of the good news of the gospel. Although there is no privileged language that is especially appropriate for communicating the significance of Jesus Christ, the categories of thought of a culture are not necessarily neutral. We pointed out in the first chapter how the categories of Neoplatonism shifted the meaning of Christology in ways that were detrimental to an emembodied Christology. By *neutral* I do not mean that any particular set of categories can be taken over uncritically. Translating the faith must be done carefully and faithfully. I simply mean that in principle, the Christian faith can be stated in a variety of ways because language as such is potentially neutral.

4. Going beyond dominant cultural norms. The dominant culture institutionalizes in its legal system the principle that one should not harm other human beings unjustifiably. Christians go beyond that requirement when they call on followers of Christ to practice Christian virtues of kindness and compassion, even though these virtues are not required by law.

5. *Creative alternative institutions.* The alternative system of restorative justice called Victim Offender Reconciliation is a process that brings victims and offenders together to provide ways for the offender to make restitution to the victim and for reconciliation to occur between victims and offenders.

6. *Revitalization of existing cultural arenas.* Here one might develop more effective ways of educating, delivering health care, or farming with stewardship of the land in mind—alternatives more consistent with the values of the Christian faith.

7. *Relativizing a cultural practice in the light of a higher principle.* Circumcision as a mark of religious identity became problematic for Paul when it served as a barrier between Gentiles and Jews. By itself, however, circumcision does not conflict with the Christian faith.

8. *Compromise.* When voting for a candidate for public office, one usually votes for someone who is "closest" or "least distant" from one's own beliefs and values. Rarely is one able to vote for someone who is in full agreement with one's own vision of the Christian faith.

9. *Conversion.* At one time people regarded slavery as a legitimate and inevitable institution of human society, much as many view war today. Today, however, due to the leadership of Christian abolitionists, that institution has been totally delegitimated. If is difficult, if not impossible, to find any person who will argue for slavery. That is quite astonishing, given the beliefs and practices of many persons just a little over a century ago. In the case of slavery, *conversion* meant abolition. We could also mean by *conversion* the transformation of a practice into something quite different, as when primitive methods for treating the mentally ill were transformed by Christians into more humane practices.

Careful use of typological methods that attend the logical classifications of positions on any given issue. I am not arguing against typologies as such or systems of classification; I use them all the time. Without such methods of classification we would be unable to think amid the complexity and variety of data we confront. Without the use of types and systems of classification, church history would be nothing more than huge lists. The key issue is whether we can develop standards objective enough to judge whether a particular typology is adequate. I am skeptical that totalistic typologies can usefully or adequately characterize a group's view of culture in general. It is more reasonable to develop good classifications of positions by attending to particular issues or arenas of culture.

John H. Yoder provides two examples—his classification of positions on war (pacifism, just war, holy war, wars in a group's self interest, and machoism), and types of religious pacifism.[37] Glen Stassen provides another good example of the use of typology in classifying "evasive tendencies"— ways in which churches evade or sidestep faithfulness to the concrete norms of the gospel. Stassen believes that "it would be an error to think we could define types that characterize particular denominations, or even particular congregations adequately."[38] He then proceeds to describe five ways a church can avoid being faithful: two types of accommodation, two types of withdrawal, and one form of dualism. He concludes with his own vision of the "transformationist church."

What standards make these uses of typology "good" or adequate? Two principles should be operative. In the first place, useful typologies grow out of careful empirical analysis. In other words, the analyst is not imposing an artificial construct on reality. The construct is informed in a decisive way by the data under consideration. For example, Yoder added "machoism" and "group self-interest" to Roland Bainton's classifications on war (pacifism, just war, and crusade) because he observed empirically the existence of these positions on war.

Second, the classification should be informed by the internal logic of the issue under consideration. For example, Stassen connects his own analysis of the evasive tendencies of the church to key theological emphases, which he argues, when ignored, lead to evasions of Christian responsibility. In other words, Stassen is able to show that there is "logic" to such evasive tendencies. If the church ignores the living God as independent judge, then it is likely to evade faithfulness by various types of accommodation to culture. If on the other hand, it ignores the reign of God over all, it will likely withdraw from responsibility.[39]

A non-Constantinian vision for the church. Both Troeltsch and Niebuhr made Constantinian assumptions. Both Niebuhr and Troeltsch developed models with biases in favor of those churches and Christians that have sought to be integrally connected with the major institutions of the dominant culture. Such a bias is reflected in Troeltsch's preference for the church type and in Niebuhr's extensive criticism of the "Christ against culture" position. As I have already argued in chapter one, a much more adequate model for the church will come out of the "sect" or "believers church" tradition. This is especially the case in our secularized and pluralistic world, where the church is increasingly a minority and stands for values in sharp opposition to many of the trends of our North American culture. A believers church model is more realistic about its place as a relatively powerless minority in the larger culture. It has no illusions about its ability to restore itself to the kind of prominence and dominance it had at the height of Christendom. With an alternative cultural vision grounded in an embodied Christology, a believers church will be able to develop a discriminating ethic as it "seeks the peace of the city where it dwells."

Bread and Meaning:

Culture and Christian Theological Reflection

Between what our body tells us and what we have to know in order to function, there is a vacuum we must fill ourselves, and we fill it with information (or misinformation) provided by our culture.
—Clifford Geertz[1]

What are needed are criteria for distinguishing God from all idols, criteria that will enable us to recognize which claims to deity are false and deceitful and misleading, and which are true. —Gordon Kaufman[2]

THE FUNCTION OF THEOLOGY
AS A UNIQUELY HUMAN ACTIVITY

For me, theological reflection is generated and energized by the experience of deep conflicts that lie at the core of my being, tensions I find hard to put into words. These tensions exist at many different levels and they crisscross with each other in complex ways. I am driven by a "fire in my bones" to be faithful to a vision of life that was passed on to me through my Mennonite heritage. This heritage passed on the conviction that at the center of the Christian life is the call to discipleship, the call to follow the way of Jesus Christ and to embody that way of life in an alternative community: the church. In seeking to live by that vision, I have felt like an alien in the various worlds in which I have lived: as the only male conscientious objector to war in my high school in American Falls, Idaho, and as a minority in a country where military service is viewed by many as the test of "real" service to country.

I am also aware that my own convictions and the truth claims I make for those convictions are historically conditioned. I live in a pluralistic world where all around me communities hold convictions very different from my own. I have come to know God as I have through my own historical and particular world, even as others have come to know God in other ways. Historical consciousness has penetrated to the core of my being.

I am aware that all views of God are human constructions. We use metaphors and stories and develop intellectual constructs to interpret life and the nature of reality from our own limited standpoints. We can easily turn our own convictions into an idol, an object of devotion that takes the place of God. Pacifism itself can become an ideology, another human dogma that can oppress and violate others. This is sometimes the experience of nonpacifist students and faculty at Bethel College, where nonpacifists are a minority. Within the Mennonite church, women, minorities, and especially gay persons, have often felt silenced by the reigning dogma. I believe we need an orientation to life—a "place" to stand—that will make us an alien in our own country. At the same time we need to be aware of the relativity of that place where we stand that makes us no different than any of our fellow citizens.

John H. Yoder and Gordon Kaufman

This tension between being aliens and citizens can be illustrated by reflecting on the theologies of John H. Yoder and Gordon Kaufman. Both were my teachers and have shaped my theological orientation. Many would see their theological orientations as radically conflicting and incompatible. But both identify an essential component of being a community of faith from a believers church perspective. I admit they really do understand the task of theology differently. Kaufman writes at Harvard for a liberal academic audience and for intellectuals beyond the academy who are trying to make sense of God talk for our time. Yoder wrote at Elkhart and Notre Dame for a Christian church audience that speaks the language of faith without basic problems with that language. They share a number of assumptions. Both Yoder and Kaufman recognize and emphasize the particularity and relativity of all human standpoints. Both are critics of "foundationalism," the assumption that humans can establish an objective, universal framework from which to judge "truth." Both have been influenced in their criticism of foundationalism by their awareness as Mennonites of holding to a minority point of view not widely shared by the larger culture.[3] This has made them profoundly aware of the pluralism of human perspectives.

Both Yoder and Kaufman disagree with the radical subjectivist, postmodern position, which rejects our ability to establish norms by which to test truth or ethical claims. Yoder is a biblical realist who employs historical reason to interpret biblical texts in cultural context in order to distinguish between more faithful and less faithful readings of the text. He believes in the possibility of translating the good news of the gospel into a variety of cultures, and in the role of analogical imagination in finding faithful ways to model the good news within the wider culture.

Kaufman uses reason in a different way than Yoder, primarily to determine the kind of language about God that can make sense of how we understand the world. He is committed to dialogue or conversation with persons of other faiths. He believes that understanding and learning is possible despite the relativity of our standpoints. But rather than appealing to the authority of texts rightly understood, he says we can employ reason to ask about the pragmatic or ethical consequences (whether a point of view is "humanizing") entailed in our particular views of the world, humans, or God.

However, Kaufman is much more aware of the precarious stance of faith in a world of particularity and relativity. In Yoder there is little indication that the awareness of relativity actually penetrated him existentially as an experiential reality. In his many books, Yoder confidently proclaimed the lordship of Christ over the world, an absolute claim on all peoples and cultures. There is no hint of doubt, of struggle, of uncertainty, or of the existential stance of the Christian who makes such a claim. There is surprisingly little reflection on the nature of the faith commitment involved in making such a radical confession. Yoder did emphasize that commitment requires a voluntary decision by the believer (symbolized by believer's baptism), yet he never placed himself in the existential situation of the person challenged to make a decision in the context of religious pluralism.

Yoder reflects from inside the circle, assuming a commitment to the lordship of Christ. Kaufman reflects more of the tension between Christian identity and being a citizen in the world. Kaufman's awareness of relativity penetrates more deeply. He examines the situation of a person confronted by alternative worldviews. From an Anabaptist perspective, Yoder addresses the Christian already baptized and committed to being a follower of Christ, whereas Kaufman addresses the human being who is not yet baptized and committed, who wants to know what is entailed in making a commitment to make Jesus Christ the orienting center of faith and life.

The style of their writings is dramatically different. Kaufman makes himself personally vulnerable. Though his writings are usually not autobiographical, the reader is drawn into a struggle, an inquiry.

Yoder's writings nowhere reflect bafflement, mystery, uncertainty, doubt, or struggle. Yoder's writings confidently answer, from within the church, why Christ's call to discipleship should not be evaded or replaced with something else. I appreciate Yoder's more concrete Christology. It provides specific norms of discipleship. However, I also find myself more in tune with Kaufman's existential sense that human life is both resident and alien, that faith entails human struggle, a search for meaning that involves the dialectic of faith and doubt.

When we do theology, we must take more seriously than we have in the past how our faith is embodied concretely in the world. Theology has often been done in abstractions that are detached from the experiential reality of being embodied selves. John H. Yoder's emphasis on the "politics of Jesus" was a recovery of a concrete, embodied Jesus that linked Jesus to our own humanity. He was also helpful in describing concrete practices that define the church. But even with this emphasis, his tendency was to develop idealized visions of the church that failed to connect with the actual reality of church life, particularly as more marginal people experienced that life. Lydia Neufeld Harder, writing from a feminist perspective, points out how even the language of discipleship can mask the abuse of authority.

> A hermeneutics of obedience may allow a misuse of human authority within a community. It can describe a commitment to the Bible, the community and the interpretive process that does not take into account the limitations embodied in a human-authored book, a human-built institution and a human-organized political practice. It can hide the fact that some interpreters with the community may be using biblical interpretation to seek their own interests. A hermeneutics of obedience can encourage an uncritical, naive acceptance of a human authority rather than promoting an openness to God.[4]

Theology must draw on three sources of wisdom: the biblical story, human experience, and reason. Through reason we seek to make sense of our lives. But we do this not through abstractions divorced from life. Theological reflection is done best by taking seriously the story of God's action revealed in the concrete, bodied, incarnate Jesus, who challenges us to live by an alternative vision of life. The human experience of limit and vulnerability we share with our fellow humans informs us as we search for meaning and purpose in our lives.

Humans live by both bread and meaning. Like all animals, we must eat in order to survive. The meaning of our lives is expressed through eating rituals, such as the Lord's Supper or a Sabbath meal. These are as essential to our survival as the physical sustenance food provides. Christian theology is the disciplined reflection on the system of meaning reflected in symbols, rituals, and ethical practices that orients the lives of a people called by God to live by a vision of life revealed in Jesus as the Christ.

Christian theological reflection is an activity of human culture. Theology is an activity of the human imagination similar to other human cultural processes, such as writing poetry or composing music. Though Christian theological reflection is an interpretation of human life and the cosmos with "God" (interpreted in the light of Christ) as the ultimate frame of reference, God talk itself is human discourse about the meaning of human existence. We are indebted to Gordon Kaufman for boldly stating this point. In the preface to *In Face of Mystery,* Kaufman says of his 1975 book, *An Essay on Theological Method*:

> I argued that theology is, and always has been, an activity of "imaginative construction" by persons attempting to put together as comprehensive and coherent a picture as they could of humanity in the world under God. This view contrasts rather sharply with more conventional conceptions according to which the work of theologians is understood to consist largely in exposition of religious doctrine or dogma (derived from the Bible and other authoritative sources).[5]

The vision of life in the Bible and the faith lived out in the history of the church provide a rich and essential resource for Christian theological reflection. In this book I draw heavily upon the rich resources of the Bible and church tradition for my own point of view. In particular, Christian theological reflection must faithfully and accurately interpret the way of God revealed through Israel and through the life, teachings, death, and resurrection of Jesus Christ. Without that orientation the church has lost its way and accommodated to cultural values alien to the good news. Examples of this losing of the way include apartheid in South Africa, German nationalism and anti-Semitism, ethnic cleansing in Bosnia, and American consumerism. All theological perspectives, including those in the New Testament writings, are nevertheless products of human thought and imagination—imaginative interpretations in response to the experience or "sense" of the living Spirit of God present in the gathered community. We must therefore take responsibility for how we put together our own thoughts for our time and place. We do not simply derive our theology from the Bible or from a given system of religious doctrine or dogma. A theology is an interpretation of God's self-disclosure in Christ for which we must take ownership and responsibility.

The function of theology is twofold. It interprets what "is" the case in the most comprehensive sense. Theology helps us make sense of things in order to orient our lives in the universe within the totality of what "is." Imagine a person on a boat in the middle of the ocean with no land in sight on a dark night. How does such a person know which way to go? Theology answers the question of being by providing humans with a guiding star in order to orient themselves in the cosmos. Theology points out the North Star or the lighthouse on the shore. Second, theology tells us what we need to know to live and to act. It answers the question of "ought": what we ought to value above all, what kind of persons we ought to be (the question of character or a theory of virtue), and what we ought to do (a theory of obligation or norms for action).

The most fundamental guiding star for Christian theology is God as revealed in Israel and Jesus Christ. As Gordon Kaufman puts it, "God" is that symbol in terms of which everything is to be interpreted and understood. If there were something beside God, then God would not be God. One would have created an idol, an object of worship and devotion that is not really God. The central task of the theologian is to aid the human community in distinguishing between God and the idols, which are penultimate realities not worthy of our devotion and worship.

GOD RELATIVIZES ALL HUMAN STANDPOINTS

So how does one talk about God, given the relativity of our human standpoints? The God symbol, first of all, relativizes all human concepts, projects, plans, ideas, and ideologies. To worship God is to view all human projects as penultimate, not objects worthy of ultimate devotion or loyalty. Mystery is therefore an integral perspective in any theology, a "bafflement of mind" that humans experience when they try to "wrap their minds around" the symbol, God. All talk about God is a "construal" of reality. Kaufman warns one who does theology, "Take special care, beware of what is being said; the speaker may be misleading you; you may be misleading yourself."[6]

Kaufman criticizes theologies that make dogma, the creeds, the Bible, or the church the primary focus or the final authority of a theology. All of these authorities are subject to critique in the light of God— and from a Christian point of view, God understood in the light of

Christ. "Serving the church … is undoubtedly of importance to Christian theologians. But this must never become theology's driving motivation: that would be putting an idol in the place where only God can rightfully be."[7] Both "believers church" and "Constantinian" models of the church are subject to "relativization" in view of God, the only reality worthy of our ultimate commitment and devotion. The believers church model I defend in this book must guard against its own form of self-righteousness. Every human construct is subject to the limits of human perspective, which is by definition finite. Sin distorts our vision, causing us to fail to honor God as God and to substitute penultimate realities for ultimate reality.

God as Model for Humans

Second, the concept of God serves to "humanize." It provides an orientation for how to live one's life. In the monotheistic world picture of the Bible, humans are called again and again to "be like God." This is dramatically stated in the Sermon on the Mount, where indiscriminate love (even love to enemies) is urged because God is like that. God makes the sun to shine and rain to come on both the just and unjust (Matt. 5:43-48). Matthew 5:48 means, "Be all-inclusive [not "be perfect"] as your Father in heaven is all-inclusive." It has the same meaning as Luke 6:36: "Be merciful as your Father is merciful," just as God gives sun and rain to God's enemies as well as friends. In 1 John we are called to love because God is love.

The call to be "like God" is ambiguous. We humans are not God and we too easily seize forms of action that are inappropriate. In Romans, Paul urges Christians to love their enemies, but not take it upon themselves to exercise God's wrath, which belongs only to God.

> "Vengeance is mine, I will repay, says the Lord." No, "if your enemies are hungry, feed them; if they are thirsty, give them something to drink; for by doing this you will heap burning coals on their heads." Do not be overcome by evil, but overcome evil with good. (Romans 12:19-21)

The Bible pictures a God who created the world, is sovereign Lord over history, and is acting in history to save the world. The problem is that this same Bible has produced both creative and destructive consequences in history. Kaufman argues that we have to both "deconstruct" and "reconstruct" this picture of God in order to develop a view of God that genuinely humanizes rather than oppresses or leads to violence. For the Christian, Christ represents the "normative" standpoint by which to evaluate any notion of God and whether that notion of God leads people and communities to live in a way that fits Christ's way of reconciliation and freedom. "By their fruits you will know them" (Matt 7:16).

Theology is Contextual and Provisional

All theology is provisional; it must be reworked again and again. Theology is thoroughly contextual. We think theologically in terms of a God revealed in Christ, a reality given through the symbols and stories of the New Testament and passed on through the traditions of the church. Nevertheless, all theology is a human cultural perspective and must constantly be reworked in relationship to the sociological and intellectual factors of the time and place. While theology reflects upon God, that ultimate reality, in terms of which all of culture is to be interpreted, it is shaped by and integrally related to the categories and the assumptions of the age in which it is developed. So are prayer, worship, and the ethical practices of the community integrally related to the assumptions of the time. This explains why theology is never a finished enterprise, but always in the process of change.

Theology was integrated with the world of Neoplatonism in Augustine's time. It was related to Aristotle by Aquinas and to African, modern, feminist, and postmodern perspectives in our time. We must therefore be fully aware of the limits to any theological worldview. It is profoundly particular, despite its claims to be talk about God, that orienting center from which we interpret the whole of reality.

In his *Church Dogmatics*, Karl Barth tried to ground a theology simply in response to the Word of God by rejecting all philosophical presuppositions. Yet Barth's very way of thinking theologically grew out of his own human understanding. Barth's theological method presupposes the Kantian distinction between the phenomenal world of nature or ordinary history (*Historie*) and the noumenal world of freedom, the special history (*Geschichte*) of God's revelation. So long as Barth presupposes this dualism of the world of "objects" and the world of "freedom," his theology is constructed to answer this problem. He argues from these dualistic presuppositions that it is no longer possible to move from the world of human experience to God as liberal theology had attempted. The "infinite qualitative distinction" between humans and God can only be bridged from God's side through revelation. But this very formulation of the problem depends upon dualist philosophical presuppositions, which Barth hoped he could transcend by beginning with revelation.

We can place our faith and loyalty only in God, not in a particular theological position. We must acknowledge our own limits as theologians. Theology begins with our human understanding and interpretation of the meaning of God for our lives. This requires us to reflect self-consciously about the point where we start. The question is not *whether* we begin with certain philosophical assumptions, but *what* they are, *why* we hold them, and *whether we are faithful* to the good news of the gospel when we use these categories of thought. These very presuppositions, the forms in which we think are not unshakeable. Another generation of theologians after us will recognize the limitations of the thinking of our time. So we must always remain open to further wisdom, aware as the writer of Ecclesiastes put it, "Even though those who are wise claim to know, they cannot find it out" (Eccl. 8:17).

THE EXISTENTIAL REALITY OF FAITH

Religious faith is a Godward orientation of humans to what they believe reality is like as a totality or a whole, reality in its most comprehensive sense. Clifford Geertz defines religion as (a) a system of symbols which (b) acts to establish powerful moods and motivations in people by (c) formulating a general view of the nature of things (d) in such a way that this view of things is seen to be really real, or more real than the ordinary routine of life.[8] The key element of Geertz's definition that distinguishes religion as a cultural system is "c", "a general view of the nature of things." Religious faith speaks to questions like the following: Is life fundamentally good or tragic? Is there any direction or purpose in the flow of cosmic time and history? What is the basis for hope? What, above all, is of value, such that it is worthy of our devotion and loyalty? In contrast to much human activity concerned with finite realities like the need for food, clothing or shelter, faith orients our lives in relation to everything that is, the ultimate framework that gives meaning to our lives.

The capacity for self-transcendence makes possible the symbolization of the meaning of life in religious terms.[9] Language enables us to "bind" time, to imagine a time before or after our time, or before or after the time of the universe as we know it. In other words, we can transcend ourselves and ask where our lives fit within the totality of what is. Through language we transcend time and space, the immediate present of our physical limitations. We have the capacity to reflect upon who we are, about the meaning of human life within the universe. Like all animals we die, but it is peculiarly human to be aware that we die, to anticipate our death, to concern ourselves with whether death is the last word, and to develop funeral rituals that interpret the meaning of death. Language enables us to ask whether death is final or whether our own capacity for self-transcendence points to realities beyond the boundaries of finite space and time.

Language enables us to develop self-awareness and self-consciousness, to become aware of ourselves as objects within the whole. At the same time, we are aware of ourselves as ecologically connected with the universe. This duality is at the root of our ambiguous relationship to nature. On the one hand, we view ourselves as one form of evolving life alongside other forms of life. On the other hand, we see ourselves as transcending nature, able to act to change and modify the natural processes and act upon nature as in some way apart from nature.

To orient our lives in relationship to the whole of reality with "God" as our point of reference requires faith. We are finite, but our sense of meaning transcends our finitude. Thus, faith is a precondition of living with meaning. Because we do not know or experience the whole of reality, we must develop a vision of "what is" and how we ought to live that goes beyond our limited experience and knowledge.

Is faith, then, simply a subjective or irrational "leap" as Søren Kierkegaard put it? No. First, faith is developed not by individuals who construe the world alone as heroic individuals, as Kierkegaard understood it, but in the context of social communities. We interpret the meaning of our lives in the context of communities of meaning and historical traditions that shape who we are. Second, even though faith must go beyond ordinary finite knowledge, faith seeks to construe reality in a way that can make sense of our experience of life. In this sense, faith is not simply a "blind leap."

Gordon Kaufman calls for a series of "small steps of faith" as we seek to construe the nature of the human and the world in relationship to which we can relate the symbol "God," that ultimate point of reference in terms of which everything else is to be understood. Though our concepts of the human and the world are also human constructions, we try to give a plausible interpretation in light of what we know and experience. To "imaginatively construct" the world is neither simply a subjective human invention nor is it the end result of an objective discovery of what is. In a Christian theological worldview, we make sense of life in the light of the concretely embodied presence of God revealed through the people of Israel and in Jesus Christ.

Because we are confronted with a plurality of views in our life pilgrimage, both as individuals and as communities, universally accepted understandings simply are not available to us. Thus an integral element of theological interpretation is to consider how the embodied presence of God in Christ engages other possible interpretations of what the world is like.[10]

In this dialogical process of engaging other worldviews, every human passion expresses a worldview and some kind of value system. In this sense, faith is universal. It is a human activity that involves our total being—intellect, will, and affections—a human activity of devotion to that which concerns humans ultimately.[11] While helpful, Tillich's views raise two further issues. Are not humans more profoundly polytheistic than Tillich seems to acknowledge, torn apart by multiple passions and loyalties, rather than oriented by an "ultimate" concern, as if there were only one object of loyalty and commitment? Second, is Tillich's view honest about the modern human condition?

With his notion of a "world come of age," Dietrich Bonhoeffer criticizes Tillich for trying to preserve a religious premise, that people are "really" religious underneath their secular commitments. Bonhoeffer argues that people need to be addressed by the gospel where they are, as completely secularized and committed to the mundane. Christian theology should not first establish humanity's "religiousness" and then build a Christian interpretation of life on this religious premise. Rather, the good news of God in Christ comes to humans in their humanness, in their strength as humans who have learned that they can get along without God, without religion, without an ultimate concern. For Bonhoeffer, Jesus Christ comes as good news in the midst of a radically secular world—a world come of age—not as an answer to human religiousness.[12]

THEOLOGY IS A PICTURE OF WHAT REALITY IS LIKE

Theology draws a comprehensive picture or model of what the whole of reality is like. Theology is a particular human interpretation of our experience that reflects the existential dialectic of faith and doubt. This is true of the world picture of the Bible as well. The Bible was developed by humans in their particular cultural context as they experienced God's presence in their midst. It too presupposes the existential commitment of faith of particular persons and communities. It too reflects the existential situation of a cosmology or worldview of its time and place.

World history shows that humans have created a plurality of world pictures, each developed in relationship to different historical and cultural conditions. The monotheistic world picture developed by the Hebrew prophets who oriented the life of Israel is one of these world pictures. It is dramatically different from the world pictures reflected in such Eastern religions as Hinduism and Buddhism and from the later religions of Judaism, Christianity, and Islam. Language makes it possible for humans to transcend themselves and reflect self-consciously on the world picture they have created. They are not simply determined by tradition, but are free to modify their world picture or even create entirely new worldviews.

However, because humans are finite creatures bounded by time and space and deeply rooted in particular histories and cultural traditions, the humanly created worlds are relative and particular. There is no mid-air position, no objective, neutral, absolute, framework "outside" of historical particularity from which one might judge the truth of a particular worldview. Those who take the biblical worldview as *the true* revelation of God on the basis of authority do so from a particular finite human standpoint. The fact that they make the *claim* that their world picture is absolute does not establish it as absolute. The same particularity is also characteristic of various Enlightenment ideas of universal reason. The so-called "universal" reason of the Enlightenment has been shown by Alasdair MacIntyre and others not really to be universal, but limited like all other views, a particular human construct developed within a particular history and tradition.[13]

Since we as finite human beings do not grasp the whole, our view of the whole is itself a human interpretation of what we imagine the whole to be. Our knowledge is highly dependent upon metaphor. We can talk only about what reality is "like." According to Sallie McFague, "a metaphor is an assertion or judgment of similarity and difference between two thoughts in permanent tension with one another which redescribes reality in an open-ended way but has structural as well as affective power."[14]

Several elements in this definition are worth noting. Metaphors assert both likeness and difference. To say, for example, that God is like a parent is to draw upon our finite experience of parenthood and our experience that God cares for us. It is to say how God is *like* that, even as we are aware that God is beyond and not quite like anything we know of human parenthood. The point is that we never grasp God apart from our interpreting, our metaphorical relationship to the one to whom we are devoted.[15]

Furthermore, metaphor is more than simply a rhetorical device that can be substituted for something we know to be true on nonmetaphorical grounds. Metaphor is foundational to knowledge in that two realities are linked together. Its meaning is a result of their interaction, not apart from it. We do not know God independent of our metaphorical relationship to God. As Tillich puts it, God is a symbol for God.[16]

In Christian theology, Jesus Christ is the "root metaphor" for our view of God and of God's relationship to the cosmos. Jesus is also the root metaphor of our understanding of what we are called to be as creatures made in God's image. We participate in this "knowing" of Christ not as detached observers, but as persons committed to following the way of life revealed in his life and teachings. The paradoxical nature of this knowledge is reflected in the Gospel of John. "If you continue in my word, you are truly my disciples; and you will know the truth, and the truth will make you free" (John 8:32). We do not first know truth arrived at in some detached manner and then proceed to act on it. We know truth in the context of our commitment to a way of life as we discover what truth is. We are not simply resident aliens, but citizens who are hungering and thirsting for justice as we act, seeking the peace of the cities where we live. Our hungering and thirsting, our acting and struggling, are essential to our living with faith and doubt. We come to commitment not simply by detachment, but by engagement in struggle. We must live with courage in spite of our lack of certainty.

Increasingly we are recognizing that all knowing is relational or participatory. This is one of the elements of what some are calling a "postmodern" perspective.[17] We know the world as a reality in which we participate, not simply as an object external to us. Knowing is analogous to how persons know each other. To know another depends upon revelation or disclosure. When we learn to know other people, we do not simply learn who they are by observing them as a spectator does an object (noting their physical characteristics, their social background). Rather, we become involved in a relational process of communication in which we open ourselves to a disclosure of who they are and we appropriate what they communicate into our own meaning system.[18] Knowledge of persons is not the same as our knowledge of non-person entities, like trees and birds. Because persons reveal themselves through language, all knowing, including knowledge of the natural world, is analogous to personal knowledge in its most fundamental sense. All knowing involves a creative interaction between the world we experience and the symbolic system with which we interpret our experience. All our knowledge presupposes relationality because it is finally rooted in the triadic nature of language: the sign, its referent, and its *meaning for us*. Because knowledge is integrally linked to language, which is language *for us*, human beings do not know things apart from their interpretation of them, but what they mean *in relationship* to us.[19] This is true in terms of how we know trees as well as how we know God.

We must overcome the sharp dichotomy between "personal" knowledge and "object" knowledge that has been so common in theology. The dichotomy is often stated in the following way: To know an object involves a relationship to what I want to know as if I am a spectator to that object. In contrast, personal knowledge is relational and involves the disclosure of one subject to another. This dichotomy has contributed to the sharp human vs. nature split: we know nature as an "object," as opposed to persons, who reveal themselves as subjects to us.

Such a way of thinking presupposes the subject/object dualism inherited from Descartes and assumes that science is "objective" knowledge as distinguished from other kinds of knowledge. This dichotomy fails to recognize that all our knowing is relational because it fails to recognize the connection of all our knowing to language. Ian Barbour and Sallie McFague have both shown how, like theology, scientific knowledge is also relational and dependent upon the symbolic systems of metaphor and paradigm. Scientific descriptions are themselves human interpretations, not simple objective descriptions of the world "as it is in itself."[20]

Metaphor describes reality in an open-ended way. The symbolizing process involves a constant process of creation and recreation. We are created by the symbol systems that give shape to our lives. At the same time, we create these symbol systems. Our lives are *gifted* by those traditions that give orientation and meaning to our lives. At the same time, our lives are an *effort* and struggle to adapt and recreate these symbols to fit ever-new experiences and understandings of life.

So religious faith involves the creative act of human imagination, which draws upon symbol systems and constantly reshapes those symbols in order to formulate our perception of the whole in both its likeness and unlikeness to our symbols.[21] Because these symbol systems order and orient our lives, they have significant power. They give fundamental shape to our basic moods, motivations, and actions.

A Normative Framework for a Christian Theology of Culture

A Christian theology of culture is a self-conscious process of assessing the appropriate metaphors for understanding God's relationship to the cosmos and our lives. We do that for our time and context in the light of the images and stories of the Bible and church tradition. A theology of culture is an interpretation of the relationship between our view and experience of the human, our understanding of the world or cosmos within which human action takes place, and how these two realities are related to "God," the ultimate frame of reference in terms of which human action and the cosmos is grounded. A specifically Christian theology of culture is fundamentally shaped by Jesus Christ as the central symbol or root metaphor for the interpretation of the other three realities. "Christ" does not simply exist as a fourth entity in addition to the other three, but as the orienting center for interpreting the other three: God, humans, and the world. Gordon Kaufman diagrams their relationship in the following way:[22]

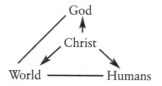

These four categories point to the four critical dimensions of the Christian life essential to an adequate interpretation of our cultural setting. These four interrelated notions provide the normative framework that can empower thoughtful Christians to know how they are to live in the world. A Christian theology of culture contributes to a normative vision that, as Geertz puts it, tells us what we have to know in order to function as Christians. With Christ as the orienting center, the four provide the leverage for interpreting what it means to seek the peace of the city where we dwell.

Christian theological reflection accepts the particularity of all human knowledge in two ways. We make the radical confession that Jesus Christ—as *sarx,* fully embodied within finitude—is the *root metaphor* for knowing God. In and through the particular Jesus of history, God is most vividly disclosed. Second, those who confess Jesus as the central integrating symbol in their lives do so within the limits of their own cultural particularity. We know and appropriate this symbol as the central paradigm of life in the context of our own limited knowledge and experience.

Theological reflection begins with particularity, with an affirmation of our rootedness in the temporal conditions of finite reality. In a pluralistic world, there seems to be no way to evaluate a particular worldview or moral position, since the validity of a worldview is defined by its own internal criteria of what is true or good. The logic of postmodernism thus seems to lead to a thoroughgoing relativism. We can choose to despair of our situation, withdrawing into our own private world of subjective experience. Or we can choose to embrace our uncertainty and begin in faith to live in response to the normative vision of life revealed to us through our own stories and tradition. We begin with the assumption that our historicity is a symbol of or pointer to the one God, who is no timeless and unchanging abstract idea. God enters into history preeminently in Jesus, is present to us as living Spirit, and risks interpretation or misinterpretation by historically particular and fallible human beings like us. We approach the one God not by abstracting ourselves from our particularity, but by glimpsing the universal through our particularity.[23]

Christian identity, then, is always a particular, temporal reality extending from the past into the present and anticipating the future. To be Christian means to be constituted by memory, to remember a past. As the book of Hebrews puts it, we belong to the people of faith. A cloud of witnesses who have gone before us surrounds us. In our remembering we experience the presence of the Spirit of God embodied in an existing community. And as a community of faith looking forward in time, giving expression to the hope that is in us, the church participates continually in the process of redefining and reshaping its system of symbolic meaning.

Having set out this general framework for a Christian theological orientation, I now need to be more specific. What specific norms guide our theological thinking?

We can divide these into two general areas: *faithfulness* to the vision of God in Christ and the *meaningfulness* of a theological vision can help us make sense of God talk in our time and place.

Faithfulness to the Vision

Commitment to the way of Jesus Christ is ultimately grounded in the attractiveness of Jesus' way as "good news"—a way that brings wholeness and healing to the world. We experience the gospel as good news, as resurrection, and as grace, as deliverance from our bondage to commitments and loyalties that are destructive of life.

The attractiveness of Jesus' way, however, does not mean that such a vision of life will automatically appeal to us in our state of addiction to powers that destroy life. Deliverance does not come easily. Anyone who has known someone with an addiction to drugs or alcohol knows how hard it is to be liberated from these powers, which literally rule people's lives. To pray as we do in the Lord's Prayer that God's kingdom may come "on earth as it is in heaven" is to pray for the delivering power of God's grace to liberate us from our bondage and addiction to powers that ultimately destroy our lives (e.g., materialism, hedonism, sexism, violence, ethnocentrism, and ecocide). To put it another way, our worship must transform us from our idolatrous commitments. It must turn us to the One revealed in Christ whose way is alone worthy of our commitment and loyalty.

This good news has "authoritative power" for those who follow Jesus. The significance of the Bible, then, is not that the book is itself the authority for how we must think or live, but that the biblical vision of life brings wholeness and healing to the world. One of the most critical theological issues is how we view the authority of the biblical story and the church tradition. How do we avoid a relativism or subjectivism on the one hand, which trusts too much in our own construction of a theological orientation, and an authoritarianism on the other hand, which appeals arbitrarily to given dogmas or metaphors as "true" simply because they are given by the tradition?

We can think of the authority of the Bible in three different ways. We can submit ourselves to it because we believe it to be true and biblical. We can regard it as a book that is more significant than any other because it provides the framework for the conversation about what it means to be faithful within the church. Or we can see it as a powerful story that enables us to make sense of our lives. I think of the authority of scripture in the second and third sense, but not in the first.[24] The Bible should continue to be an orienting center for dialogue among Christians. But more importantly, its authority lies in its power to evoke our consent because of the power of its story to change lives, to bring about resurrection, transformation.[25]

I like the way H. Richard Niebuhr puts the issue in his book, *The Meaning of Revelation*. He uses the phrase *reasons of the heart* to indicate that the appropriation of revelation in our lives is not contrary to reason, but is the way in which the story of God's action makes our lives intelligible.

> Revelation means for us that part of our inner history which illuminates the rest of it and which is itself intelligible. ... The special occasion to which we appeal in the Christian church is called Jesus Christ, in whom we see the righteousness of God, his power and wisdom. But from that special occasion we also derive the concepts which make possible the elucidation of all the events in our history. Revelation means this intelligible event which makes

all other events intelligible. Such a revelation, rather than being contrary to reason in our life, is the discovery of rational pattern in it. Revelation means the point at which we can begin to think and act as members of an intelligible and intelligent world of persons.[26]

This empowering good news can be concretely embodied in a community. In chapter five I will specify still more concrete practices and ways of living that should mark the life of the church, as a community living by an alternative cultural vision. Glen Stassen identifies seven

> concrete, historically realistic, processes of deliverance ... emphasized by the concretely incarnate Jesus ... : not judging, but forgiving, healing, and breaking down the barriers that marginalize or exclude; delivering justice; evangelism, preaching the gospel and calling for repentance and discipleship; nonviolent transforming initiatives; love of enemy; mutual servanthood; and prayer.[27]

My point here is not to describe these practices and elaborate their significance in more detail, but to emphasize that these are concrete practices that give normative guidance. We can validate through historical reason how these norms are working in the world. These are not esoteric practices available only to insiders who believe in Jesus; rather, they are concrete, doable, observable practices by a historical, sociological community—the church—that can be assessed for how they work. Even the outsider to the Christian faith can observe whether these practices are indeed good news. Do they contribute to the well-being of the city where the church dwells in bringing peace and reconciliation, and in delivering justice?[28]

Making Sense of God Talk in Our Time and Place

A second set of norms for theological thinking determines how we make sense of the Christian faith. We are called to love God with heart, soul, strength, and *mind*—in other words, to be philosophers or lovers of wisdom. Passion for the truth drives Christians to critique and evaluate the assumptions that guide living. We are called on as Christians to discern the truth. That discernment requires us to use all the mental capacities we have in the context of commitment to Jesus Christ, who serves as the most vivid standard of truth. That includes the use of logic and empirical knowledge in the service of God. A Christian theological orientation should be a dialectical one, "faith seeking understanding." A Christian view of life shapes our understanding of human experience and whatever else we know. A Christian view of the truth, then, integrates our Christian vision with human experience and knowledge. Experience shapes and changes our Christian interpretation of life even as the Christian paradigm serves as a framework for interpreting everything we know.

With this understanding of the interaction of paradigm and experience, we can understand how our normative judgments function. The Christian faith has interpretive power in helping us understand and interpret the world. If a paradigm did not have interpretive power, we could not continue to believe in it unless we were content to hold on to a claim simply on the basis of the authority of tradition. As we encounter the world, our Christian paradigm faces constant challenges. Being a Christian is a pilgrimage, an ongoing "inductive" reassessment and reinterpretation of the paradigm in the light of experience.[29] Anselm described this process as faith seeking understanding. We do not derive our faith from knowledge of sources other than the vision of life we have in Jesus Christ. Rather, we seek to relate our faith vision to all we know about history and the cosmos within which we live—from science, philosophical investigation, and the general human wisdom we learn from the wider culture.

In constructing a theology for our time, then, I believe we must incorporate the broader cultural wisdom within a Christian worldview. I do not find the approach of the postmodern confessional theologies of George Lindbeck and Stanley Hauerwas adequate in building this bridge to the wider culture. Both of these theologians do confessional theology insofar as the narrative of the Christian story defines what is true and what is the appropriate way to live. For Lindbeck the truth of the Christian faith can be judged only by its internal coherence: whether persons are faithful to the Christian story passed on through Scripture and tradition.[30] Hauerwas says that for the person outside the church, who is not within the community where the story makes sense, all one can do is tell the story or invite the person to "come and see." In *After Christendom?* Hauerwas says that becoming a Christian disciple is like learning to lay bricks. To lay bricks one must become an apprentice by participating in the brick-laying community. Similarly, to become a disciple one must "become part of a different community with a different set of practices."[31] Hauerwas is critical even of the "translation" of the meaning of the internal language of the Christian community into language that can relate to the wider culture.[32]

However, we can speak of criteria of "truth" and "moral validity" that go beyond Lindbeck's "intratextual" testability. As faith seeks understanding, we can and do appropriately employ such criteria as adequacy, comprehensiveness or interpretive power, coherence, and the practical implications for personal and social life.

Adequacy. Adequacy refers to the degree to which the fundamental issues of human existence are dealt in a Christian vision of life. How does the Christian faith interpret such perennial human issues as death, suffering, or moral failure? Our faith should be able to make sense of what we know. How does our faith relate to the insights of modern science or to the wisdom and insight of other religious traditions? Theology must take into account the full range of human experience and knowledge. It cannot simply ignore, for example, the prevalence of suffering and the horrendous evil we have experienced in this century through world wars, threatened nuclear holocaust, radical disparities between the rich and the poor, and a global market capitalism that threatens the health of the earth itself.

Interpretive power. The interpretive power of the Christian faith refers to its capacity to interpret the human enterprise. How does its account make sense of human life? Does it account for the way we experience the world? How does the Christian faith handle ambiguity or uncertainty? Christian faith can empower us to live with courage in a world where our knowledge is limited and not certain. Christian commitment to nonviolent persuasive love makes sense not because it is easy or because it is a pragmatic program to solve all human problems. It has interpretive power because it unites both commitment to a vision of nonviolent love and the recognition of human limit and uncertainty (hence the refusal to kill in the name of any penultimate idea or cause). Christian faith has incisive insights about the causes of war, the ways to make peace, and the kind of justice that restores community. It offers a prophetically realistic criticism of the injustice that comes from concentrations of power.

Coherence. A third criterion is coherence. Coherence asks about a way of formulating and living a Christian vision of life that is internally consistent. How do the parts fit together into a whole? Does it provide for creative syntheses that lead to wholeness or integration, or is its vision finally self-destructive? This criterion is analogous to the standards of symmetry, beauty, and aesthetic wholeness we use to judge a work of art or music. Is there a consistency between what we know and believe to be the case in one realm of knowledge and how we talk about God in Christ theologically? We need a holistic worldview. We should not live in separated worlds where science is compartmentalized or the marketplace separated from how we think about matters of faith. Compartmentalized worldviews violate the first article of the creed, "I believe in God." If we cannot relate a sphere of knowledge to our faith in God, then we have not done adequate thinking about God, the ultimate point of reference for *all* reality.

Ethical implications. A fourth criterion has to do with what are the implications for living if one holds to a Christian view of life. How is the good life defined? What kind of a social order is supported? Can we live with the implications of such a view? What are the ethical or practical consequences of believing a certain world picture or holding to a particular view of God? What in these pictures needs to be deconstructed because of the negative consequences they produce (e.g., God as a warrior who legitimates human violence)? What in these pictures can be appropriated for a constructive worldview (e.g., God as one who enters into compassionate solidarity with suffering to bring about a liberating justice)?

In both the Old and New Testaments we find this test used frequently. In 1 John the question posed is how one can say one knows God if one hates one's brother. In Micah we read that God requires justice and mercy, that one walk humbly with God. In Matthew 7, judgment comes to those who do not bear fruit. In the parable of the sheep and the goats in Matthew 25, the decisive difference is whether persons acted to care for the "least of these."

MARTIN LUTHER KING JR. AS A MODEL OF THEOLOGICAL REFLECTION

Martin L. King Jr. modeled the alternative culture vision I am proposing. He integrated an intellectual and moral vision that leads neither to despair nor withdrawal from society, but to action that contributes to the peace of the city.

King embraced his own particularity while addressing the universal implications of the good news for the entire world. The particular language and symbols of the black church shaped the vision of Martin L. King Jr. Out of those roots, King learned from the surrounding culture—the writings of Gandhi, Buber, Marx, Thoreau—even Nietzsche. King exercised his citizenship by seeking the well-being of America. He used the cultural language of American civil religion. However, he used it not to legitimate the violence and injustice of the dominant culture, but rather to call forth another vision: one consistent with the alternative vision of life he derived from the Hebrew prophets, Jesus, and the spirituals of the black church.

King made his contribution not by going along with the approach of the dominant culture, but by being an alternative to it. In this way he sought the peace of the society into which he was called. He spoke of injecting into the veins of history a renewing power. In "Letter from a Birmingham Jail" he puts it this way:

> Human progress never rolls in on wheels of inevitability; it comes through the tireless efforts of men willing to be co-workers with God, and without this hard work, time itself becomes an ally of the forces of social stagnation. We must use time creatively, in the knowledge that the time is always ripe to do right.[33]

King integrated philosophy, the love of wisdom, with citizenship, the quest for the social good. King was an artist nurtured by the black church. We cannot understand King without paying close attention to the black church, the roots from which he came.[34] The worship of God, especially through preaching and singing, provided the spiritual power for King's movement. King's speeches are rich in poetic metaphors and the prophetic words of the Bible. Those who participated remember the power of the music of the black spirituals and the freedom songs. Others can sense some of this when they view the films and documentaries of the civil rights movement.

In Martin Luther King Jr. we catch a glimpse of the "alternative culture" model. We see in King an example of an integrated theology of culture. King's life illuminates the three broad questions a Christian theology of culture must address, reflected in the title of this book, and the basis for the organizational structure of Part Two. How might we as philosophers (lovers of wisdom) discern what is true about reality and how might that wisdom affect our lives and the life of our culture? What is our role as citizens and how do we exercise our responsibility in seeking the good of the human community and the well-being of the earth? And what is our role as artists? How might we express a cultural vision in an aesthetically excellent way (expressed by King in image, metaphor, and poetry, and by the black church in song)?

King integrated these three elements of Christian theology. As human beings we want to know what is true. I use the image of the philosopher for this dimension of culture as loving wisdom. I mean the common human quest to know, that fundamental human quality that makes us all lovers of wisdom, or philosophers. Confronted by the limits to our knowledge, the human enterprise is a constant quest to apprehend Truth with a capital "T." Yet we know that every apprehension of truth confronts the mystery that lies beyond all human truths, and thus every attempt to express truth in symbolic form is only a limited truth, or truth with a small "t." What gives meaning and significance to the quest for truth is the conviction and hope that our limited human truths are at least approximations of Truth, and that in some sense, human truths participate in the Truth.

One of the essential elements of Gandhi's nonviolent philosophy was his view that no one can claim to possess Truth in a way that could possibly justify imposing his convictions with violence. Gandhi subtitled his autobiography "My Experiments with Truth." Yet he and Martin L. King Jr. lived out their experiments with deep conviction, believing that their own apprehension of truth was nurtured by a transcendent purpose beyond them. King said that one of the six basic elements of his own nonviolent philosophy was a conviction about truth, the nature of ultimate reality, the conviction that in the struggle for justice the nonviolent resister has cosmic companionship.[35]

Second, the creation of human culture is a social enterprise. We create who we are as citizens together with others. Just as *philosopher* symbolizes one engaged in the common human quest for wisdom, so we should understand *citizen* in a broad sense. *Citizen* describes the role all humans play in our quest for the good. By *citizen* I do not simply mean what we do when we vote or lobby for particular social policies. To be a citizen means to belong to a "city." The word *city* is a particularly apt symbol to convey what we are as humans. We belong to others and others belong to us as we self-consciously create who we are in a particular and structured form.

Martin L. King Jr. gave us a picture of citizenship. Through his speech and action he sought to create a beloved community. He said, "We are tied together in the single garment of destiny, caught in an inescapable network of mutuality. And whatever affects one directly affects all indirectly."[36] He was fond of quoting John Donne: "No man is an island entire of itself. Every man is a piece of the continent—a part of the main. ... Any man's death diminishes me because I am involved in mankind. Therefore never send to know for whom the bell tolls; it tolls for thee."[37]

He created community at several levels. The church nurtured him and the vision of the beloved community he learned as a Baptist preacher shaped his vision for the political order. He sought to help his own black people affirm their positive identity as black people. He attempted to create a social system in the United States based on political and economic justice. And at the international level he worked for peace by opposing the U.S. prosecution of the Vietnam War.

The third element in the triad is the human quest for beauty, that standard of excellence by which we judge the created world of human culture. This ability to create arises from the human capacity of language. Because of our language, we can imagine possibilities of pattern and order that do not yet exist: tools or technology to accomplish our goals, designs of the material objects to serve both functional and aesthetic needs, ways of structuring our institutions, conceptions of the organization of our living spaces, patterns of social life in our towns and cities, the patterns of our rituals.

Human beings are also artists, creators of patterns of meaning and significance. Integrally related to our search for truth as philosophers and our quest for the good as citizens is our quest for beauty as artists. The artist in us is the capacity to imagine, to create new possibilities. Artistic imagination involves the ability to "play," to be able to detach ourselves from the serious business of life in order to give shape to new possibilities. Artistic creation requires freedom, the capacity to abandon old ways, to take risks, to conceive of new ways to define issues and problems, and to interpret symbols in new ways. Without the artist, the spirit of life would die and we would cease to be, for we would cease to be fundamentally human, creators of culture, the systems of symbols that give meaning and significance to our lives.

King's movement was an aesthetic achievement. King enlivened the imagination of a nation and awakened it to new possibilities of life. He did that especially through the poetic images of the spoken word. He helped a people discover that black is beautiful. He helped people sing a new song. The documentaries from that time show that great social changes were embodied in a people who literally sang their way to jail. King empowered people to take risks, to create something new in culture.

To summarize theologically what the King movement models, being made in the image of God means that we have the gift of creative imagination, the capacity to create our own worlds of beauty, truth, and goodness. Human culture reflects the image of God, though dimly and minimally. We see the fullness of the light in Jesus Christ and in the beauty of God's created cosmos interpreted in the light of Christ. Because of sin, humans have become alienated from God and the vision of truth, goodness, and beauty that God intends for us. Nevertheless, human culture also reflects dimly the human quest for truth as an apprehension of Truth, for goodness as an intimation of Good, and for the beautiful as a reflection of Beauty. Though human culture points beyond itself to the Mystery of Being, because it participates in God's being, human culture can intimate the Mystery, Goodness and Beauty of God.[38]

In the next chapter I build on this triadic structure to develop a normative vision for a Christian theology of culture, a creative alternative from which to discriminate among the variety of cultural visions of our time. Such an alternative vision can help empower the church to participate creatively, faithfully, and responsibly in the common cultural life. Such a vision is grounded in the Trinity: God the Creator as the power and mystery of being, the source of Truth; Jesus Christ as model or standard of goodness, and the Holy Spirit as the creative power of beauty.

As we come full circle in this chapter, we stress how such a vision of life is embodied concretely. A Christian vision of culture should profoundly shape and inform our embodiment as earthlings. Such a vision can give meaning to the most ordinary of human actions, such as eating a meal together. In breaking bread together, we not only survive like animals, but we also are gifted with the possibility of expressing God's truth, goodness, and beauty.

4

A Trinitarian Model
for a Theology of Culture

*Each of God's creatures speaks to us in a kind of mystical code in
order to stimulate our curiosity. ... There is an intimation of the whole
Trinity in each of God's creations. For, if we ask whence it came, the
answer is: "God created it;" whence its wisdom, "God enlightens it;"
whence its happiness, "God is its joy." By subsisting in Him it is what
it is; by contemplating Him it receives its light; by abiding in Him it
possesses beatitude. It is; it knows; it loves. Its life is in the eternity of
God; its light is in the truth of God; its joy is in the goodness of God.[1]*
—Augustine

WHY WOULD ONE take up the doctrine of the Trinity in developing
a theology of culture for North Americans living at the turn of the millennium? Why pick such an obscure, speculative, and controversial notion? The Trinitarian controversies in church history boast of dubious
accomplishments. Are we not in the presence of mysteries about which
we would be better off not to speak at all? And why should we spend
our time and energy on something so speculative and obscure when
there are such pressing issues in our world? How is this doctrine relevant at all for how we think in order to orient our lives and know how
to live?

In what follows, I will be making three claims. First, speaking
about God in a Christian way requires Trinitarian language. Second,
Trinitarian thought is profoundly relevant to how we interpret the
larger cosmos and culture in which we live. Third, the Trinity is essential in providing us with a moral vision that can give practical guidance
to the church. I cannot enter here into the complexities of the issues

that have shaped this doctrine in the history of the church and that continue to be an important arena of discussion for Christian theologians. Instead, I will attempt only to demonstrate the "functionality" or practical necessity of Trinitarian thought for a theology of culture.[2]

WHY A TRINITARIAN MODEL

Trinitarian thinking is central to Christian theology. To speak about God in a Christian worldview requires a triadic structure of thinking. We confess our devotion to the One who is the ground of all being, the One who is most vividly revealed in the concrete embodied Jesus, and the One whom we experience as a living, present reality.

Though a doctrine of the Trinity is not developed until much later in church history, a Trinitarian structure of thought is implicit in the Bible. First, Christians confess the reality of God, the source and ground of all being. According to the Genesis 1 account of creation, God is God of the cosmos, all that is, the One who saw everything that was made and called it good (Gen. 1:31). There is no reality or dimension of being outside of God. God is the source of the "lights in the dome of the sky" (Gen. 1:14), so these "lights" are not separate divine powers that control human destiny. God created the "great sea monsters" (Gen. 1:21), so the monsters do not represent threatening powers in the universe outside of God's sovereign power.

In the words of Psalm 139, "Where can I go from your spirit? Or where can I flee from your presence? If I ascend to heaven, you are there; if I make my bed in Sheol, you are there" (Ps. 139:7-8). Everything that has being is grounded in and to be interpreted in the light of this One. God alone is worthy of our ultimate devotion and loyalty. In the words of the Shema: "Hear, O Israel, the LORD is our God, the LORD alone. You shall love the LORD your God with all your heart, and with all your soul, and with all your might" (Deut. 6:4-5).

According to the synoptic Gospels, Jesus identified the Shema as one of the two great commandments (Mark 12:29-30). Jesus called on his followers to seek first God's kingdom. Devotion to God relativizes all other values and human standpoints. God is not a dimension of being or a value alongside other values, but the ground of all being and the source of all value. We see this devotion to the one God in Paul's sermon at Athens as reported in the Acts of the Apostles: "For 'In him we live and move and have our being'; as even some of your own poets have said, 'For we too are his offspring'" (Acts: 17:28). Paul's Christology did not compromise his radical monotheistic faith. Even Christ ultimately "hands the kingdom over to God the Father, after he has destroyed every rule and every authority and power. ... When all things are subjected to him, then the Son himself will also be subjected to the one who put all things in subjection under him, so that God may be all in all" (1 Cor. 15:24, 28).

Second, God is concretely revealed in Jesus Christ. Without some concretely embodied vision of the character of God, God would remain only a distant absolute. We need a normative standpoint accessible to humans where God is vividly disclosed. Otherwise our language for God would remain in the realm of vague abstraction. God's concrete, historical presence is made known in numerous ways in the New Testament. "And the Word (*logos*) became flesh (*sarx*) and lived among us, and we have seen his glory, the glory as of a father's only son, full of grace and truth" (John 1:14). We are familiar with the passage in Paul's letter to the Philippians of self-emptying (*kenosis*) of God through Jesus, "who, though he was in the form of God, did not regard equality with God as something to be exploited, but emptied himself, taking the form of a slave, being born in human likeness. And being found in human form, he humbled himself and became obedient to the point of death—even death on a cross" (Phil. 2:6-8).

Too often the church has neglected the concrete, embodied Jesus. We need more than a vague idea of the incarnation. God was incarnate in Jesus as teacher, healer, prayer, forgiver, leader of twelve disciples, confronter of injustice, and peacemaker. The Apostles' Creed jumps from the birth of Jesus to his passion. All we confess about Jesus' humanity is that he was born, suffered under Pontius Pilate, was crucified, and died—nothing in between. Most medieval art portrays Jesus as a baby or on the cross. Luther said Jesus' teachings in the Sermon on the Mount make us aware of our sin (that we cannot follow the law), so Luther focused on Paul's doctrine of justification by grace alone.

The prevailing view of Christ for many contemporary Christians is that he died to save us from our sins—another abstraction separated from the concrete embodied Jesus who healed, taught, advocated justice, and got into trouble with the authorities because of his radical nonconformity to the values of his age. A Christian doctrine of the Trinity must recover the realization that God is present in the concretely embodied Jesus, not just in his death and resurrection abstracted from his life and teaching.

Third, God is a living, present reality. Without this third component God would remain a wholly distant "mystery," just a memory of an historical event. God would not really be God, that living reality related to and present in all reality. Luke and Acts especially emphasize the continuity of the living power of God's spirit, present to Elizabeth, Mary, Zechariah, John the Baptist, Jesus, and to the early church at Pentecost. Luke connects the same Spirit moving Jesus with the spirit of God referred to in the prophet Isaiah. This identification is evident in Jesus' inaugural message in the synagogue at Nazareth. "The Spirit of the Lord is upon me, because he has anointed me to bring good news to the poor" (Luke 4:18). In Isaiah and the prophets, the Holy Spirit inspires prophets to speak incisively and powerfully about injustice and justice, idolatry and faithfulness. Jesus is in continuity with this prophetic tradition.

We use Trinitarian language not simply because we are obligated to honor tradition that has been handed down to us. Rather, our subject matter compels us to think in a triadic way. There is a deep wisdom in the tradition. And we continue to think in a triadic way because of the insight into how one must speak about God as a Christian. Furthermore, Trinitarian thinking does real work in developing a theology of culture. These concepts are able to provide us with a framework of analysis and interpretation of the church's vision and its relationship to the wider culture that is both comprehensive and relevant for helping us discern how we as Christians should seek the peace of the city where we dwell.

Postmodern Categories for Thinking About the Trinity

We need to think about the Trinity in categories of thought that are appropriate to our own time and culture. We are not bound to the categories of thought of earlier centuries, when the church originally developed the doctrine of the Trinity. Some of the problems in thinking clearly about what we mean by Trinity are linked with the categories they used. The problem was that they were working with philosophical categories of *substance*—that reality consists of objects, "thing-like" entities that are self-enclosed or self-contained. The problem to be solved was how God could be revealed in three ways—as Creator, as present in Jesus Christ, and as present to us in the Holy Spirit, but still be one God, one substance. We still encounter this way of thinking and it creates all kinds of theological difficulties.

We see this in the debate about whether Jesus "is" God. If one says, for example, that Jesus is not God, one is subject to the charge of a low Christology, that Jesus was only a great man like Gandhi and King. Why then should he be the object of our loyalty and devotion? If, however, one says Jesus is God, then how does one preserve Jesus' full humanity, that Jesus was really sarx (flesh)? How can a "god" be a model for human beings to follow?

If one thinks in categories of substance, how can one think of God or the Spirit as a being—as a "person" in the traditional language? To attribute existence to God as a substance immediately gets one into problems; how can God exist in any meaningful sense, as an entity with boundaries in space and time? To speak of God's "existence" places God as a being beside other modes of being, and that language suggests we are placing limits on God. For we want to say that God is not a being beside other being, but the ground or source of all being, the One who is present in all other modes of being. Furthermore how can we speak of the Spirit as an "entity" or "person"? What could that mean when we talk about the Spirit's presence within a community? "Spirit" does not "appear" to us as an entity, a thing like reality, but as a presence in and among the whole community, outside of the boundaries of space and time.

Other philosophical categories can help us think about what we mean by a Trinitarian God. One of these categories is the concept of "process." At a most basic level, reality is in process. Entities do not have rigid boundaries; rather, they penetrate each other. This is true at the most microcosmic level. Particles are energy fields, according to modern physics. This is true at the human level as well. Though our bodies suggest clear boundaries within space and time, even our bodies are in process, born of the "stuff" of the cosmos and returning to the earth when we die (itself a process). Our cells are in process of birth and death. We are always in process. When we breathe oxygen, we are interacting with the larger ecosystem we share with other humans and plants. Our bodies emanate energy in the form of heat and sound waves. Our eyes process light as information, ranging from the fragment of a moment when two persons see each other to the sight of a star whose light energy reaches us only after millions of years.

At an even more profound level, we are social animals whose language is in process, shaped by others, who in turn are shaped by an evolving language tradition that goes back centuries. For example, English shares common roots with the ancient Indian language of Sanskrit. Thus the question, "Who am I?" at a common sense level, suggests a clear boundary—Duane Friesen, the personality within a particular body bounded by space and time. Yet this commonsense notion is profoundly misleading and the source of much confusion, reflecting as it does notions of an "autonomous" self, an unchanging substance, the kind of atomistic thinking which has gotten us in so many problems.

Ecological thinking is integrally connected to what we have said about process. As we learn about the earth and the larger cosmos, we are recognizing more and more that all reality is interconnected and interrelated. Everything that occurs in the universe has an impact on everything else. We belong to a whole. The challenge for modern thought is to transcend the limits of linear, sequential ways of thinking in order to develop a holistic way of thinking that reflects the ecological reality of all being.

Thus, we can think today about the Trinity in ways that are reflective of a view of reality as both process and as an ecological whole. Gordon Kaufman says that

> with the development of the idea of the *perichoresis* of three persons of the trinity (their interpenetration into one another), the notion of ultimate reality (God) as simple substance is displaced by a much more complex conception: on the one hand, the "persons" of the trinity are so involved with one another, so relationally interconnected in their very being, that it is simply not possible to conceive them as independent substances who have their being or can act in any way independently of the others (*una substantia, tres personnae*); on the other hand, the "one substance" that God is thought to be is precisely this exceedingly complex interpenetrative activity/being of the three "persons," a conception far removed from the simple oneness of unity which "substance" had previously designated.[3]

AN OUTLINE OF A TRINITARIAN MODEL

We will now consider nine motifs or themes (organized in a patchwork quilt of nine squares) to order a Christian theology of culture systematically. Our central concern is how theological reflection on the Trinity can provide a comprehensive or holistic view of Christian social ethics. Niebuhr's basic insight in *Christ and Culture*—his assessment of how various Christian attitudes to culture measure up to a Trinitarian conceptual scheme—is sound. The significant problems with how Niebuhr actually uses the Trinity to reason in *Christ and Culture*[4] do not invalidate the value of a Trinitarian conceptual scheme as a tool of description and analysis.

I use the image of a patchwork quilt to suggest the creative constructive nature of this enterprise. Quilts can be put together in many different ways. In no way can we consider this an ideal quilt in a Platonic sense or a description of the way things really are. Quilts are put together by humans, just as theological motifs can be organized in a variety of ways. Quilts also tell stories through the symbols in each block. Each of the categories and motifs developed in the grid below is a "pointer" or suggestive metaphor to tell a story. My purpose is not to set out a closed rational system.

The beauty of a quilt lies also in how the parts fit together, the appropriate blend of color and pattern. In this sense, a quilt presents us with an ordered whole. My purpose is to help us think holistically. We need to consider the broad range of dimensions of a Christian social ethic in order to avoid an unbalanced ethic that is not adequately oriented by the basic themes that are definitive in a Christian worldview. One of the problems in contemporary theological ethics is the tendency to over-generalize from a particular insight, to take a particular contribution of an ethicist (e.g., Stanley Hauerwas's view of the centrality of the church or John H. Yoder's emphasis on discipleship or Walter Wink's insights about the principalities and powers) as a launching pad for the whole job of Christian ethics.

One of the limits of the quilt metaphor is that it does not adequately suggest process. In a quilt, each block is a self-contained entity. We need to think of the quilt as a "story quilt." Each of the blocks tells a story that is integrally linked with the stories of the other blocks of the quilt. In such a quilt, the blocks are not separate self-contained stories, but are part of a larger story pattern. Each of the stories is shaped by and influences the telling and the interpretation of each of the other stories so that the stories flow into each other in a process of interaction. They are not self-contained isolated units.

The quilt grid is organized around three vertical theological motifs (God the Creator, God in Christ, and God the Holy Spirit) and three horizontal motifs (God as liberating power, Christ as the loving power of God, and the Spirit as God's creative power) to make a total of nine themes or motifs. Each of the vertical motifs tell the same story, but in three different ways. The remaining sections of this chapter will explain the content of the motifs in the grid.

The three columns of vertical blocks tell the story of God as God, God in Christ, and God as Spirit. The first vertical column is a way to think theologically about God: the transcendence or "Godness" of God, the Creator, who is the ground of all finite reality, the character of God as the power of persuasive love, when viewed in the light of Christ, and God as Spirit, the vital and creative energy of the cosmos.

The second vertical column tells the three-way story of Jesus Christ: as the one who announces God's kingdom, as the crucified one in the flesh, and as the spirit of the new humanity—a model of humanity in the new community, the church. These quilt blocks are ways to think theologically about Christ: Christ's announcement of God's kingdom of righteousness and justice, the cross of Christ as embodiment of sacrificial love, and the resurrection of Christ as the manifestation of the Spirit in a new humanity, a new community of mutuality.

The third vertical column tells the story of the Spirit in a threefold way: the Spirit as the liberating power of God, the Spirit as the renewing grace of Christ, and the Spirit as reconciling presence in the cosmos. These blocks represent ways to think theologically about the Spirit: the liberating power of God, the gift of grace through Jesus Christ, and the reconciling presence of the Spirit in the new community and the larger cosmos.

Below the line within each of the squares is a description of the human response to God, Christ, and the Spirit as viewed in each of their threefold dimensions. The bottom half of each block is divided into two parts to reflect the tension between an authentic human response and human sin. For example, in the presence of God, the ultimate reality in terms of which everything else is to be understood, we authentically experience a sense of bafflement and mystery. We confront the relativity of our own truth in the presence of the one true God. The claim to absolute certainty is a reflection of human pride and arrogance, the refusal to recognize our own finitude. The reader can look at the model below to see the basic categories of positive response and sin, which I shall describe in the remainder of the chapter.

GOD'S TRANSCENDENT, PERSUASIVE, AND CREATIVE POWER
God as Transcendence, Beyond All Limit

The central symbol of the Christian faith is Jesus Christ. As central symbol, Jesus points to the nature of God, the ground of all being. God is the Ultimate, the symbol for the reality that is "beyond" or which transcends all finite reality. God is the Source or Ground of all being. Not only Jesus, but also the entire cosmos is a symbol pointing to the reality and nature of God (as reflected in the quote from Augustine at the beginning of this chapter). Though Jesus is the norm in terms of which Christians discern what God is like, the reality of God as ground of all being is not limited to Jesus. Thus the Apostle Paul preached in Athens to those who did not know about Jesus that God is "the one in whom we live and move and have our being."

Though God is the Ground or Source of all Truth, our knowledge of that truth is relational. Our knowledge is limited by our own fini-

	God the Creator		God in Christ		God the Holy Spirit	
Transcendent Power	Transcendence of God: Godness of God; beyond all limit; absoluteness; mystery		Kingdom of God: good news; God's justice; God's domination-free order		Spirit as liberating power: engaging the powers; dying to old, rising to new	
	Negative (sin): certainty, arrogance/ pride, secure foundations	Positive (transformation): existential doubt, humility, relativity of knowledge, tolerance	Negative (sin): evasion, complacency, loss of nerve	Positive (transformation): repentance, commitment, courage, justice	Negative (sin): idolatry, bondage to powers, repression/ exclusion	Positive (transformation): devotion/ loyalty, liberation, dignity, empowerment
	God as Persuasive Love		**Jesus as Servant**		**Spirit as Gift, Grace**	
Loving Power	Suffering of God: anguish, mourning, lament		The reality of the cross: sacrificial, nonviolent love		Generosity/abundance, forgiveness, mercy	
	Negative (sin): lack of trust, domination, power over/ control	Positive (transformation): faith, consent, vulnerability, love	Negative (sin): unfaithfulness, gnosticism/abstraction, violence	Positive (transformation): discipleship, practical/ visible, concrete peacemaking/service	Negative (sin): anger/ resentment, self-centeredness, exploitation	Positive (transformation): gratitude, thanksgiving for gift of life/opportunity, generosity
	God as Creative Power		**Christ as Living Presence**		**Spirit as Reconciling Presence**	
Creative Power	Vitality, energy, life, novelty, order		New humanity/society, the church as Christ's body		Shalom/wholeness; restoring relationship	
	Negative (sin): boredom, sloth, despair, paralysis	Positive (transformation): wonder, vitality/ creativity, hope, imagination	Negative (sin): individualism/ isolation, racism/ ethnocentrism, hierarchy/ control	Positive (transformation): community solidarity, mutuality/ equality, openness /flexibility	Negative (sin): fragmentation, departmentalization, numbness	Positive (transformation): shalom/ wholeness, ecology/ linkages, joy/delight, integrity of creation

tude, our specific location in time and space within the cosmos. As ground of all time and space, God is beyond all limits. We confront therefore, the mystery, or limit of our own knowing.

The relative and the absolute are thus correlates of each other. The failure to understand this dialectic has resulted in much confusion about the issue of relativism.[5] God is the symbol of the absolute or ultimate limit in terms of which all reality is known. Thus every human construction of knowledge is but a relative approximation.

Relativity is thus a correlate of the concept of the ultimate or absolute, not a denial of it. All human knowledge is limited and cannot make the living God the possession of a set of doctrines or an institution. For human knowledge is a relative approximation of truth, and God is the living God, not a human possession. Thus every human construction, including any Christian claim that Jesus Christ is the root metaphor for God, is a faith claim that confronts mystery and the limits of human knowing.

The attempt by humans to secure a foundation for sure knowledge of God is a sign of our failure to "let God be God" and our refusal to acknowledge our limits as humans. As Paul Tillich has stated so well, doubt is an integral component of faith. He speaks not of the doubt of the skeptic who cynically refuses to commit to anything, nor the methodological doubt entailed in scientific inquiry, which appropriately resists believing in the truth of a hypothesis until it can be supported by evidence. Rather, Tillich means the existential doubt that requires a commitment to an ultimate reality beyond our finite limits. In this sense, faith is the commitment of the total person (mind, spirit, will, and emotion), yet a person who is finite, limited in perspective, and unable to guarantee that the ultimate reality to which one gives oneself is truly ultimate. Such faith requires risk and courage.[6]

The recognition of human limits can lead to another false claim, the commitment to relativism. We need to distinguish between relativity, the view we supported in the previous chapter—that truth is historically particular and relative to particular contexts—and relativism. Relativism is the leap some make from an acknowledgment of the limits of our knowing to the metaphysical claim that nothing transcends our particular context. The claim that *nothing* transcends our particular context is paradoxically a universal claim that is logically inconsistent, a denial of the very claim of relativity. It is also an idolatrous faith. It is an idolatrous faith because relativity replaces God as the absolute standard (by definition a contradiction) in terms of which all of reality is judged. The prophet Micah summarizes our responsibility before

God as a matter of doing justice, loving mercy, and walking humbly with God. To walk humbly with God means to recognize that all human truth is but an approximation before God, whom we approach as the Mystery who is beyond all human approximations of knowledge.

Gandhi subtitled his autobiography, "My Experiments with Truth." Gandhi engaged in an ongoing quest for Truth with a capital "T." He presupposed the unity of all truth in God, but saw his own understanding and action on the basis of that understanding as an approximation of truth. This is the underlying basis of Gandhi's nonviolence. We can never be so sure of our own position that we would be justified in using violent force against another person or group. The creative engagement of others through nonviolent means opens the possibility for new truth and insight to emerge. The destruction of others through violent force forecloses the future by making it impossible for a creative synthesis of new truth to emerge.

Here we see an essential polarity or tension in the Christian faith. We are called to give our lives in devotion to God. We are called to commit ourselves with passion to God's kingdom and God's righteousness. Yet we must do so in a spirit of humility, recognizing that we are not God, but frail human beings in our understanding and capacities. We see "through a glass darkly," as Paul states in 1 Corinthians 13. To be zealous for God's kingdom without a sufficient awareness of our own finitude and limits can lead to self-righteousness, fanaticism, and violence. On the other hand, if the awareness of our relativity prevents us from committing ourselves passionately to God's ways, we will vacillate and remain weak, without the power or conviction to make a difference in the cities where we dwell.

God as Persuasive Love

In genuine human communication, the hiddenness of the other is disclosed and revealed. Christians confess that Jesus is the one who most vividly reveals God's nature. Jesus is metaphorically God's Word. This is not to deny that the entire cosmos is a "Word" of God, a disclosure of God's being. While Jesus is the *root metaphor* for knowing who God is, the entire cosmos also reveals God, since its being is derived from God's creating action and God participates in all being. While ordinary persons reveal themselves most vividly at certain times in their lives, they also reveal themselves in manifold words and actions throughout their lives. But if we want to know them most clearly, we turn to those events that are most revealing. Christians make the claim that Jesus most vividly reveals God without denying that God is revealed elsewhere throughout the cosmos.

If we take Jesus as the one who most vividly reveals who God is, then love is the symbol that most adequately expresses the truth about who God is. In seeking to illuminate what characterizes this love, we look to Jesus' life and teaching, death, and resurrection. We also search for metaphors or analogies within human experience that best convey the nature of God's love.

Parental love is one of the most vivid and powerful expressions of human love. God's relationship to the universe is analogous to the relationship of loving parents to their children.[7] To give birth to a child is an act of faith, a commitment to affirm life, yet with no guarantee about the outcome. God gives birth to the universe. This act does not happen all at once; like the growth of a child into adulthood, it is a process that develops over time. Intentional parenthood requires an act on the parents' part to conceive a child. So the universe does not arise from itself, but is intended by God and brought into being. The creative process of bringing the universe into being is itself an act of creative love, a yearning on the part of God to affirm life. The act of redemption in Christ to restore the universe to the intention God has for it and the creative process of bringing the universe into being are both actions that arise from the one God who is the power of love both in creating and redeeming the universe.

The child who develops over time into an adult human being becomes who he or she is not just in interaction with the parents. In the early stages of life within the womb, a loving mother provides the environment for the development of a healthy child. The child who is born, however, is a result not just of the intentions of the mother and father, but also of the interaction within its environment: the air the mother breathes, the food she eats, and even the impact of sounds and vibrations on the womb during pregnancy.

The birth of the universe is a similar process. Over billions of years, processes developed that made possible the kind of universe that sustains life as we know it today. We can speak of God's purposes for the universe, yet the outcome is not the result of the deterministic control of God. For biological life, the engine of change is the result of chance variation in the DNA molecule. The universe that is emerging over billions of years arises from the interaction of a great variety of forces within the framework of God's loving purpose, a persuasive power that seeks to influence but does not control the outcome. Like the birth and development of a child, however, the universe is not completely the result of chance. Parents must seek to provide an environment that will produce a healthy child.

Theology has struggled with how to understand the relationship of God to an evolving universe. This evolutionary process arises either from chance variation or completely under the control of God. Neither position seems plausible. It is difficult to account for the order and beauty of the cosmos simply on the basis of chance. On the other hand, to think of God as an absolutely controlling power fails to account for events that seem to lack any purposeful explanation. It also destroys human freedom and thus undermines human responsibility.[8]

Persuasive love is analogous to the relationship of parents and children. Parents want their children's lives to flourish, but they cannot control the outcome. If God is ultimately love, we must rethink our understanding of power. One kind of power is controlling or dictatorial power, the kind of power I have in relationship to a chair when I determine to move it. Another kind of power is persuasive power, the kind of power I have in relationship to other persons when I persuade them to act in a certain way. My power in relationship to them is interactive, and depends upon their consent to my persuasion.

This metaphor makes sense when we think of God's relationship to humans. God relates to us through Jesus Christ who is God's agent of creative and persuasive love. Through Christ, God seeks to persuade us to act in accord with God's intention for human beings in the universe. We must give consent to God. God respects human freedom and thus does not intervene in the universe to "save" us from the consequences of our decisions. As human freedom emerges in the process of evolution, the possibility for horrendous evil exists. The twentieth century is evidence of what human beings can do to each other and to the universe when they fail to give consent to God's love.[9]

In the biblical picture of God, there is a tension between the God of persuasive love revealed in Christ who overcomes evil through sacrificial love and the God who intervenes in judgment and wrath to defeat evil through violent power. We see this tension in Miroslav Volf's profound and brilliant book, *Exclusion and Embrace: A Theological Exploration of Identity, Otherness, and Reconciliation*. In this book, which was born out of the suffering of his people in the Balkans, Volf argues for a God who forgives and does not remember forever, a God who creates a new community out of enemies through the sacrificial love of the cross. But in the final chapter Volf introduces the "other hand" of God, a side of God we are not prepared for in the argument of the rest of the book. Volf argues that in the end, Christian nonvio-

lence and the embrace of enemies is possible because of an eschatological hope in a God who will ultimately destroy evil through violent force and set things right. We do not have to do it because God will
see to it that justice is done. "Vengeance is mine, I will repay says the
Lord" (Rom. 12:19). In other words, wrath belongs to God alone, not
to us.[10] Volf argues that this is the only way he can respond to the deep
sense of violation felt by persons in the Balkans who cry out for justice.
God too is angry and does not ignore the evil done in history. There is
judgment, and justice will be done.

What are we to make of this tension, which is certainly present in
the Bible? Volf rightly argues that we must take evil seriously, as well as
the violation people have experienced. Weak sentimental love will not
do. Genuine love and compassion for others entails anger at evil and
the naming of injustice. Nonviolence is not a sentimental love. In the
tradition of Martin Luther King Jr. and Gandhi, compassionate nonviolence confronts evil vigorously and actively. But in history, tragedy
often prevails. An ethic of nonviolence that is based on the premise
that sacrificial love will always succeed in winning over one's enemies
is unrealistic about the depth of evil. This is why Volf says that ultimately God must intervene in an extraordinary way.

Volf's argument is problematic for several reasons. In the first
place, it raises serious problems with a Trinitarian notion of God, which
he argued for cogently earlier in the book. If we are to accept Volf's argument, there is another God than the God we know in Jesus Christ.
Besides the God of Jesus, there is a righteous and just God who destroys evil by violence.

Second, this ultimate appeal to violent force as the only way in
which evil can be defeated undermines Volf's argument in the rest of
his book—that the way of the cross and forgiveness is the only way in
which the escalating cycle of evil can be broken in history. If the slain
lamb is not ultimately victorious over evil because only a God on a
"white horse" can defeat evil, then how can it be credible to believe
that the way of the cross should be followed in history?

Third, Volf's argument assumes a miraculous intervention of God
at the end of history that does not square with the relationship of God
to the cosmos the previous 15 billion years. On what grounds do we
postulate an intervention that suddenly calls the evolutionary process
and freedom to an end through some kind of miraculous intervention,
a controlling power that ends human freedom? While such a violent eschatological vision is present in the Bible, is it theologically credible?
Should we not rather agree with Walter Wink who argues that if we

take Christ's "domination-free order" as the revelation of God, then the appeal to a wrathful, violent God is a residue of the old myth of redemptive violence, a myth that has not been fully overcome in the minds of some of the biblical writers?[11]

How should we understand God's power? Many theologians have challenged views of God's power because they are idolatrous projections shaped by our assumptions about power. Such theologians as Dietrich Bonfoeffer, Dorothee Soelle, Martin Luther King Jr., Kazo Kitamori, Keosuke Koyama, Jon Sobrino, and Larry Rasmussen have all suggested ways to understand God's power in the light of the cross where God enters into our pain and suffering.[12] We assume that power means control, that power is the ability to accomplish any purpose by any means necessary. We therefore also assume that an all-powerful God must be able to accomplish anything God wills and will accomplish it by whatever means it takes.

Such human preconceptions of power are not shaped by the vision of power of suffering love we see revealed in Christ. If God is really the God we see in Jesus Christ, then our preconceptions of power must change. God's power is revealed on the cross where God is most vulnerable; it is not defined by control or being in charge. Christ revealed his power in his identification with the human condition. He entered into the suffering of the world and saved us there in that weakness and vulnerability.

We do not worship a God who pulls strings like a puppeteer to save us out of our predicament, if God so wills. We do not worship a God who magically decides whether to exercise power to heal or not to heal. Rather, we see revealed in Jesus a God whose way of salvation comes through a loving presence within our suffering. Within our vulnerable human condition we are invited to consent to that love, to respond freely to God and offer that same love to others. There is no magical intervention or formula for salvation, only the hard and joyful work of sacrificial love. In Jesus we see the God for others and we are invited to be that presence to others as well.

We see this vision of God's power in the cross in the ethics of Paul.

> Consider your own call, brothers and sisters: not many of you were wise by human standards, not many were powerful, not many were of noble birth. But God chose what is foolish in the world to shame the wise; God chose what is weak in the world to shame the strong. God chose what is low and despised in the world, things that are not, to reduce to nothing things that are, so that no one might boast in the presence of God. He is the source

of your life in Christ Jesus, who became for us wisdom from God, and righteousness and sanctification and redemption, in order that, as it is written, "Let the one who boasts, boast in the Lord." ... For no one can lay any foundation other than the one already laid, which is Jesus Christ. (1 Cor. 1:26-31; 3:11)

We see it again in Philippians 2, where Paul uses the paradigm of God's emptying himself and taking on the likeness of a servant to the point of death on the cross as an argument for humility (Phil. 2:1-11). In Paul's vision, resurrection is not something added to or different from God's love revealed in the cross. It is precisely this servant love that makes Jesus "Lord" and an enduring, living reality in the cosmos (Phil. 2:9-11).

Process theologians, dependent upon the work of Alfred N. Whitehead, use the model of persuasive love also to account for God's relationship to the physical and biological universe as well. God is in relationship to all entities in the universe, from simple particles to biological organisms. All entities possess an elementary freedom, the possibility of "choosing" to act in relationship to that with which they interact. As persuasive power, God acts upon all entities in the universe. According to Charles Birch, "God confronts what is actual in the world with what is possible for it."[13] The universe is not programmed to act in a predetermined way, but is capable of responding to the possibility put before it by God.

Furthermore, God responds to the world that emerges. Just as parents respond to the decisions made by their children, so God continues to respond to and interact with the universe.[14]

Therefore, we appropriately refer to the suffering and pathos of God. Jesus stood on the Mount of Olives and wept as he longed that the city of Jerusalem would do those things that make for peace (Luke 19:41-42). So also God suffers with the universe and continues to seek to persuade it to decide for those things that affirm life rather than death. Matthew uses the parental metaphor: "Jerusalem, Jerusalem, the city that kills the prophets and stones those who are sent to it! How often have I desired to gather your children together as a hen gathers her brood under her wings, and you were not willing!" (Matt. 23:37).

Though this is only the bare outline of a description of a Christian understanding of God, this account illuminates the way in which "faith seeks understanding." The persuasiveness of the metaphor of God as loving parent is dependent both upon how faithful it is in illuminating God's nature as revealed in Jesus Christ and also how well it enables us to make sense of the world as we experience it. The metaphor has interpretive power: it helps us account for the world adequately, it provides coherence to a Christian vision of life, and it has practical implications that are appropriate and consistent with the Christian faith. This metaphor helps us to interpret the world of evolutionary biology. It can also integrate a vision of the Christian life. Above all, this metaphor encourages Christian responsibility by affirming human freedom. God relates to human beings not by saving us out of our predicaments, but by calling us to cooperate with God's loving purpose by seeking the peace God intends for the universe.

God as Creative Power

The Spirit is God's creative power present in the cosmos. The presence of God in Christ, in the flesh, is the ground for the astonishing claim that the transcendent God is at the same time immanent in the entire cosmos. The earth and human flesh are not alien to God; they are the very locus of God's presence. We do not "see" and "know" God by an escape to another realm of reality, by ascending to some other sphere beyond the world (as in various forms of Neoplatonic philosophy), but by embracing the cosmos, the earth, the earthy sensuous reality in which our bodies live and move in our daily activities. The heart of the Christian faith, the incarnation, is the audacious claim that the Logos, the very Word of God, is present in flesh (sarx).

Two errors have contributed to the failure to emphasize the divine creativity in the cosmos. The one is a false spiritualization, a kind of gnosticism that diminishes the body and the earth as a locus of God's presence. In so much Christian piety, especially in more conservative and fundamentalist forms of Christianity, salvation has been understood as eternal life with God after death. A soul/body dualism has been presupposed, which places the emphasis upon salvation of the soul (devoid of embodiment).

The other error is a secular or materialistic philosophy. The divine presence in all of reality is difficult to imagine in a culture where the cosmos has been desacralized. We have inherited hierarchical dualisms of God/world, mind/body, and spirit/nature that have robbed us of a sense of God's spirit immanent in all reality. We tend to look upon the natural world as an "object" distinct from us to be "used" for human benefit. We see it as an object "out there" to be studied, manipulated for our benefit. Christian theology has contributed to this view of the world as devoid of God's presence in several ways. Emphasizing that God is the creator of the world and therefore distinct from the world distances God's presence and creativity from all reality. Another problem area has been the emphasis in so much twentieth-century theology (influenced by Kant's distinction between the phenomenal and noumenal realm) upon God as an actor in history, with nature as a kind of theater or stage on which the drama of human history takes place.

Both of these positions are contrary to the emphases of the Bible. "The heavens are telling the glory of God; and the firmament proclaims his handiwork. Day to day pours forth speech, and night to night declares knowledge" (Ps. 19:1-2). Isaiah's experience of the transcendence of God in the temple, with God sitting on a throne, high and lofty, is correlated with the divine immanence in all reality. "Holy, holy, holy is the Lord of hosts; the whole earth is full of his glory" (Isa. 6:1-3).

Or, in the words of Psalm 139,

> Where can I go from your spirit? Or where can I flee from your presence? If I ascend to heaven, you are there; if I make my bed in Sheol, you are there. If I take the wings of the morning and settle in the farthest limits of the sea, even there your hand shall lead me, and your right hand shall hold me fast. ... My frame was not hidden from you, when I was being made in secret, intricately woven in the depths of the earth. Your eyes behold my unformed substance. (Ps. 139:7-9; 15-16a)

Feminist theologians have noted that the most extended instance of female imagery for God in the Bible is the presence of God's Spirit in Wisdom. "The Spirit's functions are depicted as Woman Wisdom."[15] In the second story of creation in Genesis the Spirit of God is "breathed into" humans. We are not persons who *have* a body, as if it were external to us. We are not spiritual beings with a soul distinct from the body. In the biblical understanding, we *are* "spirited bodies." That is why the eschatological vision of Paul is a resurrected *body*. Paul does not accept the Greek notion of an immortal soul separate from the body. This dualism of soul and body would develop later and be a detriment to an adequate understanding of the human person. Elizabeth Johnson beautifully summarizes the biblical emphasis on the presence of God's Spirit in the whole creation.

> The continuous changing of historical life reveals that the Spirit moves. From the beginning of the cosmos, when the Spirit moves over the water (Gen. 1:2) to the end, when God will make all things new (Rev. 21:5), standing still is an unknown stance. The long and unfinished development known as evolution testifies to just how much novelty, just how much surprise, the universe is ca-

pable of spawning out of pre-given order or chaos. In every instance the living Spirit empowers, lures, prods, dances on ahead. Throughout the process, the Spirit characteristically sets up bonds of kinship among all creatures, human and non-human alike, all of whom are energized by this one Source. A Christian liturgical greeting expresses this very beautifully. "The grace of our Lord Jesus Christ, and the love of God, and the fellowship of the Holy Spirit be with you all." Fellowship, community, koinonia is the primordial design of existence, as all creatures are connected through the indwelling, renewing, moving Creator Spirit.[16]

This Christian worldview has been characterized by a number of theologians as "pan-en-theism.[17] God is present in the whole cosmos (to distinguish the position from dualism) yet not identical with the cosmos (to distinguish the position from pantheism). Sallie McFague uses the metaphor of the "world as God's body" to stress the way in which God is present in the whole body and dependent upon the body, yet not identical with the body. This is analogous to the mind, which cannot be reduced to the body, yet is dependent upon it. Though I find her metaphor suggestive, I agree with James Nash's warning that McFague's metaphor is in danger of undermining the transcendence of God, since it suggests that God is dependent upon the body.

> The "body" metaphor seems to compromise divine independence, and deny the distinctive integrity of creation and its creatures. It may contribute to animism and idolatry. It certainly adds nothing to the value and lovableness of nature that is not already accomplished through the traditional affirmation of the sacramental presence of the Spirit.[18]

"Sacramental presence" is the conviction that all material reality is holy because God is present in it. This conviction is essential to a theological orientation that seeks the peace of the city. Larry Rasmussen's analysis of the different ways Karl Barth and Dietrich Bonhoeffer responded to the cultural crisis of Europe in the midst of the suffering and pain of World War I can help us as we reflect on our cultural crisis at the turn of the millennium. Both Barth's and Bonhoeffer's perspectives are important, as both together reflect the polarity and tension in a Christian understanding of God. Barth responded to the crises with a theology of transcendence.

> An infinite qualitative distance separated divine from human ways. ... Theology's task was deep and unrelenting cultural critique. The even younger Dietrich Bonhoeffer, desiring to pro-

claim the same majesty, began by bringing God into the closest possible, but also awesome, proximity. Barth was drawing from the Calvinist insistence that the finite cannot hold the infinite (*finitum non capax infiniti*) while Bonhoeffer insisted, with Luther, that the finite bears the infinite and the transcendent is utterly immanent (*finitum capax infiniti*). "God is in the facts themselves," said Bonhoeffer, asserting his conviction that God is amidst the living events of nature and history. His favorite quotation from F. C. Oetinger said much the same. "The end of the ways of God is bodiliness."[19]

Bodiliness means for us respect and care for the earth. The cosmos, both in its grandeur as a totality as well as in the minuteness of each small particle, should evoke in us a sense of wonder and delight at the mysterious creativity and beauty of God. It should evoke in us a sense of awe and reverence, a profound humility to counter our arrogance and our desire to conquer and control. It should induce gratitude and an enthusiasm for life to counter our sloth and loss of energy. Despair and hopelessness result when we lose touch with the sacred mystery of the cosmos, when we live one-dimensional lives by seeking material goals and hedonistic pleasures. Such a way of life leads to paralysis and cynicism. We lose our capacity to be creative partners with God.

Bodiliness means for us a respect and care for the image of God in every person. The Quakers speak of "that of God in every person." This means respect and care even for the enemy, the stranger, and the least of these. In the powerful and challenging words of Matthew 25, "I was hungry and you gave me food, I was thirsty and you gave me something to drink, I was a stranger and you welcomed me, I was naked and you gave me clothing, I was sick and you took care of me, I was in prison and you visited me" (Matt. 25:35-36). God is present not just in the "good" or in the beauty of the cosmos, but in pain and suffering. God becomes flesh. In Christ, God enters into the suffering and pain of the universe. In that solidarity with us lies our hope.

JESUS CHRIST: EMBODIMENT OF THE GOOD

"I give you a new commandment, that you love one another. Just as I have loved you, you also should love one another" (John 13:34). Foundational to the Christian faith is the claim that in Jesus we find the most complete manifestation of what we are called to be as human beings. Though said in a different language, the great creeds of Nicea and Chalcedon, still held as authoritative by most Christians, make these two affirmations: that in Jesus we find God and our humanity most vividly illuminated. Christians also confess that in Jesus the "human" is most fully known and lived out. Jesus is the norm for what it means to be fully human, and thus the historical Jesus as Son of God illuminates what we are called to be as children of God. Jesus Christ is not only a metaphor pointing us to God's Truth, but also the norm or standard of the good.

Jesus Christ is God's disclosure of what it means to be fully human. This standard is presented to us historically in the human life of Jesus the Jew who lived in the particular time and space of first-century Palestine. As a norm or standard for our own humanity, Jesus is a symbol. Knowing who we are called to be through Jesus is not like knowing an object of historical study, though historical study is helpful and important. Knowing Jesus as norm is not like knowing a text (e.g., the Bible) as an object of study, though rigorous study of the text is helpful and important. For it is not Jesus as historical object or the Bible as text that is the foundation for our faith, but Jesus as metaphor, symbol, norm, and standard for us.

We appropriate Jesus Christ into our lives to orient us and to show us what it means to live a well-lived life. It is in the lives of the people of God, who view Jesus as the foundational metaphor both for God and humanity, that the Spirit of God in Jesus Christ is *embodied* or appropriated in the worship of the community as well as in the life of its members in the world where they are residents.

To describe theologically what it means to hold Jesus Christ as norm for our humanity is, however, not a simple procedure. The interpretation of who Jesus is for us must be constructed anew in each generation and in every context. Our knowing of Jesus is integrally connected with how we "confess" Jesus, or appropriate Jesus in our lives. The task of discerning who Jesus is for our lives therefore involves a complex interpretive process. The church is the context in which we discern what it means to be faithful to the story of Jesus. Commitment to Christ as norm means to commit as a people to an ongoing conversational process under the guidance of Scripture in the face of a multitude of challenges.[20]

An adequate theology of culture is one that has an "embodied" Christology. We need a Christology that can provide a vivid picture of a Christ who is not disembodied from cultural formation, but who is concrete enough to provide leverage for assessing how we should engage the particularities of culture. The Christology of many Christians conveniently relegates Jesus to a "separate" sphere of life (the spiritual) or to the afterlife as an answer to their special concern about eternal life. Jesus is disconnected from culture, from living life responsibly before God in the world. When Christ is relegated to the "spiritual" or salvation deferred beyond the grave, Christians tend uncritically to legitimate the dominant political and economic system, since Jesus is defined as "acultural" and therefore irrelevant to culture.

It is important, then, for the church to rethink its Christology in the light of the alternative model I have presented. Such a rethinking will also be a more faithful reading of the New Testament itself, since the early church viewed Jesus in the light of its call to be an "alternative society" in the world.[21] The Jesus of the Gospels represents a specific and concrete alternative way of life.

We get a colorful picture or model of who Jesus is in the New Testament through a variety of images and stories, sayings, teachings, accounts of Jesus' life, and the encounters that led to his crucifixion. It is difficult and problematic to summarize what principles we can learn from this story to guide our discernment of how to engage our own culture. The task is difficult and problematic because of the richness and variety of the images and stories. We must not reduce who Jesus is to a list of abstractions. The variety of stories and images can stimulate our imaginations to bring Jesus Christ to life in our own communities in ever new and creative ways. The Trinitarian model introduced earlier suggests that Christ is the one who proclaims God's kingdom of justice and righteousness, the servant who is faithful to death on the cross, and the living spirit in the new community, the church. This Trinitarian structure functions as a compass or guide for our appropriation of Jesus as norm for the church's engagement with culture.

The One Who Proclaims God's Kingdom

Jesus Christ is God's anointed one (Messiah), commissioned to bring God's kingdom or rule into the world. The kingdom of God represents the wholeness God intends for the entire cosmos. The kingdom of God is not, as so often has been understood, a reference to heaven, a reality "off the map" of the world in which we live. Rather that kingdom is God's rule in all of life. Jesus taught his disciples to pray that the kingdom of God might come *on earth* as it is in heaven (Matt. 6:10).

The kingdom entails liberation from bondage to powers that are destructive of life. We see this vividly demonstrated in two stories in the Gospel of Luke. A person enslaved by demonic power is healed. Jesus says, "If it is by the finger of God that I cast out the demons, then the kingdom of God has come to you" (Luke 11: 20). Here the kingdom is a present reality. The larger corporate or structural dimension of God's kingdom is evident in the story of Zacchaeus. The context is Zacchaeus's participation as a tax collector in the system of Roman oppression. By being a tax collector, Zacchaeus had benefited from a system that enabled some to get rich at the expense of the poor. So people murmured when Jesus invited himself to Zacchaeus's house.

Zacchaeus's encounter with Jesus caused his repentance, a genuine turning around of his life in a different direction. He made restitution to those whom he wronged. Zacchaeus promised to give half his goods to the poor and to restore fourfold to anyone he had cheated. Jesus responds, "Today salvation has come to this house, since he also is a son of Abraham. For the Son of Man came to seek and save the lost" (Luke 19:9-10). Zacchaeus symbolizes liberation from a corporate system of exploitation and from his complicity in that system by virtue of his own greed. He is liberated to become a person who practices justice by a redistribution of his resources to those in need. This brings his salvation *today*, not in some distant future.

Of course, the liberating power of God is not fully present within the world. The reality of the kingdom is still future in terms of its full manifestation; yet it is already present where God's wholeness breaks into the cosmos. The kingdom becomes present through Jesus when he gives sight to the blind, feeds the hungry, liberates people from demonic possession, forgives sin so that people can live a life of wholeness—and in many other ways.

Luke 4:18-19 expresses the purpose of Jesus' messiahship:

> The Spirit of the Lord is upon me,
>> because he has anointed me to bring good
>>> news to the poor.
> He has sent me to proclaim release to the captives
>> and recovery of sight to the blind,
>>> to let the oppressed go free,
> to proclaim the year of the Lord's favor.

Jesus identifies with or stands in solidarity with the marginalized. Those treated as outcasts in the social context of Jesus' time were the very ones for whom Jesus had compassion: the poor, widows, the sick, Samaritans, and those labeled "sinners." We observe, in particular, Jesus' revolutionary attitude and behavior toward women, especially when viewed in the cultural context of first century Palestine. Letha Scanzoni and Nancy Hardesty summarize Jesus' attitude to women:

> He treated women not primarily as females but as human beings. Without sentimentality, condescension, or undemanding indul-

gence, he accepted them as persons in a way that moved them to repentance and love. ... Thus Jesus' life on earth from beginning to end outlines a paradigm for women's place. His actions upset and appalled his contemporaries, dumbfounded his critics, and flabbergasted his disciples.[22]

Jesus taught and practiced a total devotion to God's kingdom that challenged human devotion to lesser ends. This is particularly evident in Jesus' teaching on wealth and material well-being. Jesus did not deny the importance of bodily needs like bread and drink; he fed the hungry and calls us to do likewise. But he severely condemned devotion to the accumulation of wealth. Walter Wink summarizes Jesus' teachings:

> Jesus ... pours scorn on those who are clothed in soft raiment and dwell in king's houses (Matt. 11:8 and Luke 7:25). He challenges creditors, not only to forgo interest, but to ask no repayment whatever. To those who wish to follow him, he counsels selling everything, and warns the rich that they have no access whatever to the new society coming. Those who hoard luxuries and neglect the poor at their doors are presented with the prospect of their own death and divine judgment (Luke 12:13-21; 16:19-31). To the religionist's dream of being able to be "spiritual" and still amass wealth within an unjust system, Jesus pronounces an unconditional no. "You cannot serve God and wealth" (Matt. 6:24 and Luke 16:13)."[23]

Walter Wink characterizes the kingdom as "God's domination-free order." Among the many characteristics he lists are the following: mutuality rather than hierarchy and control; partnership and cooperation rather than power over and the desire to dominate others; sharing and generosity rather than exploitation and greed; cultural transformation rather than holding on to the status quo; ecological attitudes of respect toward creation rather than anthropocentric attitudes; and nonviolent conflict resolution rather than violence and war.[24] Glen Stassen points out that "the reign of God (or kingdom of God) is not a place, it is a process—a process of turning and deliverance—a process of peace, justice, and the reign of God. In our language, a better translation is 'God's reigning' or 'God's delivering' than 'kingdom of God.'"[25]

Jesus' call to "seek first God's kingdom and God's righteousness" (Matt. 6:33) "means the restoring of just relations among us personally and societally, and with God. It points to God's gracious initiative in delivering us from sin, guilt, and oppression into a new community of justice, peace and freedom and our obedient participation in God's way of deliverance."[26]

The kingdom of God therefore calls us to repentance. We are called to turn our lives around through the power of God's gracious deliverance, to commit ourselves to an alternative vision of life. The opposite of repentance is evasion and complacency. Some choose to seek happiness by giving themselves to the idols of the dominant culture: personal satisfaction and well-being, material self-indulgence and pleasure, comfort and security—at the expense of God's kingdom of justice and peace.

Jesus the Servant

At the heart of the Christian faith is compassionate presence, Jesus' incarnate presence in the middle of the suffering and anguish of life. Jesus reveals a God who is not a detached sovereign ruling over the universe from a distance. The Greek word for compassion in the New Testament, *splagchnoisomai*, a word that perhaps best characterizes Jesus, means literally "to be moved in one's bowels." Compassion means to let one's innards embrace the feeling or situation of the other. Jesus is a compassionate presence to those who suffer. This is evident in many of the stories of the Gospels.

Jesus' solidarity with those who suffer leads him into direct conflict with the powers and authorities that keep people in bondage. In his preaching, teaching, and living this good news, Jesus clashed with the religious, political, and economic establishment that saw him as a threat to their vested interests and social order. Jesus struggled throughout his life with the question of how to bring in his kingdom, whether by the traditional methods of political power and revolutionary violence or in other ways. Ultimately, he accepted the way of suffering and death, becoming obedient unto death (Phil. 2:8). The resurrection vindicated the way of the suffering servant, which led to Jesus' death on the cross. The slain lamb is the Lord, the victor over evil (Phil. 2:8-11; Rev. 5:6-14).[27] We see in Jesus a concrete vision of what God's kingdom might look like. We also get a picture of the *means* by which that kingdom comes.

Jesus offers a model, both in his own life and in his teachings, particularly in the Sermon on the Mount, of how to confront evil nonviolently. Instead of legitimating the dominant culture's view that pathological evil must finally be confronted with violence, Jesus offers a creative third way, an alternative to the use of violent force and passive resignation to evil. John H. Yoder's *Politics of Jesus*, Walter Wink's *En-*

gaging the Powers, and Glen Stassen's *Just Peacemaking* are examples of recent books that spell out Jesus' model of nonviolent engagement in more detail than I can do here.

Stassen points out that most interpretations of the Sermon on the Mount view Jesus as teaching an impossible ideal that cannot be realized in a sinful world. He argues that they misinterpret Jesus' teachings as dyadic: (1) You have heard of old, don't kill, (2) but I say don't even be angry. Stassen instead points out that in the Sermon on the Mount there are fourteen triads organized around three categories: (1) traditional piety (e.g., you shall not kill); (2) the mechanism of bondage (e.g., nursing anger or saying, "you fool!"); and (3) transforming initiative (e.g., go, be reconciled while there's time). He summarizes:

> We see that the third element is always an initiative, not merely a prohibition. It is always a practical participation in deliverance from a vicious cycle of bondage, hostility, idolatry, and judgment. ... Each moves us away from the "hard saying" or "high ideal" kind of interpretation that has caused resistance, evasion, and a dualistic split between inner intentions in the heart and outer deeds in society. Each moves us instead into participation in God's grace, God's deliverance, God's reign."[28]

This suggests that to be a follower of Christ means to search for concrete initiatives within one's culture that can creatively and nonviolently transform conditions of injustice and violence into occasions of justice and peace.

Jesus' way of life that led to the cross is a model for our own humanity. Unfortunately, many of the prevailing views of Jesus' death and resurrection are disconnected from Jesus' life and teaching. These views indirectly contribute to a legitimizing of the dominant culture rather than projecting a concrete alternative cultural vision from which to engage the dominant culture.

Three atonement metaphors have been prominent in traditional theology. In the satisfaction theory, the basic problem that must be satisfied is God's justice, God's just demand for punishment for sin. An innocent man, Jesus, must pay the debt owed to God. Jesus receives the punishment sinners deserve as a substitution for us. A second view draws upon the Old Testament images of expiatory sacrifice or blood atonement (see Lev. 4:27-31). God is angry with people because of sin. People express sorrow (Heb. 9:11-14) for their sin by sacrificing their best to God. God turns toward people favorably, forgiving their sin. So Christ offers himself to God (in his death) as the supreme sacrifice.

Through his sacrifice for sinners as the slain lamb who sheds his blood, Christians who believe are forgiven and accepted by God. A third view is known as the ransom theory. In this view, human beings are captured by sin and held in bondage. The devil must be paid a ransom in order to release sinners. Christ pays the price by giving his innocent life. Sinners who believe are released from bondage.

In each of these views of the meaning of Christ's death, the death of Christ is *necessary* in order to satisfy God or the devil. An innocent victim must die. In each case death is a necessity for salvation in a way that is unrelated to the life and teachings of Jesus. Jesus' life is significant only in the sense that it demonstrates that Jesus is an innocent victim. In all of these cases, the death of Jesus is unrelated to ethics, to our responsibility before God. The purpose of Jesus' death is related to our salvation beyond death.

Another way of understanding Christ is more in harmony with the New Testament and undergirds the "alternative" culture model we have proposed. The work of Christ should be understood primarily as aimed at *transforming people* rather than primarily satisfying God or the devil. Christians who believe in Jesus—not just in the sense of intellectual assent, but who trust in his way and in his power—are called to a life of faithfulness to the way of Jesus. Thus Jesus' life and death are directly connected to ethical responsibility. Jesus' life and death are models for the kind of people Christians are to be—to love like Jesus, even our enemies, to be servants to others like him, and to be willing to lay down our lives for others as he did for us. In other words, Jesus' way becomes a model or standard for a community that is an alternative to the values of the dominant culture. Through Christ, Christians are set free from bondage to the old age and called to be participants with Christ in inaugurating a new age (Col. 2:13-15; Gal. 3:23-28).[29]

The implication of this view of Christ is that the church should not divide the spiritual and ethical, this life and the life to come. Both dimensions are integrally connected to the one salvation brought about by God in Christ. Being a new community of peace in the world, and seeking the peace of the city where the church dwells is therefore central and integral to the gospel, the good news.

In the light of this understanding of Christ as the one who brings shalom, I will reinterpret the three models of atonement discussed above and link them to the transformation of humans toward wholeness. The dominant image in the satisfaction theory is of Jesus as the suffering servant who sacrifices his life for sinners. Jesus died not to appease an angry God but because he challenged our sin, he confronted the status quo, he called for a new way of life. Instead of judging us with his wrath or seeking our end through holy war, he laid down his life for us. He forgives us even when we reject him. In other words, his sacrifice is the price of his nonconformity and his willingness to suffer for us rather than engage in holy war against us. In that sacrifice he reveals to us a God who seeks to restore the world to the life God intended for it through the persuasive power of love, not through wrath and violence.

The dominant image in the expiatory sacrifice or substitution theory is that humans deserve God's wrath for their disobedience. But instead of God's wrath being directed to them, Jesus takes the wrath of evil systems upon himself, substituting for humans and suffering the consequences of human sin. The price Jesus pays for his nonconformity in his confrontation with human sin results in his crucifixion and death. What this reveals is a God of immeasurable love who is willing to pay the ultimate sacrifice of life in order to restore humans to life. In other words, God's love is victorious over God's justified wrath. Just as a parent does not forever maintain her anger toward a child even when the child cannot make amends for the wrong done, so God is willing to forgive and accept sinners so that life can start anew. This has significant implications for the mission of the church. God's love for the cosmos (John 3:16) cannot be carried out authentically when we divide the world into the good and the evil and direct our hostility to the evil. God's aim is to transform the evil into the good. God makes it rain on the just and unjust. God is indiscriminate in God's love, and Christian people are called to be like God, loving even their enemies (Matt. 5:48) with a view toward reconciliation. What Christ reveals is a God whose love is patient and endures, even when that love is continually spurned.

The main image in the ransom theory is that Christians are released from bondage in Christ. Jesus pays the price of nonconformity with his life, which gives us a new lease on life. Christians are set free to love, to reject self-centered lives, to turn away from the cycle of violence. A new option is available to people. Most revolutionaries want to make the enemy pay the price of revolution by destroying the enemy and his institutions. In such a scheme, the cycle of violence simply continues. In Jesus, who loves his enemies, we see the cycle of violence broken. Christians who trust in his power are set free from the bondage of the friend/enemy dichotomy.

The traditional ideas of the atonement support the myth of redemptive violence, the belief that for salvation to occur, for God's wrath to be satisfied, an innocent victim must die. Is it any wonder that so many Christians support capital punishment on the grounds that for justice to be "satisfied," the one who commits a crime must die? The common assumption behind capital punishment and traditional theories of the atonement is that violence is required for justice to be satisfied. What a sad commentary on the history of the church! Jesus' life, teachings, and death showed us a way of liberation from the powers of violence! But for millennia the church has rejected Jesus' way in the false conviction that God's justice can be satisfied and our salvation can be achieved only through an act of violence!

Indeed, the costly sacrifice of Jesus on the cross is integral to our liberation, but not to satisfy a God "out there," detached from the cross. God is there "in" the cross, present in Christ's suffering, revealing the way of liberation through sacrificial love, not through redemptive violence.

> The nonviolent God of Jesus comes to be depicted as a God of unequaled violence, since God not only allegedly demands the blood of the victim who is closest and most precious to him, but also holds the whole of humanity accountable for a death that God both anticipated and required. Against such an image of God the revolt of atheism is an act of pure religion.[30]

Jesus Christ as Living Presence in the New Society, the Church

Through the narrative of God's action in history, culminating in the story of Jesus, we come to know who we are and what we are called to be. The biblical story shows us that we are creatures dependent upon God, that we receive this story within the context of our own particularity or historicity, and that this story is given to us through God's self-disclosure in the people of Israel, a self-disclosure that is fulfilled in Jesus Christ. This story teaches us that we are dependent upon God. We are a community of grace, a gifted community. The story teaches us that we are sinners in need of repentance, but that we are empowered to live in faith and trust.

As a gifted community that lives in trust, Christians recognize that they do not control the world. The church is called to live faithfully after the pattern of life revealed in Jesus, rather than to impose their vision on the world by force. Communities that take this story as normative for their lives give shape to certain kinds of people. The story of Jesus socializes people into a set of virtues that describe what it means to live well-formed lives: love, joy, peace, longsuffering, gentleness (Gal. 5:22). These qualities entail certain kinds of actions in the world. Paul describes what it means to have been transformed by Christ: to think soberly, to use gifts wisely, to contribute to the needs of the saints, to practice hospitality, to bless those who persecute, to repay no one evil for evil, and to feed hungry enemies.[31]

What happened at Pentecost? In a culture preoccupied with "empirical" reality, we may be inclined to focus on what is reported in Acts about the sound of a rushing wind, tongues of fire, and people speaking in other languages. Our culture tends to respond to such reports in various ways. Many dismiss such realities as empirically unverifiable or unreal. Others are fascinated and attracted by so-called "miraculous" powers of forces that seem to go beyond our ordinary experience of reality. Both kinds of responses assume that the answer to the question, "What happened at Pentecost?" is to be found in what happened "literally" or empirically.

C. Norman Kraus argues that "what really happened at Pentecost was the forming of the new covenant community of the Spirit."[32] The two wings of modern American evangelicalism that emphasize the Spirit (Pietism and Pentecostalism) both view Pentecost as an experience that comes to individuals.

> Pentecostals have stressed the importance of the ecstatic manifestations as signs to the believer. The Pietists have stressed the inner resources which the filling of the Spirit provides for personal piety and witness. Neither has seen that the fundamental work of the Spirit at Pentecost was the formation of the new community itself.[33]

Kraus argues that Pentecost reveals a new understanding of the relationship of the individual and the community.

On the one hand, the power of the Spirit confers a new dignity and identity to the person moved by God's Spirit to become part of the new community. Baptism symbolizes this new membership. Being empowered by the Spirit confers on the person certain gifts that are be exercised for the benefit of the community (1 Cor. 12). On the other hand, to become a member of this new community means to become a participant in a new humanity. Old divisions that have divided people are overcome in a new vision of oneness in Christ. In Christ there is neither Jew nor Greek, male nor female, slave nor free (Gal. 3:28).

In the Pentecost story of Acts 2, the impact of the Spirit has economic consequences that remind one of the Zacchaeus story of Luke. "All who believed were together and had all things in common; they would sell their possessions and goods and distribute the proceeds to all, as any had need" (Acts 2:44). The Spirit of Christ in the community is a power that liberates people to have a generous spirit. It breaks the bondage of those preoccupied with the idea that the goods and resources of this world belong to them. The coming of the Spirit is a fulfillment of Jesus' inaugural sermon at Nazareth. When the Spirit comes, it is good news for the poor and liberty to the captives, for in the new community of the Spirit people are liberated to have a generous spirit of sharing.

This is the good news of the gospel. It explains why the kingdom of God is good news to the poor (Luke 6:20).[34] It is good news not because sometime in heaven the poor will receive the resources for life to flourish, as this text has too often been interpreted. Marx rightly revolted against that kind of an "opiate," which promises salvation only in the "sweet by-and-by," but not in this world. The gospel is good news to the poor because the Spirit liberates people to a generous spirit of giving so that in the new community people's basic needs are met.

A community that embodies the Spirit of Christ will acknowledge the significance of the individual person who is made in God's image and restored to dignity and responsibility through the power of God's Spirit. The individual person with gifts to build up the community should simply not be absorbed into the group, into a kind of repressive collectivism. On the other hand, the greater danger today is probably individualism and isolation from each other. A community empowered by Christ's Spirit will be in solidarity with each other, living together in mutuality and service to each other.

The authors of *Habits of the Heart* rightly recognize the destructive consequences of a radical individualism in our culture. They call for the intentional creation of "communities of memory."

> A "community of memory" is involved in retelling its story, its constitutive narrative, and in so doing, it offers examples of the men and women who have embodied and exemplified the meaning of the community. ... The stories that make up a tradition contain concepts of character, of what a good person is like, and the virtues that define such character. ... Communities of memory ... also turn us toward the future as communities of hope ... that can allow us to connect our aspirations for ourselves and those closest to us with the aspirations of a larger whole and see our own efforts as being in part contributions to a common good.[35]

This last sentence suggests the significance of a communal vision of the church in contributing to the larger well-being of the city where the church dwells.

The authors of *Habits of the Heart* distinguish between a "community of memory" and a "lifestyle enclave," where people are joined to others at a superficial level because they share a certain living area or have similar patterns of consumption and leisure. A "lifestyle enclave" may express certain values about leisure and consumption, perhaps even similar "family values" or similar inclinations to a particular political philosophy. Unlike a religious community empowered by the Spirit of Christ, however, it does not have an integrating center that links persons together by virtue of a shared vision about the nature of reality.

The best hope for our individualist culture is a vision deeply grounded in a view of God, concretely embodied in the Jesus of history, and lived out in an alternative community. God calls us to be citizens, to join together in the household of God to create social arrangements based upon the normative vision of the good we know in Jesus Christ. Such a vision should give shape to our social lives as we live together in families, work within the market place, and carry out our political responsibilities within nations and in the larger world community.

The Spirit as Liberating Power, Forgiving Grace, and Reconciling Presence

This third section of our elaboration of a Trinitarian theological model will necessarily be briefer than the preceding two sections. If the Trinity is a relation, an ecological whole, then the motifs we elaborate here will have already been described in a variety of ways. God is living Spirit present in the entire cosmos. Christ is the living Spirit present in the new community, the one who reveals the character of God's spiritual presence. Second, we have already said that the meaning of Pentecost is the formation of a new community. In the next chapter, on the significance of the church, we will elaborate more fully the practical implications of this third section of a Trinitarian structure.

God As Liberating Power

To develop this section on God's liberating power, we need to reflect briefly on the "principalities and powers," the fundamental structures of human culture that make human life possible. *Powers* can refer to a wide variety of human structures: educational institutions that pass on knowledge and wisdom, domestic and kinship structures for the nurture and the care of the young, economic institutions through which goods and services are made available and people use their skills and energies to make a living, institutions of government through which we organize our common life together, technological systems that extend the control and management of our lives as we interact with natural and human forces in the world, and such systems as the arts and religion, which give meaning to our lives.[36]

The New Testament uses various terms (*powers* and *principalities* are two of these) to refer to the fundamental social institutions through which we organize our lives as social animals. In the ancient worldview, which the New Testament writers shared with their surrounding culture, it was believed that behind social institutions is a heavenly counterpart, angelic beings that shape and control these institutions.

Walter Wink seeks to make sense of this New Testament language for a modern worldview at variance with an ancient worldview. Wink argues that the powers have essentially two dimensions. On the one hand, we can see the physical or external things that make up a power, such as its visible institutional form or such physical elements as buildings and equipment. But equally important are the "spiritual" dimensions of a power: the ethos, the atmosphere, the values inherent in a structure. The system of Nazism, for example, included not only the visible structures of the German system of government and its leaders, but the ideology of Nazism and its power over people's lives that led to one of the most destructive periods humankind has ever seen. He argues that we should not reduce our understanding of powers to "materialistic" explanations (e.g., that the powers consist only of the external physical structures). Neither should we "spiritualize" the meaning of the powers by ignoring their real physical manifestation.

Wink argues for an "integral worldview." The powers have both an "inner" spiritual dimension as well as an "outer" physical dimension. Both of these dimensions are integrally connected to each other. To engage the powers requires that one take seriously this complex reality that includes both the external, physical and inner, spiritual dimension. God is "liberating power" in this integral way.

In the language of the New Testament, the powers are good, fallen, and in need of transformation or redemption. By *good* we mean that these structures do serve a positive good—that their purpose is to meet basic human needs and to order human life in a positive way so that life can flourish. The powers are fallen insofar as humans have devoted themselves to idolatrous values destructive of the cosmos and all that supports the flourishing of life.

The powers are simultaneously good and fallen. This fallenness has permeated all institutional structures, including even the church, which is not immune from the effect of sin. God's liberating power is therefore essential to a creative engagement of the powers so that they can be transformed to serve again their God-intended functions. One of the central functions of the church is to discern how to engage the powers through the power of the Spirit: In what sense can these structures be affirmed? In what sense must they be resisted? Where and how can they be transformed? To commit oneself to God as liberating power means to be reoriented in one's loyalty and devotion to God. This liberation from idolatry, from the bondage to gods not worthy of our devotion, can free us to recreate culture in a way that leads to the flourishing of life.

The Spirit and a Life of Thanksgiving

The central ritual of the Christian faith is the Eucharist, a meal of thanksgiving. What could be more fitting? The Christian life is at its core thanksgiving, gratitude. At the deepest level, our lives are filled with gratitude for being itself, the mystery that there is something rather than nothing. We live with awe in the presence of the mystery of the cosmos, a process of billions of years that makes human life and culture possible. We live in gratitude as we remember the story of God's gracious intervention into human culture and history to create a people and restore humanity so that life can flourish. We celebrate in the Eucharist the life, death, and resurrection of Jesus Christ, who offers us grace despite our failure and weakness, and a liberating vision of life.

We are all who we are because of the gifts of the many who have gone before us and surround us. My own story is shaped by Anabaptist forebears who gave up their lives as martyrs for the faith. This is a rich inheritance that continues to shape the Mennonite church into which I was baptized and contributes to the larger ecumenical vision of the church. My own forebears left the Ukraine in Russia in the 1870s to settle in central Kansas, seeking both economic opportunity and the religious liberty to live peaceable lives in faithfulness to Jesus Christ. My own family passed these values on to me. I am grateful for the numerous ways in which "that great cloud of witnesses"—especially teachers in college, seminary, and graduate school—has surrounded me.

We take much for granted at a more mundane level. We are dependent upon thousands of people and numerous systems that sustain our lives and enable us to live comfortably, from the food on the table each meal to the electricity that lights and heats our homes. Most North Americans are privileged with economic systems and governmental structures that make life predictable and enable us to meet our basic needs. It is important that those of us for whom the institutions of our culture work for our benefit most of the time acknowledge the gift and privilege we have.

In this context of undeserved privilege we must confront the deep flaw and injustice in our culture. Growing numbers are marginalized and poor. Thousands of children do not grow up in systems that make their lives flourish.

Just weeks before I wrote this chapter, six poor black children were killed in a house fire in Elkhart, Indiana, on a cold January night, the day before we remembered the birthday of Martin Luther King Jr. King died in Memphis, where he was supporting poor black garbage workers on strike. He was in the middle of helping to organize a poor people's campaign to Washington, D.C. Thirty years later a fire in Elkhart killed six black children, a fire that was due to a combination of poverty and adult negligence. Because the gas was not hooked up to heat the home in the middle of the cold winter in Elkhart, Indiana, the grandmother who was caring for the children (and who was also charged with drug abuse) had hooked up a stove burner to an electric cord to keep warm, which caused the fire that proved fatal. One of the local television stations interviewed a black man whose words haunt me: "There is no mercy for the poor."

I raise the issue of deep injustice in the context of our experience of undeserved privilege because we will be empowered to respond to the needs of others with a generous spirit only if our response flows out of gratitude and thanksgiving for the grace and giftedness of our lives. Response to the needs of others out of the grace we have received lies at the heart of the gospel. It is disconcerting and shameful how many in our culture believe that they deserve what they have. And since they have earned what they have, others should prove their merit as well. Even previously privileged groups (e.g., white males of European background) exhibit attitudes of resentment and anger when others threaten their position of privilege. Such views breed mean and tight-fisted attitudes and behavior that are reflected in public policies toward the poor and the marginalized.

At a deeper level, we know ourselves as sinners, persons who are deeply flawed in our relationships to God, the larger cosmos, and our neighbors both far and near. The gospel is the good news that we can be forgiven and that resurrection to a new life is possible. If there were no forgiveness, we would forever be caught in a vicious cycle of failure and recrimination. In situations of personal violation, forgiveness is a symbol of hope. Where serious violations of other persons occur, the process of personal reconciliation is often arduous and painful. But because forgiveness is possible, we can risk acknowledging our violation of another. We are empowered to repent and ask another person to accept us again as brothers and sisters. Forgiveness is the good news that resurrection is possible. In the next chapter, on the church, we will return to forgiveness as one of the practices that marks the life of the church. Later we will see that forgiveness is also an essential component of peacemaking among the nations.

The Spirit as Reconciling Presence

All that we have said so far is an ecological whole, not nine separate stories unrelated to each other. The Spirit of the living God moves and lures us toward a future where everything is connected. Instead of living our lives by separated fragments isolated from each other, we are called to imagine a future where everything is integrally linked together. Nothing can be isolated or separate, for if God is God, then nothing in the universe or in human culture lies outside of or beyond a unified vision of life.

The integration of all reality within the divine Spirit is captured in the Hebrew word *shalom*. The word *peace* in our culture is used in ways that are limited and far removed from this Trinitarian vision. Sometimes, for example, *peace* is used in the context of military preparedness to call for "peace through strength." A weapon can even be named "the peacemaker." Such a view of life is necessarily fragmented, for it assumes that reconciliation is impossible and violent force is required. Often *peace* is used negatively to describe the mere absence of conflict or war. This fragmented view lacks a more comprehensive and positive vision of life to guide our energies.

In the biblical worldview, peace as shalom is a multi-layered and comprehensive eschatological vision. Peace is a vision of God's future for the cosmos. It is a vision of an alternative future, not simply "pie in the sky," but a vision that serves as a motivating power and direction for our lives. If our lives envision only the American dream or material success or a life of self-gratification and pleasure, then from day to day and year to year we will put into practice that for which we hope. But we will not live by an alternative set of practices if we do not have an alternative hope for the future. We are what we hope for: visions of the future have a powerful impact on people's lives.

If we really do hope for peace with justice, then it is possible to put that reality into practice in our lives. In the biblical vision, peace is not the mere absence of conflict, but the presence of justice and righteousness. If we hope for a more peaceful relationship with the earth, we might put into practice an alternative relationship to the earth. The prophet Hosea envisioned a shalom that includes even the birds and the beasts. "I will make for you a covenant on that day with the wild animals, the birds of the air, and the creeping things on the ground; and I will abolish the bow, the sword, and war from the land; and I will make you lie down in safety" (Hos. 2:18-19).

If we can imagine the possibility of nonviolent processes that can make peace between people and nations in conflict, we are more likely to put this hoped-for alternative into practice. The biblical vision imagines the blessing that comes to peacemakers who are called "the children of God" (Matt. 5:9). We cannot hope for reconciliation if we cannot imagine a future where strangers and enemies can become friends. If the biblical vision of an alternative relationship between Jews and Gentiles had shaped the practice of the church, we might have spared the world centuries of hatred and violence to Jews by Christians.

> For he is himself our peace. Gentiles and Jews, he has made the two one, and in his own body of flesh and blood has broken down the enmity which stood like a dividing wall between them; for he annulled the law with its rules and regulations, so as to create out of the two a single new humanity in himself, thereby making peace. This was his purpose, to reconcile the two in a single body to God through the cross, on which he killed the enmity. (Eph. 2:14-16, NEB)

God's peace involves reconciliation of the whole universe to Godself (Col. 1:20). These hopes, when put into practice, can awaken us to a sense of wonder and delight, the fullness of life intended by God. This possibility is vividly portrayed in Isaiah's eschatological vision:

> For I am about to create new heavens
> and a new earth;
> the former things shall not be remembered
> or come to mind.
> But be glad and rejoice forever
> in what I am creating,
> for I am about to create Jerusalem as a joy,
> and its people as a delight.
> I will rejoice in Jerusalem
> and delight in my people;
> no more shall the sound of weeping be heard in it,
> or the cry of distress. (Isa. 65:17-25)

The Church
as an Alternative Society

I appeal to you therefore, brothers and sisters, by the mercies of God, to present your bodies as a living sacrifice, holy and acceptable to God, which is your spiritual worship. Do not be conformed to this world, but be transformed by the renewing of your minds, so that you may discern what is the will of God-what is good and acceptable and perfect. —Romans 12:1-2

INTRODUCTORY REFLECTIONS:
WHAT DO WE MEAN BY CHURCH?

The church must first be a new society for it to contribute meaningfully to the peace of the city where it dwells. We must think creatively about how to imagine and construct the life of the church so that it can more faithfully embody Christ within culture. The church should be understood theologically from two poles. There is a creative tension between God's initiative to embody Christ in the world through the Spirit and the flawed human institutional life of a particular community in time and space. Liturgy is the dynamic integration of these two dimensions of the life of the church.

The word *liturgy* suggests a vision for the church as a whole. *Liturgy* derives from the Hellenistic Greek word *leitourgia*, which means an act of public service. Liturgy is not only the symbolic or ritual action of the church, but is also the holistic life of the church as a new society living in response to God. Ethics (our way of living), worldview (our way of believing), and symbolic action (our manner of worship) are not three separate spheres, but are integrally linked in the response of the church to God.[1]

Liturgy is both a fundamentally public action reflected in a visible, corporate structure, and a creative action. It requires of human beings to form their life together in imaginative ways, to find a language and a way of living that adequately expresses their vision of life. To sing God's song in word and deed in the midst of a broken and alienated world requires imaginative construction, a creative public action, the modeling of a new vision of life within the old.[2]

The establishment of an alternative community is what makes the Christian faith a potent force in the world, not simply the ideas or the teachings of Jesus. Margaret Mead says, "Never doubt that a small group of thoughtful committed citizens can change the world; indeed it's the only thing that ever has."[3] Larry Rasmussen replies, "The word *only* in that sentence need not be defended in order to affirm the rest." He goes on to cite John H. Yoder, who makes the same point with respect to Jesus' founding of a new social reality with the calling of the disciples (Luke 6:12-13).

> To organized opposition, [Jesus] responds with the formal found-ing of a new social reality. New teachings are no threat as long as the teacher stands alone; a movement, extending his personality in both time and space, presenting an alternative to the structures that were there before, challenges the system as no mere words could.[4]

According to Daniel Smith, the Jewish community carried into exile by Nebuchadnezzar developed a fourfold response to the threat of destruction by the Babylonians or the danger of assimilation into their society.[5] They adopted a pattern of social organization, with tightly knit groups of people under family or clan heads who had authority to provide leadership in maintaining group identity. Second, leaders mediated between the entire exiled community and the domi-nating group without selling out to the dominant culture. Examples of such counter-cultural leaders in the Bible include Moses in Pharaoh's court, David among the Philistines, and Jeremiah. A third response was to develop stories or a folklore of heroic figures whose cleverness and courage saved the Jews from their enemies. Such are the stories of Joseph, Esther, and Daniel. These representative biblical figures serve as models for the persons we need today—persons who live "on the boundary." As "insiders," they are called to be faithful; as "collabora-tors," they must negotiate the relationship of the community to the dominant culture.

Fourth, the community develops rituals that mark it off from the dominant society. The purity laws in Leviticus reflect such a strategy. In the course of their long history in the Diaspora, Jews developed an elaborate system of rituals that marked the Jewish community from others and gave them a clear identity. Some examples are the weekly Sabbath meal, the dietary laws, and the yearly rituals of Passover, Purim, Sukkoth, Hanukkah, and others. Smith uses the work of social scientists to compare similar patterns found in other minority communities: African-American slaves in antebellum America, Japanese prisoners interned in camps in the Western United States during World War II, and South African movements of black Africans to Bantustans and the religious response of the "Zionist" churches.

It may be harder to establish a clear identity for the church in modern America, with its tolerant pluralism and its comfortable blend of Christianity and American culture. The church needs to develop a sense of identity by recreating itself in four areas. It must develop a social structure and process that can respond to modern tolerance and pluralism. It needs a competent and inspired leadership that can help guide the discerning process of cultural engagement. It needs an imaginative recital of the rich narrative traditions of the Bible and church history to offer paradigms for the interpretation of modern life. And it needs a system of symbols and rituals to provide a clear vision and alternative to the symbols and rituals of the dominant culture. All of these factors contribute to a practice of faith that can offer wholeness and hope to the surrounding culture.

We need to distinguish a number of layers of meaning to the word *church* as we begin our reflections. Historically, four key words have characterized the church: *one, holy, catholic, apostolic church.* As we have already said, the church is the body in the world formed in response to God. *Apostolicity* distinguishes the church as a people formed by a story handed down through the witness of the first followers of Christ. Though the church is a human institution, it is also a response to the activity of God in history that culminated in the life, death, and resurrection of Jesus Christ. The *oneness* of the church is grounded in the church's common loyalty and commitment to Jesus Christ, the mystical body united in its one Lord. This vision of oneness is stated most vividly in Jesus' prayer in the Gospel of John:

> I ask not only on behalf of these, but also on behalf of those who will believe in me through their word, that they may all be one. As you, Father, are in me and I am in you, may they also be in us, so that the world may believe that you have sent me. The glory that you have given me I have given them, so that they may be one, as we are one, I in them and you in me, that they may become completely one, so that the world may know that you have sent me

and have loved them even as you have loved me." (John 17:20-23)

The desire to overcome the scandal of the splintering of the church into its many denominational traditions and sectarian divisions has, especially in the last century, spawned the ecumenical movement. *Catholicity* refers to the recognition that the church is a universal community spread over the entire world—a society of persons among the many nations, within the variety of races, ethnic groups, and cultural traditions in the world. The *holiness* of the church reflects the church's commitment to live faithfully in response to the way of Christ. The church is called not simply to be like the world around it, but to live out an ethical vision that contrasts with the way of life of the surrounding culture where it lives.

This one, holy, apostolic, catholic church exists in a variety of specific institutional structures in different historical and cultural contexts. The denominational structure is the predominant form of the church in the North American context. Though denominations vary, given the different theological and ecclesiological traditions with which they identify, significant commonalities in the bureaucratic structures are common to the denominational form of the church. And although the denomination is the primary form of the church in North America, there are many other kinds of churches, making *church* an extremely varied and complex phenomenon. For example, there are quasi-denominational associations of Christians whose loyalties form around Bible schools, radio programs, or publishing houses. And increasingly we see the formation of independent churches that identify with no particular denomination or theological tradition.

Common to all forms, however, is the fact that church must finally be embodied in a specific, concrete, group of people who meet regularly in a local congregation. The form these local gatherings takes can be extremely varied, ranging from house and storefront churches to large parish congregations meeting in a church building. But if they are the church, they are all called to live faithfully in response to Christ, who calls them into being. The focus of this chapter is on these local gathered bodies of Christians and the networks of congregations in various local contexts.

What are the marks of authentic congregations? What practices give structure to their embodied life so that they represent an alternative vision of life within the dominant North American culture that contributes to the peace of the city where they dwell?

This chapter proposes a model, a human construction for our time and place. This model draws heavily on the New Testament, on historical and contemporary practices of the church, and on the ideas of contemporary theologians, ethicists, and practitioners. I do not wish to suggest, however, that there is only one institutional form of the church. The New Testament writings reflect a variety of understandings of the meaning and significance of Jesus for faith. Models of the early church vary because of the tension between what the church shares in common and the varied images of Jesus that relate to specific contexts and issues and which the church puts into practice in a variety of ways.[6]

Expressions of the Christian faith have varied from the beginning of Christianity, since each form of the faith is itself a particular cultural embodiment of that faith. Each expression uses a particular language or set of symbols to express its understanding of Jesus. Each is a particular response to the issues within the context in which that particular apostle or church is living. No pure essence or pristine ideal of the Christian faith exists to which we can return or appeal as a basis for our own normative vision of the church.[7] This does not mean that we cannot or should not search for a common standard of faith. However, there is no privileged position from which we can define a Christian ideal or essence. All we can do is offer specific proposals, which are subject to further discernment by the church catholic.

The view I present is a particular cultural expression of the Christian faith that is part of a larger mosaic. I view the living traditions of Christianity (Roman Catholic, Lutheran, Orthodox, Reformed, and many others) as representative of the gifts of the church, all of which contribute to and enrich the whole. Each of these particular perspectives is a vehicle or symbol that points to the vision Christians have in common. Although participation in ecumenical conversation with other Christians is an essential mark of a faithful church, the gift of pluralism does not entail the kind of mutual appreciation that fails to take seriously the truth claims of each tradition. Rather, each interpretation should be taken seriously as a vehicle that expresses a dimension of the truth of the one, apostolic, holy, catholic church.

The Anabaptist-Mennonite tradition has fundamentally shaped my understanding of the church, though many other traditions and factors have influenced me as well. My view of the church emphasizes the importance of the local, gathered congregation, a believing community that seeks to model an alternative society in faithfulness to Christ. This does not mean that larger church bodies are unimportant. In fact, churches cooperate together in key ways as they faithfully carry out their mission in the world. I am simply saying that the health of the church depends on flourishing congregations of local believers.

I do not present my perspective simply for Mennonites or other churches within the believers church or free church tradition. I mean to take the catholicity of the church as a discerning community more seriously than that. I wish to take seriously the gifts others offer as a possible "truth" for me and for the larger church. Many of the practices I name later in this chapter have in fact been shared widely across ecclesiological traditions. I commend my perspective on the church as a model for the North American church, lived out within Roman Catholic, Presbyterian, or other polities.[8]

"REPENTANCE" AND "BALANCED REALISM"
AS A CONTEXT FOR DEVELOPING A MODEL OF THE CHURCH

Gathered congregations are human institutions. Paul refers to them as a "treasure in earthen vessels" or "clay jars" (2 Cor. 4:7). How can we speak about the church as an "alternative society" with a "creative" vision? Is it not just the opposite, an institution that is particularly alien to creativity as it seeks to protect tradition and the status quo?

We begin with confession. It is important that we give voice to our deep ambivalence toward the church. Many of us love the church and believe it can offer hope for the world. But the church often disappoints us. The church is often closed-minded and rigid. It is frequently prejudiced against those who are different. It often legitimates racism, sexism, and war. It has bred indifference to the world, to the earth. We must reexamine the ways in which the church has related to those of other faiths, most notably its relationship to Jews. Larry Rasmussen states the issue forcefully:

> Developments after the ecumenical councils, including the Reformation, only solidified the massive shift from the God-centered Christology of an alternative servant community with the wider world to the Christ-centered theology of a universalizing empire. ... This absorption of virtually all of God into the Jesus of imperial Christianity is at the greatest possible remove from the theocentric Jesus and his yeasty, salty, seedy community way. Deadly results for Jews, pagans, indigenous people and cultures would eventually follow.[9]

The church is hypocritical when it constantly appeals to the forgiveness of God while unable to forgive those who seek reconciliation.

Our memory is flooded with the recollection of wounded souls who have been rejected by the church. We think of the gifts of creative artists whose visual or musical language did not fit. We weep as we recall the rejection of women with creative gifts and ministries to offer to the church. I will not soon forget the tears in the eyes of the parents of a young gay man who served the church well as a minister of the gospel … until he came out of the closet. The dispute about homosexuality is tearing the church apart. We seem incapable of modeling an alternative to the world's handling of conflict. I confess, therefore, that the church has often been a rigid, fearful, defensive, and hypocritical institution.

Many of us experience life in the church "on the boundary." We believe in God, yet we are unclear about what it means to confess such belief in a postmodern world. We learn much from the wisdom of scientists and philosophers and from other religions, yet we are not sure that the church is able to incorporate human wisdom beyond its boundaries. We search for appropriate images and metaphors that take into account our experience of the world. Much God talk is too restrictive, stifling, and rigid to contain what God must be for our world. Some struggle with images of God as Father, or as a Sovereign Lord over the world, a being separate from the cosmos. Such metaphors no longer seem capable of containing the vision of God we need to overcome our alienation from each other as men and women—or our alienation from the earth.[10]

Many have a deep ambivalence toward the church because of its inadequate understanding of salvation and of hope. Too many churches lack compassion for the well-being of this planet and fail to identify with people's suffering because of a self-centered view of salvation. Too many people are primarily preoccupied with whether *I* am saved, whether *I* will go to heaven. Instead of linking salvation to the renewal of creation and the restoration of wholeness, the church often thinks of salvation and hope primarily in terms of "fire insurance," life beyond the grave. Ignoring the threat to life symbolized by "the bomb," oblivious to racial hatred, to economic injustice, unemployment, and homelessness, too many churches are content with a narrow view of salvation. The hope for personal salvation becomes disconnected from compassion for this world and its people, who suffer from hunger, disease, injustice, and war.

Moreover, the liturgy of the church often serves the egotistical self-interest of individuals. Liturgy is not primarily about having our hearts warmed by good music or our minds stimulated by a good sermon. Genuine liturgy is not about how I can believe or do the right things in order to gain God's favor. It is not mouthing the right creedal formulas or going through the proper rituals. Such a liturgy is distorted because it is disconnected from discipleship, from being a new people in the world who are seeking the peace of the city where they dwell. The prophet Amos has harsh words for such disconnected worship.[11]

> I hate, I despise your festivals,
>> and I take no delight in your solemn assemblies.
> Even though you offer me your burnt offerings and grain offerings,
>> I will not accept them;
> and the offerings of well-being of your fatted animals
>> I will not look upon.
> Take away from me the noise of your songs;
>> I will not listen to the melody of your harps.
> But let justice roll down like waters,
>> and righteousness like an ever flowing stream.
>> (Amos 5:21-24)

The quest for "personal salvation" is particularly disturbing among comfortable, complacent, economically and politically well-situated North Americans. Too often these Christians conveniently relegate Christ and salvation to the realm of the spiritual or life beyond the grave. For such Christians, worship preserves their life of complacency. The black slaves cried out to God for a time when there would be no more weeping or wailing. In the context of the oppression of slavery, such a cry represented for slaves the recognition that before God they were somebody, and that the white system of slavery was wrong in the eyes of God. Rather than being a "pie in the sky" escape from this world, the black spirituals affirmed black identity within the world. The spirituals were a means toward the delegitimating of the white system of slavery, in contrast to which they affirmed a God of supreme justice and love.[12]

The church is a "treasure in clay jars" (2 Cor. 4:7), a treasure to be cherished and nourished. Though we experience the church as an institution of clay, many of us also love the church. As children we learned the stories of faith: Abraham and Sarah, Moses, Elijah, Ruth, Job, Amos, Mary, Peter, and Paul. Through the stories of Jesus we learned a vision of life that gave us an identity and sense of purpose. If we were to abandon these stories, these images and metaphors, we would cease to be. The cloud of witnesses that surrounds my life is incomplete without the men and women of the church—St. Augustine and St. Francis, Felix Mantz and Martin Luther, Dorothy Day and Elise Boulding. Each Sabbath Christians participate in the worship of imperfect churches to sing and pray, surrounded by visual symbols of stained glass, banner, and communion table. We listen to the words of Scripture, hear the word preached, discern what it means to live faithfully, and discuss theology. We are made aware of our own sinfulness and brokenness. We hear the word of forgiveness and the call to repentance. We hear the stories of suffering people—fellow church members and people near and far over the face of the globe—and we are challenged to respond. Again and again, we are challenged by a vision of life—what it means to live faithfully in a world of violence, injustice, suffering, and death. How could we ever leave this church, despite its imperfections?

I use the term *balanced realism* to introduce this section of the chapter. As we think about the life of the church, we should avoid a utopian style of thinking that fails to take into account how institutions work. The church is a treasure in *clay jars*. If we absolutize the communal dimensions of the church at the expense of the individual, or the individual at the expense of the community, we will end up in trouble.

We need balance to counter the divisive polarizing tendencies in our time. Congregational life can be developed well only if we realistically assess the situation of the church in our time and context. The model I propose looks quite different from either of the two sides that James Davison Hunter describes in his book, *Culture Wars: The Struggle to Define America*. In the first chapter, I argued that the church cannot and should not try to retrieve the status it had within Christendom. The church must recognize itself as a minority in a pluralistic context. Many evangelical Christians still think of America as a Christian nation and seek to use the power of government to legislate practices that further that vision, such as restoring prayer in the public schools or outlawing abortion. Such an approach reduces Christians to one lobby group alongside others.

The church fails to model an alternative vision of life when it becomes politicized by adopting the power tactics of any other lobby. The church needs to think of itself as a "pilgrim" people of an alternative way. The cross of Christ, who renounced traditional forms of political power by making himself vulnerable, models such a way. I am not suggesting that the church withdraw from politics. But what would happen if the church were to model an alternative nonviolent politics of solidarity with the weak and the marginalized that still respects the dignity and the humanity of those in positions of power who violate the weak? How would such a model look if, in responding to the issue of abortion, the church were motivated less by the abstraction "right to life" and more by its identification with the unborn as well as with the often isolated and vulnerable women who seek abortions? How can the church minister and serve out of a deep compassion for the vulnerability and plight of prospective mothers who cannot see how to care for a child, whether because of poverty, physical danger to their lives, pregnancies resulting from rape or incest, or feeling abandoned and alone with no one to care for and nurture a child?

Such a church would be an alternative to secularized individualism, which reduces life to the slogan "freedom to choose" anything and everything within the limits of the law. The church must find an alternative to relativism and an ethic of tolerance based on an appeal to individual freedom. Such an ethic lacks a transcendent frame of reference to guide us in what we should choose, an ethic grounded in a vision of the good beyond ourselves. An ethic of self-interest, in which individual well-being (convenience, self-realization, success, and self-fulfillment) is the ultimate value, undermines communities that nurture cooperation and the larger corporate goods and values. Consumer capitalism and a market economy has had the effect of "socializing" us to think in terms of calculating self-interest.

> All society and its decisions can be fashioned and executed in the manner economic actors do—with the calculation of self- and group interest in relationships that are fundamentally instrumental in character. Stripped down, ... rational self-interest is the one language everyone understands and ought to apply to decisions and actions in every domain.[13]

Decisions about abortion are often based on a calculating self-interest. Individualistic consumerism erodes commitment to the weak and the marginalized and to the larger common good. Politics in North America has degenerated into cynical appeals to self-interest. Politicians appeal to us to vote for them out of our self-interest, not because a policy might in the long run benefit the common good, even though it might be painful and require sacrifice. It is a sad commentary of the acculturation of Christianity to consumer capitalism when so many Christians simply leave behind any alternative Christian vision of life when they enter the polling booth, where they vote out of calculated self-interest like everyone else.

The key issue for the church is how people can be morally formed to live by an alternative vision of life in a culture where the forces of modernity are eroding the very elements essential to the development of character. The great moral traditions of the Enlightenment—Kantian deontological rationalism and utilitarianism—do not help us respond to the issue of moral formation. Both assumed "that good games depend on good rules more than they depend on good players."[14] Kant held that morality can be known in abstraction from actual conversation and communities of discernment by imagining what rules one would follow in an abstract universal community. Larry Rasmussen argues that both these traditions

> assumed the ethics of character. ... Here they replicated modernity's naive expropriation of civil society and its communities of moral formation. Communities of civil society make the players who make and keep, change and break, the rules. Perhaps Kant, Bentham, and company simply forgot that we are children before we are adults and that the moral life does not begin in "reason": but in childhood.[15]

Moral formation of a people of character takes place in more intimate communities. The acids of modernity have eroded the very communities that are essential to moral formation (i.e., the family, neighborhoods, the church). The individualism of our culture has caused us to slight the gospel's emphasis on community. The larger social forces of consumer capitalism, the power of large corporations and a globalized economy, technologies that reduce intimate contacts between humans, the impersonal forces of large nation-states that impact our lives in so many areas, urbanization, mobility, specialization, and the separation of our work spaces and living spaces—all of these forces reduce the more intimate communities that are critical for moral formation.

In developing intimate communities of moral formation, we must adequately balance four critical tensions in order for these communities to function well. The Enlightenment was in part a reaction against a repressive dogmatism and authoritarianism. Authoritarianism is one of the great dangers of intimate communities. We gain nothing if we substitute a repressive legalism for individualism. We must find an alternative to repressive collectivism on the one side and the isolating rationalization of the individual on the other. The church must maintain a healthy tension between the dignity and value of each individual and the gifts and creativity each has to offer as children of God on the one hand, and on the other, the importance of belonging to the body of Christ, where each individual takes responsibility for the well-being of the whole and love binds everything together (1 Cor. 13).

Second, how do we balance a need for clear boundaries that define the identity of a community with also being a welcoming community to persons of diverse cultural, ethnic, religious, and socioeconomic backgrounds and lifestyles? In his book, *The Social Sources of Denominationalism,* H. Richard Niebuhr pointed out how race, class, economic level, and national identity have marked the history of denominational identity more than the gospel that welcomes people of all conditions. One of the great problems of our world is that strong identity often leads to the projection of indifference, prejudice, and then hostility and violence to the "other."

Miroslav Volf, a theologian of Croatian background, lived in Los Angeles when he wrote his book, *Exclusion and Embrace.* In it he reflects theologically on this issue in the light of these dual contexts. His book is a search for an alternative to the dominant options of our time: exclusivist identities that underlie the conflicts in the former Yugoslavia or cities like Los Angeles; a homogenized Enlightenment rationalism that does not adequately account for particular identity; and the relativist tendencies of some forms of postmodernism that undermine commitment to anything. He describes this postmodern option as follows:

> We should flee both universal values and particular identities and seek refuge from oppression in the radical autonomy of individuals; we should create spaces in which persons can keep creating 'larger and freer selves' by acquiring new and losing old identities—wayward and erratic vagabonds, ambivalent and fragmented, always on the move and never doing much more than making moves.[16]

In other words, such postmodernism fails to accept the limit and responsibility of an identity that requires us to stand somewhere.

The key issue is how communities can form people of moral character who can make enduring commitments to each other and the common good, and yet be welcoming and open to those who are different. Communities do draw boundaries; complete openness is an impossibility. Larry Rasmussen cites the work of such authors as Philip Selznick and Michael Walzer, who argue that "communities of character require stable, ongoing associations of persons with special commitments to one another, a common purpose, and a common sense of life; we only underscore that all this assumes and requires reasonably clear community boundaries."

Thus, while tolerance is an important liberal virtue essential to a civil society, it "does not of itself generate community, though it often saves and preserves it. It is an important brake on oppressive community boundaries; on its own, however, tolerance does not establish boundaries." Rasmussen argues that "a clearer minimum requirement for community definition (and thus boundaries) is loyalty. Loyalty is faithfulness and a studied commitment to take others seriously in season and out."[17] This loyalty is grounded in respect, a dignity bestowed on the person by virtue of our humanity as persons created in God's image and as recipients of God's love and grace.

A third issue is how Christians can develop a clear sense of identity and vision while recognizing how much we live on boundaries between identities, how much we share with the larger culture around us, and how much we can learn from it. In her critique of the post-liberal theology of George Lindbeck, Kathryn Tanner argues that we do not first define a Christian identity and only then cross the boundaries to the larger culture. The relationship between the church and the larger culture is much more fluid. "The boundary has already been crossed in and through the very processes by which Christians come to believe anything at all."[18]

I share some of Tanner's postmodern emphasis on the fluidity of boundaries, but her position is overdone. She is reluctant to name moral practices that mark the life of the church as a distinctive community. Tanner's Barthian theology of the Word of God relativizes all cultural forms and critiques all idolatries. Before God we are all sinners. A postmodern perspective on "sin and grace blur any difference between Christians and non-Christians drawn on social grounds."[19] Because of Tanner's postmodern emphasis on process, she is reluctant to identify distinctive moral practices that define a Christian community as a result of the new being in Christ.

> Even without agreement in results, unity among Christian practices is therefore sustained by a continuity of fellowship, by a willingness, displayed across differences of time and space, to admonish, learn from, and be corrected by all persons similarly concerned about the true meaning of discipleship. ... Christianity has its identity as a task; it has its identity in the form of a task of looking for one.[20]

While I share Tanner's concern for openness and ongoing inquiry in a spirit of humility, we need to say much more about the content of a Christian way of life that marks a Christian vision of life. Tanner tends to absolutize a postmodern style of thought despite her own Barthian caution against idolatry. In Tanner, postmodernism ironically looms as a "plumb line" by which to evaluate all theological endeavor.

Fourth, we need to balance the emphasis upon *being* the church with *doing the work* of mission in the larger society. This is a point we have already made several times in our critique of Stanley Hauerwas and William H. Willimon in *Resident Aliens,* who argue that the "political task of Christians is to be the church *rather than* to transform the world" (emphasis mine). The Christian vision is both/and, to be the church, and in being that church to seek the peace of the city where we dwell.

A COMMUNITY OF FOCAL PRACTICES

The Concept of "Focal Practice"

Focal practices are ways of being, living, and behaving that express the vision of the good of a community or a group of practitioners of a particular discipline or profession. To use an analogy, those skilled at playing the piano have developed over time the practices that define good piano playing. Focal practices are ways in which Christians embody or put into practice the virtues, those qualities of character that identity a Christian way of life. Paul's letter to the Galatians contains such a list of virtues: "The fruit of the Spirit is love, joy, peace, patience, kindness, generosity, faithfulness, gentleness, and self-control" (Gal. 5:22-23). Virtues as ideals alone are not sufficient, nor are they really virtues if they are not "bodied" or put into action. The word

> *practices* is not simply a synonym for "actions" as though anything we might do, if repeated a few times and worked up as a routine would constitute a practice. Practices are those particularly pregnant actions ... intrinsic to a way of life that center, sustain, and order that way of living. ... They are the engaging, reenacted actions of a certain ritual quality, if not always a ritual format.[21]

Practices are performed. They are not simply abstract ideas or ideals; they are observable ways of being or living. They are socially defined by a community of practitioners over time. The traditions of what constitute good practices may change, but in continuity with what has gone on before. Through practices, persons are socialized or catechized into a disciplined community. We learn (i.e., are "disciples") by experiencing the modeling of others, by practicing the discipline with others who seek to be practitioners. These practices are "bodied" in visible, concrete ways of living that can be observed and evaluated by others, even those outside the circle of the community of faith. The function of theology in this view is pragmatic, oriented to helping us act in ways that are appropriate to a Christian way of life. Such theology is one of the essential "gifts" in the life of an alternative community.

The function of theology in relationship to practice is illuminated nicely by Phil Stoltzfus's analysis of Gordon Kaufman's view of theology as imaginative construction. He argues that Kaufman overemphasizes linguistic self-consciousness and deliberateness in developing his understanding of the term *imaginative construction*. Drawing from the philosophy of Ludwig Wittgenstein, Stoltzfus uses an idea from musical aesthetics, "performance practice," to argue for the practical function of theology to support more strongly Kaufman's own understanding of the pragmatic function of theology. "Music-making is to be treated neither as a fixed essence nor a relativistic experience, but rather as a series of public performances which are in continual critique, so to speak, of each other." He says we ask of a performance not so much whether it is faithful to some prescribed pattern, but whether it displays musicality, a freshness that invites further performances.

> Even if we assume that Kaufman is right, that theology really is a self-conscious, deliberate imaginative construction of a symbolic frame of reference to orient our lives, we have to acknowledge, with Kaufman, that the proof of the adequacy of one's theologizing takes place when the linguistic assertivenesses have stopped, and the pragmatic effects of those assertions can be clearly seen and responded to. We might even go so far as to say, along with the Pragmatists, Gandhi, and King, that an evaluation of two theological/ metaphysical proposals takes place not so much through a conversation between symbol systems as it does through an interactive attunement between practices. In the theological enterprise there may be times—perhaps more often than we like to think—where we must rein in the urge to construct things. Instead of a discipline which argues from constructs, then, theology might take a cue from certain aspects of the Anabaptist-Mennonite experience, and become a demonstration of itself through the totality of life practices, both linguistic and non-linguistic, which interact with and critique one another through their public performances.

Stoltzfus makes his point by using the examples of Kaufman's and Wittgenstein's own lives. Wittgenstein quit teaching philosophy in 1941 at age 52 to take up manual labor in a hospital in an area of London vulnerable to the German aerial bombardment.

Wittgenstein was doing philosophy, so to speak, through the act of placing his body within a particular setting of human need. In one journal entry, he used the word "praxis" to describe how one is to understand what it means to "believe in God." Not long after Wittgenstein, an 18-year-old conscientious objector named Gordon Kaufman began similar work in a hospital ... in the U.S. If we were to apply Wittgenstein more radically than Kaufman has done in his own writing, then I think we would need to acknowledge that which Kaufman himself has shown in his life; i.e., when we really have a societal crisis on our hands which effects the viability of life as we know it, the proper theological 'move' may in fact be to stop constructing linguistic things and to demonstrate theology through the everyday labor—the performance praxis—of one's body.[22]

Performance practice is inherently communal, not individualistic. We "perform" within a community where together we seek to embody Christ. As we act together in this community we discern over time how to be and how not to be Christ's body in the world in faithful ways.

Some practices are central to the life of the church. In briefly describing these practices, I will attempt to paint an overall picture with the broad brushstrokes of a vision of life. Given the specialization that is characteristic of our lives today, we often see these practices described in piecemeal ways. We need to see these practices as an integrated whole that provides a more comprehensive alternative cultural vision. I see the list below as suggestive, a list of practices intended to invite further imagination and reflection by others. This list should help theology enable us to practice an alternative vision of the Christian life so that we can indeed contribute to the peace of the cities where we dwell.[23]

Rituals of Moral Formation

One kind of focal practice is ritual. In such sacred or religious rituals as baptism and the Lord's Supper, the church is reoriented with reference to its ultimate center of concern (Tillich) and by the vision of life reflected in its view of reality (Geertz).[24] Christian rituals or rites

differ from secular or profane ceremonies in that they are intended to link the ordinary and the nonordinary. Holy rites charge the commonplace and instrumental world with ultimate meaning. Clifford Geertz has used "leaping" as a metaphor for understanding the sacred dimension of ceremonies. Through sacred ritual, humans leap into the framework of the sacred. When the ritual

Roger Schmidt, Exploring Religion

ends and the communicant returns to the ordinary world, the person is, as Geertz notes, changed "unless, as sometimes happens the experience fails to register." ... And, as he is changed so also is the common sense world, for it is now seen as but the partial form of a wider reality which corrects and completes it.[25]

Religious ritual enables people to transcend themselves, to go "outside" themselves in order to view life in terms of the sacred realities that give meaning to their lives. When Christians use water in baptism and ordinary bread and wine in the meal of the Lord's Supper, the church enters into the "sacred world" of God as revealed in Jesus Christ and made present to the community in God's living Spirit. If the ritual "registers," the participant returns to the daily routine of life transformed, aware that the living of profane existence has been profoundly altered by the drama of God's action in Jesus Christ.

Our rituals are very powerful. They express our priorities, the values we hold most dear in our lives. Rituals can be idolatrous. They can draw us into identities that are parochial or even violent to those who are not participants in the rituals that mark off the group. Rituals direct our time and energy. Consequently a church that is concerned about being a new society in the world and about being transformed rather than conformed to distorted and false values must concern itself with ritual. To what groups do we belong? Are they worthy of our commitments of time, energy, and money? Do they bring healing to the cosmos that God intends? What rituals dominate our lives, and how can we be discriminating in how we participate in them?[26]

Baptism. Baptism is one of the more important and critical rituals of moral formation if the church rightly understands its significance. An understanding of baptism is central in developing a right understanding of the church's relationship to culture. Baptism balances four important polarities in a Christian vision of life.

Baptism is a rite of passage that marks movement from one identity to another. Baptism signals the individual's desire to participate in a new identity, the new humanity that has been formed by Jesus Christ. This desire does not simply arise from an individual self, similar to the desire to join a club or community organization. The desire for baptism arises out of the power of the gospel, the good news of God's way in the world, made vivid in Jesus Christ. A right understanding of baptism requires us to balance the paradoxical relationship between grace, the story that has moved the individual to desire, and free consent, the personal response of faith. We cannot decide without coming to know God's gracious power, yet grace must be responded to freely in faith.

The Anabaptist, Hans Denck, expressed this paradoxical relationship beautifully. "No one can truly know Christ unless one follows Him in life. And no one can follow Him except inasmuch as one has already known him."[27]

Second, baptism balances individual freedom and consent with corporate identity and responsibility. On the one hand, baptism is a commitment of the individual person, a voluntary decision to become a member of the church, to make Jesus Christ the orienting center of life. Baptism presupposes the dignity and responsibility of the individual person before God. Genuine baptism should not arise out of social pressure. It should not be a ritual of conformity, a sign that a person has participated actively in the Christian environment into which she has grown up. It should not simply bless what a person has been born into by virtue of a person's cultural or family heritage. Baptism should be the free decision of a person who has been attracted by the way of Jesus Christ, who desires to give her free consent to follow him in the ongoing pilgrimage of life.

On the other hand, baptism signals an individual's participation in the church, a commitment to offer one's gifts for the edification of the body, a willingness to listen to the insight and counsel of others and to discipline one's life as a disciple of Christ. The church is not simply a collection of individuals; it is a corporate reality, a visible new society, a vision of a way to live together. John H. Yoder argues that the believers church tradition of radical Protestantism offers an alternative to individualism and authoritarianism.

> Communities which are genuinely voluntary can affirm individual dignity (at the point of the uncoerced adherence of the member) without enshrining individualism. They can likewise realize community without authorizing lordship or establishment. The alternative to arbitrary individualism is not established authority but an authority in which the individual participates and to which he or she consents.[28]

Third, baptism is the incorporation into a new identity in Christ in which there is neither Jew nor Greek, slave nor free, male nor female. Yet this new identity does not abolish one's cultural, ethnic, racial, or sexual identity. Membership in the church is not a melting pot that dissolves ethnicity, race, or nationality. Paul envisions a new inter-ethnic social reality of Jews and Gentiles. Unfortunately, the community of Jews and Gentiles was gradually reduced to a Gentile identity after the second century, which would later have disastrous consequences for the relationship of Christians and Jews. We have already seen how the Epistle to Diognetus treats the dialectical tension between an alternative identity, a new kind of citizenship, and the church's continuity with the life of non-Christian members of society. Miroslav Volf insightfully explores Paul's understanding of this special relationship between membership in the Body of Christ and ethnic identity.

> The resurrected Christ, in whom Jews and Greeks are united through baptism, is not a spiritual refuge from pluralizing corporeality, a pure spiritual space into which only the undifferentiated sameness of a universal human essence is admitted. Rather, baptism into Christ creates a people as the differentiated body of Christ. Bodily inscribed differences are brought together, not removed. The body of Christ lives as a complex interplay of different bodies—Jewish and Gentile, female and male, slave and free— of those who have partaken in Christ's self-sacrifice. The Pauline move is not from the particularity of the body to the universality of the spirit, but from separated bodies to the community of interrelated bodies—the one *body in the Spirit* with many *discrete members*.[29]

The church has not done a good job of practicing this Pauline insight. Nevertheless, Paul's vision is an answer to some of the most significant problems of our time. It shows how one can affirm the particularities of cultural identity while relativizing the ultimacy of these loyalties within an alternative new society grounded in our oneness in Christ. The very existence of a church where diversity is experienced and appreciated out of mutual respect and a commitment to reconciliation puts the lie to racism and ethnic cleansing. Those of us who are white Europeans must learn how to incorporate the painful history of blacks into our history and cultural identity in order to explore together, out of mutual respect and recognition, how to be a new society in which our blackness and whiteness is not abolished, but can flourish together in a new society of justice and reconciliation.

Fourth, baptism is a ritual that balances the tension between ethical practices that mark our new identity as Christians and those practices that are integral to the dominant culture, some of which as Christians we need to renounce. Baptism presupposes a discriminating ethic. Because the church in North America has become so acculturated to the dominant culture, it would be good if we could do it without authoritarianism and legalism, to revive a sense of what it means to "renounce" the world and participate in an alternative community. Larry

Rasmussen describes how baptism was practiced in the third century in North Africa. After catechumens had gone through two years of instruction, the ritual of baptism included

> standing and facing Rome to "renounce the devil and all his works and all his ways" and turning toward Jerusalem to confess the faith one would now walk by. Baptism was a declaration of "no" to one way of life and "yes" to another, a schooling in the latter, and a ritual enactment of it. ... The first thing the rites disclose is that the task of conversion was to reshape an entire way of living and system of values, and that the community was an encircling presence in all the rites. Indeed the community was "renewed in the rites" as members joined the competents at every stage in this elaborate journey. This is baptism as a focal practice. The connections from center outward were made, and moral character was formed and reformed around this center. A way of life was ordered and sustained in a ritual performance of its faith.[30]

We need to find a way in our own context to ritualize baptism so that it might become a more potent rite that can help form us as an alternative community with vision.

The Lord's Supper. Eating a meal together is one of the most basic, elemental acts in which human beings share their solidarity with each other. Disciples should break bread together and they should do it often. Disciples shared meals together with their leader again and again, culminating in that last Passover meal, a meal that has formed the practice of the ritual of the Lord's Supper ever since. In the post-resurrection accounts of Jesus' appearance to the disciples, many of the experiences of presence occur in the context of a meal. In the Lukan account of the disciples on the road to Emmaus, Jesus is recognized when they stop and break bread together. In the longer ending of the Gospel of Mark, Jesus appears to the disciples at a meal. In the concluding story in the Gospel of John where Jesus commissions Peter to tend his sheep, Jesus makes breakfast for the disciples on the Sea of Galilee.

This special ritual meal of the Lord's Supper is central to Christian worship. At the same time, it is a practice that forms us ethically as people. In the Lord's Supper we share together the memory of Christ in thanksgiving for bread and for the life Christ shared with us. The meal we share is not primarily an individualistic remembrance of how we have been saved by God's grace. This meal, eaten together, is a corporate meal of thanksgiving for the new community that has been brought together in Christ. We remember that we have been made whole through the sacrificial love of the one who gave his life on the cross. The meal invites us to share Christ's suffering as we, like Christ, are called to a life of solidarity with others and to the practice of sacrificial love.

The sharing of bread is a matter of economic ethics. At the table, material sustenance is shared and no one is excluded based on rank. This connection between the Lord's Supper and ethics is made vivid in Paul's first letter to the Corinthians. He criticizes them for eating scandalously when some who have an abundance of food do not share with those who have little.

> When you come together, it is not really to eat the Lord's supper. For when the time comes to eat, each of your goes ahead with your own supper, and one goes hungry and another becomes drunk. What! Do you not have homes to eat and drink in? Or do you show contempt for the church of God and humiliate those who have nothing? What should I say to you? Should I commend you? In this matter I do not commend you!" (1 Cor. 11:20-22)

The meal together should remind us of our baptism, our incorporation into a new humanity that in Christ transcends old divisions. It should also remind us of our anticipation of the messianic banquet, that new society of justice in which all will be fed and where no more hunger will exist. The supper is a symbol of hospitality to all. It points forward to the vision of a messianic banquet where all are welcome that is reflected in the biblical idea of the jubilee. Many visionaries in church history have made the connection between this supper and hospitality to the poor: Peter Waldo; St. Francis; the Hutterian Brethren; Girrard Winstanley and the Diggers in Puritan England; Dorothy Day and the Catholic Worker Movement, with its houses of hospitality; and Mother Teresa of Calcutta, whose daily participation in the Mass was connected integrally with her ministry among the poor.

Such rituals as baptism and the Lord's Supper point to a vision of life "beyond" ordinary profane life of our culture. Yet they use ordinary symbols like water, bread, and wine in expressing this alternative meaning. In the symbol and in the ritual, celebrants become participants in the world of sacred meaning. In that sense, the ritual participates in the reality it represents. The ritual is not itself the sacred reality, but it points beyond itself.

In the light of this understanding of symbol and ritual, we can move beyond a traditional debate that has occurred in the history of

Christian thought. This debate is symbolized best by the disputation at Marburg between Ulrich Zwingli and Martin Luther about the meaning of the Lord's Supper. Zwingli insisted that the bread and wine only "represent" the holy. The bread and wine are simply ordinary elements that point beyond themselves to enable the people of God to remember Jesus' death and resurrection. Martin Luther insisted that Jesus Christ is really present in the sacrament of communion. Yes, the bread and wine "signify" the events of long ago. But in the eating of the bread and the drinking of the cup, Christ is also present among the people.

One takes both Zwingli and Luther seriously when one recognizes that a powerful symbol is both representational and presentational. It points beyond itself (represents) even as it participates in that to which it points (presents).[31] To be taken up into the realm of the sacred through ritual is to be brought into God's presence. If the ritual registers in people's lives, the people will experience a sacred power beyond the group to which the ritual can only point.

The failure to keep a dynamic tension between these two aspects of ritual leads to either of two distortions. In the Zwinglian stream, worship can easily lose its power. Because Zwingli recognized the power of symbols, he reduced symbols to a bare minimum by throwing out of the church all artistic forms, including music. Worship was in danger of being reduced to the profane. Of course, Zwingli was reacting to the other danger, when the sacred becomes identified with the symbol or ritual itself. When that happens, ritual can become superstition or pure form. People begin to believe that they can control the sacred by repeating the proper formulas. As in the previous distortion, the result is the same. The sacred is reduced to the profane. A kind of magic begins to operate: the rite is used as a means of control toward a particular end.[32]

The Protestant Reformation was a reaction against a kind of magic that had crept into the Roman Catholic sacramental system. Luther saw this magic most vividly in the sale of indulgences within the sacrament of penance. Later Protestantism has its own forms of abuse. Simple recitation of creedal formulas has become for many the means of salvation. Dietrich Bonhoeffer identified that as cheap grace. In modern American Christianity, some forms of Evangelicalism reduce the Christian faith to a kind of magic, where one's "ticket to heaven" is predicated on confessing the right things or saying the right formulas.

The liturgy of the Orthodox tradition is a powerful, moral forming ritual. The drama of one expression of this liturgy begins when one enters into the quiet of a dark church on a late Saturday night before

Easter. After a candlelight procession led by the priest and choir around the church, the congregation gathers at the door of the church. The priest knocks on the door of the church and repeats several times the words of Psalm 24: "Lift up your heads, O gates! and be lifted up, O ancient doors! that the King of glory may come in." When the doors open, the bells on the church begin to ring and the people move into the now brightly lit church. The priest repeats again and again the phrase, "Christ is risen!" and the congregation responds, "He is risen indeed!"

In the congregation I visited, the resurrection affirmation was repeated in four languages: Greek, Slavonic, Arabic, and English. The worshipers participated for about two hours in the rhythms of liturgical drama, particularly the movement back-and-forth between priest and choir, joined by the congregation singing, "Christ is risen from the dead, trampling down death by death, and upon those in the tombs bestowing life." The mystery of the liturgical drama was highlighted by the organization of space. Doors opened to the altar located behind the wall of icons (the iconostasis). Throughout the liturgy, the priest moved back-and-forth through this space, mediating the sacred presence of Christ to the congregation.

The liturgical drama, the priest, and the visual images—all in effect become icons, images that embody the presence of the Holy. According to Anthony Ulgonik, the icon is an emblem of the incarnation.

> Christ took upon himself flesh, the "stuff" of this world, and thereby redeemed us. He called upon us ... to take the flesh, the "stuff" of this world, and sanctify it for his service. The icon is fashioned, in a prescribed way, of wood and paint. It is an "incarnation" of Christ's image and that of his saints. It is a sanctification of materiality, meant to remind us of its Prototype, "the image of the invisible God, the first born of all creation." Icons "image forth" the majesty of God, just as we are called to "image forth" in turn Christ our Savior.[33]

The drama climaxes when Orthodox Christians move to the front of the church to receive the chalice of Holy Communion. This ritual marks Orthodox Christians. Members of the congregation offer guests the congregation bread. Thus all Christians share in Holy Communion. This motif of Christian unity continues as the drama concludes. All receive an Easter greeting from the priest as they leave the sanctuary and an Easter egg, symbolizing also the break of the fast begun at Lent, and all join in a great feast and time of fellowship together.

In the Easter liturgy of the Roman Catholic tradition, after the service of light, seven Scripture readings summarize the entire history of salvation. The final reading is from Romans 6: "Do you not know that all of us who have been baptized into Christ Jesus were baptized into his death? Therefore we have been buried with him by baptism into death, so that, just as Christ was raised from the dead by the glory of the Father, so we too might walk in newness of life" (Rom. 6:3-4). A renewal of baptismal vows and the profession of faith, ritually enacted in the sprinkling of the congregation by the priest, follow this reading. I found this particularly significant as a member of a believers church with a tradition of adult baptism. Not only does one make a commitment at the time of initial baptism into the church; but also each Easter the members of the church renew their baptismal vows.

In the Lord's Supper we offer the work of our hands, symbolized by the bread and the wine, as a sign of thanksgiving (Eucharist) for the work of God in Jesus Christ. A common meal of food and drink, drawn from the earth and transformed by the work of human hands, becomes an offering to God through which we experience the presence of Christ among us as we remember and look forward with hope.

In the liturgy of the St. John's Benedictine Abbey, the worshiping congregation is taken up into the holy week drama, when the abbot symbolically washes the feet of one of the monks. In the Mennonite Church and the Church of the Brethren, footwashing used to be an important ritual. I believe the church needs to revive the footwashing ritual in connection with the Maundy Thursday communion meal. Through the concrete physical realities of basin, water, and towel, by touching each other in the washing of feet, we appropriate powerful and rich symbols that suggest humility, mutual subordination, and our call to care for each other.

Such a service of footwashing appropriately precedes a communion meal, especially within the believers church tradition, for which "communion" (being reconciled and at peace with each other) is a central meaning of the Lord's Supper. One eats a meal, not with enemies, but with persons at peace with each other. The congregation I grew up in took the Lord's Supper so seriously that sometimes persons unable to resolve a dispute with another member of the congregation would not take communion "lest they profane the body and blood of the Lord" (1 Cor. 11:27). In the Roman Catholic Mass, the "sign of peace" thus appropriately precedes the taking of communion. Ritually, the action of the congregation of greeting each other with the sign of peace expresses a profound truth of the meaning of the Eucharist.

Sabbath.[34] A proper rhythm of Sabbath and labor is an essential practice in a Christian way of life. Human beings are invited to fulfill their identity by celebrating the Sabbath in their lives, honoring God through restful delight in all that God has created. It is a particularly important witness to an alternative way of living in a North American cultural context where so much of life has been reduced to a calculated interest in personal and material benefit. The Sabbath is a special time within the flow of chronological time simply to *be* rather than to *do*, to enjoy the beauty of God and God's creation. To seek the shalom of the city is to invite our fellow humans into this same peace and joy of the Sabbath. It is significant that the practice of the Sabbath was developed as a powerful Jewish institution in exile. The seven-day rhythm served as a critical marker of Jewish identity within a hostile culture. Elie Wiesel points out how important the Sabbath was for Jews during the holocaust, who even in the concentration camps would save a piece of bread to celebrate the Sabbath. His statement of the significance of the Sabbath for Jews is powerful: "More than the Jews observed the Sabbath, the Sabbath preserved the Jews."

The Sabbath is not an oppressive legalism, as it has unfortunately often been viewed and practiced; it is a gift to us of "transcendence." We ignore the rhythm of work and rest at our peril. We desperately need the Sabbath for humanitarian reasons of rest and relaxation, for such renewal is important for our health and well-being. But more than that, the Sabbath is the occasion for us to worship God, the ultimate reality of our lives. The Sabbath allows us to reorient ourselves and reestablish our priorities.

The purpose of the Sabbath is not to provide the rest we need so that we will have new energy to work when the Sabbath comes to an end. That would make an idol of our work. Such an instrumental view of the Sabbath misses the main point. The renewal of life by God's spirit is nothing less than the return to holiness of the Sabbath, God's joy and delight in the created cosmos. We are invited to worship God and enjoy God's creation when we honor God in the sanctification of the Sabbath. In the words of the King James Version, we are invited to "worship God in the beauty of holiness" (1 Chron. 16:29).

If viewed rightly, the Sabbath is a special time within the flow of ordinary time. In the creation story of Genesis 1, the climax of the perfectly ordered creation is the sanctification of a special time within time. Abraham Heschel, Jewish theologian, calls the Sabbath a "cathedral in time."

He who wants to enter the holiness of the day must first lay down the profanity of clattering commerce, of being yoked to toil. He must go away from the screech of dissonant days, from the nervousness and fury of acquisitiveness and the betrayal in embezzling his own life. He must say farewell to manual work and learn to understand that the world has already been created and will survive without the help of man. Six days a week we wrestle with the world, wringing profit from the earth; on the Sabbath we especially care for the seed of eternity planted in the soul.[35]

Larry Rasmussen calls for a renewal of the Sabbath as a feature in an adequate earth ethic that can empower us to resist our exploitation and rape of the environment. In an interesting chapter entitled, "The Gift of Darkness," he captures the spirit of Sabbath.

[Christians] don't know when Sabbath begins. We think it begins by dawn's early light on the first day of the week, the Big Work Week. Jesus knew better. Of course Sabbath begins at dusk, when shadows rise and candles and quiet and night and God comes. And when stillness subtly, in the very last hours, saves the day and the week from sure death by efficiency. Of course Sabbath comes as a gift of darkness, and not light and day. For it is by night and candlelight that we cease our cravings and are taught to open ourselves, allow ourselves to be empty and receptive. Our egos, busy all day and all week, somehow miraculously recede in darkness, darkness with prayers centuries old and chants without composers' names, prayers and chants known only by the smooth tones of a communion of countless saints gathered in quiet worship over umpteen centuries.[36]

Prayer. The habit of prayer is integral to an alternative cultural vision. In his book, *Just Peacemaking: Transforming Initiatives for Justice and Peace,* Glen Stassen points out that Matthew's Sermon on the Mount is not about abstract ideals that are difficult or impossible to implement. As noted in chapter four, Stassen holds that the Sermon consists of a series of fourteen imperatives or transforming initiatives made possible by God's delivering grace that are concrete, practical, and doable. One of these imperatives is the call to prayer.

It is striking how often prayer is discussed in the Sermon on the Mount, a text many assume to be primarily about human responsibility to the neighbor. Prayer is mentioned three times in the Sermon: the imperative to pray for one's enemies and those who persecute (Matt. 5:44); imperatives about how to pray, including the Lord's Prayer (Matt. 6:5-13); and the imperative to make one's requests known to

God (Matt. 7:6-11). Stassen summarizes: "Prayer is asking God's delivering grace to happen; and it is participating in that grace and deliverance." It includes facing the evil that is in us. It is not only speaking, but also listening to the Spirit of God praying in us. In the Lord's Prayer we pray for God's rule (the transforming power of God's justice and peace) to come on earth "as it is in heaven." And in the second section of the prayer, we pray "for God to deliver us from four concrete threats—hunger, debt, temptation, and evil. 'Give us our daily bread; forgive us our debts; lead us not into temptation; deliver us from evil' (Matt. 6:11-13)."[37] Prayer is not a substitute for action. Rather, it places human action and responsibility within the framework of God's transforming power. Martin Luther King Jr. expresses the fundamental meaning of prayer with his conviction that in the struggle for justice, humans have cosmic companionship.[38]

For Walter Wink, prayer is an existential struggle with the authorities and powers "against an antihuman collective atmosphere, against images of worth and value that stunt and wither human life."[39] Prayer struggles with the powers outside oneself as well as with the demons within that hold us in bondage. Our obsession with our hostility and hatred of our enemies is one of those powers that can keep us in bondage and lead to our own self-destruction. If we cannot let go of that hatred, we will be determined by it. The imperative to pray for our enemies is a call to imagine an alternative future, to see the image of God in the one we hate and wish to destroy.

> Intercession is spiritual defiance of what is, in the name of what God has promised. ... History belongs to the intercessors, who believe the future into being. ... This is the politics of hope. Hope envisages its future and then acts as if that future is now irresistible, thus helping to create the reality for which it longs.[40]

Wink warns us that all of this sounds like arrogant bravado "unless we recognize that it is God rather than ourselves who initiates prayer, and that it is God's power, not ours, that answers to the world needs."[41] Paul puts it this way: "The Spirit helps us in our weakness; for we do not know how to pray as we ought, but that very Spirit intercedes with sighs too deep for words" (Rom. 8:26).

In the context of corporate worship, prayer is not primarily a private act of the individual, but functions as a powerful ritual to order and reorder our lives. Prayer is not a turning away from the world to warm feelings of ecstasy. To be brought into the presence of Christ means to experience anew the meaning of incarnation, God's full and complete identification with the world. Churches that are an alternative cultural presence in the world view worship not as a warm fuzzy, but as a time in which Christian people interpret the world in a new way, a way different from the surrounding culture. Worship encourages movement back into profane time with new hope and energy. In a world of suffering, misery, self-indulgence, materialism, faithlessness, and hopelessness, if ritual has registered, the church should enter into the world filled with the Spirit of God. The church will then seek to make Christ present to the world. That is why Henri Nouwen has said that genuine prayer is the most radical form of peace action.

> Prayer—living in the presence of God—is the most radical peace action we can imagine. Prayer is peacemaking and not simply the preparation before, the support during, and the thanksgiving after. ... Prayer is not primarily a way to get something done. In prayer we undo the fear of death and therefore the basis of all human destruction. ... The act of prayer is the basis and source of all action. When our actions against the arms race are not based on the act of prayer, they easily become fearful, fanatical, bitter, and more of an expression of survival instincts than of our faith in God and the God of the living.[42]

Singing. We are formed to be the people of God through the corporate act of singing hymns together. Hymns can be a powerful force in shaping us to be the kind of people we are. Hymns can play a particularly powerful role in enlarging our pictures and images of God so as to be more inclusive of human and cosmic realities. We need both to deconstruct old images of God that are no longer helpful or are downright destructive and to replace these old metaphors with new or neglected ones that are more adequate for our experience. Through singing hymns we expand our metaphorical language, both to help us preserve the transcendence or Godness of God, and to give voice to the immanence of God present in the cosmos.

Jointly published by Mennonites and the Church of the Brethren, *Hymnal: A Worship Book* is a valuable resource for expanding our sense of the global church as we learn Native American, Japanese, African, Russian, Latin American musical styles, and more. Through singing such hymns from many traditions in the history of the church, we come to know the church catholic. The hymnbook is probably the most ecumenical of all our sources for worship. One hymn able to expand theological horizons is the hymn text of Jean Janzen based on writings of Julian of Norwich that embraces feminine images of God.

Mothering God, you gave me birth
    in the bright morning of this world.
Creator, Source of every breath,
    you are my rain, my wind, my sun;
you are my rain, my wind, my sun.

Another example is the Brian Wren hymn that uses the image of darkness as a symbol for God's presence.

Joyful is the dark, holy hidden God,
    rolling cloud of night beyond all naming,
    majesty in darkness, energy of love,
    Word-in-flesh, the mystery proclaiming.
Joyful is the dark, spirit of the deep,
    winging wildly o'er the world's creation,
    silken sheen of midnight, plumage black and bright,
    swooping with the beauty of a raven.[43]

The linkage of proclamation and performative, participatory music making is central to the practice of African-American worship. The church can learn much from the flow of action back-and-forth across space in the call and response patterns in African-American worship—preacher and congregation, choir or lead singer and congregation. In African-American worship, meaning is expressed through a pattern or rhythm of interaction through space, which creates a sense of a conversation between God and the people. The people hear and respond to the Word of God; the preacher or music makers are moved by the Spirit of God among the people.

Irene Jackson Brown describes a number of the factors that are significant in the organization of space in African-American worship. People crowd together in the pews to create a sense of community and connectedness. The congregation participates broadly in performance through singing, dancing, or playing an instrument.

Affiliation is determined by proximity to the pulpit or altar and visibility in the sanctuary, not by musical proficiency. The core category—the most visible music makers are situated within or near the "sacred space"—the elevated altar space or pulpit. The core music-makers encourage the Spirit. Specific tempos, rhythmic and harmonic patterns are used to heighten worship—to the point where shouting or possession begins. ... The supportive category of music makers includes the congregation who sing, clap, shout, play tambourines, and/or sway. Supportive music makers usually perform the response to the choir's call or the preacher's call. Within the sanctuary, the core and supportive music-makers are separated spatially. Yet connectedness, community, is achieved because the call and response pattern is used, providing dialogue between choir/preacher and the congregation. The third category, marginal music-makers, are not incidental, but participate occasionally or episodically by either singing, humming or clapping.[44]

Powerful rituals "register" in the lives of people in such a way that they return to the ordinary or profane world changed or transformed as the life and struggle of the people are "taken up" into worship. The power of the spiritual in African-American worship was its ability to address the suffering of people, just as the doxology of praise in the book of Revelation has the power to create a new sense of reality for people negotiating between competing allegiances.

Other Important Ritual Practices. Ritual "practices" are therefore significant for moral formation. The offering is also a significant ritual in worship in the context of the disciplined practice of stewardship. Historically, the offering is a particularly significant practice in the believers church tradition. We offer a portion of the money of our labor to be used in our participation in God's continued work in the world. The offering of money is central particularly for a church that understands itself as a voluntary community (as in North America), independent from the political system in which it exists and thus dependent upon voluntary contributions for its continued existence as a community and its mission in the world.

The church is a community of memory. It is nourished through proclamation and storytelling. Forgetfulness is one of the hazards of the church in a culture oriented by the values of consumerism and self-gratification. The church needs to follow the lead of the Bible itself, where the stories of the heroes and heroines of the faith show their shadow sides as well. We need to learn not only from the stories of triumph and faithfulness, but from stories of failure and tragedy as well.

Process Practices

A number of focal practices are central to the processes of congregational life. John H. Yoder in particular has contributed to our understanding of the nature of the church's structure and social process.[45] The church is based upon voluntary membership, "the choice to confess oneself a disciple of Jesus and to commit oneself to hearing the counsel of one's fellow disciples."[46] Yoder's position is deeply indebted to the Anabaptists of the sixteenth century, whose views became the occasion for intense conflict about infant and adult baptism because they challenged the medieval idea of the corpus Christianum, the unity of church and society, which had its roots in Constantine. In modern pluralistic America, the choice to join the church and become a disciple does not seem very radical. Hardly anyone notices the ritual of baptism, which marks this choice.[47] However, distinctive focal practices follow from the believers church idea.

The Dialogical Process of Discernment. The radical dimension in Yoder's position is the idea of "hearing the counsel of one's fellow believers," which at other points Yoder calls "dialogical liberty." Yoder believes that this view of the church was not just an Anabaptist position, but that it "marked the common Protestant origins in the early 1520s."[48] A process of "practical moral reasoning" marks such a church, where people engage in conversation about what their faith commitments entail for their lives.

Yoder refers to Paul's exhortation in 1 Corinthians, which he says Ulrich Zwingli once referred to as the "rule of Paul": "When you come together, each one has a hymn, a lesson, a revelation, a tongue, or an interpretation. Let all things be done for building up. ... Let two or three prophets speak, and let the others weigh what is said" (1 Cor. 14:26, 29). This approach challenges an individualism that says it is my business alone to discern what it means to follow Christ faithfully.

With the concept of dialogical liberty, Yoder seeks a position that recognizes the dignity of the individual person while accepting the discipline of a community. Neither individualism nor collectivism can be the reigning principle. All are free to speak in the meetings. The community, from whom the individual receives counsel, weighs the various positions. "The moral validity of a choice one makes is connected to the freedom with which one has first of all made the choice to confess oneself a disciple of Jesus and to commit oneself to hearing the counsel of one's fellow disciples."[49]

So long as persons in a congregation are genuinely seeking to follow Christ and are willing to listen to others, a congregation should keep the dialogical process open to ongoing ethical discernment on matters where Christians conscientiously disagree. We live in a time when issues like homosexuality and abortion are tearing apart the church. We must find a way for Christians who disagree on conscientious grounds to keep the process open to ongoing discernment. This is difficult for those who believe that the church's moral position is not subject to question on a particular issue. They interpret the openness to ongoing dialogue as a compromise of the church's clear moral teaching. The position of such persons must be respected and heard conscientiously. Both the minority and the majority must be ready to entertain the possibility that the one with whom they disagree is really speaking the truth.

On the other hand, neither side in a debate should be expected to accept the position of those with whom they disagree until they are persuaded by the Spirit what God is calling them to do. All must be free to speak without being judged. All must be willing to listen. The unity of the church does not reside in the propositional agreements Christians have on doctrine or ethical issues. The unity of the church is ultimately grounded in the covenant members make to each other at baptism to follow Christ and to be guided by the Holy Spirit as they discern together God's guidance.

I see no grounds for excluding anyone from the church who desires to continue to discern God's will in a spirit of humble sharing and patient listening to others. Only those who exclude themselves should be separated from this process, either because they freely choose to do so because they are no longer conscientiously committed to the vows they made at baptism, or because they are no longer willing to submit to the discipline of ongoing discernment under the guidance of the Spirit.

This same spirit of dialogical liberty should hold at other levels of the church: within denominations when congregations meet together, when church leaders and committees gather together to make decisions, and in the larger ecumenical conversations between church bodies. We are all "on the way." Our unity resides in a common commitment to follow Christ and in the process to speak and listen to each other to discern what it means to be faithful.

The church should be a safe space for dialogue and discernment. Unfortunately, the church has been anything but that kind of space. For many persons, the church is the last place they can experience "dialogical liberty," the freedom of inquiry to discern what it means to be faithful to God in our time and place. Unfortunately, the church has not practiced an alternative cultural vision. Institutions of secular society, like colleges and universities, have often done better at being "sanctuaries" where free conversation and inquiry can take place.

The practice of reconciliation. Another mark of the church is a reconciling process, referred to by the Anabaptists and other Reformers as the "Rule of Christ" of Matthew 18:15-18:

> If another member of the church sins against you, go and point
> out the fault when the two of you are alone. If the member listens
> to you, you have regained that one. But if you are not listened to,

take one or two others along with you, so that every word may be confirmed by the evidence of two or three witnesses. If the member refuses to listen to them, tell it to the church; and if the offender refuses to listen even to the church, let such a one be to you as a Gentile and a tax collector. Truly I tell you, whatever you bind on earth will be bound in heaven, and whatever you loose on earth will be loosed in heaven.

This text outlines a reconciling process of admonition. To be a member of the church is to agree to accept the counsel of others with the goal of reconciliation. The process is realistic in that it acknowledges that members of the church sin. The text does not say that people should be treated as "tax collectors" because they conscientiously disagree. The only cause for a breach in the community is when the conversation stops, "if a member refuses to listen."

The goal of the process is not punishment or discipline, but reconciliation and restoration. The text emphasizes the *process* that is to occur, not the *standards* by which people are to live. The procedure requires that the offender and the violated go through the process together (as opposed to a private confession or a prayer for forgiveness). The terms *bind* and *loose* come from rabbinic usage and refer to holding accountable and freeing from obligation. In explaining this passage, John H. Yoder notes that Matthew links what the community does on earth to what God does in heaven. "When human and divine activity coincide in this way, that is what some denominations call a sacrament. ... The community action is God's action."[50] In summary, to be a member of the church is to commit oneself to a process of ongoing reconciliation, involving both taking responsibility for the other members of the community and being willing to listen and learn from others.

Yoder argues that this practice can be a model for other social relationships and it parallels what we have learned about conflict resolution:

> (a) the process begins at the point of concrete offense, with a real problem;
> (b) the intention is not punishment but resolution;
> (c) the frame of reference is a value communally posited as binding on the parties;
> (d) the process is not a zero-sum game, but a mediator trusts that a solution is available whereby both parties will win;
> (e) the first efforts are made in ways that minimize publicity and threat, and maximize flexibility without risk of shame;

(f) the process makes use of a variety or roles and perspectives carried out by competent, caring, yet objective interveners;

(g) the skills and the credibility of interveners can be validated by experience and accredited by colleagues and clients;

(h) the ultimate sanction, if negotiations fail, is public disavowal of the party refusing reconciliation, and what is left is either to let the injustice stand or to see the civil powers intervene their ordinary way.[51]

Related to but not identical with this reconciling communal process is the practice of forgiveness. When one party has violated another and a communal process of reconciliation has occurred, forgiveness is an integral part of that reconciling process. However, sometimes the process of reconciliation described above does not work out. One of the parties may refuse to participate and may leave the church.

Some within the church have experienced violations of their being by forces and powers that happened long ago. Others have been the victims of torture or participated in torture themselves, refugees who have fled from situations of war, revolution, or unjust systems of oppression; minorities like Native or African Americans, whose people have been the victims of genocide or slavery and who continue to experience injustice and lack of recognition and respect as persons. A process of reconciliation such as we have described may not be available. What then?

The practice of forgiveness is one of the most important for our time and situation. Forgiveness pervades the biblical text.[52] It is named as a central practice in the life of the church many times. We ask for the power to forgive in the Lord's Prayer. In the Gospel of John, the responsibility and authority to forgive is made explicit. "Receive the Holy Spirit. If you forgive the sins of any, they are forgiven them; if you retain the sins of any, they are retained" (John 20:23). Such a responsibility and power can be healing; it is also subject to the dangers of the abuse of power.

Hannah Arendt states the importance of forgiveness well and succinctly:

Without being forgiven, released from the consequences of what we have done, our capacity to act would, as it were, be confined to one single deed from which we could never recover; we would remain the victims of its consequences forever, not unlike the sorcerer's apprentice who lacks the magic formula to break the spell.[53]

The ability to go on with our lives so that we can flourish is necessary for both the victims and the perpetrators of wrong. Forgiveness is the process whereby we come to terms with having been violated so that we can say, as Jesus did on the cross, "Father forgive them for they know not what they do." It is the process whereby we can acknowledge our wrong and ask for forgiveness of those we have violated. Such a process is essential if we are to break the vicious cycles of resentment, recrimination, and violence. The process can easily be subverted, however. The violated party must be allowed to go through a period of grieving, anger and separation, and must be able to choose a reconciliation process freely. Otherwise the process can be manipulative.

If we can learn this practice in an alternative community, the church, it can have significant relevance as we seek the peace of the city where we dwell. Donald Shriver, Alan Geyer, and Bishop Desmond Tutu all make convincing cases for how this practice is relevant to politics, how forgiveness is an essential practice if nations and peoples locked in bitter struggles can learn to live together in peace.[54]

Recognition of Gifts. The New Testament strongly emphasizes the contribution of the gifts of the members to the building up of the church. Yoder describes the exercise of various gifts in the church: agents of direction, of memory, of linguistic self-consciousness, and of order and due process.

> "Agents of Direction" are referred to in 1 Corinthians: One who prophesies talks to others, to their improvement, encouragement and consolation. ... Let two or three of them speak, and the others weigh what they say ... (1 Cor. 14:3, 29). Another function in the community is to keep alive the collective memory that provides a rich resource for discernment. "Agents of Memory" draw upon the Scriptures as well as the rich church tradition. "Agents of Linguistic Self-Consciousness" are the teachers or theologians who scrutinize open-mindedly, but skeptically, typologies that dichotomize the complementary and formulae that reconcile the incompatible.[55]

> The "Agent of Due Process and Order," far from being a monarchical authority, appears in the New Testament in the plural. Their ministry is not self-contained but consists in enabling the open conversational process. ... The moderator or facilitator as practical moral reasoner is accountable for assuring that everyone else is heard and that the conclusions reached are genuinely consensual. The nearest modern example is the Clerk of a Friends' Meeting.[56]

Yoder's description of the gifts essential to community places the emphasis on linguistic and organizational roles. We must be careful not to develop a hierarchical ordering of importance by honoring gifts that are more visible over others that are less visible. We must not forget the important ordinary tasks performed by janitors and trustees, the work of numerous committees, those who make and bring food to church suppers, persons who visit the sick and the dying, those who contribute to worship through music or visual symbol, the ones who bring food for distribution to local charities, those who care for children in the nursery, teachers of Sunday School classes, and the work of quilters and woodworkers, who contribute their labor for the benefit of organizations that carry out the church's mission in the world.

Yoder describes a process of ongoing conversation in the church that is based upon the commitment to follow Christ and being subject to the counsel of others. Such a process is essential to the church, which must discern what it means to seek the peace of the city where it dwells. This model of the church within culture requires a constant process of discernment. But discerning without prayer and worship is inadequate. If this approach is going to work, it cannot presuppose a one-dimensional rationality. This discerning process must include practices of worship (described above) that place our lives in relationship to those symbolic actions that orient the life of a congregation. Through prayer in the context of worship, people are enabled to transcend the limits of rational discussion and debate. Each congregation is called to discern Micah's exhortation to love mercy and do justice in our communities and in the world.

We will not always agree what that means. Those disagreements must be taken up into the life of worship, so that in the process of discernment, a congregation can also be faithful to the third element in the triad of Micah's admonition, to "walk humbly with God." Worship that ignores our debates about the meaning of faithfulness or that enables us to escape from discerning our responsibility with respect to such issues as the role of women in the church, homosexuality, war, or injustice is not genuine worship. Only if our worship integrates the discerning process with a sense of the transcendent will Christians be empowered with the patience to continue the conversation with brothers and sisters with whom we disagree.

Pastoral Care Practices

The words *pastoral care practices* do not refer to the work done by professional ministers, though professional leadership is certainly important to the life of the church. Pastoral care practices are focal practices that mark the life of the faith community as a corporate body. Such practices are important for the care of the household. Two metaphors, *household* and *body* suggest the corporate care practices of the church. We catch such a vision in the book of Acts, where Luke reports that after Pentecost "all who believed were together and had all things in common; they would sell their possessions and goods and distribute the proceeds to all, as any had need" (Acts 2:44-45).

One need not advocate communal ownership of property as the only pattern for the church to recognize that a mark of the church is a mutual aid that treats fellow Christians in need as if they were brothers and sisters in a common household. The underlying assumption is that where one member of the body suffers, all suffer. One cannot simply ignore a member of the body if it is hurting or suffering. Membership in the body of Christ calls us to a life of solidarity expressed in mutual service to one other. Corporate care of the household of faith can cover a wide range of needs: physical needs of food, clothing, and shelter; the experience of loss from fire and storm; help for those suffering from illness; participation in the nurture of children and the care of the elderly to ease the burden of individual families; and care for those who are dying and experience grief from death and tragedy. Just as important is the fundamental need people have for love, for belonging to an intimate community where people know each other by name.

One of the significant roles the church needs to play in our time, argues Larry Rasmussen, is that of "community haven or way station." In the midst of the anomie and fragmentation of modern culture, where people's lives are marked by frenzy and dislocation, "we need sanctuaries, sacred spaces and places of safe retreat and balm very close to home, places of prayer, consolation, and the company of those who understand."[57] However, these way stations should not be seen, as they often have been in the past, simply as a legitimating or conserving of society as it is.

> What is in view here ... is the church community as haven in the manner of base communities on the margins. ... They are havens of refreshment and of celebration around simple gifts. They are places of song, dance, and not a little silliness. They know how to do feasts, just as they know how to pray and be quiet and merciful to one another. They know how to resist the powers of death and make of their "homeplace communities" solid sites of resistance and reconstruction. The people here are pastoral people present to one another in time of trouble and joy.[58]

Practices of Service to the Wider Community

In the last section of this book, I will address more directly the way in which the church relates to the larger culture through the bridge concepts of *artist*, *citizen*, and *philosopher*. It is important to emphasize, however, that the church is not genuinely the church without mission. Just as Christ is the man for others (to use Dietrich Bonhoeffer's language), so the church as Christ's body is authentic only when it lives for others rather than for itself.

Miscellaneous Practices that Address the Needs of the World. Persons are formed morally through practices that address the needs of the world. To address these needs effectively requires that we give our time, money, and energy to voluntary organizations that empower people to work for common causes. One of the church's most important practices is advocacy of the poor and the marginalized. It is not enough for the church to address the symptoms of injustice by responding to the needs of people on a one-to-one basis. The church must also address the larger structural conditions that cause injustice. Another practice is community service: giving our time and energy to address the common good of the communities where we live. Christians can join with other citizens in supporting the common good by nurturing the quality of institutions like the public schools or supporting the arts in a community.

A third way we can address the needs of the world is through the development of alternative institutions. Many institutions now taken for granted in our society, such as hospitals and mental health centers, were originally created by the church to address needs that were not being met. A fourth practice is the call to be peacemakers, to contribute to the peace of the city where we dwell by enabling persons to respond to conflict with nonviolent processes of conflict resolution. Even our daily work and professions are vehicles for creative intervention in our culture with an alternative vision of life.

Hospitality. We close by describing in a bit more detail one of these practices, the practice of hospitality. Hospitality is the welcoming of needy strangers and offering them food, protection, clothing, warmth, and safety. The central New Testament text for the practice of hospitality is the well-known passage of Matthew 25.

> For I was hungry and you gave me food, I was thirsty and you gave me something to drink, I was a stranger and you welcomed me, I was naked and you gave me clothing, I was sick and you took care of me, I was in prison and you visited me. (Matt. 25:35-36)

Hospitality has deep roots in the Old Testament. Abraham's offer of hospitality to strangers contrasts with the story of the men of Sodom and Gomorrah, who asked Lot to turn over strangers to whom he had provided hospitality in his own household (Gen. 18–19). The book of Hebrews builds the exhortation to hospitality on the Abrahamic model. "Do not neglect to show hospitality to strangers, for by doing that some have entertained angels without knowing it" (Heb.13:2). Hospitality is grounded in God's character. Even as God had compassion on Israel in Egypt, so Israel should practice similar compassion. "You shall not oppress a resident alien; you know the heart of an alien, for you were aliens in the land of Egypt" (Exod. 23:9).

Christine Pohl believes that the central theological themes of hospitality come together in the practice of the Lord's Supper. Christ is both the host who welcomes all to the table and the guest who is present at the table in the stranger who has been welcomed.[59]

According to Pohl, Christ's presence in the person of the guest is a common theme in the literature on hospitality. This is vividly portrayed in Leo Tolstoy's story, "Where Love is, God Is." In this story Christ comes in a dream to the cobbler, Martin Aveich, who has lost hope in life. He comes through three strangers to whom he offers hospitality: a poor old soldier to whom Martin offers a cup of tea, a woman in shabby clothes with a baby in her arms whom Martin invites in from the cold for soup and a warm fire, and through an intervention that leads to forgiveness and reconciliation between in an old woman and a boy who had stolen an apple from her basket. Tolstoy closes his story with the text of Matthew 25 and the words: "And Martin understood that his dream had come true; and that the Savior had really come to him that day, and he had welcomed him."[60]

Hospitality is hard work. It requires the practical unrelenting work of sustained attention to both the earthy needs of shelter, food, clothing *and* the emotional needs of listening to and respecting persons who are not always very lovable. Dorothy Day, founder of the Catholic Worker Movement, established houses of hospitality. She had as one of her mottoes, "a harsh and dreadful love," one of the wise sayings of Father Zosima in Dostoyevsky's novel *The Brothers Karamazov*. The nature of love is discussed when Madam Khoklakov comes to Father Zosima with her doubts.

"But the future life, it is such an enigma. ... What if I've been believing all my life, and when I come to die there's nothing but the burdocks growing on my grave?" Zosima responds to her by acknowledging that although one cannot prove it, one can be convinced.

"How?" she asks.

"By the experience of active love. Strive to love your neighbor actively and indefatigably. Insofar as you advance in love you will grow surer of the reality of God of the immortality of your soul."

This prompts Madam Khoklakov to say, "You see, I so love humanity that—would you believe it?—I often dream of forsaking all that I have, leaving Lise, and becoming a sister of mercy. I close my eyes and think and dream, and at that moment I feel full strength to overcome all obstacles."

But then she wonders whether she would persevere in such a path. "And do you know, I came with horror to the conclusion that, if anything could dissipate my love to humanity, it would be ingratitude. In short, I am a hired servant, I expect my payment at once—that is, praise, and the repayment of love with love. Otherwise I am incapable of loving any one."

Father Zosima then tells her a story about a doctor who sounds like Madame Khoklakov.

> "I love humanity," he said, "but I wonder at myself. The more I love humanity in general, the less I love man in particular. In my dreams," he said, "... as soon as any one is near me, his personality disturbs my self-complacency and restricts my freedom. ... I become hostile to people the moment they come close to me. But it has always happened that the more I detest men individually the more ardent becomes my love for humanity."

Madame Khoklakov, exposed, replies, "You have seen through me and explained me to myself!"

After urging Madam Khoklakov to be truthful to herself, Zosima penetrates to the heart of the matter.

> I am sorry that I can say nothing more consoling to you, for love in action is a harsh and dreadful thing compared with love in dreams. Love in dreams is greedy for immediate action, rapidly performed and in the sight of all. Men will even give their lives if only the ordeal does not last long but is soon over, with all looking on and applauding as though on the stage. But active love is labor and fortitude, and for some people too, perhaps, a complete science.[61]

The practice of hospitality requires courage. One of the most inspiring examples of hospitality is that shown by the French Huguenot community, under the leadership of Andre and Madga Trocmé, in LeChambon, France, during World War II. Under the watchful and threatening eyes of the Nazis and the French Vichy government, this community took in several thousand Jewish refugees, gave them a place to live, and protected them from the ovens of Auschwitz. They used as their motto the text from Deuteronomy 19:10: "So that the blood of an innocent person may not be shed in the land."

In his marvelous account of the story of this community, *Lest Innocent Blood Be Shed*, Philip Hallie asks the challenging question, "Why did goodness happen here?" The answer to that question has many dimensions to it, which Hallie explores in his book. However we answer the big question, we do know that the process began with a simple act of hospitality, when the first refugee came to the door and Magda Trocmé said, "Come in, and come in!"[62]

Part 2

Engaging Culture:

Seeking
the
Peace
of the City

Artistic Imagination
and the Life of the Spirit

Nathan Soderblom has remarked that Bach's St. Matthew's Passion music should be called the Fifth Evangelist. So was Bach for me. One night after singing ... in the Mass in B Minor under Koussevitsky at Symphony Hall, Boston, a renewed conviction came over me that here in the Mass, beginning with the Kyrie and proceeding through the Crucifixion to the Agnus Dei and Dona Nobis Pacem, all that was essential in the human and the divine was expressed. My love of the music awakened in me a profound sense of gratitude to Bach for having displayed as through a prism and in a way which was irresistible for me, the essence of Christianity. —James Luther Adams[1]

THE AESTHETIC DIMENSION OF LIFE IS integral to a cultural vision that seeks the peace of the city where we dwell. First, aesthetic experience is an integral part of our response to God, the Creator of the cosmos. Aesthetic experience is our sensual response to the way the cosmos and our world is ordered. Aesthetic experience is grounded in the sensual experience of sight, touch, smell, taste, movement, and sound. It is complex and many-faceted. We can experience sensual delight through the composition of sound and silence in music, the ordering of words in poetry and story, or the visual impact of sculpted wood or a Kansas sky. But our world is also profoundly alienated from God. The word *beauty* does not adequately describe the aesthetic experience we derive from a painting or a poem that can upset us and cause us to feel pain, anguish, or profound uncertainty.

Second, all Christians are called to be artists. When we honor God with our heart, soul, and mind, we order the cosmos to be in tune with God's intention for it. We can demonstrate our lack of faithfulness by creating that which is aesthetically inferior, or we can honor God by aesthetically excellent form. We "order" our words through poetry and

169

story, create and play music, and give order and structure to our households, farms and cities. We can honor God as well by poetry and art that challenges our complacency, jars us to "see" the world in its brokenness and alienation from God, and moves us to repentance.

Third, as already stated in the preceding chapter, aesthetic form is an integral component of worship. Worship is an invitation to respond to God with poetry, stained glass and banner, song, drama, and dance. In worship we express joy and delight in knowing God as Creator and Redeemer as we give aesthetic form to our spiritual yearnings. We also express the awareness of our own sin and alienation.

Fourth, we experience the arts in the larger culture beyond the church—in museum, concert hall, and city plaza, as well as in the myriad forms of aesthetic expression of ordinary people in all their cultural diversity (from clothing and jewelry to popular music). The arts can awaken us from our complacency and numbness to awareness and wonder. The arts foster the exercise of the imagination. They can also mislead us or seduce us with values that detract from an authentic vision of life. In our response to the arts in our culture, we must delicately balance openness and tolerance so that we may grow, while developing skills of discriminating judgment so that we know what is "good, acceptable, and perfect" (Rom. 12:2).

Making discriminating judgments about what is "good" aesthetically is complex and difficult. Can we do it? How can what is "good, acceptable, and perfect" be anything more than a matter of taste, relative to the context and setting in which a particular aesthetic form is developed? Later in this chapter I will address how a Christian theology of culture can help us discriminate between aesthetic excellence and aesthetic expressions of inferior quality.

AESTHETIC DELIGHT: BEING WHOLE PERSONS

Aesthetic delight is an integral part of being whole persons before God. Aesthetic delight is central to an embodied, incarnational vision of life that embraces the full range of sensual experience. A Trinitarian view of God nourishes sensual delight. The creator God is the ground of all that is, the one most vividly present in the concrete, historical Jesus, and the one whose Spirit is present in and participates in the cosmos. Consequently, any particular material form can become for us a "sacrament," a vehicle through which the gift of God's grace can come to us.[2]

Every day on my way to work I pass a large cottonwood. Planted near Kidron Creek, it is a wounded survivor of Kansas' droughts, wind, and ice storms. Its large, gnarled trunk (two of us cannot encircle the tree with outstretched arms) and broken limbs testify to the wounds it has suffered from the forces of nature, which are both hostile and life-giving. It rises majestically over 100 feet into the sky. I watch it change throughout the seasons—its stark form against gray winter sky, the yellow of autumn against blue, and the blanket of cotton it sends to earth each spring. The cottonwood is a nesting place for birds and squirrels. It provides shade in hot Kansas summers, and it could provide fire-wood in the middle of a blizzard.

But that is not why the tree is there; it is simply there for its own sake, a thing of beauty, a delight to the senses. It is a magnificent beauty, a study in the tension between symmetry when seen as a totality in the sky and the particularity of its parts. Its beauty lies in the juxtaposition of the perfectly ordered harmony of the whole and the jarring and un-settling bruises of the particular parts. The aesthetic experience of the cottonwood symbolizes the joy and delight God intends for humans, whose brokenness and alienation have been transformed by the renew-ing power of God's Spirit.

This linkage between personal transformation and aesthetic de-light is vivid in Alice Walker's *The Color Purple*. The main character, Celie, was nearly destroyed by the brutality she experienced from the oppressive structures of racism and violent patriarchalism. For a time she preserved her sanity by writing letters to God. Eventually she came to the insight that her image of God was so integrally linked to these structures that "God" could be of no help to her. "The God I been praying and writing to is a man. And just like all the other mens I know. Trifling, forgitful, and lowdown." In a letter to her sister, Nettie, Celie reports her change in consciousness after a conversation she had with her friend, Shug. Shug, too, used to see God as

> big and old and tall and gray-bearded and white. ... This old white man is the same God she used to see when she prayed. ... That's the one that's in the white folks' white Bible. ... When I found out I thought God was white, and a man, I lost interest. You mad cause he don't seem to listen to your prayers. Hump! Do the mayor listen to anything colored say? You have to git man off your eyeball before you can see anything a'tall. Man corrupt everything. ... He on your box of grits, in your head, and all over the radio. He try to make you think he everywhere. Soon as you think he everywhere, you think he God."[3]

The transformation of Shug comes when she begins to see again the beauty of the world.

My first stop from the old white man was trees. Then air. Then birds. Then other people. But one day when I was sitting quiet and feeling like a motherless child, which I was, it come to me: that feeling of being part of everything, not separate at all. I knew that if I cut a tree, my arm would bleed. And I laughed and I cried and I run all around the house. ... God love everything you love—and a mess of stuff you don't. But more than anything else, God love admiration. ... I think it pisses God off if you walk by the color purple in a field somewhere and don't notice it.[4]

The last letter of the book, when Celie is able again to write a letter to God, begins, "Dear God. Dear stars, dear trees, dear sky, dear people. Dear everything. Dear God."[5]

Though some might criticize the tendency to pantheism in Walker, the nearly complete identification of God with everything, her position can more appropriately be labeled panentheism. God is present in the cosmos, though not identical with it. Whatever Walker's theology, the novel presents a profound insight. The renewal of life by God's Spirit experienced by Celie and Shug is nothing less than the return to holiness of the Sabbath, when we step back to enjoy and delight in the cosmos that has been created. Such delight is one of the dimensions of shalom. Our end is to dwell in peace in all relationships: with ourselves, with nature, with our fellow human beings, and with God. When we ask in the Lord's Prayer for God's kingdom to come on earth as it is in heaven, the prayer expresses our longing not only for the creation of a new moral order, but also an order in which human beings take aesthetic delight. This longing is expressed in the eschatological vision of the prophet Isaiah:

> For I am about to create new heavens
>   and a new earth;
> the former things shall not be remembered
>   or come to mind.
> But be glad and rejoice forever
>   in what I am creating;
> for I am about to create Jerusalem as a joy,
>   and its people as a delight.
> I will rejoice in Jerusalem,
>   and delight in my people;
> no more shall the sound of weeping be heard in it,
>   or the cry of distress. (Isa. 65:17-19)

Interest in aesthetic form is central in Scripture. The Bible is essentially a large dramatic narrative with many smaller narratives. These stories shape us not primarily through the moral they teach or the abstract theology they convey, but through the drama of the narrative. In the first creation account, we see the constant repetition of the word *good*, climaxing with the phrase at the end of the six-day cycle, "and it was very good" (Gen. 1:31). *Good* cannot be restricted to moral goodness, since the word not only describes human beings, but also a properly ordered cosmos.

The Bible reflects an interest in the aesthetic form of offerings (Exod. 25:1-9), institutions like the ark of the covenant (Exod. 25:10-22), and the temple (1 Kings 6:14-38). The poetry of the Psalms expresses the fundamental affections of the religious life, from praise and thanksgiving to anguish and anger. We know Christ through the written language of a text. But that written language arose first out of an oral discourse integrally connected to the senses: sight, sound, smell, taste, and touch.

To grasp the textual meaning of the Bible, therefore, we must attend to the meaning of sensual symbols—mustard seeds, trees, shepherds, wine, bread, lilies, coins, fathers and sons, leaven, grain, chaff, sowers, widows, vines, and branches. In Isaiah, beauty is one of the elements of an eschatological vision, the future to which humans look forward in hope. The book of Revelation reflects a similar eschatological vision, an aesthetic yearning that includes both visual form and music. Central in the book are powerful visual images of a new city, Jerusalem, and a doxology, a hymn of praise: Worthy is the Lamb that was slain to receive honor, power, glory, and wisdom. It is not surprising that Karl Barth lauded the music of Mozart as a "symbol" or foretaste of the age to come, music that "is at once 'beautiful play' and virtually the equivalent of a parable."[6]

A selection from the poetry of the Song of Solomon illustrates the Hebraic affirmation of the beauty of the human body. The poetry is a dialogue between two lovers. Here the woman responds to her beloved:

> My beloved is all radiant and ruddy,
>   distinguished among ten thousand.
> His head is the finest gold;
>   his locks are wavy,
>   black as a raven.
> His eyes are like doves
>   beside springs of water,
> bathed in milk,
>   fitly set.

His cheeks are like beds of spices,
  yielding fragrance.
His lips are lilies,
  distilling liquid myrrh.
His arms are rounded gold,
  set with jewels.
His body is ivory work,
  encrusted with sapphires.
His legs are alabaster columns,
  set upon bases of gold.
His appearance is like Lebanon,
  choice as the cedars.
His speech is most sweet,
  and he is altogether desirable.
This is my beloved and this is my friend,
  O daughters of Jerusalem. (Song of Sol. 5:10-16)

Similarly, the man responds to his beloved:

How graceful are your feet in sandals,
  O queenly maiden!
Your rounded thighs are like jewels,
  the work of a master hand.
Your navel is a rounded bowl
  that never lacks mixed wine.
Your belly is a heap of wheat,
  encircled with lilies.
Your breasts are like two fawns,
  twins of a gazelle.
Your neck is like an ivory tower.
Your eyes are pools in Heshbon,
  by the gate of Bath-rabbim.
Your nose is like a tower of Lebanon,
  overlooking Damascus.
Your head crowns you like Carmel,
  and your flowing locks are like purple;
  a king is held captive in the tresses.

How fair and pleasant you are,
  O loved one, delectable maiden!
You are stately as a palm tree,
  and your breasts are like its clusters.
I say I will climb the palm tree
  and lay hold of its branches.

O may your breasts be like clusters of the vine,
    and the scent of your breath like apples,
and your kisses like the best wine
    that goes down smoothly,
gliding over lips and teeth. (Song of Sol. 7:1-9)

Nicholas Wolterstorff argues that humans are to continue God's work of bringing forth order (cosmos) that is "very good." For what purpose? For the sake of sheer joy and delight.

> For if the physical creation available to our sensory apparatus is good, and if joy is not only permitted man but is in fact his fulfillment, then there is no further charge to be brought against joy grounded in the sensory and the physical. So it can be said emphatically: This world of colors and textures and shapes and sounds is good for us, food for us in many ways, good also in that it provides us with refreshing delight. It is the Platonist and not the Christian who is committed to avoiding the delights of the senses, to taking no joy in colors, to avoiding the pleasures to be found in sounds. Delight in the colors and textures of eucalyptus seed pods, as well as in the sculptures of Henry Moore; delight in the sounds of the sea, as well as in the music of Debussy's *La Mer*; delight in the rhythms of John Donne's poetry, as well as in the movement of flowing streams—all contribute to human fulfillment.[7]

When we experience aesthetic delight, we can interpret that experience theologically or simply understand it as a rich aesthetic experience. Aesthetic experiences do not of themselves produce a religious interpretation of reality. I take delight in the patterns of light that are filtered through the windows in my home. These patterns of light and shadow are aesthetically pleasing, though the patterns do not necessarily communicate religious meaning or significance.

I would not call this "work of art" religious, though I may give my aesthetic experience a theological interpretation. As one who lives with a sense of religious wonder in the fundamental beauty and goodness of existence, I interpret the light and shadow form as a gift of God. Someone else who sees the same form may interpret the perceptual experience in strictly aesthetic terms. We treat scientific knowledge in a similar way. I may interpret the biological understanding of ecosystems theologically, whereas a biologist may not consciously attempt to do so. If she is a religious person, she may then give her understanding of biology a theological interpretation.

SOME ISSUES IN AESTHETIC THEORY

I digress for a moment to define terms and clarify some theoretical issues that have concerned those who reflect on the arts. We can distinguish between an *aesthetic experience*, which we described above as the sensuous experience of an object or art form, and *aesthetic form.*

Aesthetic form refers to the shape or structure of an object, poem, or composition—the way it is put together. Aesthetic form concerns the way in which words are chosen and ordered within a poem, how a composer creates the desired affect by rhythmic patterns of sound and silence, and the arrangement of notes to produce melodic line or harsh dissonance. Aesthetic form concerns the use of color, light and dark, texture and line, balance and organization in a painting or sculpture, or the way light is filtered through the windows in my home and the shadows it casts on the ceilings and walls.

Aesthetic quality refers to how well a particular form (a poem, a sculpture, or a musical composition) is put together. The aesthetic quality of a form should not be confused with whether it expresses truth, whether it produces morally good effects, or whether it is useful or functional. A house functions to keep us warm, but its aesthetic qualities have to do with how it looks, or how its space is arranged, judged by standards of aesthetic excellence.

Aesthetic form is, then, a kind of symbol system or system of communication. We use symbols to communicate in many different ways. Scientific language is descriptive and often uses the mathematical language of probability. Sometimes language describes past or current events and states of affairs. Philosophical and theological discourses use highly abstract language to reflect on the meaning and relationship of concepts to each other. Mathematics is the most abstract form of language, used to represent symbolically formal or logical relationships. Visual and audible aesthetics have their own languages too.

The language of music, for example, communicates with the overall structure and dynamic of a work created by the composer. A composer creates the desired aesthetic experience by using the musical language of rhythmic patterns, the arrangement of notes to create a certain mood, or a variety of instruments in an orchestra to produce different qualities or textures of sound. The language of the music consists of the specific elements the artist employs and the dynamic interaction among these elements.[8]

Theologians, pastors, and church leaders should be educated to interpret the nonverbal symbols of communication of music and the visual arts, even as now they learn to interpret the verbal language of

Scripture and the creeds and the language of psychology for pastoral counseling.[9] All of us can benefit by learning to interpret the variety of ways in which artists use aesthetic form. All of us can be broadened and opened to new dimensions of insight and aesthetic awareness by encountering unfamiliar forms. Too many of us respond to visual form in terms of whether it is an "accurate" duplication of the world as we see it naturally. Or we will listen only to music that has a clear melody, or a chord structure that fits our conventional sense of harmony. We are unwilling to take the risk or spend the energy to learn unfamiliar languages used by artists in every culture and time period, and especially by many contemporary artists.

By its very nature, the gift of artistry challenges our conventions, for it is the essence of the creative process to call into question what is and to imagine what could be. In her book, *Image as Insight*, Margaret Miles argues that learning the language of visual communication is as important as learning verbal language.[10] It is particularly critical in our society, where visual images play a powerful role in communicating who and what we are. Advertising and photographic image play powerful roles in our society. If we do not understand the way this language is being used, we are more likely to be manipulated.[11]

Susanne Langer objects to referring to artistic form as language.[12] However, the question of whether the arts are a form of language is largely an issue of semantics. Langer defines language as "discourse" and restricts the term to discursive reason. For her, language communicates ideas. She then defines the arts—too narrowly, I think—as those symbolic forms that express the life of feeling. Music is for Langer the primary art form that shapes her ideas about the arts in general. For Langer music is the

> tonal analogue of the emotive life. Music does not copy feeling, but gives a symbolic representation of it. The tonal structures we call "music" bear a close logical similarity to the forms of human feeling—forms of growth and of attenuation, flowing and stowing, conflict and resolution, speed, arrest, terrific excitement, calm, or subtle activation and dreamy lapses—not joy and sorrow perhaps, but the poignancy of either and both—the greatness and brevity and eternal passing of everything vitally felt. Such is the pattern, or logical form, of sentience; and the pattern of music is that same form worked out in pure, measured sound and silence.[13]

Langer's definition is not broad enough to encompass the arts in general. The arts do not simply represent the life of feeling symbolically; they portray more broadly the inner life of the spirit. Through a variety of artistic forms we communicate our basic underlying moods and motivations in life. We reflect on and communicate the underlying ambiguities and tensions of human existence. The arts express our fundamental values, commitments, and identities as human beings. Sometimes the arts express patterns and relationships among colors or forms. The "life of feeling" is too narrow an understanding of the arts. The arts express how we feel, but they also link our feelings to how we perceive reality, the world in which we live. Aesthetic forms of expression—poetry, story, drama, painting, sculpture, dance, and music—express, nurture, and enrich the human spirit. The arts feed the soul of human beings and are as important to our wholeness as bread and water.

Sometimes the arts link our feelings and moods with our moral sensibilities. Francisco Goya's *Disasters of War* vividly illuminates the horrors of war and communicates outrage at the suffering caused by war. Goya's work expresses feeling, yes, but also a view of the world. Such works symbolically "reveal," "open up," or illuminate dimensions of reality we may have ignored or not been sensitive to until we experience the work of art. The work communicates something about life. In this sense, art is a type of language, a language used primarily to communicate how we interpret the meaning and significance of our lives.

When artistic communication expresses our deepest values and commitments, the arts function in a way similar to religious language. In fact, the expression of religious truth and meaning is almost always integrally connected with artistic form. We employ artistic language in the expression of religious meaning by using metaphor and poetry, story and drama, dance, music, and visual and architectural form.

Some aesthetic theorists would object to my description of the arts as a language through which we express the meaning and significance of our lives. According to some theories, art does not express meaning, rather it simply *is*, and should be judged by purely formal criteria. From poetry to painting, the preoccupation of critics is with *how* a work is expressed, not *what* it expresses.[14] A nonreductionist attempt to identify the aesthetic dimension of an object or experience can lead to a pure aestheticism, the autonomy of the aesthetic or "art for art's sake." Frank Burch Brown traces from Kant the modern tendency to view the beautiful as inherently isolated from moral, theoretical, and practical functions.[15] It is certainly valid and essential to approach artistic works by asking *how* a work communicates, but we need not reduce our response to art by limiting ourselves to that question. Some postmodern theories have challenged "pure aestheticism." Today aesthetic theories are fluid and marked by a variety of points of view.

In modern theory, the arts have become increasingly separated from our daily living. Many theories about the function of the arts reflect this separation. Frank Burch Brown shows how modern theories of aesthetics correlate with the development of the "institution of high art." Nicholas Wolterstorff uses this phrase to designate the development of institutions of art like museums and concert halls, separated from the rest of life, where persons go to contemplate and enjoy the arts. The modern age could be characterized by the development of aesthetic theories in which the function of art is to provide aesthetic satisfaction for its own sake. So all types of artistic expression—music, poetry, painting, and sculpture—are judged by standards of aesthetic excellence that are severed from functions the arts may have performed. Brown identifies three assumptions that underlie this modern aesthetic theory:

> First, that the value of art qua art derives from nothing other than its capacity to maximize purely aesthetic qualities and pleasures; second, that all aesthetic qualities are ones apprehended in the act of "free" contemplation and thus never appeal to genuinely conceptual thinking or practical impulse, or therefore to any aspect of morality or religion that is not already essentially aesthetic and thus sheerly "felt"; and third, that as a consequence the exercise of taste is unalloyed and exclusive, entirely concerned with form or with a unique sort of feeling expressed by the "object itself," which one values "for its own sake."[16]

Postmodern perspectives have challenged these assumptions. The arts are objects of perceptual contemplation that give us aesthetic satisfaction. They are made available to us in museums and concert halls and certainly enrich our lives. But like both Wolterstorff and Brown I view the role of the arts in our lives in a much broader sense. They reflect the creative spirit as we yearn to embody wholeness in our daily lives. They sensitize us to moral concerns, jar us from our insensitivities, open us up to levels of insight we have overlooked or repressed, and communicate the ambiguities and tensions of human life, such as anguish and hope. One of the impulses of postmodern theories is to reconnect artistic expression more holistically with our experience of life in all its dimensions, including our need to deconstruct, destroy, and pull apart our certainties and conventions.

Theological reflection on the arts cannot be limited to the "institution of high art." Aesthetic expression is also an integral dimension of popular culture—from pop music and the visual communication of advertising and cartoons to the way we build homes and plan cities. The arts also function in religious worship to express the deepest yearnings of the human spirit. As a Christian ethicist, I am searching for ways to connect aesthetic experience with our relationships to God, to our neighbor, and to the larger cosmos. Artistic creativity contributes to our lives by making possible a richer aesthetic experience that can touch the deepest levels of our spirituality and moral concern.

Therefore, we should be able to look at a visual form or listen to music with a view to the multiple levels of value an object or work may have. These meanings are shaped by the context in which they are seen and heard. Different angles of vision offer different layers of meaning or value in an aesthetic form. This relationship is like the intersection of two circles. Depending upon what a person brings to a musical or visual experience, the circles might overlap in different ways.

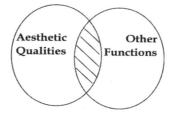

Worship itself is not necessarily one-dimensional. Eastern Orthodox liturgy's focus on worship is not extraneous to appreciation and evaluation of its obvious aesthetic dimensions. The same is true of Chartres Cathedral, an aesthetically lovely place of worship. Depending on context, Handel's Messiah might serve primarily an aesthetic function or be central in the church's liturgical calendar. A secular musical work, not originally associated with worship, can if carefully chosen contribute a mood suitable to worship. Or Shaker furniture, which has a pragmatic function, can also provide aesthetic delight. I grow a vegetable garden partly because we enjoy eating fresh, home-grown vegetables but derive pleasure mostly from planning the space and from simply enjoying the garden's intrinsic beauty. The point is that the significance of an object is integrally linked to context. It is a mistake to isolate the "aesthetic" from other functions. Aesthetic properties relate to how things function holistically, the "felt" sense of an object that may give us delight while serving a pragmatic or religious purpose.

THE RESPONSIBILITY FOR AESTHETIC EXCELLENCE

Christians are called by God to know the truth, to witness to it, and to live well with Jesus as their norm. But they are also called to create beauty or aesthetic excellence. As actors in the world, Christians participate with their fellow human beings in many tasks. We design, build, live, and work in homes. We worship in churches. We design, build, and use furniture, eating utensils, and tools to accomplish tasks from gardening and farming to fixing our bicycles and cars. We design, build, and use various types of technology from transportation to communication. We design and construct the space in and around our homes, our farms, our institutions, our communities, and our cities.

We often ask what it means to be ethically responsible in the performance of these tasks. But seldom do we ask whether we have any aesthetic responsibility. Does it make any difference what appearance we give to our cities, our institutions, our communities, our cars, or our furniture? Should we judge the things we design and use simply by how well they perform their function to meet our material needs or satisfy our pleasures?

The visible, outward form of culture should express the spirit within, the underlying values that orient our lives. Insofar as the visible, outward form expresses the Spirit of God within, our lives should honor God not only in living the truth and by living ethically responsible lives, but also by creating beauty, or aesthetically excellent form.

The expression of our lives in aesthetic form is inevitable even when we are not self-conscious about it.

> Just as all behaviors have an ethical dimension, so all dimensions of expressive and material culture possess an aesthetic sense. There are no aesthetically neutral customs. Even those behaviors which are overtly technical have a dimension of symbolic expressiveness which reveals the ethics as well as the aesthetics of a community.[17]

The issue, then, is not *whether* we will express ourselves aesthetically in material culture, but *how*. Not every aesthetic expression expresses or nurtures the human spirit. Not every aesthetic expression is excellent. As with other areas of culture, a Christian theology of culture should help us develop skill at discriminating excellence from shoddiness, superficiality, and pretentiousness.

But is it possible to develop community standards of aesthetic excellence? Can aesthetic excellence be anything more than a matter of private opinion or personal taste? Does the Christian faith have anything distinctive to offer in this area? Given the difficulties of developing clear standards and practices in ethics, is it not even more presumptuous to attempt to develop standards of aesthetics that can guide us in our judgments and behavior as Christians?

What I propose here is to open a dialogue on these questions. The suggestions I make are tentative and are intended to invite further discussion. Indeed I have more questions than answers about how to develop norms of aesthetic judgment. I can only briefly introduce this topic here as one component in a larger theology of culture. We need our artists to help us become more self-conscious and responsible in this area of our lives.

So why begin a dialogue, why open these questions? I raise these issues because I believe it is critical that the church not simply abandon aesthetic issues to the dominant forces of the larger culture. We cannot simply accept what the dominant cultural elites define as high culture or excellence. We cannot uncritically assimilate to the cultural standards of delight and pleasure as defined by advertising, the mass media, or Hollywood. Nor can we simply give in to a pragmatic functionalism that fails to include aesthetic form as a significant consideration in how we shape the communities and cities in which we live. We must find a way to be discerning, to resist destructive forces in the dominant culture, and to learn from, support, and help create those aesthetic forms that contribute to the well-being of the city where we dwell.

I quite agree with Frank Burch Brown, who connects "bad taste" with sin.

> Aesthetic sensitivity and judgment [are] so integral to the moral and religious life that people whose aesthetic sense is dull or perverse are in an unenviable position. The possibility that bad taste may be a moral liability is suggested in fact by the quite traditional notion that sin—which is not only wrong but also profoundly ugly—looks alluring to the unwary, whereas virtue—which is not only right but also profoundly beautiful—frequently appears drab at first sight. It follows that failure to distinguish genuine beauty from counterfeit can lead to moral error. Moral and aesthetic discernment often go hand in hand.[18]

A high aesthetic standard by itself certainly does not guarantee moral sensitivity. The Nazis are a prime example of an idolatrous aestheticism divorced from the moral life. The Nazis loved classical music and even brought Jews together to play for them, while treating the Jews as vermin.

We have emphasized that the Christian faith affirms our embodiment, that we are earthy creatures who touch, taste, smell, see, hear, and express ourselves in bodily movement. But how do we distinguish between the joy and delight of the Sabbath and the delight and pleasure offered by the dominant North American culture, which also is ready to embrace a superficial sensuality? Goods and services are marketed to us for the way they can give us pleasure and meet our material needs. We lack a standard for making critical distinctions between materialism and an aesthetically responsible expression of our lives in material culture that gives honor to God.

Materialism is an idolatrous commitment to things as a means to ego-centered satisfaction. Materialism is the self-centered attachment to things that results in neglecting to share our resources with others. Materialism leads to one-dimensional lives oriented to the profane at the expense of spirituality. To express human spirituality and beauty within material culture is not to view things as objects of our devotion, but as vehicles for the expression of the image of God. We seek to create not one-dimensional, profane objects valued only for their function or their ability to fulfill selfish interests. Our calling is to create a material culture that reflects our attunement and coherence with God's intention for the cosmos. We are called to create a material culture in response to the beauty of the cosmos God has created, one that grows out of attentive seeing and listening, based on profound respect for what is.

Some Christians bring to these issues a dualism of body and soul that denigrates the sensual and that assumes human salvation is an escape from our earthy, embodied existence. In the absence of an aesthetic vision that embraces earthy sensuality as an integral element of the Christian faith, these Christians lack a standard of critical judgment by which to assess aesthetic issues. They tend to reduce "material" existence to a pragmatic functionalism. What matters to them is whether something is useful for its intended function. A chair is simply to provide a place to sit, or a house a place of shelter. While aesthetics may be important to them, the aesthetic qualities of a chair or house are simply a matter of private taste, not a component of Christian theological reflection. Inevitably, the dominant cultural forces around them—the advertising media, television, the movies, entertainment, and sports celebrities—form these tastes.

Therefore, since aesthetic form concerns the very substance of our everyday lives, we must discern how to honor God with the form we create. Our task is to find a way to integrate form and function coherently, so that the aesthetic excellence of something is integrated with its function. We live in the midst of aesthetic squalor, and Christians often participate unconsciously in producing that squalor. Is it possible to recover a sense of what it means to be faithful to God in this sphere of our lives, so that the church can contribute to a shalom that includes the kind of delight envisioned in the eschatological vision of Isaiah?

In developing aesthetic norms, our judgments will inevitably be contextual. They will vary according to time, cultural setting, and experience. Standards of excellence change over time. When we participate in this dialogue, we should not presume to make definitive, universal judgments. However, it is important that we be clear about what we mean by standards of aesthetic excellence. People's tastes in art obviously differ. Some prefer baroque music, others the music of the Romantic period. Some like modern art, others the art of the Renaissance. Some prefer Amsterdam over London. We differ about whether we prefer Victorian or Colonial architecture. But standards of excellence get behind these particular preferences to ask what makes any or all of them "excellent." Can we identify formal qualities of excellence that endure despite changes in style from period to period? What makes a city or our dwellings "good" or aesthetically excellent despite differences in style?

Should we equate beauty with aesthetic excellence? Much depends on what we mean by beauty. It is important to distinguish between two different meanings of aesthetic excellence. When we speak of aesthetic excellence theologically, we mean the ideal forms God calls humans to create, to express what humans and the universe were intended to be. Aesthetic excellence means the ideal form God intended for creation, or the new eschatological age for which we hope. The images of form in Genesis 1 and visions of the New Jerusalem in the book of Revelation both suggest such an ideal of aesthetic excellence. Such an ideal suggests a norm or standard for our human activity as we construct a world of forms in the light of the image of God in us. The word *beauty* is appropriate for aesthetic excellence in this sense. Thomas Aquinas defines beauty in the *Summa Theologica*: "Beauty includes three conditions: integrity or perfection, since those things which are impaired are by the very fact ugly; due proportion or harmony; and lastly brightness, or clarity, when things are called beautiful which have bright color."[19]

Contemporary artists sometimes create works that suggest such an ideal. Wilson Yates refers to sculptor Barbara Hepworth, who says of her work:

I think that the very nature of art is affirmation, and in being so reflects the laws and the evolution of the universe both in the power and rhythms of growth and structure as well as the infinitude of ideas which reveal themselves when one is in accord with the cosmos and the personality is free to develop.[20]

What is beauty? The experience of beauty includes both a sensory feeling as well as the intellectual sense of the "rightness" of the relationship of any object to its surroundings.[21] Robert Regier defines beauty as

"dynamic wholeness." It is not merely a subjective response to a fragment, but rather a response to an organic or man-made system in which many fragments are interrelated (interdependent) in a dynamic way. This interrelatedness is dynamic when both unity and variety (diversity) are present in the form of a delicate tension. If the tension breaks either boredom (sameness) or chaos is the result. An aesthetic response occurs when one intuitively or consciously experiences dynamic wholeness.[22]

As we become increasingly conscious of the environmental threat to our planet and disturbed by the aesthetic squalor of a materialistic culture, one of the functions of the artist is to help us develop a more adequate notion of "dynamic wholeness" so that we might give form to our life on the earth that more nearly fulfills God's intention for humans and the cosmos.

Aesthetic form may also express brokenness, alienation, disharmony, feelings of loneliness, anger, or anguish. If by *beauty* we mean "pretty" or "nicely decorated," then the word is misleading and can contribute to a false standard of excellence. For too many of us, beauty has been reduced to prettiness or ornamentation. For example, we build the basic structure of our homes with little thought to aesthetic form until we are about finished and then decide it is now time to "decorate" what we have done.

The consequence is that much of what counts as beauty is simply gaudy, excessive, and pretentious. An aesthetic form can be anything but "pretty," jarring us into recognizing a truth that we have ignored or suppressed. My colleague, Merrill Kraybill, a sculptor, uses rusty pieces of metal, broken chunks of cement, rusty wire, and blackened clay to construct sculptures to represent the passion of Christ. Kraybill does not resist the word *beauty* if understood in the right way. One of the themes in his work is to explore rather than avoid the pain and deep sadness that lie at the core of life. In speaking of his work he says:

None of these images are ugly or represent an evil to be avoided. They are all beautiful in their way, if you are willing to use the word as describing an ideal rather than as being without flaw. ... Somehow all the work is connected to a search for how to live well in a broken world. The pieces are bound with wire and chain, but that binding also holds them together. They are broken and the barbed wire, the bent and twisted metal, the broken clay, the broken glass and the red stains are all painful images, but the pieces are put back together and they are healing.[23]

These works invite deeper reflection because they present us with the stark reality of the cross. The word *beauty*, with its usual connotation seems inappropriate to describe his work, yet we can call a work such as his aesthetically excellent.

We should not, therefore, necessarily equate beauty and aesthetic excellence. We can appreciate an aesthetically excellent work because of the way it portrays brokenness and pain. Speaking theologically, the artist, like the prophet or preacher, describes both the fallenness of the human condition and the need of human beings and the earth to be healed.

What standards can we use, then, to judge aesthetic excellence? Wolterstorff suggests three broad categories: unity and coherence; richness and intensity; and the "fittingness" of a work. By *fittingness* he means whether the aesthetic qualities of an art form are appropriate for the function the work is to perform. Wolterstorff illustrates this concept in a reference to a quote from Gustave Flaubert about his novel, *Madam Bovary*. "The story, the plot of a novel is of no interest to me. When I write a novel I aim at rendering a color, a shade. ... In *Madam Bovary*, all I wanted to do was to render a grey color, the mold color of a wood-louse's existence."[24]

One aspect of aesthetic excellence, then, has to do with whether the form of a work fittingly renders what is expressed in the work. Though truth and aesthetic excellence or form should not be equated, we also cannot separate them. We can then say that a work is aesthetically excellent insofar as a work's aesthetic qualities are fitting in relation to what the work is trying to do or communicate. Grünewald's or Merrill Kraybill's portrayal of the cross, for example, can be said to be excellent insofar as the aesthetic forms express appropriately the truth of suffering and brokenness, which the cross symbolizes. Insofar as a work communicates something about the human condition, its excellence consists in the appropriateness of the aesthetic form to the truth it reveals.

What about church buildings, hymns, liturgical forms, sermons, or organ music? In what sense are the forms used suitable or fitting for the purpose of Christian worship? When we go to a concert hall to hear Beethoven, we expect the performance to satisfy our aesthetic interests. When we hear the organ or sing a hymn in the context of worship, it should "fit" with the purposes of the liturgy. We are not at a performance. At the same time, the aesthetic qualities of the organ music or the hymn should be excellent. The hymn text and tune should utilize appropriate aesthetical form to express the mood or idea of the liturgy. Brian Wren, theologian, poet, and hymn-writer says:

> At its best, the hymn is a complex minor art form, combining theology, poetry, and music. As such it merits attention from theologians and artists. ... When read aloud, as a poem, a hymn text is time art. Each such reading is similar, yet unrepeatable. When the poem is sung as a solo or choral item, it moves the listener as songs do. When sung by a congregation, it invites commitment. Though some congregations behave as if they didn't have bodies, singing together is an intensely corporeal, as well as corporate activity. Diaphragm, lungs, larynx, tongue, lips, jawbone, nasal cavities, ribcage, shoulders, eyes, and ears come into play. When body attitude combines with deepest beliefs, singers are taken out of themselves into a heightened awareness of God, beauty, faith, and each other. ... Hymns deserve to be seen as visual art: like other poems, their appearance on the page enhances their attractiveness, or detracts from it.[25]

In addition to this general criterion of aesthetic excellence, which asks whether a form is suitable to its message or function, internal standards of excellence also apply. Though our tastes may differ, and though we may disagree about whether a particular aesthetic language chosen by an artist or a community fits our standards, Wolterstorff argues that two broad standards usually emerge in accounts of aesthetic excellence. On the one hand, we expect coherence. Do the parts fit into the whole? How are the parts arranged in relationship to each other?[26] Coherence can include dissonance and contrast. A beautiful church built by Russian Mennonites soon after they came to Kansas in the late nineteenth century illustrates the principle of coherence. When the congregation added an educational wing much later, they tacked on what looks like a "box" to the rest of the building. Although the addition may serve its pragmatic function well, there is no coherence between the addition and the original church building. Though contrast and dissonance can be elements of coherence, the addition simply clashes with the original church building and fails to enhance the aesthetic impact of the whole.

Unity alone can also be bland. Wolterstorff says that aesthetic forms should be internally rich, varied, and complex. Coherence and richness come in degrees. Often the excellence of a form has much to do with how richness and coherence are balanced or proportioned to each other. One can achieve unity at the expense of richness and vice versa.[27]

Pete Seeger's well-known folk song (lyrics by Malvina Reynolds) about middle class American suburban culture illustrates in a vivid way bland unity and conformity at the expense of richness and diversity.

> Little boxes on the hillside, little boxes made of ticky tacky, little boxes all the same.
> There's a green one and a pink one and a blue one and a yellow one,
> And they're all made out of ticky tacky and they all look just the same.[28]

By contrast, a prairie ecosystem reveals a dynamic balance between ecological wholeness and coherence, and richness and diversity.

Learning aesthetic norms from the natural world suggests another important principle we must be sensitive to in our relationship with our material culture: Everything in nature is recycled. What is both suitable aesthetically and responsibly built, given the threat to the well-being of our earth? The production of "junk" that ends up in the dump within a few years is irresponsible. Such junk includes homes, cars, furniture, clothes, dishes, and appliances that do not have enduring quality, both in a functional and aesthetic sense. We need to ask ourselves not only what stories and traditions we want to pass on to future generations, but also what kind of material culture we are leaving them that has enduring quality. How can the material culture we pass on continue to enrich the human spirit generations after those of us who created it are gone?

In addition to Wolterstorff's standards, I would like to add the term *integrity*, a term in Aquinas' definition of beauty. What would it mean to have integrity in how we express ourselves? We would not try to make material forms look like something else, such as synthetic products made to look like wood or stone. We would also choose forms that are appropriate to the environment where we live. Is there any rationale for imitation English Tudor in the middle of Kansas? In the late '40s and '50s some Mennonite churches in central Kansas copied neo-

Gothic architecture. These forms may have had integrity at the time and expressed the values of those Mennonites who chose these forms. On the other hand, these examples also illustrate a lack of attention to the distinctive values of the Anabaptist tradition. The long narrow nave in these churches with elevated pulpit and straight rows may be appropriate for an emphasis on the proclamation of the Word, but the form is not suitable to Anabaptist emphases on community and corporate discernment.

I question the integrity of contemporary postmodern architecture, where malls, shopping centers, retirement complexes, and schools are blessed with pointed nonfunctional medieval arches, turrets, and towers. How can the appropriation of medieval forms within a consumerist society be an appropriate use of geography and history?[29]

I like the sensitivity to integrity reflected in Sylvia Judson's report of a Quaker aesthetic. Originally an outsider to the Quaker tradition, she reports that she was attracted to Quaker simplicity, honesty, and personal mysticism, but bothered by their unconcern for art. On the surface, Quakerism seems largely devoid of aesthetic expression when compared with the emphasis upon aesthetic form in the Roman Catholic tradition. But Judson discovered this gem from the Book of Discipline of the Philadelphia Yearly Meeting of 1927:

> True simplicity consists not in the use of particular forms, but in foregoing over-indulgence, in maintaining humility of spirit, and in keeping the material surroundings of our lives directly serviceable to necessary ends, even though these surroundings may properly be characterized by grace, symmetry and beauty.[30]

Much of the quotation above expresses well the traditional understanding of Radical Reformation social responsibility. What strikes me is the last phrase—that truly simple material surroundings "may properly be characterized by grace, symmetry and beauty." Judson goes on to describe the integrity of some Quaker meetinghouses, with their good proportions, quiet calm, and restful lighting, and the purity of line in honestly fashioned furniture. Meetinghouses are forms of abstract art, where relationship of line, color, and especially of space express the spirit within. The Quakers experience the power of God as Inner Light or Truth, and express that Spirit outwardly, not only in a life of social responsibility, but in the construction of their meetinghouses.

These standards of excellence have important implications for how we view and design our cities. Although this topic is large and complex,

I want to make a few connections for the reader. My wife and I spent a semester in Toronto while I was working on this book. One of our favorite places was Nathan Philips Square, a wonderful open space linked to the new city hall, placed among the skyscrapers of the downtown. The focus of the square is a public ice skating rink that serves as a "welcoming" place of meeting for the diversity of peoples that make up the city of Toronto. Cities are places where strangers meet. In the design of our cities, it is critical that we prepare spaces where strangers can meet in safety and enjoy each other's company. The Boston Commons was another of our favorite spaces, to which we were often drawn in the four years we spent in the Boston area.

While we were there, Toronto celebrated the life and work of Jane Jacobs, author of the well-known book, *The Death and Life of American Cities*. Jacobs makes us aware of how important the organization of space in a city is for safety and the flourishing of life. She is critical of city planners who have mistakenly created spaces that are aesthetically uninteresting and unsafe.

The first several chapters of the book discuss sidewalks—sidewalks that are safe and draw people to them because they are places of joy and delight. She argues that the key to safe sidewalks is many "eyes on the sidewalk," day and night. The most dangerous places in large cities, especially after dark, are public playgrounds and parks near large housing complexes. She argues that the way we design our cities impacts whether we will have "eyes on the sidewalk." If we zone a city so as to separate living spaces from all the functions people need, we make people dependent upon the automobile or public transportation. We also create empty spaces that can become dangerous and unwelcome for many times of the day and night.

People need a reason to be on the sidewalk: local restaurants, sidewalk cafes where one can enjoy the art of people watching, drug stores, laundromats, tailors, cabinet makers, electricians, churches with their array of services from day cares to food banks, small corner grocery stores, and magazine and newspaper stands. All of these should be integrated with or in close proximity to living spaces—small apartments above stores, or houses nearby, with children playing on the sidewalk. Toronto has many such safe neighborhoods, which makes it an attractive city and which draws people into these spaces. Rather than fleeing the city, many Torontonians who grow up in the city want to go back to live.

Soon after Jacobs arrived in Toronto, she led in the resistance to stop construction of the Spadina Expressway, a super expressway that would have cut the center of Toronto in half. Many U.S. cities have been ruined by such projects. Cities cut in half develop strips of blight right through their center. The expressways contribute to the flight to suburbs, as commuters leave central cities on the weekends and evenings only to return to the cathedrals of capitalism during the week, such as banks and insurance companies.

Wolterstorff outlines some of the aesthetic principles that he believes should govern how we put together our cities. He argues that the principles of aesthetic excellence in urban space are not different than other aesthetic forms. We should seek to balance unity and coherence with richness, complexity, variety, and contrast.

> Most Midwestern American cities are aesthetically bad. What is almost invariably missing is any strong unity in the individual spaces and any significant variety among the spaces. Buildings are separated from each other to such a degree that the definition of space is minimal; and everywhere one gets the same feeling of openness and slackness. The streets are just as open as the plazas, the only significant difference being that they have a stronger axial orientation. And lacking any significant degree of completeness, the spaces of these cities are singularly lacking in any intensity of character. They are bland, the epitome of blandness. Moving through them is anti-dramatic. It is as if there were a hatred of the city at work, a deep wish to be done with it as soon as possible. ... The ideal of almost all urban Americans is to acquire enough money to live out in the country; failing that, to live in the suburbs; failing that, at least to escape from the city on weekends and holidays. ... The Midwestern American has an abhorrence for what is absolutely indispensable to a city—shaped space.[31]

The standards of aesthetic excellence we have identified above are not unique to the church or to a Christian view of life. Norms or standards in aesthetics are similar to the judgments we make about truth in scientific research. We cannot say that there is such a thing as a "Christian" science or "Christian" aesthetics. What we can say, though, is that through the creation of aesthetic excellence, Christians honor God. Insofar as we create form in the world that is untrue, deceptive, unauthentic, aesthetically mediocre, not fitted to the cosmos in which we live, or inauthentic to our humanity as God intended it, we dishonor God by creating aesthetic squalor. But aesthetic excellence is an integral component of seeking the peace of the city where we dwell.

As we fulfill our responsibility to God as persons filled with God's Spirit of life, we also nurture our spirits and the spirits of those around us in the creation of beauty and aesthetic excellence. Our responsibility to God will not be fulfilled if we only seek the truth and act ethically. We also honor God in the creation of aesthetic excellence. The material culture we will create serves not only our utilitarian needs, but it also enriches our spirit and overcomes the sensory squalor of our lives.

The Gift of the Artist in an Alternative Cultural Vision

We must open our lives to the gifts offered by the artist: poets, musicians, painters, and sculptors. We must listen to what they have to say as they exercise their gifts both inside and outside the church. We learn from the artistic work they produce and from what the artistic process itself teaches us about a holistic alternative cultural vision.

My friend, faculty colleague, and visual artist, Robert Regier, uses three words to characterize his work as an artist: *process, polarity*, and *risk*. He reminds us of the importance of remaining in tune with and open to process. "Act can precede thought. There is no correct formula for sequencing eye, mind, and hand. Thought and reflection can occur before, during, or after the gesture. The result can be a genuine surprise."[32]

The ambiguity in giving form to something is that form is not properly static, but seeks to express the dynamic of movement and novelty. The creativity of the artist lies in the ability to remain open to novelty that is always emerging even as the artist gives structure to things. Underlying all novelty is the element of mystery that no form can contain what is. We constantly live with the tension between fleeting order and the novelty that emerges out of every form. If we cannot endure that tension, we risk bringing premature closure to our work and repressing creative possibilities.

> In the making of a gesture, any closure is only a momentary pause in a continuous opening-closing rhythm—a rhythm that expresses the dynamic tension between polar opposites. But it is a rhythm, not mere repetition. Rhythm is repetition (which is predictable) visited by novelty (the unpredictable). The interplay between predictability and surprise may be the needed cadence that sustains us.[33]

Artists often use jarring and unconventional forms to give us a window, an insight into our culture that we would otherwise not know. An example of such a window was given to me in a 1990 exhibit of sixteen artists at the Stedelijk Museum in Amsterdam entitled, "Energieen."

The organizer of the exhibit, Wim Beeren, describes the exhibit:

> I have sought and found art which—I contend—affects our world
> of thought in its concept and form in such a way that we still feel
> able to exert an influence on our reality and to shape our time.
> These works of art function as energies on our life, in our intel-
> lectual, spiritual, and emotional discourse.[34]

Each artist's work was placed in a separate room. Most of the
exhibits employed a variety of media: human voice, music, side and
upside-down television images, electronic banners, flashing colors, and
patterns of slide and movie images projected simultaneously on a wall.
Other exhibits employed a dark room containing a variety of sculptured forms with a light in a tube slowly turning that cast shadows in
the room, sculptured forms of cloth, human figures made of fabric, and
a row of seven granite coffin structures for four adults, two children,
and a baby, with laments chiseled into their lids.

As I moved from room to room, I experienced becoming a participant in the work itself. In the exhibit of the Japanese artist, Issey
Miyake, the observer becomes a participant by taking off one's shoes
and entering the room by walking on a raised floor, then wandering
about among the forms. On the floor is finely pleated fabric with geo-
metrical cutouts of flat oval or rectangular form. These forms are con-
trasted with four human figures wearing the same shapes as clothing.
In the silence of the room, one experiences the interplay of the lifeless
form of fabric on the floor and the fabric as it is brought to life when
draped on the four figures.

In another exhibit, a dark room has a slowly revolving tube reflecting light. One's own shadow and those in the room become part of the
exhibit. This experience spoke to me powerfully that we create the reality we become part of, that we cannot be neutral spectators or observers. Anselm Kiefer's work had an ominous prophetic quality about
it. He portrayed

> a fighter plane of lead, pitifully defenseless, with a dead snake in
> the cockpit. Behind is a lead painting with captions left and right:
> Euphrates-Tigris. The land in between is treated with chemicals
> and oxidized: Zweistromland [Mesopotamia]. ... Zweistromland
> is the title of the huge two-piece bookcase which Kiefer made be-
> tween 1984 and 1989 and which was recently on show in Lon-
> don. It held two hundred books with lead pages, seventy specially
> treated. Copper wires and test tubes filled with water turn the
> whole thing into a battery-like producer of current.[35]

Kiefer's exhibit evoked in me a sense of the profound ambiguity of life in the twentieth century. It stirred in me an awareness of the vital and life-giving roots of civilization and at the same time a sense of our contemporary suicidal destructiveness. This profound feeling of ambiguity was heightened by my memory of this exhibit as I watched the Persian Gulf War unfold a few months later.

In her composition, *Missa Gaia: Mass for the Earth*, contemporary American composer Libby Larsen uses a musical language that can express circularity rather than traditional patterns of linear flow. Through this musical language she expresses the poetic images of Wendell Berry:

> Within the circles of our lives
> We dance the circles of the years,
> The circles of the seasons
> Within the cycles of the years,
> The cycles of the moon
> Within the circles of the seasons
> The circles of our reasons
> Within the cycles of the moon.[36]

Sculptor Paul Soldner has developed a visual language to express asymmetry and process. In his search for a visual language, he found the tendency to symmetry in Western art too confining, sterile, and static, so he turned to Japan and Zen Buddhism. His work allows for the unintentional to emerge by allowing material to speak for itself. His pottery does not conform to the conventional forms of pots and bowls that we are used to seeing. I find his work aesthetically pleasing and illuminating, akin to the aesthetic pleasure I derive from the cottonwood tree I described earlier. His work expresses vividly the organic forms so evident in the natural world, a blend and juxtaposition of symmetry and asymmetry, of structure and process.[37]

Little artistic expression is explicitly religious or intentionally "Christian." Many artists are purely secular or even anti-religious in sentiment. But the arts function in a variety of ways in our culture. One strand is the "institution of high art." Nicholas Wolterstorff argues that as we move toward the modern era, the "institution of high art" serves primarily an aesthetic purpose of "perceptual contemplation," divorced from any larger meaning or purpose.[38] From the eighteenth century onward, he argues, high art has become more and more dissociated from our daily lives. It is located primarily in museums or concert halls and experienced primarily in leisure time. Such artistic works express significant form, but give meaning to many people primarily in terms of satisfying standards of aesthetic excellence, however they define aesthetic excellence.

The Spirit of God can speak to us through works of art that may not be explicitly religious. Just as we may interpret theologically knowledge we gain from the natural sciences about the physical universe, so artistic works that are not intentionally religious may communicate a profound theological insight. For example, Paul Tillich saw Picasso's *Guernica* as one of the greatest religious paintings of all times because of what it reveals about the human condition.

We must be careful not to claim for artists or artistic works what they are not. Paul Tillich's broad and loose understanding of religion as the expression of ultimate concern leads him to interpret artistic works theologically where it is perhaps unwarranted. Though both religious and artistic language seek to communicate the meaning and significance of our lives, religious language does this by an explicit linkage of the meaning of our lives to a general view of reality, to some sense of how our lives are connected to that which we regard as ultimate or absolute.

In many cases artistic forms do communicate our underlying worldview, our sense of the ultimate or of what transcends our finite existence. But we may also appreciate a work of art simply for aesthetic reasons, for the way in which some pop art uses irony, or the way in which some artists organize space or use color, line, or texture. Examples are Mark Rothko's "Yellow and Red" or Kandinsky's "Farbestudie Quadrate mit Koncentrischen Ringen." We must be open to the variety of ways art functions and not adopt too restrictive a theory of what art is.[39]

Another strand of contemporary art is folk and grassroots art—art that is closely connected with the daily lives of people The contemplation of the art of museum and concert hall can have significance for the church, but that surely is not the only or even primary locus of the aesthetic dimension of life, nor the primary significance of the arts for a Christian theology of culture. A person could attend a festival in a Kansas community almost every weekend through the spring, summer, and fall months where a variety of folk arts are prominent. Thousands of persons come to Winfield, Kansas, each September to participate in the Walnut Valley Bluegrass Festival. And we are profoundly aware of the power of visual image, which impacts us through movies, television, and advertising.

How material culture expresses the creative Spirit of God can profoundly shape relationships in a family. Creatively designed material objects that are expressive of God's Spirit through the human spirit create connecting links between people and with the world around us. A table beautifully set and food prepared with love and care are integral to the building of relationships in a family.

Our home is surrounded by symbols that connect us to those most dear to us. Hanging on the walls in our home is a painting done by our niece and a mixed-media work by our daughter that weaves together clay and fibers. In my office is a pencil holder with the word *Daddy* and a flower drawn on it that I have used for many years. On my desk is a clay paperweight made years ago with the initials of our daughter on the back. A rocker connects us to my wife's sister, given to us the last Christmas before she died of cancer. On the counter in the kitchen is a round tile trivet with the imprint of the feet of our granddaughter.

Every birthday and Christmas in our family involves the giving of a gift that someone has made. For many years our grandmothers and mothers sewed children's clothes, knitted sweaters, and designed and made quilts that remain integral to our family's material culture. On one of our shelves is a hand-made dulcimer crafted by my brother. My wife's brother designed and made a beautiful small table from cherry wood that stands in our living room. In the garage is a sled my brother and I used as boys. Long ago my father fixed it up, repainted it, and gave it to us as a Christmas gift. I am now waiting to pass it on to a grandchild.

My ninety-year-old father-in-law is a wood craftsman who is constantly designing and making gifts to give to children, grandchildren, and great-grandchildren. Every room of our home and of the other homes in our extended family are filled with the gifts he has designed and made over the years: a small walnut wood clock that runs on a battery, wood puzzles and games, bookshelves and book holders, paper and pen holders, an end table whose base is designed to fit under a bed or chair so that it will extend over a person's lap, a walnut paper towel holder, a coat rack, a child's bench, a rocking horse, a carousel with carved wooden figures that spins, a rocker, trucks and cars with wooden figures sitting inside, carved birds of many shapes and colors, a carved sheep and lamb, and his specially designed lawn chairs, table, and purple martin house for our backyard.

Our nephew and granddaughter are fascinated with a smooth, beautifully carved walnut duck made by my wife's brother. Our granddaughter is especially attracted to the small knot in the wood that can represent the eye on the duck. Almost every time they go in and out of our home, our nephew and granddaughter stop to see the bird mobile in the entrance as well as the chimes by the front entrance. Through the sensuous delight of taste, sight, touch, and sound, we connect with each other as a family, with the world around us, and with the Spirit of God.

I conclude this chapter by identifying five ways in which the arts connect with a religious vision.

Aesthetic Experience and "Religious Affections"

The arts illuminate the religious dimension of human life by symbolically representing the underlying tones or moods of human existence, what some have called the "religious affections." Faith is commonly understood as a way of knowing or seeing the truth, or a way of willing the good. To speak of the religious affections in the tradition of Friedrich Schleiermacher and Jonathan Edwards is to think of religious faith in still another dimension: the relationship of our being to the totality of reality as we experience it. Religious affections are different from passion or human emotions. Emotions are responses to particular events in our lives, such as rage at injustice or sorrow and grief in the face of death. Richard R. Niebuhr says that *affection* refers to a much more encompassing phenomenon. He believes this is expressed by the German word *Stimmung*,

> which the English language can best render as attunement. The attunement of the self is the basic and all-including frame of mind that gives to the whole of personal existence its determinate quality, color, and tone. An affection, so conceived, is not a specific response to a stimulus or object, although a particular object may elicit in us a consciousness of the pervasive tone of our existence. Rather, it tempers the rapid succession of stimuli and response in personal existence and superimposes on them a degree and quality of order.[40]

It is significant that Niebuhr uses aesthetic language to describe the religious affections: tonality, resonance, attunement, color. Many have recognized the close connection between religious and aesthetic experience.

The language of religious affections refers to basic moods or dispositions of life: trust as opposed to despair, or joy and gratitude as opposed to bitterness and cynicism. The arts are vehicles for expressing the religious affections. They open our spirits to a sense of wonder, to the sheer mystery of being itself, before which we stand in amazement. Or they put us in touch with our imperfection and brokenness, the fragility of life, our underlying sense that our lives are utterly dependent upon God or that we live in the context of powers beyond our control.

The Psalms poetically reflect these underlying tonalities in our lives: joy, gratitude, anguish, and our sense of brokenness. Claus Westermann, a biblical scholar, discovered the Psalms while in a prison camp during World II. He says that

> the two main groups, psalms of praise and psalms of lament, correspond to the rhythm of joy and grief which characterizes all human life, grounded as it is in human creatureliness and its limitation. Joy and grief, however, are here not human emotions which are then brought into relationship with God; rather, praising God means joy finding words, lament to God is grief's self-expression.[41]

The rhythm Westermann refers to is developed by the Hebrew poets in a distinctive poetic form consisting of the balance of sentences, technically named *parallelismus membrorum*.[42] Westermann says, "What we have is a rhythm of sentences, not a rhyming of words or syllables, not determined by sound but by sense."[43]

Westermann argues that the purpose of this poetic structure is not aesthetic; its function is to serve worship. But we need not create a dichotomy between worship and aesthetics. His distinction is correct only if we understand aesthetics in the modern sense as the beauty of form for its own sake. The excellence of the Psalm structure lies in its suitability or fittingness for its function. Form and content are integrated for purposes of worship, but at a deeper level, form is a response to the rhythm of life itself.

Our experience of nature often brings together the aesthetic and religious. The immensity and beauty of the sea, the vastness of a prairie landscape, the power and energy of a thunderstorm, or the order and perfection of a tiny cell or spider web—all can symbolically represent the nature of human being in the universe. Paul Tillich's description of the sea, the infinite bordering on the finite, is an appropriate theological metaphor for my experience.

> I can remember sitting all day at Scoodic Point on the coast of Maine, watching the waves batter the shore. The swells would build and build until a massive wave would hit the rocks and send white spray into the air. Then the sea would subside, a sense of calm would prevail, until again the swells would build. This goes on and on. The sea is a symbol of infinity. It is a symbol of God— the Alpha and Omega. The land is a symbol of the human condi-

tion—finite, battered, and beaten by the waves, vulnerable and subject to erosion.[44]

Religious affections, the underlying tonalities, moods, and motivations in our lives, are constantly in search of a language to give them expression. Foundational to this language is metaphor or symbol. And it is through the arts especially that religious people symbolically represent who they are.

Humans as "Earthlings"

Nicholas Wolterstorff grounds his theology of art in the notion of human beings as earthlings. Arguing against the "heaven-storming" or "Promethean" view of human beings made in the image of God and thus "godlike" in their creative capacity, Wolterstorff places human beings in God's world as finite creatures, made of the physical stuff of the universe. He critiques the tendency in the history of Christianity to denigrate the material or physical. "Every such form of devaluation flies in the face of God's affirmation of His creation. The sheer physicality or materiality of something is never a legitimate ground for assigning to it a lower value in our lives."[45]

Since Augustine, Western Christianity has developed a deep suspicion of the body. For Augustine, the primary form of sin was "concupiscence," particularly evident in grasping for meaning through the delight of the senses of sight, sound, smell, and taste. Augustine believed that the delights of the senses directed our love to earthly things rather than to God. Sexual passion was for him one of the most vivid signs of the fall, because in sexual passion, the body is not under the full control of reason. Augustine speculates that in the paradisiacal state before the fall, humans would have copulated without any passion whatsoever.

> Surely, every member of the body was equally submissive to the mind, and surely, a man and his wife could play their active and passive roles in the drama of conception without the lecherous promptings of lust, with perfect serenity of soul and with no sense of disintegration between body and soul.[46]

Discomfort with our materiality is reflected in the way in which Christian exegetes throughout the centuries have interpreted the Song of Solomon. It was frequently interpreted spiritually or allegorically to symbolize a relationship between God and Israel, or Christ and the church, but hardly ever the sexual relationship of an actual man and woman.

The Song of Solomon is a vivid reminder of the Hebraic affirmation of the beauty and goodness of the human body, of embodied human relationships, where sexuality is integral to our humanness. The creation story of Genesis 2 does not hold a dualism of body and soul. We do not *have* bodies in which there is a soul. Humans are enlivened or inspirited bodies. We *are* our bodies, enlivened and "spirited" by God. Thus in answer to the view that the Christian theology gives a much higher place to the soul or the spiritual, Wolterstorff refers to the views of St. Paul:

> When Paul insists on our avoiding the works of the flesh, he is not preaching that the physical is evil, nor even that it is inferior to the nonphysical. He is not following in the footsteps of the Socrates of Plato's *Phaedo*. Rather, he is urging us to avoid lives of total secularity and worldliness, to live lives open to the Spirit of God. He cites jealousy, scarcely a sin of sensuality, as one of the works of the flesh.[47]

But humans are not simply earthlings. As earthlings we are called to responsibility before God, to affirm the beauty of the human body and of sexual love, and to love each other genuinely. Human beings were placed in a garden to take care of it. In the care of this garden, human beings give order and form to the world. But they should care for the earth responsibly before God, not despising or assaulting the physical, or escaping from the physical to a higher level of spirituality. The vocation of the artist, as one responsible to God, is a symbol of what human beings are called to be. To give aesthetic form to sounds, colors, shapes, textures, light and shadow, bodily movement, and gesture, the artist must have a profound respect for the material stuff of the universe and engage in an intimate dialogue with it.

We fulfill our vocation as earthlings when we recognize limits. In the context of limit, we seek to know truth, live goodness, and create aesthetic excellence. This dynamic tension between our limits and our godlike creativity is held together in creative tension in Psalm 8:

> When I look at thy heavens, the work of thy fingers,
> the moon and the stars which thou has established;
> what is man that thou art mindful of him,
> and the son of man that thou dost care for him?
> Yet thou hast made him little less than God,
> and dost crown him with glory and honor. (Ps. 8:3-5, KJV)

Artistic creativity results from the mystery and dynamic of the interaction of finitude and the human capacity to create new form. We are bound by givens—the limits of words, the qualities and strength of stone and wood, the textures of cloth and paint. Although bound by the length of a line, a poet chooses and uses words to give meaning to an experience. A painter has available a canvas, some brushes and paints, but within the confines of the canvas creates an image not seen before. A sculptor accepts the limits of a piece of marble, knowing that each piece chipped away cannot be replaced. But within that limit the sculptor shapes a new form. Poet Derek Walcott in his dialogue with Bill Moyers puts it well:

> If you're planing a piece of board, you know that it has an edge and that you can only go as far as the edge where you are planing. In a sense, as you are writing a poem, you are aware of a coming margin. Metrically, it's going to terminate at some point. So between then and the end of the margin there is a very ecstatic panic. The joy of the construction of the poem lies in the ecstasy of keeping the discipline of the poem.[48]

Life is a poem. The work of the creative artist is symbolic of our lives. We are bounded by birth and death. Within those limits we experience the "ecstatic panic" of living. Our joy comes in accepting the discipline of living responsibly before God as we remain open in our search for truth, goodness, and beauty.

Transcendence

I referred earlier in this chapter to the way in which the "Energieen" exhibit in Amsterdam drew the observer into the exhibit so that one figuratively became a participant in another world. In the experience of drama, we are drawn into the world of the dramatic action as we become participants symbolically in another world. Through music we are invited to participate in a world of special time, a time within time. Music is a symbolic representation or "tonal analogue" of the life of feeling, as Susanne Langer puts it. It expresses the ebb and flow of dissonance and resolution, the pulsating rhythms of life's energies, the occasional calm and serenity, the alterations of anguish and joy, the mystical qualities of contemplation, the passions of love and rage, and the detachment of delightful play.

Bounded by limits, human beings have the capacity to experience the "other" or the "beyond" through symbolical representation. Langer points out the essential element of semblance or illusion in all artistic creation. As symbolic forms with import or meaning, artistic works are fundamentally different from physical objects.

Herein lies the "strangeness" or "otherness" that characterizes an artistic object. The form is immediately given to perception, and yet it reaches beyond itself; it is semblance, but seems to be charged with reality. Like speech, that is physically nothing but little buzzing sounds, it is filled with its meaning, and its meaning is a reality.[49]

There is a close parallel between transcendence, the arts, and religious experience and ritual. For example, Black Elk reports a vision he had as a young boy where he experienced himself being carried to the "center of the world," there to be with the "grandfathers." He reports that he was able to see and understand things in a new way, "as they are in the spirit." So powerful was this vision that Black Elk viewed the vision as more real than his ordinary life. Later he and his tribe reenacted the vision, and in the process of ritual enactment he reports that they experienced again the power and healing of the vision.[50] On frequent occasions in a variety of cultural contexts, religious persons report similar types of experiences: of being transported or being carried into another world. While in that world they report having a powerful experience that then has an impact upon their ordinary life when they return to the world. Common to these experiences is that persons seem to have some reference beyond the ordinary, a world not simply understandable or reducible to what is manageable or practical within ordinary life.

When the arts do their work, they have the capacity to bring us to a similar state of ecstasy, to a state of being outside ourselves. These experiences can have a powerful impact on our lives. Paul Tillich says,

> The artist brings to our senses and through them to our whole being something of the depth of our world and of ourselves, something of the mystery of being. When we are grasped by a work of art things appear to us which were unknown before—possibilities of being, unthought-of powers, hidden in the depth of life which take hold of us.[51]

As a young soldier in the trenches of World War I, Tillich was comforted amidst "mud, blood, and death" by works of art he was able to find in a magazine at a field bookstore. One painting that particularly affected him was Botticelli's *Madonna and Child*. After the war was over, he went to Berlin to see the painting itself for the first time. He writes,

> In the beauty of the painting there was Beauty itself. It shone through the colors of the paint as the light of day shines through

the stained-glass windows of a medieval church. As I stood there, bathed in the beauty its painter had envisioned so long ago, something of the divine source of all things came through to me. I turned away shaken. That moment has affected my whole life, given me the keys for the interpretation of human existence, brought vital joy and spiritual truth.[52]

The playwright and president of Czechoslovakia Václav Havel also points to this experience of transcendence. Unlike Tillich, he does not interpret his experience of art theologically. In a letter written to his wife, Olga, while in prison, he reflects on the importance of the "conventions" of the theater (e.g., the arrangement of the stage, the actors, the curtain, and the audience) in a "performance."

> It seems to me that the convention of "performance"—an outgrowth of theater's ancient roots in ritual—is precisely the "trick" on which that miraculous "enactment" of the mystery of human existence is based: it is only as a person who is physically present "here and now" begins to perform that he takes that "fateful" step "outside himself" that allows him "here and now," to demonstrate the mystery of his own humanity, i.e., the mystery of human existence altogether. In other words: it is only by consciously making theatrical convention a part of our enterprise that we can create a springboard to a "flight of the spirit."[53]

The mystery of the arts is their capacity to invite us into another world to be enlivened and transformed. The arts are like humor and play in our lives, which can become signals of transcendence.[54] In order for us to create and enjoy humor, in order for us to play, we cannot be too attached to the mundane. We cannot become completely burdened down by the serious business of the profane—making money and seeking material well-being, manipulating power, or trying to secure and control our future. The arts enrich our lives, not by escape from the profane, but by questioning and reinterpreting the profane in terms of another frame of reference.

Transcendence through aesthetic experience is a dimension of life that can transform our ordinary affairs. Many in my community take great delight in our flower and vegetable gardens. A former faculty colleague, Paul McKay, who has worked with refugees in Central America, reports that almost immediately after coming to a refugee camp, the people would plant flowers, even in front of a makeshift shack. Another former colleague, Reinhild Janzen, art historian, tells the story of a Laotian refugee who had come to live in Kansas. Her first concern was to locate needle and thread so she could carry on her needlework. My wife's great-grandmother, who lived to be 100, quilted into her upper nineties. Why do we take such delight in sports? Surely the beauty of a Michael Jordan soaring through the air, or Barry Sanders weaving his way through tacklers, or the perfectly executed squeeze play in baseball are symbols of the beauty of creation as God intended it.

Prophetic Imagination

We live in the tension between our experience of finitude and of transcendence. We live between the times: immersed in suffering and brokenness, with some foretaste or inkling of a new order of truth, goodness, and beauty. The arts are also linked to religious imagination when they open our eyes to see the brokenness of our world, the suffering of those around us. The arts can help us overcome the numbing effect of our culture. They can urge us to weep and mourn with those who suffer, those who experience pain and injustice, whose lives are destroyed by famine and war. The arts can nurture in us a sense of the fragility of life on our planet, a sense of our precarious existence as we hover in the solar system, protected by a fragile ozone layer, treading the earth on a thin layer of topsoil, as we become aware of the perfectly ordered balance of vegetation and animal life that provides us with a rich supply of oxygen.

The Radical Reformation tradition has attuned me to artistic forms that express a prophetic religious consciousness. One powerful promoter of such a prophetic awareness is Thieleman van Braght's *Martyr's Mirror*. No book other than the Bible has been more important to Mennonite identity. Mennonites have carried this book with them as they migrated from country to country. The second edition of 1685 brings together the stories of the martyrs collected by the Dutch pastor, van Braght, and 104 etchings of a Mennonite artist, Jan Luyken. The stories of the martyrs, collected under the title, *The Bloody Theater of Defenseless Christians*, together with the vivid images of torture, suffering, and death, are powerful symbols of a community of Christians living "between the times."

A traveling exhibit based on the *Martyr's Mirror*, and occasioned by the recent finding of twenty-three of Luyken's plates in the hands of a Rhineland art dealer, provokes those who view the exhibit to ponder what it means to live responsibly before God in a world of violence and torture, where it is estimated that over one-third of the world's governments torture or tolerate the torture of prisoners.[55]

The term *prophetic imagination* is inspired in part by Walter Brueggemann's book by that title.[56] Brueggemann contrasts "royal" consciousness with "prophetic" consciousness. Royal consciousness has three central characteristics. It is characterized by wealth, power, and affluence. Second, it maintains itself through repression, oppression and violence. And third, it legitimates the social order through religious symbols in which God or the gods "bless" a status quo suitable to an economics of affluence, injustice, and a politics of oppression. Brueggemann analyzes three periods of royal consciousness in biblical history: the slavery in Egypt at the time of Moses, the kingdom period in Israel, symbolized by Solomon, and the Herodian establishment at the time of Jesus.

The prophetic consciousness of Moses, the Hebrew prophets, and Jesus dares to imagine another way to live and structure society. This prophetic consciousness is characterized by an economics of social justice, a politics of covenant, and a religion of God's freedom. Such a religious imagination inspires hope for a new order and motivates people to seek change rather than use God to bless the status quo. It is not easy to develop prophetic imagination, for people have become so immersed in the royal consciousness that they cannot even imagine an alternative. They have been so numbed by their immersion in the royal consciousness that they can no longer see or hear pain and anguish.

Brueggemann indirectly suggests the powerful role the arts can play in our lives. The arts help us overcome the numbing effect of a culture where the preciousness of life is taken for granted as we preserve "our way of life" at the expense of others. In the summer of 1991 the majority of Americans seemed oblivious to the death and suffering of thousands of Iraqi citizens as they celebrated the "renewal" of America and the return of American soldiers to a society almost undisturbed by the Persian Gulf War. The callousness continues as thousands of Iraqi children have now died as a result of the sanctions imposed on Iraq after the war.

War is often out of sight and out of mind. We sanitize it with euphemisms like *missions* and *collateral damage*. It takes the artist to break through our blindness and our numbness, to open our eyes and ears so that we can see and hear again. Such is the power of Picasso's *Guernica*, a work that protests Franco's use of Nazi bombers to destroy the city of Guernica during the Spanish Civil War. Wilson Yates describes the painting:

> A woman with a dead child is screaming, a second woman is holding a lamp as if to show what has been done, a soldier is fallen as

a tortured victim. There is light bulb that seems to offer no illumination—a symbol of the eye of God or civilization that lends little light on the act of brutality. Two central figures are the bull and the horse. In a conversation with Jerome Seckler, Picasso acknowledges that the bull represents brutality, the horse the people. He insisted that the bull is not an explicit symbol of fascism, but more broadly a symbol of "brutality and darkness." The bull stands in stoic fierce pose, the horse writhes with the agony of having fallen at the hands of the sword. In the work there is no door, "no exit" from which to escape. The symbols of hope are few if any: a small flower in the lower part of the work and an almost indistinguishable dove, the woman and her light.[57]

The candor of the language of the prophet causes us to weep and mourn. Brueggemann says the "language of grief" is frequently the mode in which the prophet communicates. A work of Kathe Kollwitz expresses the deep pathos of human existence in the context of a war. In 1942, during World War II, Kollwitz created her last print, a lithograph entitled "Seeds for the Planting Shall Not Be Ground Up." She named it after one of her favorite poets, Goethe, "saatfruchte sollen nicht vermahlen werden," from the *Wilhelm Meister*. Kollwitz portrays a mother hovering over her children. Her arms and hands are stretched out as she tries to protect them from danger. Her eyes haunt us as she looks out to the terrifying world around her with a mix of foreboding, of impending death. Yet she offers an intentional gesture of compassion. Above all, she seems determined to protect and nourish the precious lives of her children. Her three children clutch her skirt and peer out underneath her arms. The eyes of the two littlest ones still reflect an innocent trust. The older one, like the mother, already has eyes opened to the darkness of the world around them.

Kollwitz brings to mind Jesus' weeping over the city of Jerusalem. Abraham Heschel's insightful commentary on the Hebrew prophets notes repeatedly the pathos of the prophet as he suffers for his people and mourns with them.[58] Heschel says that through complete identification with God, the prophet represents not only his own pathos, but also the pathos of God. We see this especially in the prophet Jeremiah, who lived during the time of the destruction of Jerusalem and the beginning of the exile.

My joy is gone, grief is upon me,
   My heart is sick. ...
For the hurt of my poor people I am hurt,
   I mourn, and dismay has taken hold of me,

Is there no balm in Gilead?
　　Is there no physician there?
Why then has the health of my poor people
　　not been restored?
O that my head were a spring of water,
　　And my eyes a fountain of tears,
so that I might weep day and night
　　for the slain of my poor people! ...
Who will have pity on you, O Jerusalem,
　　or who will bemoan you?
Who will turn aside
　　to ask about your welfare? (Jer. 8:18–9:1; 15:5)

Brueggemann argues that only by embracing pathos, by becoming deeply aware that the old must die, can we begin to be energized toward new possibilities. The old order of war and trust in military power has such a grip on people that it is impossible for a new order to emerge. Only after we weep and mourn and allow the old to die, says Brueggemann, can the amazing wonder of alternative possibilities emerge. Thus the prophetic imagination gives birth to symbols of hope and yearnings that have been so long repressed. The prophet has two tasks. One is "to mine the memory of this people and educate them to use the tools of hope. The other is to recognize how singularly words, speech, language, and phrase shape consciousness and define reality."[59] And, I would add emphatically, the language of the arts. Humanity desperately needs the artist to break through the numbing impact of our culture, to invite us to weep and mourn, and to call us to an alternative vision of the good.

The Arts as "Gift"

Artists contribute to the human community by enriching our lives and enlivening our spirits to what we are called to be as human beings. If I were to rewrite Paul's discussion of the variety of gifts or roles in the church—teachers, apostles, prophets, healers, miracle workers, administrators—I would certainly want to add the artist to the list.

Lewis Hyde's book *The Gift* states well the function of the arts as "gift" in society to enrich our lives.[60] Hyde's work is structured around a typology that distinguishes between the role of gift-giving and commodities that are sold or bartered in the market. Gifts are given without regard for reward or the expectation of reciprocation. A product on the market is "owned" by a person who benefits from selling that product and appropriates the benefits for himself or his business.

But gifts are *given*, not owned. By their very nature, gifts are circulated. They belong not to the private sphere, but are donated for the benefit of the public sphere. In a market economy, money circulates as persons buy and sell. This too benefits the public sphere. The motivation in a transaction, however, is the personal gain or profit that can be appropriated to a person or business. The essential function of gifts is circulation without motivation for personal gain or appropriation. Gift-giving that seeks to manipulate or control is thus not a genuine gift. True gift-giving arises from gratitude. Though persons who give usually experience personal benefits in satisfaction and sometimes a return gift, that *byproduct* of the gift should not be confused with the *motivation* for giving.

In placing the arts within the sphere of gift-giving, Hyde uses the counterexample of the mass-produced romance novel, which society produces primarily for market reasons. Market research determines the characteristics the hero or heroine should have in order to attract readers to buy them. He contrasts such novels with enduring works of art. Enduring works of art belong to the category of "gift" because they endure even when there is not a market.

We do not wish to idealize art. Some artists rightly do make a living through their art. Art also functions within the economy, is bought and sold, and for some becomes "big business." But it is easy for artistic creation to be subverted by economic motives, just as the other professions can be subverted when the calling to serve others is demoted by interest primarily in meeting the demands of the market. The value of artistic works lies in their ability to enrich, enliven, inspire appreciation, or provide insight into life. The artist, if genuinely in the service of her creative impulse, does not produce music, a poem, a sculpture to satisfy the whims of the market. That may happen to the work produced, but that is not the purpose of such a work. The creative artist is rather responding to a spirit within herself, motivated by a sense of truth or beauty, which has integrity for its own sake, independent of the marketability of the product.[61]

Van Gogh revolted against his early work as a seller of "art" to fit the tastes of the public. He chose instead to live a life of poverty, depending on financial support from his brother, Theo. Only after his death did Van Gogh's work become valuable in the marketplace. Many artists see the work they produce as a gift to them, not simply something produced through their own talent and effort. So poets refer to the inspiration of the muse, or Bach acknowledges the creative gift from beyond himself and thus dedicates his work "to the glory of

God." That does not mean that artists do not engage in intense self-discipline (witness Van Gogh) to try to perfect the gift. Yet when they produce something satisfying, many refer to something that "happened" to them.

The gift, then, has three dimensions—the gift given to the artist, the expression of that gift in a work (a novel, poem, painting), and the appropriation and enjoyment of those who receive the gift with gratitude. The third dimension brings gift-giving to its fruition, as the gift performs its crucial function in the creation of a spirit of community. The gift is shared with and appropriated by the society, rather than kept and owned by the individual. In this process, people are brought together in a common spirit of gratitude and appreciation. The artist thus contributes to the peace of the city.[62]

Hyde's ideas suggest basic connections to the Trinitarian structure that informs this book: the artist, the work created by the artist, and the meaning of the work that the community appropriates. Hyde's ideas also suggest connections to basic Christian theological notions of grace and ethical responsibility. Gifts are given away, sacrificed, given up, and made available to be consumed by others. Sacrifice and death are inherent in gift-giving. The gift then nurtures life and the community. The grain of wheat must die in order for new life to emerge. People sacrifice themselves to carry on the gift of life. Christ gives himself for us in order that we may live. We, in turn, give that others may live.[63]

We can interpret the "gift" of an artistic creation in a strictly humanistic way, or we can place it in a broader theological framework. As gifts are created, received, and passed on, they nurture our lives and foster community. But artistic creation can also be understood in the context of the giftedness of human existence, the wonder and mystery of being itself, and the thanksgiving for life as a gift of God. In that context, the artist's work is an expression of gratitude for existence, and it can be received by the human community, both the church and the larger society, as one of the gifts of the Spirit.

The Dynamics
of Dual Citizenship

"Paul replied, 'I am a Jew, from Tarsus in Cilicia, a citizen of an important city; I beg you, let me speak to the people.'" —Acts 21:39

"Paul said to the centurion who was standing by, 'Is it legal for you to flog a Roman citizen who is uncondemned?'" —Acts 22:25

"So then you are no longer strangers and aliens, but you are citizens with the saints and also members of the household of God, built upon the foundation of the apostles and prophets, with Christ Jesus himself as the cornerstone." —Ephesians 2:19-20

ON THE BOUNDARY BETWEEN TWO CITIES

To be a citizen is to belong to a city, to be a member of a society. With citizenship come certain rights and duties. In modern Western societies, a person is a citizen simply by virtue of being born in a particular territory or by becoming naturalized. However, citizenship has not always been defined by birth. Luke's account of the life of Paul in Acts reflects the ambiguity of living within the Roman Empire. Not everyone born within the Roman Empire was a citizen. Slaves, who made up a large share of the population, were not citizens. For many, citizenship was not an option. They were resident aliens. Paul was in the minority when he indicated he was a citizen. The tribune, a Roman official charged with keeping order, who Paul met in Jerusalem, paid a large sum of money to get his citizenship (Acts 22:28). Few persons in the first century had the option of becoming citizens.

The book of Ephesians reflects another kind of citizenship: "So then you are *no longer* strangers and aliens, but you are citizens with the saints and also members of the household of God, built upon the foundation of the apostles and prophets, with Christ Jesus himself as the cornerstone" (Eph. 2:19-20). Citizenship is neither by birth nor a matter of free choice, but a complex response to a vision of life to which one is called by God. For the Apostle Paul, being a citizen meant to live on the boundary in the dynamic tension of dual citizenship. He was born a Roman citizen. Paul appealed to rights he had as a Roman citizen. He asked to speak in public (Acts 21:39). He questioned Roman officials about whether they were upholding their own law when they flogged him (Acts 22:25). Before Festus, Paul asked to be tried by the emperor's tribunal (Acts 25:10).

These passages in Acts indicate that to be a citizen meant to be part of a humanly constructed social order, to inherit a system of law and morality, and to be part of a society with an understanding of the good. But this Roman vision clashed with Paul's citizenship in another society, the church. According to Acts, Festus challenged Paul's claims: "You are out of your mind, Paul! Too much learning is driving you insane!" During the last years of his life, Paul was a prisoner of Rome. He was allowed to live by himself with the soldier who was guarding him (Acts 28:16). The conflict between the two cities to which Christians belong is made vivid in the story of Acts 5. "'We gave you strict orders not to teach in this name, yet here you have filled Jerusalem with your teaching and you are determined to bring this man's blood on us.' But Peter and the apostles answered, 'We must obey God rather than any human authority'" (Acts 5:28-29). To be a Christian is to live on a boundary, a citizen of two societies.[1]

This tension between citizenship in two societies is concrete and sociological. Our identity as Christians is shaped by membership in two different sociological structures: the nation-state and the church. This tension between two social identities is central to a believers church model of the sixteenth-century Radical Reformation (especially Anabaptists) on the Continent, and the seventeenth-century separatist stream of Puritanism (Baptists and Quakers) in England.

This model is particularly relevant for our contemporary post-Constantinian pluralistic context, where the church can no longer presuppose that society as a whole is basically Christian. In the believers church model, membership in the church is a voluntary commitment of faith, symbolized in adult or believers baptism. Becoming a member of the church means committing to a life of discipleship, the decision to take on an alternative identity distinct from the dominant culture. This distinctive identity, however, is not necessarily an exclusive identity. Like the Apostle Paul, members of the church participate in various ways as citizens in the societies where they live. The relationship between citizenship in the church and citizenship in the larger society is complex and fluid. The Christian must discern, based on the vision of life defined by membership in the church, how and on what terms a person will act as a citizen in the larger society.

The tension is often the greatest on matters of war and peace, where following Christ's way of nonviolent love clashes directly with the call of the nation to participate in armed force. I felt this tension as an 18-year-old when I was the only person in my high school in American Falls, Idaho, to register as a conscientious objector to war. But we were not "against" culture. My parents voted. My father was active on the Soil Conservation Service and the local hospital board. An uncle was a member of the school board. Though war and peace always seems to highlight the issue of dual citizenship most vividly, it is not the only test case to determine a particular group's relationship to culture. John H. Yoder makes this point in his critique of H. Richard Niebuhr, who seems to have held this assumption in his description of the "Christ against culture" type.

> The state, or even the violence of the state, is pre-eminently representative of culture, so that pacifists who reject that are described as being against culture "as such" or as a whole (even though they are in fact affirmative about agriculture, the arts, marriage, communication, and social justice). H. Richard Niebuhr does not make the state (or war) nearly as important for his whole system as does his brother Reinhold, to whom he dedicated *Christ and Culture*, yet in his portrayal of both Tolstoy and Tertullian it is their challenging the Empire (Roman and Russian) and its wars which best exemplify the "against culture" posture.[2]

The Christian faces the question of the relationship of Christian identity and citizenship on many levels other than the assumed "defining" issue of war and peace. The church addresses many issues in the public arena that concern the shalom (basic well-being) of the city where it dwells. War and peace is a critical issue. Just as important are how we respond to poverty and to the needs of the marginalized, how we respond to issues of safety in the work place and in our neighborhoods, or how we educate and nurture our children. Given the collapse of nurturing structures for so many children, the work of teaching effectively does not end in the classroom. Children who come to school without breakfast, or who live in abusive situations, cannot learn. What is a fair tax system, one that allocates resources within a state or nation to make it possible for all children to be educated well? How should scarce tax resources be spent? What obligations do citizens have toward the poor, to children without proper systems of nurture, or to underemployed or unemployed parents?

We exercise our citizenship at many levels: national, state or provincial, and local. A city-wide recycling program for North Newton, Kansas (where I live), was mandated by law in January 1993. Recycling originally began as a voluntary project. After several years of a successful voluntary program, where citizens paid for the service directly to the trash hauler, the city council decided to charge all citizens an extra fee in order to pay a local business to pick up recyclable materials. This law was a significant achievement, given the atmosphere of resistance by so many Americans to higher costs of government services.

At another level, citizens participate in the symbolic and ritual actions of the American civil religion. Saluting the flag, standing for and singing the national anthem, and swearing oaths of loyalty are rituals in tension with Christian identity. When the Wichita Symphony opens its concert season each year with the National Anthem, I stand and participate. However, when the Symphony broke tradition by playing the National Anthem in the middle of its concert season during the height of the Persian Gulf War and urged us all to stand in support of "our soldiers in the Gulf," I could not stand. I felt the concert had become politicized, that I was being pressured to declare my support for the war by standing.

During World War I, the local American Legion put an American flag inside the sanctuary of the First Mennonite Church in Aberdeen, Idaho. They wanted to make sure that the German immigrants in the church were patriotic Americans. The flag is an ambivalent symbol for Christians. Loyalty to the red, white, and blue does not easily harmonize with loyalty to Jesus Christ and citizenship in the church. The presence of the American flag in my boyhood Mennonite Church in Idaho was analogous to the requirement to burn incense to Caesar in the first century. Some might question the analogy, since the American flag symbolizes democracy and, for many, that the U.S. is a "Christian" nation, not a pagan imperial power like Rome, which demanded that it be treated like a god. Though not as violent as Rome's, the American Legion still used coercive force to make sure that these Mennonite

Christians were loyal Americans and would not let their loyalty to Christ interfere with loyalty to their country.

WAYS OF BEING CITIZENS

Too often we think of citizenship in too restrictive a way as having to do primarily with paying taxes or voting. Citizenship is not simply a matter of how Christians relate to the civil government. Just as war and peace is not *the* defining issue, so our relationship to the state does not define the meaning of citizenship. To be a citizen is much broader and more complex. Below is a summary of six ways we as Christians can engage the culture as citizens.

Ethos

We participate in shaping the attitudes and beliefs of our culture in a myriad of ways by simply being a people who respond to life with an alternative vision of what could be. The church can help shape public opinion through its witness in the society, especially by how it names and unmasks the principalities and powers. Cultural criticism needs to be concrete and specific. Walter Wink demonstrates this by unmasking the myth of redemptive violence that has such a hold on our culture through his analysis of the basic storyline of so many of our cartoons, TV programs, and movies.[3]

The subtlety of this myth is evident in the aesthetically powerful, but untruthful movie, *Mississippi Burning*. In the movie, the FBI finds the killers of three young civil rights workers who died because of their participation in a nonviolent campaign to register black voters in Mississippi. The counter-terror tactics of the head FBI man (played by Gene Hackman) against the Ku Klux Klan is what gives the movie its power. The movie confirms the myth of redemptive violence: one should defeat evil by any means necessary, using even the same kinds of terror tactics employed by the Ku Klux Klan. The difference is that the FBI is serving a good cause and that justifies its tactics. The FBI is thus the hero in the story. Evil is defeated through redemptive violence. Completely lost in this telling is that the civil rights movement and Martin Luther King Jr. challenged that very myth and broke the chain of racism and violence, not with mimetic violence, but through alternative nonviolent processes of confrontation and transformation.

The movie also rewrites history for the sake of the myth. We know from the historical record that under the leadership of J. Edgar Hoover, the FBI not only resisted the civil rights movement, but also tried to subvert it. They were anything but heroic in the struggle against racism.

We need to be liberated from our bondage to powers that legitimate violence and oppression. The church contributes to the peace of the city by unmasking the myths that legitimate power and domination and that offer shallow views of fulfillment and salvation through self-gratification and material self-indulgence.

Modeling and Example

The church engages the culture around it with an alternative model of citizenship simply by being itself. In Clarence Jordan's Koinonia Farm in Georgia, blacks and whites lived and worked together in the 1950s in the context of the racist and segregated South. Their very existence as an alternative community was a powerful witness to an alternative social vision that put the lie to racist structures. Their very *being* was a threat to the status quo and often led to acts of violence against Jordan's group.

The church can also develop institutions to address the needs of the larger culture by modeling an alternative approach. Churches took the lead in the development of hospitals for the care of the sick. Some of the most innovative models of care for the mentally ill were developed in church institutions.[4] The church has taken the lead with Victim Offender Reconciliation programs, which provide models of restorative justice. In these models, victims of crime are given the opportunity to process their experience of being violated by confronting a perpetrator of a crime with the consequences of their criminal act. The criminal is also given the opportunity to take responsibility for his action, to repent, and, where possible, to make restitution to the victim. This meeting of victim and offender, facilitated by skilled mediators, provides a space to acknowledge the pain of the victims as well as space for the offender to take responsibility for their action, and perhaps begin the road to recovery. This model offers an alternative to the traditional criminal justice system, where victims are often lost in the process because crime is viewed as a violation of the state. It also makes possible the transformation of the violator by shifting the focus away from punishment. This model attempts to respond to evidence that traditional forms of punishment, like imprisonment, only socialize violators into further criminal behavior.[5]

Participatory Democracy

While electoral politics is important, the electoral process receives far too much attention as the primary locus for citizenship participation. We do the work of peacemaking and justice in the larger society especially through voluntary associations of citizens who organize themselves to address concerns of justice and peace.[6] Christians sometimes act through their own church institutions. More often they make common cause with others in the larger culture who share their commitment on a particular issue.

We who live in less repressive societies are in a position to stand in solidarity with people in other parts of the world who are more vulnerable. Numerous examples could be cited from the interface of North American Christians and Central America: Witness for Peace, a North American ecumenical grassroots organization that challenged U.S. policy in Nicaragua through the 1980s; the Roman Catholic Church, influenced by liberation theology, which served as a vehicle for lay leadership training and development through Catholic Action groups and Christian base communities; the Human Rights Resource Office for Latin America for the World Council of Churches; the American Baptist Churches, which challenged the injustice of U.S. refugee policy toward Central America by bringing a lawsuit against the Immigration and Naturalization Service;[7] and the role in the late 1980s of Moravian church leaders in Nicaragua and John Paul Lederach of the Mennonite Central Committee in North America to mediate the conflict between the Atlantic Coast Indians and the Sandinista government in Nicaragua.[8]

According to Daniel Buttry, "the link in partnerships between the Nicaraguan Baptist Convention and the American Baptist Church had a definite impact upon the question for peace."[9] The Nicaraguan bishops sent a series of pastoral letters to the churches in the United States. North American missionaries returned to the United State to provide a critique of U.S. policy toward Nicaragua, which lent support to resistance against U.S. policy. American Baptists also were inspired to participate in Witness for Peace and the Pledge of Resistance.

Robert Putnam, international relations scholar and political scientist, has shown the important interaction between achievements in international negotiations and the pressures of domestic politics:

> The politics of many international negotiations can usefully be conceived as a two-level game. At the national level, domestic groups pursue their interests by pressuring the government to adopt favorable policies, and politicians seek power by constructing coalitions among those groups. At the international level, national governments seek to maximize their own ability to satisfy domestic pressures while minimizing the adverse consequences of foreign developments. Neither of the two games can be ignored

by central decision-makers so long as their countries remain interdependent, yet sovereign.[10]

In his book, *Peace Works: The Citizen's Role in Ending the Cold War*, David Cortright argues that grassroots social movements have the power to shape history. From 1980 to 1987, citizen peace activists played a significant role in ending the Cold War. Though the factors that influence policy were varied and complex, "if citizens groups had not campaigned constantly to prevent nuclear war, the military standoff between East and West might have become much more dangerous."[11]

The Politics of Protest and Resistance

Throughout history, but especially in this century, the world has seen the extraordinary success of nonviolent movements of social change. When social institutions are unresponsive to change, when the normal procedures of democratic process have been exhausted, and when the powers of evil are strong and intransigent, many have learned that there is another way to wage conflict without using violent force. Through the leadership of Mohandas K. Gandhi and Martin Luther King Jr., we have become aware of an alternative kind of power that changes reality not by meeting violence with violence, but through alternative nonviolent methods of waging conflict.

According to Gene Sharp, the power of nonviolence arises from people's capacity (1) to do what they are not expected or required to do, and (2) from their ability to withhold consent from what they are supposed to do.[12] Since governments can govern only if most people obey most of the time, the power of government to impose an unjust and violent order on people is more fragile than is normally assumed. When people who are repressed are empowered to overcome fear and are willing to accept the consequences of their behavior by their willingness to suffer and die for their convictions, the ability to impose an unjust order by force is limited. This does not mean that nonviolent struggles will always be successful, but neither are most struggles waged through violent means. In armed struggles, at least half of those who wage conflicts lose, whereas most nonviolent struggles can be turned into "win-win" outcomes.

Community Service

One area of cultural involvement can easily be taken for granted. Healthy communities depend upon a great variety of volunteer activity to meet human needs, such as providing clothing and food banks for the poor, disaster relief, recycling, parental support of the public schools, service on school boards and hospital boards, tutoring services, services for the homeless and the mentally and physically handicapped, shelters for abused persons, parks and recreation activities, and meals on wheels for the elderly. While such voluntary action is essential in a healthy community, Christians must not become so completely absorbed with their time and energy that they forget to give time to the underlying structural causes of issues like poverty, homelessness, or illiteracy. Compassion for human need can be misdirected if we respond to symptoms or crises only when they arise or fail to address deeper structural issues of justice or the distribution of power in a society.

Vocation

Work is a social activity in which we cooperate with other human beings by contributing to the common good and the well-being of the cosmos. When we look at work as a calling, we interpret what we do with our time and energy as a response to God's purpose for our lives. As Luther put it, our work is the context for neighbor love. To see our work as a calling means to link our work to its social purpose, to move beyond work as a means for our individual well-being and personal satisfaction. To view work as a calling means to understand what we do in the creation of human culture as beings made in the image of God. From this perspective, the purpose of our work is to "image" God in both the goods we produce and the services we perform.

We "image" God in the world in the context of boundaries, our limited space and time as human beings. Within those limits we may be able to do a few things well. Though it is important to keep in mind the links between our work, the work of others, and other spheres of life, developing a sense of responsibility for the world and honoring God with our work is to accept the fact that we can only image God within a concrete and particular sphere of operation. Responsibility for the world in which we live often paralyzes us from acting responsibly before God within our particular sphere of responsibility. Karl Barth developed this notion of our limit within time in his discussion of vocation in the *Church Dogmatics*. Barth is worth quoting at length because he warns humans of the hubris of presuming to exceed the boundaries of our limited sphere of operation.

> Faithfulness in vocation first means that we are to remember its particularity and ... its frontiers, and that we must be willing to keep to them. In this respect faithfulness implies restraint. ...

None must play the Atlas and take everything on his shoulders. None must try to do everything himself or act as if everything was waiting for him to take it up or to speak the decisive word. ... A man may suffer from an excessive urge for activity in virtue of his endowment. He may see only too clearly the imperfection of the world, the profound contrariety of all or at least most of the human things around him, the personal inadequacy with which most or all of his fellows are encumbered. And he now feels that he is summoned like Hamlet, and also enabled, to rearrange or to hold together by his work, according to ideas which he thinks illuminating and means which seem to be serviceable, the great or little world which is now so out of joint. There are noble spirits of this kind. But we can only warn them against attempting general activity instead of specific activity in a single sphere of operation. ... Where there is no modesty there is no greatness either. ... There is genuine operation for each of us only in his own limited circle.[13]

Barth's comments could be dangerous if interpreted to mean that one need simply do one's own specific work well. His perspective needs to be balanced by an awareness of the larger social purpose served by one's work. If we are to approach a profession from a Christian point of view, we need a place to stand, a framework for assessment that transcends both the standards of competence provided by a profession as well as our own personal standards of success and satisfaction. Without that transcendent framework, the workspace becomes an autonomous sphere of life no longer subject to interpretation within a world created and sustained by God. The workspace can then easily become an occasion for the expression of the demonic rather than service to the neighbor or the common good.

James Luther Adams refers to the misguided energy and devotion of Thomas Mann's Faustus, who made a compact with the devil, agreeing that in return for fame as a composer he would sever the bonds of normal affection and social responsibility. Adams argues that some of us have made this compact with the devil

under the aegis of a pseudo-Protestant doctrine of vocation: we are prone to take seriously only the responsibility of doing our own professional or vocational work well. In this fashion we evade a costly responsibility for the social policies of the common life. One can find physicians, lawyers, professors, workers who believe that their public responsibilities consist almost entirely in their vocational activity.[14]

The same issue is raised by the authors of *Habits of the Heart*. The American middle class is failing to take responsibility for the common good as Americans seek personal advancement and success within the workspace without concern for the shape of the larger society.[15]

Stanley Hauerwas points out the limits of a narrow understanding of vocation in his reflection on the memoirs of Albert Speer, state architect under Hitler. He describes how Speer chose to define himself as "only" an architect. Speer lived a life of self-deception, deliberately concealing from himself the significance of the connections of his work to the political purposes of the Nazis. Hauerwas argues that Speer's story was not rich enough to illuminate his real identity. He clung to the story that he was simply being Hitler's apolitical architect. Hauerwas points out that nothing in Speer's background would have led one to think he would join the company of Nazis. He was humanistically trained and he seems to have been a humane and loving father. But Hitler gave him the opportunity to lose himself in his work. He joined the party and was increasingly drawn into its activities. As Speer puts it:

> My position as Hitler's architect had soon become indispensable to me. Not yet thirty, I saw before me the most exciting prospects an architect can dream of. I did not see any moral ground outside the system where I should have taken my stand. ... My new political interests played a subsidiary part in my thinking. I was above all an architect.[16]

Though most of us do not serve demonic ends equivalent to Nazi ideology, many Christians are vulnerable to the same kind of distortion in their lives as we see in Albert Speer. Many of us increasingly view the workspace as an autonomous sphere isolated from our larger commitments as Christians. So Christians serve uncritically in workspaces for the good of the company or the organization. By deceiving themselves into thinking they are not responsible, persons deliberately overlook the fact that a research grant may be tainted by narrow military or nationalistic interests, a company may be making arms that are sold to dictators, nuclear triggers for nuclear weapons, or products that are unsafe or waste scarce resources of the environment.

DIFFERENT WAYS OF CONCEIVING DUAL CITIZENSHIP

This believers church sociological view is fundamentally different from Augustine's understanding of the two cities and Luther's two-kingdom theology. Augustine's thought is organized around the notion of two cities defined by what people love: a heavenly city, where love is oriented toward God; and the earthly city, where love is oriented toward everything that is less than God. Because Augustine divides humankind by what they love, the two cities are abstractions. They are not linked to specific sociological structures. For Augustine, the earthly city is not equivalent to the state nor is the heavenly city equivalent to the church. On earth, where sin is a powerful force that has been passed on since Adam's fall, the cities are commingled. We cannot identify a specific sociological group whose identity is defined by the love of God. Living nearly a century after Constantine, Augustine no longer held to the distinctive sociological identity of the church. Infant baptism was already a prevalent practice. Thus, people were "born into" the church. The wheat and the tares are mixed together in the church. The true church is invisible, or visible only to God. Thus, Augustine did not understand the church as a society of believers whose membership is distinct from the larger culture.[17]

Luther divided the "children of Adam" into two classes of people—the righteous, who belong to the kingdom of God; and the wicked, who belong to the kingdom of the world. God governs the world in two ways. The good news of the gospel of God's grace is offered to all those persons who put their faith and trust in God. Sinners need the law to convict them of their sin, to show them that they cannot fulfill the law by their own power, and to order their common life through civil government, which protects the good and punishes the evil.

For Luther, the church is where the gospel is preached and the sacraments are administered. Sociologically, however, membership is based on birth (infant baptism), not voluntary membership based on faith. The church is not a distinctive sociological identity from the dominant culture. Because of the fall, civil government is necessary to protect the good and punish the evil. Christians are called to serve their neighbors through the offices of civil government. The tension for Luther is internal: it lies within the Christian person, who before God is "spiritually" saved by grace. "Externally," the Christian serves his neighbor through his calling. Luther limits the teaching of the Sermon on the Mount to interpersonal relationships. The worldly calling dictates public behavior (e.g., doing one's duty as a prince, a hangman, or a soldier who serves the prince). The tension in Luther is located not between the church as a distinctive alternative institution and the larger social order, but *within* the Christian—between his "private" and his "public" spaces.[18]

The believers church model has more affinities with John Calvin and the Reformed tradition, with its vision of a holy commonwealth. Calvin and his followers wanted to create a concrete, visible new society. The issue with the believers church traditions was whether this new society could encompass the entire social order (as Calvin held) or whether it entailed creating a believers church distinct from the dominant culture (as the Anabaptists held). The basis of Calvinism's encompassing vision is what H. Richard Niebuhr calls its "universalism." As Niebuhr puts it,

> Despite its doctrine of predestination, or because of its acknowledgment that only God predestined his creatures, it resolutely refused to give up any part of human life as beyond hope of redemption. Not economics, nor politics, nor church, nor the physical life could be regarded as merely temporal in significance, as not involved in corruption or beyond need of restoration to the harmony of God's kingdom.[19]

The vision of a holy commonwealth is deeply embedded in the American moral fabric. This Calvinism was mediated through the Puritan tradition, which significantly shaped a view of citizenship that continues to be a powerful model for many Christians in America. It has shaped denominations as diverse as the Baptists, Quakers, and Methodists. It has had a profound impact on more conservative forms of evangelicalism as well as the social gospel movement. Two of the most important moral theologians of this century, H. Richard and Reinhold Niebuhr, cannot be understood apart from this influence. Reinhold Niebuhr is a complex blend of the social gospel and Lutheran realism.

An example of this vision is the Puritan John Winthrop. Just before landing in the new world in 1630, Winthrop preached a sermon in Salem harbor in which he said that he and his fellow Puritans intended to found a "city set on a hill." While the Puritans were interested in material well-being and religious liberty for themselves, their primary objective was to create a holy commonwealth,

> a community in which a genuine ethical and spiritual life could be lived. … He decried what he called "natural liberty," which is the freedom to do whatever one wants, evil as well as good. True freedom—what he called "moral" freedom, "in reference to the covenant between God and man"—is a liberty "to do that only which is good, just, and honest.[20]

The Calvinist/Puritan vision of a holy commonwealth shaped both the established churches, which held to an identity of church and society membership as in the Massachusetts Bay Colony, and the separatist or believers churches, such as the Baptists and Quakers who believed in voluntary church membership. One issue that divided these churches was the degree to which coercion was an appropriate means to bring about the holy commonwealth. The Baptist Roger Williams, and the Quaker William Penn sought to accomplish their goals by recognizing and protecting religious liberty. They accepted in their colonies people of diverse belief and conviction and had a much more positive relationship to native peoples. On the other hand, the Massachusetts Bay Colony did not tolerate Baptists and Quakers. They were expelled from the colony.

A second major difference is that the believers churches also stress the importance of the church as a distinctive community of disciples, an identity distinct from membership in the larger society. From the believers church perspective, Calvinism inevitably leads to unacceptable compromises in the search for a common consensus that results from its lack of differentiation between membership in the church and the larger society.

Nevertheless, there are significant commonalities. Most significant is that both establishment churches and believers churches appeal to a vision of God's kingdom. The reign of God is not simply "spiritual." It is a concrete sociological reality that is made partially visible in the world through a community that is faithful to God.

FOUNDATIONS OF CITIZENSHIP: HOW DOES THE CHURCH LINK ITS VISION TO THE LARGER CULTURE?

Christians contribute to the well-being of the society in which they dwell by being the church, by living by the practices described in chapter five. Christians seek the peace of their society through their involvement as citizens in their civil society, by contributing to political discourse on the issues society faces and by participating in the political process. But what is the basis of this participation?

Participation within civil society is a complex issue. There is a fundamental tension between the values and purposes of the church and social institutions like the economy or civil government. The purpose of civil government is to order the common good for all members of a society. The church is a voluntary community, a society within the larger society, in which persons have committed themselves to follow

Christ. Civil governments serve all people who are born into a society. The masses do not share a common commitment, but hold to a plurality of worldviews and values.

Christians should bring to their thinking and activity as citizens their vision of the "new" society. The church is a model for society. But this model cannot simply be applied directly, given the pluralism of civil society and its lack of shared commitment to Jesus Christ. In applying a Christian vision to civic responsibility, therefore, a mediating process of thought must take place. The Christian vision must be "translated" to a situation where different presuppositions are operative. This mediating process is not unique to civil government. The person who works in a business organization, educational institution, in a medical practice, or on a farm must "translate" what it means to be faithful within those institutions as well.

Citizenship Grounded in Analogical Imagination

A Christian understanding of the citizen is founded on two principles. It is based on: (1) a vision or model of the good society that grows out of the view of the church elaborated in chapter five; and (2) a commitment to the process of analogical thinking that draws norms from that vision for how other societies beyond the church might work and be structured. Such analogical thinking requires both faithfulness to the vision of the church and imaginative thinking in how to translate that vision into other languages that will link us with other human beings as we seek the peace of the city where we dwell. My position has some affinities with Karl Barth, who believes that Christians should relate to political institutions by means of analogy with the kingdom of God. I would apply the concept of analogy more broadly, however, and not restrict the concept to the Christian's relationship to the state. Barth says that since Christ is Lord over the entire world, the church

> desires that the shape and reality of the State in this fleeting world should point towards the kingdom of God, not away from it. Its desire is not that human politics should cross the politics of God, but that they should proceed, however distantly, on parallel lines. ... It desires that the active grace of God ... be reflected in the earthly material of the external, relative, and provisional actions and modes of action of the political community. It therefore makes itself responsible in the first and last place to God—the one God whose grace is revealed in Jesus Christ—by making itself responsible for the cause of the State. ... It sets in motion the historical process whose aim and content are the molding of the state

into the likeness of the kingdom of God and hence the fulfillment of the State's own righteous purposes.[21]

The church is a modest foretaste of the kingdom of God. Though it is not the kingdom of God on earth, it seeks to embody that kingdom in a distinctive way. The church's vision of the kingdom is the basis for the process of analogical thinking as it relates to the larger society. A Christian understanding of justice will draw "analogically" from a corporate vision of church where the well-being of the whole body requires that human needs be met by mutual aid. Since membership in the church is based on respect for the dignity of each individual who has made a voluntary commitment to be a member of the church, by analogy the church will work in the larger society for the respect and safeguard of religious liberty. Based on the discerning process of respectful dialogue, by analogy the church will support democratic structures of participation and decision-making in the larger society. Based on the church's vision of a nonviolent process of confronting an erring brother or sister (Matt. 18:15-18), the church by analogy will search for and model nonviolent methods for confronting evil in the larger society.

Stephen Mott points out that the seventeenth-century Puritans

> used normative analogies from the order of the church to justify democracy: As in the order of grace all believers are equal, so in the order of nature all people are equal. The Levellers applied this analogy only to participation in government. Their conservative opponents, however, pointed to the economic implications of such thought: the same argument for a right of elections would validate a right to land and any other good necessary for sustenance. A group on the left fringe of the Puritans, the Diggers, also saw that the analogy extended to participation in property, but they approved it. They went and dug up the town commons, planted their crops, and waited in anticipation for the Reign of God.[22]

Working out an ethical position by analogy, however, is not something that happens in the abstract; it develops in the context of a discerning process as Christians live with the tension of their dual citizenship. Over time case studies (like precedents in the field of law) provide guidance for ongoing future discernment.[23]

The function of these case studies is somewhat analogous to the function of the Talmud for Jews. The Talmud provides an account of the way the rabbis applied the Torah to daily life. Case studies do not provide abstract principles or rules to follow in all cases. Rather, they serve as resources for the community to draw on in the process of on-going discernment. Citizenship based on analogical imagination is not one in which we can develop a set of abstract universal principles from which we can deduce a course of action for every available situation. Rather, it is based on conversation, a process of practical moral reasoning by which we are constantly engaging the issues of the wider culture in the light of the church's vision.

Another reason we cannot directly apply general guidelines that flow from a vision of the church to social policy is that to apply guidelines to specific social policies involves complex empirical analysis of any given issue. Furthermore, we must make judgments about strategies of action not logically entailed in a "guideline." I accept the same kind of caution the Roman Catholic bishops gave in their pastoral letter on war and peace. "When making applications of these principles [in their case they are referring to principles of just war theory] we realize—and we wish readers to recognize—that prudential judgments are involved based on specific circumstances which can change or which can be interpreted differently by people of good will."[24]

The church shares the ideas and models it has worked out with the larger culture and forms alliances with others of similar perspective. In this process the church also makes itself vulnerable by opening itself to learn as well from persons and groups with other cultural visions. In this process, new insights can be gained, and the church may modify its views based on what it has learned from others. The basis for cooperation, however, does not arise from first looking for some common denominator or watered-down version of a universal ethic that persons of secular or different religious faiths can share. Rather Christians contribute to the peace of the city by modestly sharing the distinctives of their vision in the larger process of cultural interaction.

As noted above, no one brings a universal vision to the conversation in society. Rather, all share distinctive perspectives. We must recognize our particularity and share it without embarrassment or apology. With such a framework, we can respect the individuality of different visions of life while learning from each other.

Comparison With Other Approaches to Grounding Citizenship Responsibility

THE COMMON SENSE VIEW OF CIVIC DUTY

The common sense view, taught in the public schools, is that simply by virtue of living in a democracy, one has civic duties. Citizenship entails obligations to contribute to the common life by paying taxes, contributing to the national defense, supporting and participating in democratic institutions, and especially by voting. In our culture so much media attention focuses on the electoral process and voting that we tend to ignore the broader and deeper understanding of the responsibilities of citizenship outlined above. We are taught that "the people" are the government, and that government legitimacy resides in "the people" because we elect our leaders. Consequently, we the people are ultimately accountable for what our government is and what it does.

This is, however, a naïve view. Governments are authorities and powers, to use biblical language. Governmental structures are good insofar as they serve the common good, respond to the people they serve, and make it possible for human life to flourish. But they are also fallen. Elites and large bureaucracies run all governments, including democratic ones. Interest groups and lobbyists with vast sums of money make more of a difference in how governments function than the ballot. Elections are won and lost based on who has the money to develop the best marketing images. In this sense, the governmental structures in North America, particularly the larger ones, are dominated by elites who are very good at protecting their own privileges and self-interests at the expense of "we the people," particularly those who are marginalized and poor. Because of the power of these elites, large numbers of people no longer participate in the electoral process in the United States.

The vote, while not irrelevant, is one of the less significant ways we contribute to the peace of the city where we dwell. The common sense civic lesson that Christians should participate like all other citizens through the electoral process gives us little moral guidance for *how* we should be responsible citizens. Such a position is unrealistic about how governments work. It assumes that the vote is what matters most. And the civic lesson that tells us we should vote gives us little or no guidance on *how* we should vote or whether we should vote when our choices are between "bad" and "still worse." The assumption that we are obligated to participate in the electoral process simple because we live in a democracy begs the question of what is responsible citizenship.

NATURAL LAW POSITIONS

1. Classic Natural Law in the Roman Catholic Tradition. Thomas Aquinas's position on natural law theory was shaped by Aristotle.

Aquinas believed that one could ascertain the ends for humans through rational reflection on human nature. This view of natural law assumes that basic moral law can be known by reason and that this moral law is universal because it is grounded in the eternal law of God. This moral law can thus be a basis for developing positive law, that is, those policies that determine how governments and citizens should act. Aquinas says, "Human law has the nature of law insofar as it partakes of right reason; and it is clear that, in this respect, it is derived from the eternal law. But insofar as it deviates from reason, it is called an unjust law, and has the nature, not of law, but of violence."[25]

This classic tradition of natural law is assumed in the 1983 National Conference Catholic Bishops Pastoral Letter on War and Peace:

> The wider civil community, although it does not share the same vision of faith, is equally bound by certain key moral principles. For all men and women find in the depth of their consciences a law written on the human heart by God. From this law reason draws moral norms.[26]

The language of the "law written on the human heart by God" is a reference to the Apostle Paul's view in Romans 2:15 (cf. also Ps. 37:31; 40:8; Jer. 31:33). The Reformers Luther and Calvin, while not developing an Aristotelian view of natural law like Aquinas, also continued the classic tradition. John Calvin believed that human sin had not extinguished the basic law of God written on the heart. Further, this basic moral law was equivalent to the Decalogue. Calvin asserted, therefore, that even pagan civil governments had a basic knowledge of the moral law by which to govern even though knowledge of this moral law had been "partly weakened and partly corrupted, so that its misshapen ruins appear."[27]

Can an adequate view of Christian citizenship be grounded in this minimalist "law written on the heart" that is common to all human beings? Classic natural law theory raises two issues. It fails to account adequately for particularity and cultural diversity. Can it be said that there is a common moral law that can be known by all persons through the exercise of reason? Is reason not always culturally situated and particular?

The second problem is related to the first. In order to develop a universal moral law, the principles of moral law inevitably tend to become formal and abstract, without the richness of specific cultural content. The distinctive contribution of Christian ethics is lost when the church resorts to such a formal and minimalist ethic. Because the classic natural law position develops a foundation for citizenship by abstracting universal moral concepts, the distinctive vision of shalom of an alternative vision is minimized and the distinctive contribution Christians can make to public moral discourse is lost. The alternative position I am developing in this book is that we can develop a basic civic responsibility in a pluralistic cultural context where people do not share a common worldview.

2. *Post-Enlightenment Views of Natural Law.* Liberalism is the philosophy that has most shaped modern American political thought. Its basic underlying premise is commitment to the freedom of the individual. Liberal ideology has two key intellectual sources: the Protestant tradition (particularly Puritanism) and the secular Enlightenment. Both of these intellectual traditions are correlated with the rise of the middle class and its aspirations for freedom from the bondage of tradition.[28]

In the modern era, natural law theories or their equivalents are linked less to explicit theological claims than classic natural law theory. The Declaration of Independence (1776) and the French Revolution Declaration of the Rights of Man (1789) were based on a concept of individual rights grounded in nature. Whether in Locke's version or Rousseau's version, these rights belonged to nature prior to the social contract or formation of human society. Since human beings are rational, and these rights are grounded in nature, which is rational, natural rights are self-evident. And so we have the familiar words of the Declaration of Independence: "We hold these truths to be self-evident that all men are endowed by their creator with certain inalienable rights."

In the area of politics, this classic liberal philosophy led to the emphasis on the freedom of conscience and religious tolerance, freedom of speech and the press, and the right of opposition to tyranny. In economics, it meant a view of limited government. Ownership of property was protected and the right to pursue individual economic self-interest was subject only to the impersonal rule of the market. The modern welfare state has adapted classic liberalism by placing a stronger emphasis on the role of government. The core value of the individual, however, remains the underlying premise: "achieving the free expression of the individual personality by upholding those institutions that foster and protect free expression."[29] Government is the one institution that can enable persons to achieve such freedom.

In their study of the middle class in the United States, the authors of *Habits of the Heart* illuminate the negative consequences of this individualism. The U.S. middle class is convinced that freedom is a value they all want, but they do not know toward what end this freedom should be directed. People can agree on a minimalist idea of procedural justice, that political processes should be fair and that every individual should have equal opportunity to pursue whatever goals they want that are compatible with the freedom of others. But there is no substantive moral framework. What should we commit our lives to substantively and why? What is our freedom *for*? This individualism translates into the loss of any substantive view of justice. The question of what the common life should look like is unanswerable for many because a liberal theory is incapable of a vision for the common life apart from the protection of freedom. Liberalism is incapable of providing a substantive view of the common good.[30]

John Rawls's *A Theory of Justice* is a kind of natural law theory in this liberal tradition, which begins with the primacy of the individual. The essential components of his theory are: (1) that a theory of justice can be arrived at by reason, and (2) that these principles of justice can serve as norms for civil society. Rawls proposes that we put ourselves in an "original position" behind a "veil of ignorance" to arrive at principles of justice. We should put ourselves in a position where we do not know what our circumstances will be as individuals, whether rich or poor, black or white, powerful or weak. He asks, then, to what principles of justice we would agree. The two principles Rawls arrives at are: (1) "equal right to the most extensive liberty compatible with a similar liberty for others,"[31] and (2) "social and economic inequalities are to be arranged so that they are both (a) to the greatest benefit of the least advantaged and (b) attached to offices and positions upon all under conditions of fair equality of opportunity."[32]

Though Rawls claims to arrive at his principles of justice through a purely detached rational process behind a "veil of ignorance," Rawls's theory turns out to be a rational defense of liberalism built on industrial capitalism's theory of justice. His position "corresponds strikingly to the context in which the position was developed."[33] The claim to be a universal theory of justice is actually a proposal that reflects one particular cultural perspective. Rawls's theory presupposes the Enlightenment liberalism that begins with the individual—the particular kind of individual who operates out of rational self-interest. The primary obligation of the state is to preserve and protect the rights of this individual. The liberal concept of freedom is based on the premise that an individual's right to choose should be protected above all and that it is compatible with liberty for others.

A number of the values of liberalism overlap with a Christian vision of life. There is an analogy between a vision of the church and particularly those values that affirm respect for the dignity of the individual: freedom of conscience, religious tolerance, and protection of freedom of speech. Protection of the right to assembly and to hold views contrary to the dominant values of the culture (such as conscientious objection to war) is a precious value that overlaps with emphases in liberal philosophy.

However, in a Christian vision, the protection of the individual is grounded not in "inalienable natural rights," but in several theological claims. One of these claims is that each person is created in the image of God. A second is the way the individual and community are balanced in a Trinitarian vision that affirms the individual "persons" in the Trinity while seeing them in their relationship.[34] A third theological conviction is that God's love and grace are made available to all humans beings, even the most wicked. This Christian vision of God's love and grace, which values all humans, is a more universal grounding of the value and dignity of the individual than modern liberalism, with its emphasis on our common dignity in reason. Because God loves all people, we can recognize the full humanity and dignity of each individual person, even those whose reason has been captivated by irrational desire. Enemies are to be loved because they are recipients of God's love. They do not forfeit their right to life and respect.

Another weaknesse of liberal philosophy is that it fails to take into account adequately that we are social beings—that we are joined to each other in a common solidarity of mutuality. The individual is defined by rational self-interest, rather than by mutuality and care for each other. If a view of citizenship is informed by a vision of the church, then by analogy we will develop a political philosophy that takes into account our corporate identity, that we belong to each other. We find our meaning and identity in relationship. The very being of God is relational, as we saw in the development of the Trinity in chapter four. The social is not simply a secondary or derived entity that arises out of our individuality. Our very being as individuals is integrally linked with our social nature. Emphasis on the individual at the expense of community leads to serious weaknesses in ethical reasoning. Since individual self-interest is the driving motivation of liberal politics and economics, it is difficult to sustain the development of policies whose goal is the common good.

Liberal philosophy also fails to take into account adequately the problem of sin, particularly the way in which corporate interests shape social reality. Individuals do not have an even playing field. Our identity is shaped by factors such as class and race. To work for the common good, we need to consider not only individual freedom, but also how corporate structures continue to perpetuate racism, poverty, and the assault on the earth. These structures must be modified to allow life to flourish, both for individuals and for the community.

Stephen Mott argues that liberalism places too much confidence in reason and education. Liberalism veils the "hard struggle that justice requires. ... [It] also neglects the fact that social transformation is not possible without a transformation of human beings."[35] We noted this critique earlier in discussing the church. The good society requires moral formation of persons. This presupposes the existence of communities of character and vision, the soil for individuals' formation.

3. The Politics of Remedial Action. One social philosophy has had a profound effect on Christian understandings of citizenship: accepting the structures of the fallen order as ordained by God. This position has its origin in the thought of the Apostle Paul in Romans 13:1-7 and is generally more "conservative." In a world of sin, the role of government is to protect the good and punish the evil. Paul views the one who carries the "sword," the symbol of judicial authority, "as the servant of God to execute wrath on the wrongdoer" (Rom. 13:4).

This view of government as a remedial institution was developed first most thoroughly in the early fifth century by St. Augustine. As stated earlier, Augustine's thought is structured around the idea of two cities—the heavenly, where love is oriented to God; and the earthly, where love is oriented toward what is less than God. Because of the permanent condition of the human fallen state, these two cities will remain commingled with each other until the return of Christ. Through the operation of God's providence, the state provides some modicum of peace and order in the interim until the final judgment, when the heavenly city triumphs. Herbert Deane summarizes Augustine's view:

> The state ... is an external order; the peace that it maintains is external peace—the absence, or at least the diminution, of overt violence. The state is also a coercive order, maintained by the use of force and relying on the fear of pain as its major sanction for compliance to its commands. ... It does not seek to make men truly good or virtuous. ... It attempts ... to restrain its citizens from performing certain kinds of harmful and criminal acts.[36]

Martin Luther continued the Augustinian tradition. He said that it is God's will that the sword and secular law be used for the punishment of the wicked and the protection of the upright.[37] Luther divided persons into two classes, the righteous and the unrighteous. He said that if all were true Christians, we would have no need of civil government. God has ordained two governments, the spiritual and secular. The one produces true piety; the other brings about "external peace and prevents evil deeds; neither is sufficient in the world without the other."[38]

For Luther, Christians carry out God's love and care for the world by serving the needs of their neighbors through the administration of secular government. Through the instrument of the sword, the good are protected from the evil. The duty of the prince—and of his hangman, if necessary—is to use the sword to restrain evil. Thus subjects of the prince are to obey him and to serve in a just war, when necessary to restrain evil. Particularly in Lutheranism, with its emphasis on obedience to authority, this philosophy functioned conservatively to protect the established order. Luther saw no role for government, as Calvin did, to create a holy commonwealth.[39]

My critique of this point of view is threefold. Its interpretation of Romans 13: 1-7 in legitimating its position is weak. Its understanding of the function of the sword in relationship to a view of God is problematic. And its theological view of government as an order of the fall is narrow.

1. Romans 13:1-7. As inheritors of the Constantinian synthesis of church and society, both Augustine and Luther interpreted Romans 13:1-7 as legitimating the sword as a necessity in a world of sin and, therefore, a necessary tool in the hands of Christians to provide order in a world of sin.

The central message of Romans is that good news has come into the world in Christ. Romans 12 calls on Christians not to be conformed to the world, but to operate by a different standard in the world. In the context of what precedes and follows Romans 13:1-7, Paul calls on Christians to love their enemies, to leave the wrath of the sword to God. In the larger context of the book of Romans, Paul is calling for Christians to love their enemies and not to take up the sword.

Romans 13 does not support the preservation of any particular government, no matter how oppressive or violent. Christians should not be tempted to overthrow Rome with violence. They are to respect the state, even the state of pagan Rome. Christians who have heard the call of Christ are to respect that order as they seek to live by another standard, the call of Christ to love their enemies.[40] To be subject to or to submit to the authorities means to respect their authority, to allow oneself as citizen to come under the rule of law even if that means to suffer for one's convictions. However, being subject does not mean always obeying the state. It is possible to be subject even in an act of civil disobedience, if one commits the act of disobedience openly and is willing to submit to the consequences of one's action. In other words, Romans 13 does not justify passive compliance with anything a state does; it might require civil disobedience and nonviolent resistance.

2. Does the Sword Legitimate Violent Force? What does Paul mean that government is a servant of God to protect the good and punish the evil? Paul is referring to the pagan Roman state. Just prior to this passage he has urged the believers to give food and drink to their enemies and to overcome evil with good (Rom. 12:20-21), so it would be a contradiction for him now to tell them to take up the sword to protect the good and punish the evil. In a world of sin, God providentially uses the pagan state to order human life. The sword symbolizes the judicial authority of government. This is a fact of governments: they have authority and exercise their authority through the use of coercive force. The sword is not a symbol for the approval of war or of capital punishment.

Theologically speaking, Paul's claim is that nothing in the world, including the sword, falls outside of God's providential ordering. Even the freely chosen wrath of people can work to serve God's purposes in the universe, though God does not will or approve of wrathful behavior. For instance, by crucifying Jesus, Pilate unwittingly served God's cause of human salvation.

In our contemporary world, the use of violent force to solve problems is paradoxical. While it may provide some limited kind of order or accomplish limited short-range goals, the resort to armed force, even in defense of just causes and for the sake of order, perpetuates the cycle of violence. For example, it is clear now that the 1991 Persian Gulf War did not secure the promised new world order, nor did it provide even a minimum of stable order and justice in the Middle East. The short-run gains, such as expelling the Iraqis from Kuwait, are being offset by the long-term consequences. Thousands of people met death and destruction. The destruction of the infrastructure of Iraq has turned it into a third world country. The very resort to violence undermines the global political goal of nonviolent conflict resolution. The war continued the long history of mutual humiliation and hatred between Muslims and non-Muslims. The environment was destroyed, thousands of refugees were created, and the Israeli/Palestinian conflict was ignored. Above all, the war did not solve the persistent problem of biological and chemical weapons.

To summarize, God does not will the sword of government. There is no other God who wills that some people exercise the sword, while other people, the disciples of Christ, practice nonviolence.

3. *Need for a Broader View of Civil Government.* To resolve the question of Christian civil responsibility, we must develop a theological perspective on government that encompasses a broad range of theological perspectives. If Jesus Christ is the root metaphor for an understanding of God, there is no other "hand" of God, no violent hand completely contrary to the God revealed in Christ. God wills for all human beings to live peaceably with each other. The purpose of government is to order people's common life together. Civil government is not just an institution that arises as a result of human sin; it is also inherent to God's good creation, designed to order human social life. Though the "politics of remedial action" should keep us sober and realistic about the sinful human condition, a more complete theological understanding of citizenship should keep in mind four theological motifs that contribute to our view of civil government.

First, government is an institution created by human beings. It reflects the creativity given by God to humans to order our lives together as good stewards of God's creation. The purpose of politics is to coordinate human social behavior in service of the common good.

Second, governments are nevertheless institutions corrupted by sin. The sword is a sign of that fallenness. It is an empirical fact that political institutions resort either to the threat of force or to its actual use in order to preserve their function. But the God-intended function or essence of politics is to order human behavior in service of the common good. The sword is not the essence of government, for the purpose of the sword lies only in serving the common good. Those who make the sword the essence of government turn things upside-down and make secondary the primary, defining role of civil government.

It is crucial that Christians have an adequate doctrine of sin. But this doctrine of sin should not be self-serving. An adequate doctrine of sin will recognize that any nation is capable of self-righteousness and pride, self-deception about its motives, and a tendency to abuse violent force. Even the noble commitment to democracy can be pursued arrogantly and self-righteously, without regard for historical conditions. The attempt to impose democracy by violent force has produced terrible suffering. Reinhold Niebuhr has pointed out how frequently self-interest, deceit, and arrogance are clothed or masked in high-sounding moral idealism. It is particularly difficult for the church to speak the truth when its own nation is at war, since the tendency of political leaders who support the war is to paint the enemy as totally evil and their own motives as pure. The church that exercises its civic responsibility will, even if unpopular, call attention to the truth in Jesus statement: "Why do you see the speck that is in your brother's eye, and not notice the log in your own eye?" (Matt. 7:3).

Third, from the standpoint of the doctrine of redemption, politics must be transformed to serve its God-intended function. This is the distinctive contribution made by a Christian interpretation of political institutions. The "sword" function of government dare not legitimate the inevitability of the status quo. The prevalence of the sword must be reduced in order to serve human ends without resort to force. The Christian seeks to be involved in the political process in practical ways that can contribute to the just and peaceful resolution of conflict. For example, I have participated the last several years in the development of a just peacemaking theory. This is the work of twenty-three scholars—mostly Christian ethicists, along with well-known international relations scholars, peace activists, and conflict resolution practitioners—all of whom have specialized in peacemaking. The theory does not replace just war theory or pacifism, but it is an attempt to identify actual practices that contribute to the peaceful and just resolution of conflict. The ten practices we have identified are the following:

1. Support nonviolent direct action;
2. take indepdendent initiatives to reduce threat;
3. use cooperative conflict resolution;
4. acknowledge responsiblity for conflict and injustice and seek repentance and forgiveness;
5. advance democracy, human rights, and religious liberty;
6. foster just and sustainiable economic development;
7. work with emerging cooperative forces in the international system;
8. strengthen the United Nations and international efforts for cooperation and human rights;
9. reduce offensive weapons and weapons trade;
10. encourage grassroots peacemaking groups and voluntary associations.[41]

Fourth, since perfect redemption is an eschatological hope that has not yet been fully realized in history, the redemptive process is therefore incomplete. This important perspective on citizenship restrains utopian fanaticism. We need to accept the limits of what humans can accomplish in history. As Stephen Mott puts it: "The fallen inheritance of the human race cannot be removed in a couple of generations—or in many generations. It will not be removed in history. The only power to do so is Christ's, which non-Christians reject and Christians neglect."[42] Nevertheless, the church lives in the world as a new society to bring to civil government a vision for a new redemptive order. It cannot do this in a triumphalist way, but in modesty and humility, aware of its own need for repentance.[43]

God calls on Christians who seek the peace of the city where they dwell *not* to withdraw from participation in government simply because it is the will of God that governments use the sword (as some Mennonites have done). The church should not try to impose a utopian vision on the world (as Marxism does). Rather, it should be a creative witness to government and within governmental structures for justice, and it should work to resolve conflict nonviolently. Many persons in the dominant culture regard such a goal as unrealistic or irrelevant. It is true that nonviolent solutions may not always be readily apparent. But this is true when violent force is used as well. Christian participation is not primarily based on the ability to predict success, but on hope in the kingdom of God, the coming of God's rule in Christ through persuasive love. The Christian believes that the future is secured nonviolently. That is what it means to believe that the Lamb that was slain is the Lord of history.[44]

CITIZENS OF A HOLY COMMONWEALTH

There is a sharp tension in American society today between the liberal view of citizenship we described above, which places primary emphasis on freedom of the individual, and the position we are about to describe, which envisions a holy commonwealth, a good society in which freedom is one value alongside others. This tension emerges in the intense debates about abortion and whether public prayer should be allowed in public schools. Though the debate on abortion is often framed in terms of "rights" language, those who hold this position in fact do not place the highest value on freedom to choose, but on the sanctity of unborn life. In their vision of the good society, the freedom of the individual is restricted in order to uphold other values. The same persons argue that a good society is one in which we should acknowledge our dependence as a society upon God. So the rights of individuals or groups that oppose public prayer in public institutions can be compromised by the general social ethos of the majority that believes in God and desires to acknowledge that belief in public prayer. Some want to place limits on pornography or nude dancing. In a good society, it is argued, the right of an individual to look at and read what they want should be overridden by general societal values of wholesome sexuality and decency.

The deep contradiction in American society is that, depending on the issue, people switch sides between a liberal view of human freedom and a vision for a holy commonwealth. When it comes to issues like gun control, economic freedom versus government regulation, environmental policy, or affirmative action, those who wish to *restrict* human freedom on issues like abortion and prayer appeal to the *rights* of individuals to do what they want without government interference. Alternatively, persons who argue for freedom of choice on abortion or sexual expression shift the grounds of their argument on issues like economic justice or environmental quality, where, they argue, the regulation of freedom is appropriate in the name of the good society.

The vision of a holy commonwealth is as deeply embedded in the American moral fabric as is the "rights" language of the Enlightenment. It has its roots in the Calvinist and Puritan traditions described above. The complexity of the moral fabric that informs citizenship in American society is complicated even further by the believers church tradition, which draws its inspiration from neither the Enlightenment nor a Calvinist vision of the holy commonwealth. Quaker William Penn and Baptist Roger Williams diverged from the establishment Puritans of the Massachusetts Bay Colony in defending religious liberty and toleration.

Failure to understand this divergence in perspective contributes to the confusion in the contemporary debates about abortion and prayer in the schools. Persons shaped by these different traditions may share an abhorrence for the widespread practice of abortion while disagreeing whether one should prevent abortion through the force of law. Those in the believers church tradition, when consistent with their view of religious liberty, prefer to convince persons of the sanctity of life through witness or persuasion. Those influenced more by the establishment Puritan stream are prepared to use the force of law to bring about compliance. This divergence is often not understood. "Freedom of choice," with its roots in Enlightenment liberalism, is confused with opposition toward the legislation of morality out of believers church assumptions.[45] While some oppose prayer in the public schools on grounds of religious liberty, believers churches oppose it because it reflects a form of religious establishment rather than an expression of voluntary commitment.[46]

In the debates about these issues in American society, reasons people give for positions often involve a mix of arguments. Sometimes people are simply confused. There is a "good" confusion that comes from the mixing of the grounds for moral argument. This mixing arises from the fact that there is a convergence between some of the ideals of Enlightenment liberalism and believers church convictions. Although Stanley Hauerwas sees Enlightenment liberalism as an unmitigated evil,[47] I take the subtler and more nuanced position developed by Glen H. Stassen. The Baptist Richard Overton shows how one can bring together different streams of moral argument. Stassen writes:

> The story of his creative discovery of the language of human rights comes out of Christian and specifically Mennonite and Baptist faith in dialogue with pluralistic political, class, and faith loyalties. Overton does not "give up" his biblically based ethic. He grounds his human rights ethic in biblical faith. At the same time he translates his biblically based ethic into a language persons of other faiths or unfaiths can speak and uses both languages to analyze our empirical social experience and social struggles for human rights. In our pluralistic world, our very selfhoods are multilingual: We belong to various communities, and translate our concerns into the language of those communities as we move from one community to another.[48]

THE CONTRIBUTION OF SOCIALISM

Socialism has taken many forms.[49] We take up here only one form, the vision of Karl Marx. Karl Marx's passion for justice is in several ways consistent with the vision of justice in the Bible.[50] Marx's concern for the disadvantaged is biblical. His concern for the plight of workers in the context of the industrial revolution parallels biblical themes. The passion for the poor and weak is deeply rooted in the story of the Exodus. The passion for justice is one the central themes in such Hebrew prophets as Micah and Amos.

> Therefore because you trample on the poor
>> and take from them levies of grain,
> you have built houses of hewn stone,
>> but you shall not live in them;
> you have planted pleasant vineyards,
>> but you shall not drink their wine.
> For I know how many are your transgressions,
>> and how great are your sins—
> you who afflict the righteous, who take a bribe,
>> and push aside the needy in the gate.
> Therefore the prudent will keep silent in such a time;
>> for it is an evil time. ...

But let justice roll down like waters,
    and righteousness like an ever-flowing stream.
        (Amos 5:11-13, 24)

The theme of the Jubilee in Leviticus 25 is based on the premise that the earth belongs to the Lord. The Jubilee entails the redistribution of land and capital (the cancellation of debts) to ensure that basic human needs are met and that persons not be permanently dispossessed. In the Gospel of Luke, Jesus picked up the same theme in the inaugural message at the synagogue at Nazareth that begins his ministry.

The Spirit of the Lord is upon me,
    because he has anointed me
        to bring good news to the poor. (Luke 4:18)

Marx's emphasis on the distribution of material resources in order to meet human need is also biblical. Marx's slogan, "from each according to his ability, to each according to his needs," echoes a theme in the book of Acts, where the coming of the Spirit in the new community led to the sharing of material resources as each had need. "All who believed were together and had all things in common; they would sell their possessions and goods and distribute the proceeds to all, as any had need" (Acts 2:44-45). This is repeated in Acts 4.

> Now the whole group of those who believed were of one heart and soul, and no one claimed private ownership of any possessions, but everything they owned was held in common. With great power the apostles gave their testimony to the resurrection of the Lord Jesus, and great grace was upon them all. There was not a needy person among them, for as many as owned lands or houses sold them and brought the proceeds of what was sold. They laid it at the apostles' feet, and it was distributed to each as any had need. (Acts 4:32-35)

In response to the famine in Judea, "the disciples determined that according to their ability, each would send relief to the believers living in Judea" (Acts 11:29).

In addition to distributive justice, Marx also emphasized commutative justice. Economic exchange should be reciprocal so that the interests of each party are met. If power resides in the hands of the few at the expense of the many, exploitation results. For Marx, commutative justice was more than simply meeting the self-interest of both parties. "Justice requires mutuality in which the self-realization of the other party is sought. ... Mutuality insures individual participation in communal control over the processes of social life and over social production."[51]

Marx supported democracy, but others later exploited other dimensions of his thought to produce the terror of communism. According to Mott, when Marx used the unfortunate and reckless phrase, "the class dictatorship of the proletariat," "dictatorship did not have the pejorative associations that is has for us. It meant the direction of society by the proletariat, who were the majority."[52] Nevertheless, Marx did not have an adequate ethic of means. With his emphasis on the goal of distributive justice and his utopian vision of a new communist society, he did not reflect sufficiently enough on how means and ends are interconnected—that the means used are the ends in the making. Marx's ethical reasoning was connected to his inadequate view of human nature. Marx believed that structural change would change people and produce the good society. As Mott puts it, "Marx's anticipated social framework is not sufficient for the continuing occurrence of group and personal exploitation, materialism, and sloth that is inevitable because of the permanence of evil."[53]

An adequate Christian view of citizenship must take seriously the biblical (and Marxist) passion for justice. Yet it must also recognize that in an imperfect world, complete justice is not possible. One of the deep roots of violent conflict in our world is the anger and hatred that is expressed when those who have been exploited rise up against their oppressors. In the process, new victims are created and the cycle of violence is perpetuated. Though Christians must work for justice, the unjust deeds of the past cannot be erased.

The injustice done to blacks, to Jews during the holocaust, to Hutus and Tutsis in Rwanda, or to Serbians and Bosnians in the former Yugoslavia cannot ever be completely corrected. The memory and continued impact of the injustice can be carried for generations. A Christian view of citizenship can contribute to politics the possibility of a community beyond the limited categories of oppressor and oppressed. We see this vision in Martin Luther King Jr.'s vision of the "beloved community," which led King to seek reconciliation with his opponents. Though he did not shrink from his passion for justice, justice in King was tempered by love. Forgiveness is essential to a politics of healing.

> Without being forgiven, released from the consequences of what
> we have done, our capacity to act would, as it were, be confined
> to one single deed from which we could never recover; we would

remain the victims of its consequences forever, not unlike the sorcerer's apprentice who lacks the magic formula to break the spell.[54]

In Jesus Christ we have a model of one who identified with the poor and the marginal in the cross while offering forgiveness to his enemies. So justice must be tempered by or understood in the light of love. As put by Miroslav Volf: "In the presence of God our rage over injustice may give way to forgiveness, which in turn will make the search for justice *for all* possible. If forgiveness does take place it will be but an echo of the forgiveness granted by the just and loving God."[55]

GUIDELINES FOR CHRISTIAN CITIZENSHIP

The following is a partial list of guidelines for Christian citizenship. Since many were discussed earlier, we simply summarize them here. These axioms are not exhaustive. Persons of other religions or of secular persuasion will also agree with a number of these guidelines. The ecclesiological framework of my view does not rule out the possibility of significant agreement with those who are not church members. If the God made most vivid in Jesus Christ is indeed God of the cosmos and all peoples, which I claim, and if basic moral knowledge is not extinguished by human sin, which I also claim, then we should expect areas of agreement with persons who are not members of the church.

Balance of Individual Dignity and Community

The church respects the individual who is a member by voluntary choice based on conviction. The individual dignity of each person is affirmed by the concept that each person is created in the image of God and that God offers the free grace of God's love to each individual. To be a member of the church means to belong to a "body," to enter a relationship of mutuality and solidarity in that body. The church is a body where the well-being of the whole and the needs of each member are of paramount concern. By analogy, Christian citizens seek a proper balance between respect for individual dignity and the well-being of the community as a whole. Christians should avoid both autonomous individualism and repressive forms of collectivism.

We need to act out of a sense of corporate identity, of understanding at the deepest level that in God we belong to the earth and to each other. Dostoyevsky powerfully expresses this solidarity with all being, both in its wholeness and in its brokenness, in his great novel, *The Brothers Karamazov*. In reflecting on the experiences of his life, Father Zossima says that the key to redemption is that we acknowledge our corporate identity and take responsibility for the sin and guilt of all. "We are responsible to all for all, apart from our own sins."[56] Zossima goes on to lament the individuality and isolation he finds all around.

> Everywhere in these days men have, in their mockery, ceased to understand that the true security is to be found in social solidarity rather than in isolated individual effort.[57]

> There is only one means of salvation, then take yourself and make yourself responsible for all men's sins, ... for as soon as you sincerely make yourself responsible for everything and for all men, you will see at once that it is really so, and that you are to blame for every one and for all things.[58]

This insight has direct relevance for how we deal with the historical memory of slavery and its consequences in the United States and with the corporate reality of racism with all its destructive consequences. If we truly belong to each other, this problem is *my* problem as a white person, even though my ancestors did not arrive in America until the 1870s. Because blacks and whites are called to live in solidarity with each other, the destructive consequences wreaked on blacks by the historical experience of slavery and by its memory represent a history for which I am also responsible. Healing can come only if we all take responsibility for the sin and guilt we share when we own the history of slavery and racism as "our" history.

If we are participants in the triune God, then the memory of the "sixty million and more" to whom Toni Morrison dedicated her novel *Beloved* belong to the memory of God and therefore to us. "It was a story not to pass on. ... So they forgot her. Like an unpleasant dream during a troubling sleep. ..."[59] And yet Morrison told the story of Beloved, whose story becomes part of our memory and our responsibility for healing. Morrison's quote from the book of Romans at the beginning of her novel is a call to begin the journey of healing: "I will call them my people, which were not my people; and her beloved, which was not beloved" (Rom. 9:25, KJV).

Dostoyevsky's insight of our profound solidarity with all being is expressed in his account of Alyosha's conversion after Alyosha leaves the room that contained the coffin of his dead hero, Father Zossima.

> His soul, overflowing with rapture, yearned for freedom, space, openness. The vault of heaven, full of soft, shining stars, stretched vast and fathomless above him. The Milky Way ran in two pale streams from the zenith to the horizon. The fresh, motionless, still night enfolded the earth. The white towers and golden domes of

the cathedral gleamed out against the sapphire sky. The gorgeous autumn flowers, in the beds round the house, were slumbering till morning. The silence of earth seemed to melt into the silence of the heavens. The mystery of earth was one with the mystery of the stars. ...

Alyosha stood, gazed, and suddenly threw himself down on the earth. He did not know why he embraced it. He could not have told why he longed so irresistibly to kiss it, to kiss it all. But he kissed it weeping, sobbing and watering it with his tears, and vowed passionately to love it, to love it for ever and ever. "Water the earth with the tears of your joy and love those tears," echoed in his soul. What was he weeping over? Oh! In his rapture he was weeping even over those stars, which were shining to him from the abyss of space, and "he was not ashamed of that ecstasy." There seemed to be threads from all those innumerable worlds of God, linking his soul to them, and it was trembling all over "in contact with other worlds." He longed to forgive every one and for everything, and to beg forgiveness. Oh, not for himself, but for all men, for all and for everything. "And others are praying for me too," echoed again in his soul. But with every instant he felt clearly and, as it were, tangibly, that something firm and unshakable as that vault of heaven had entered into his soul. It was as though some idea had seized the sovereignty of his mind—and it was for all his life and for ever and ever. He had fallen on the earth a weak boy, but he rose up a resolute champion, and he knew and felt it suddenly at the very moment of his ecstasy. And never, never, all his life long, could Alyosha forget that minute.[60]

Compassion and Wholeness Toward the Weak and Powerless

The church is driven by compassion, based on the Jesus story and the vision of the prophets, to seek wholeness in all dimensions of life on earth. This concern for people's well-being should lead the church to work actively in the public arena against public policies that cater to the self-interest of the powerful and wealthy at the expense of the poor and less powerful. Justice in the biblical story is decisively tilted toward concern for the poor and the voiceless in society. The church should ask of every social policy, Who decides and who benefits? The church must have as one of its highest priorities that it be an advocate, a voice for the weakest and most vulnerable members of society.

The church's view of economic justice has two sources: the biblical narrative, which expresses again and again God's compassion for the poor, and a vision of its own common life, its commitment to mutual aid for those within its own midst who are in need. In the new society, the church, the resources of the community should be made available to meet the basic needs of members who have suffered loss or whose life conditions have created severe hardship. In the early church, the principle of mutual aid was evident when the community gathered their resources for famine relief for the church in Jerusalem.

By analogy, compassion should extend beyond the boundaries of the church. Social justice is not based primarily on merit, on the inevitable consequences of the operation of a free market, or on the greatest good for the greatest number. Justice is based on basic needs. It is the obligation of a society to care for every member of the society because everyone is a child of God. Private property is not an absolute to dispose of as one sees fit. The earth belongs to God for the benefit of all God's creatures. The church must therefore favor social policies that enhance the basic well-being of all members of the society, not those based primarily on the preservation of individual self-interest.[61]

Love and the Practice of Forgiveness

However, the passion for justice must be tempered by love. Perfect justice is not possible in a fallen world. The cycles of rage and violence can be broken only by a politics that transcends the categories of oppressor and oppressed. The creation of a "beloved community," to use Martin Luther King Jr.'s phrase, requires forgiveness and a love that can embrace even the enemy.

Religious Liberty

The church is a voluntary society based on the freedom to respond noncoercively to God's love. Both because of its understanding of freedom as a correlate of love and its understanding of community as a voluntary society, the church must support public policies that protect religious liberty and the exercise of conscience. Mennonites have become involved in politics for this principle to protect their own community interest. In recent times, they have also supported liberty of conscience for persons of secular or humanitarian orientation.[62] As noted above, Glen Stassen argues that "the concept and the term 'human rights' originated more than a half-century prior to the Enlightenment and the French Revolution, among the free churches at the time of the Puritan Revolution, as an affirmation of the religious liberty of all persons.[63]

Equality

In Christ there is neither Jew nor Greek, slave nor free, male nor female (Gal. 3:28). Baptism places all persons in equal status before

God. This vision of the church has significant implications for the church's involvement in society. John H. Yoder writes,

> Baptism inducts persons into a new people, and one of the distinguishing marks of this new people is that all prior given or chosen definitions of identity are transcended. ... The concrete social-functional meaning of these statements is that social definitions based upon class and category are no longer basic.[64]

From this ecclesial vision, one can derive guidelines that challenge social policies that promote discriminatory patterns of sexism, racism, and classism based on economic or educational status.

Respect for the Contribution of Each Person to the Public Good

Each member of the church is valued and has gifts for building up the entire community. Yoder suggests what this might mean ethically beyond the boundaries of the church.[65] The Christian seeks to support a workplace where the dignity and contribution of each person are valued. This can apply to a business or a corporation where the workers participate in the decision-making process. In a school setting, instead of a top-down management, one can imagine a more participatory role for teachers and parents. There is evidence that schools perform better where there is site-based management, rather than control of schools by administrators far removed from the decisions that affect the teachers, parents, and students.

Restorative Justice

Chapter five identified the reconciling process the church is called to practice in order to deal with the sinner (Matt. 18:15-18). The presupposition of this reconciling process is the good news of compassion, which comes to people who do not deserve it. The church knows that Christians are sinners who deserve death from the perspective of God's righteousness and justice. Yet God has compassion and has given people the opportunity to repent. In the reconciling process, the church refuses to end a conversation with a deviant member until he or she refuses to listen. So by analogy the church works to bring healing to "rehabilitate" rather than destroy through capital punishment those who have done such a dastardly deed as to deserve death.[66]

Because of the church's compassion for victims of evil, it will also work for the development of *restorative* justice in society. A society that practices restorative justice recognizes that when a victim is violated, that violation must be acknowledged and confessed. Genuine repentance for the violation must issue in a sincere desire to make amends—

if possible, through some type of reparation or the restoration of what was violated or destroyed. In cases of loss and damage to property, direct reparation may be possible. In the case of the destruction of human life, reparation is possible only indirectly: by service on behalf of the well-being of the community. This vision of restorative justice is not based on a philosophy of punishment, or justice through retribution. Rather, it is based on the conviction that healing can come only when persons begin to take responsibility for what they have done. Restoration can happen if offenders face the victims of their crime, acknowledge what they have done, and do something specific to make amends.[67]

Nonviolent Resolution of Conflict

The Sermon on the Mount summarizes a central practice and teaching of the church in the statement: "Blessed are the peacemakers, for they will be called the children of God" (Matt. 5:9).[68] Christian nonviolence is grounded in the character of God, who is revealed in the cross as one who reaches out in love to both the just and the unjust (Matt. 5:43-48). We are called to practice God's indiscriminate love, to seek the well-being of all persons, including our enemies.

Peacemaking is a central vocation of Christian citizenship. We have already identified a list of ten normative criteria for a new and just peacemaking paradigm. Christians join with many others in the world who recognize the power of nonviolent social change in the traditions of Gandhi and Martin Luther King Jr., most recently made vivid in the collapse of the Soviet empire. Christians can participate in citizen groups to resist governments when they behave unjustly, are shortsighted or arrogant, or when they think they can control the future.

Christians can help to initiate, foster, or support transforming initiatives where existing parties need support and courage to take risks to break out of the cycles that perpetuate violence and injustice. Glen Stassen develops an excellent example of how the church should do analogical thinking. Working with fourteen triads in the Sermon on the Mount, Stassen shows how each triad suggests a transforming initiative that a Christian should take in the world.[69] For example, traditional piety calls for an "eye for an eye, a tooth for a tooth." The bondage in which such persons are caught is the cycle of violent resistance. The alternative is the transforming initiative Jesus suggests of turning the other cheek, going the second mile, and giving to one who begs.

Walter Wink shows that, if we understand these actions in their first-century context, Jesus is not recommending passivity, but a creative third way between passivity and violence.[70] Stassen takes the New Testament language of transforming initiatives and "translates" it into the language of "just peacemaking." In the case of a conflict between two adversaries, Stassen argues that a transforming initiative is one where we "affirm our common security partnership with our adversaries and build an order of peace and justice that affirms their and our valid interests."[71] Stassen points out how the political pressure of citizen groups who took seriously the common interest of security of both the Soviets and the West encouraged the adoption of the "zero solution" in the late '80s on intermediate-range missiles in Europe.[72]

Citizen Movements for Social Change

Christians will participate in the building of a "global civic culture."[73] They will seek to build a worldwide citizens movement of peacemakers and peacemaking groups. Such a network of people organized to learn from each other and to act in concert holds potential to partially transcend the narrow self-interest and myopia that often characterizes groups in conflict. A citizens movement that is committed more to peacemaking than to defense of governmental or bureaucratic processes or to quick fixes in a single conflict can help keep the long view before people. Such perseverance is needed if a just peace is to emerge over generations. Citizens groups can be advocates for those voices often not heard, especially those who are poor and powerless.

A citizens network of Non-Governmental Organizations (NGOs) and International NGOs can often be a source of information that persons in positions of governmental authority lack. The primary service performed by the Office of the Mennonite Central Committee, Washington, D.C., is to circulate returned workers from around the globe to the U.S. Congress. I have seen the power and significance of such testimony on a number of issues, as well as their impact in informing their home communities. A transnational people's network has less investment in defending what has been. Persons in the movement can free our imaginations to think of alternatives to established patterns of behavior and the narrow range of options we often consider in resolving conflict. People in a citizens movement can play a servant role, working behind the scene in mediating conflict without needing to be in the limelight or to take credit. People without strong attachments to governments or who do not bring to a conflict a strong self-interest can gain the trust of parties and serve a mediating role.

Citizens networks (particularly those that are institutionalized in voluntary associations) can keep alive concerns and can sustain interest when the media and world opinion are unaware, forget, or flit about from one thing to the next. In 1993 our attention was on Somalia. In 1991 and again in 1998 it was on Iraq. Churches can serve a special role in nurturing a spirituality that sustains courage when just peacemaking is unpopular, hope when despair or cynicism is tempting, and a sense of grace and the possibility of forgiveness when just peacemaking fails.[74]

A Transnational Network
that Transcends Boundaries of Nation States

Christian citizens should challenge the idolatry of an exclusive national identity. As the body of Christ, the church represents a transnational network. As the Epistle to Diognetus puts it, "every foreign land is to them a fatherland, and every fatherland a foreign land." If the church were to take its identity as a transnational reality more seriously, it would challenge the idolization of nations that use religious symbols to sanctify national ideology and practice. The loss of a sense of the church as a transnational body is most evident when Christians kill each other in war after war, putting the lie to their profession of oneness in Christ.

The inability to think straight about identity is a great failure of American evangelicalism. The scandal is that so many American evangelical statements are made or written for Americans. Such nationalistic focus distresses brothers and sisters in the faith in other lands by not taking them into account. One blatant example of this failure is with respect to the Middle East. Most evangelical statements simply ignore Arab brothers and sisters in Christ. Christian Zionism legitimates Israeli nationalism and the repression of Palestinians in the name of speculative projections about how God's kingdom is expected to come in the future.

Many evangelicals defend capitalism as if it were God-ordained. They defend American military power in the world as a nonbiblical secularist humanist might defend the politics of "realism." Such views are so dominant it is hard to see distinctions between believers and non-Christian political conservatives. The forty-eight-page National Association of Evangelicals guidelines, "Peace, Freedom and Security," has a biblical section of just three pages, mostly refuting pacifism. But it is full of terms like *values, responsibility, complexity, democracy,* and *human rights*—"terms that seem to be more appropriate for the vocabulary of 'secular humanism' than of biblical theology."[75] As a consequence, most evangelicals in America bless American foreign policy.

Christians are rarely able to transcend what is in the national economic and political interest because they have become secularized by the prevailing values of capitalism and power politics.

Support for Democracy

Although Christians may support democracy, they do not do it in the way the U.S. State Department uses its power to support democracy in the world, including the occasional use of military force. We support it not from the standpoint of the Constantinian assumption that dominance and power are what shapes the world. Our framework is an alternative community, which is not in a position to impose its form of democracy on the world. Instead, its ethic is the practice of mutual servanthood.

The support of democracy should be modest. We are simply reflecting the ecclesiological experience of dialogical liberty in the context of the church, where all are free to speak and everyone is heard in the process of discernment and decision-making—a process marked not by the exercise of coercive power, but by the free exchange of ideas. Behind this process is the conviction that human beings really can listen to each other and make decisions and that sober realism suggests that we need each other to correct the partial insights and self-interest of individual persons. Reinhold Niebuhr caught this dialectic in his famous statement, "Man's capacity for justice makes democracy possible; but man's inclination to injustice makes democracy necessary."[76] We can rephrase Niebuhr's insight for an ecclesiology as follows: The human capacity for dialogue makes democracy possible, but the human inclination to partial knowledge and self-serving ideas makes democracy necessary.

Based on this understanding of how a "new" society should work, we support those processes of governance in the broader culture that reflect a similar process of decision-making. As John H. Yoder remarks, "There is widely recognized evidence for a historic link between the Christian congregation [as a prototype] and the town meeting, between the Christian hermeneutic of dialogue in the Holy Spirit and free speech and parliament."[77]

CONCLUSION

These guidelines are by no means complete. They are meant to illustrate a method. For example, I have not developed adequate guidelines for how citizens should relate to the earth and to the larger cosmos.[78] Another area is the Christian responsibility of "truth-telling," or of naming political, economic, and social realities for what they are instead of hiding or masking evil with various ideologies; or sugarcoating evil in the name of morality.[79]

We are participants in an ongoing conversation, a discerning process, as we seek the peace of the city where we dwell. We do not possess the Truth, but are participants with our fellow citizens, who also are seekers. Truth belongs only to God, who transcends our finite understanding. We know the truth only in limited ways, for our time, "through a glass darkly." The church does not have an answer for every question. We must avoid the Promethean temptation that because we are the people of God, we always know best. History shows clearly that the church has often been wrong. The first step the church must take is to repent and to be what we are called to be. Then we might be able to contribute as citizens to the peace of the city.

Philosophers,
Christian Faith,
and Human Wisdom

"If there is any excellence and if there is anything worthy of praise, think about these things." —Philippians 4:8

IN SEEKING THE PEACE OF THE CITY where they dwell, Christians incorporate human wisdom from a variety of sources into their vision for the city. The word *philosopher* in the chapter title describes one of the fundamental dimensions of a Christian theology of culture, the love of wisdom. By *philosopher* we mean the love (*philia*) of wisdom (*sophia*) in the generic sense. We do not confine the word to the particular specialized discipline of philosophy, though philosophical wisdom is one dimension of the wisdom Christians include in an alternative cultural vision.

Theology is one kind of human wisdom. In doing theology, the way in which we think is dependent upon the wisdom of our culture. The question is not *whether* we incorporate human wisdom within a theological perspective, but *how* we do it. In chapter three we argued that one of the central functions of theology is to interpret what is the nature of reality in the most comprehensive sense. In theology we interpret the cosmos and the place and responsibility of humans in the cosmos in the light of God, our ultimate point of reference. Theology is both a kind of knowledge about reality and a method or way of knowing.

We assume in this chapter the ideas developed in chapter three about the role of metaphor in theological knowledge and the participatory nature of knowing. Knowing is not primarily about something objective, but is relational. In our relationship to people of different faiths, practicing the truth of nonviolent love is foundational to how

252

we relate to the other. In this chapter we clarify more fully the task of the church to discern how to incorporate wisdom into a Christian vision of life so that this wisdom can contribute to the peace of the city. We begin with a summary of the role of wisdom in the biblical tradition and then take up two issues: the discernment of wisdom in the encounter between the Christian faith and people of other religious faiths, and the relationship of a discerning Christian ethic to empirical knowledge and scientific wisdom.

THE BIBLICAL WISDOM TRADITION

In the biblical wisdom tradition, God's wisdom is understood to be universal, available to all human beings, irrespective of particular cultural or social identities. This wisdom tradition provides a counterpoint to the emphasis in theology on narrative, the particular story of God's action in history, which shapes the distinctive identity of Israel and the church. The basis for this underlying unity and universality of all truth is the implicit biblical Trinitarian understanding of reality. The creator God who is God of the whole cosmos; the Christ who is the logos, the universal Word present in the world; and the Spirit, God's creative energy and power present within all of reality.[1]

In the last two decades, scholars have reaffirmed the significance of this wisdom tradition alongside the priestly, prophetic, and narrative material of Scripture.[2] As Roland Murphy puts it, "Wisdom literature provides a biblical model for understanding divine revelation apart from the historical mode (salvation history) in which it is usually cast."[3] Wisdom in the biblical material: (1) carefully observes nature for what it teaches humans about life; (2) consists of prudence, wise advice about how to live; (3) reflects on puzzling questions about the meaning of human existence; and (4) is connected to Christology in the personification of "Lady Wisdom" (Sophia). Murphy characterizes this Sophia as "divine communication: God's communication, extension of self, to human beings."[4]

Careful Observation of Nature

One layer of wisdom in biblical material is the careful observation of the natural world. According to Murphy "this is a 'worldly' understanding, an appreciation of the autonomy, the independence, of created things. It is not the same as 'secularism.' The autonomy of creation is recognized for what it can teach humans about themselves, about God's creation, and even about God's own self."[5] From careful observation, a person can draw lessons about how to live. One could argue that this emphasis parallels the point made by ecologists today about humans learning from the way ecosystems work to guide humans in their own behavior. Murphy summarizes this point:

> Wisdom recognizes a dynamic relationship between humans and their environment. Gerhard von Rad has written that "the most characteristic feature of [Israel's] understanding of reality lay, in the first instance, in the fact that she believed man to stand in a quite specific highly dynamic existential relationship with his environment." The sages analyzed the environment—the created world and its inhabitants—for signs and for conclusions (Prov. 17:1; 25:13). They drew analogies and made comparisons between things, living and nonliving (Prov. 25:14; 26:2). In the animal world there were the very small that were, at the same time, very wise: ants, locusts, and lizards (Prov. 30:24-38). Job could taunt the three friends to ask the beasts and birds of the air to teach them (Job 12:7). It has been well said that when the Lord "replies" to Job he lets nature do the talking (Job 38-41).[6]

Wisdom as Prudence

At a second level, wisdom appeals to human experience, the traditions that have been handed down by family and teachers about what people have learned practically about how to live. This is wisdom based on experience, without appeal to the authority of Torah or the authority of tradition, though the assumption is that all such wisdom comes from God.

Wisdom is equivalent to prudence. What leads to success or well-being in life? The book of Proverbs is filled with such wisdom. An example is Proverbs 12:1: "Whoever loves discipline loves knowledge, but those who hate to be rebuked are stupid." Another example is Proverbs 12:15: "Fools think their own way is right, but the wise listen to advice." The linkage of nature as a teacher to prudence is reflected in Proverbs 6:6-11:

> Go to the ant, you lazybones;
>> consider its ways, and be wise.
> Without having any chief
>> or officer or ruler,
> it prepares its food in summer,
>> and gathers its sustenance in harvest.
> How long will you lie there, O lazybones?
>> When will you rise from your sleep?
> A little sleep, a little slumber,
>> a little folding of the hands to rest,

and poverty will come upon you like a robber,
and want, like an armed warrior.

In the Gospels Jesus used the wisdom tradition frequently in his teaching. Jesus' stories about the wise man who built his house on a rock, or the people who start building a tower and cannot finish it are two examples.

Pondering the Meaning of Human Existence

Third, the Bible views wisdom as lessons derived from human experience about how to understand human existence. Wisdom is based on the common or shared experience of being human. The book of Job invites the reader to participate vicariously in the dramatic dialogue between Job and his three friends, who are trying to interpret human suffering. Job challenges the idea that suffering is caused by sin or human fault. In the course of the dialogue, Job challenges his friends' interpretation of suffering by an appeal to common sense, reasons that might be persuasive to anyone regardless of their particular cultural or social identity.

One of the essential characteristics of wisdom literature in the Bible and in the Ancient Near East is that it is no respecter of national, cultural, linguistic, or geographical barriers. Wisdom is universal. It belongs to the human race. Within the plurality of human cultures is embedded a folk wisdom about how people should deal with the puzzling questions of human life—questions like the purpose for humans in the universe, what is the good life, the roles of men and women, or what happens when humans die. Answers to these questions are reflected in the stories or myths of the culture. They are passed on in the process of story telling and modeled in the way people live.

Wisdom literature in the Bible also reflects skepticism about what humans can know about the mysteries of life. Ecclesiastes 8:16-18 even describes the folly of the pursuit of wisdom.

> When I applied my mind to know wisdom, and to see the business that is done on earth, how one's eyes see sleep neither day nor night, then I saw all the work of God, that no one can find out what is happening under the sun. However much they may toil in seeking, they will not find it out; even though those who are wise claim to know, they cannot find it out.

Alongside the certainty of the prophet who claims, "thus says the word of the Lord," is the skeptical sage. The author of the book of Job, who after probing the issues of theodicy at length in a series of poetic dialogues concludes in the speeches from the whirlwind by confronting the reader with mystery: "Who is this that darkens counsel by words without knowledge?" (Job 38:2).

Wisdom and New Testament Christology

In the New Testament, Christ, the Logos, is God's wisdom made flesh. A Christian theology of wisdom is paradoxical: the particular is universal and the universal is particular. The Christ who becomes flesh is the universal logos (John 1:1). Christ "is the image of the invisible God, the firstborn of all creation; for in him all things in heaven and on earth were created ... all things have been created through him and for him" (Col. 1:15-16). On the other hand, we know God through the historically embodied Jesus of Nazareth. God's wisdom is revealed most vividly in the cross. According to Paul, this radical particularity is foolishness to the world.

> For the message about the cross is foolishness to those who are perishing, but to us who are being saved it is the power of God. For it is written, "I will destroy the wisdom of the wise, and the discernment of the discerning I will thwart." Where is the one who is wise? Where is the scribe? Where is the debater of this age? Has not God made foolish the wisdom of the world? (1 Cor. 1:18-20)

How can wisdom be foolishness, and foolishness wisdom? What are we to make of the statement in Colossians, "See to it that no one takes you captive through philosophy and empty deceit, according to human tradition" (Col. 2:8)? Do these texts suggest that Christians possess an esoteric wisdom that only a member of a sect can know through special insight not accessible to everyone? One can see how the logic of gnosticism (a special wisdom available only to the initiated) could develop from the interpretation of such texts.

These texts have also been used by Christians to question the validity of reason in matters of faith. Many have heard it said, "Do not question so much; just accept things on faith." Sometimes these texts have been used by the church to support anti-intellectualism, a preference for feeling and a rejection of the use of the mind for rigorous and clear thinking in matters of faith.

It is a misreading of Corinthians to argue against the use of the mind or reason. As a Pharisee trained at the feet of Gamaliel, Paul employed all the mental skill he could muster in making the case for a Christian understanding of the world. The issue Paul addresses in 1 Corinthians 1 is not whether the use of reason is appropriate, but who

God is. The notion that the Son of God could suffer and die challenged traditional Greek ideas of God's immutability and Jewish notions of the messiah. For those operating out of those assumptions, the "wisdom" Paul was advocating was "foolishness."[7] But Paul was not anti-intellectual. Rather, Paul employed reason in the service of faith. From the perspective of his vision of truth in Jesus Christ, Paul sought to understand and interpret the world. He was not advocating esoteric knowledge, but was interpreting a publicly available event.

In his letter to the Corinthians, he comments on the ecstatic utterance of tongues. He brags that he has spoken in tongues more than anyone else. Yet he relativizes ecstatic utterance with his appeal to reason: "I would rather speak five words with my mind, in order to instruct others also, than ten thousand words in a tongue. Brothers and sisters, do not be children in your thinking; rather, be infants in evil, but in thinking be adults" (1 Cor. 14:19-20).

The texts from the Gospel of John and Colossians 1:15-16 express the conviction that the particular Jesus has cosmic and universal significance. Although the Christian confesses that she knows the truth through a particular narrative culminating in the Christ event, the Christian also confesses that in the light of this special history, she can discover and embrace wisdom from whatever source, because Christ is the logos, the firstborn of all creation. In Jesus Christ, all truth is included and illuminated. This is the meaning of the logos Christology in the New Testament. Jesus Christ is the Word or the wisdom that illuminates the entire universe. Jesus Christ is the root metaphor for God, the One in whom all truth is united. So the insights of human wisdom are ultimately in harmony with Jesus Christ. For where truth is, there God is, and where God is in Christ, there is truth.

To understand Christ as logos is to claim that the heart of reality is Word or wisdom. Christ is the light that illumines all other truth. Like the sun, Christ illuminates everything that is. In the light of Christ, therefore, wisdom from the sciences or from the plurality and variety of human cultures or from world religions can be acknowledged and affirmed. To confess Christ is not to deny the truth of human wisdom, wherever it is found. Rather, a christological perspective includes all truth, including the insights of the religions other than Christianity.

The relationship between the universal and the particular is analogous to the relationship of the sun and the earth. The sun is the source of energy for the entire earth. All energy derives from the sun, yet it exists independently from the sun, such as in fossil fuel or in forests. Like the sun, Christ as universal logos is ultimately the source of all truth.

But that truth is expressed in an orderly universe, one that humans can study and know independent of its source. Non-Christians who probe the mysteries of the universe as scientists or philosophers discover truth that can be acknowledged by and incorporated within a Christian vision of life.

A DISCRIMINATING ETHIC IN THE CONTEXT OF RELIGIOUS PLURALISM

Given the particularity of every cultural and religious perspective, what is the basis for how we humans can relate to each other? Though a logos Christology provides a universal framework for Christians, so does the Torah for Jews, the Qur'an for Muslims, and the principles of the Four Noble Truths for Buddhists. How should Christians relate to others who also make universal claims?

The world has always been religiously pluralistic. Religions existing side-by-side simultaneously make universal claims for their particular vision of life. Though a variety of religious traditions have dominated certain territories of the globe historically (e.g., Christianity in Europe, Islam in the Middle East, Hinduism in India, and Shinto in Japan), no religious tradition has even approached carrying out its universal vision for the entire globe, though around 1900, some Christians dreamed that the twentieth would be the "Christian century." What is new about our era is not religious pluralism as such, but our increased awareness of pluralism. The world has shrunk through modern communications technology and increased contact between religious faiths. Even *within* almost every community and nation we see religious pluralism.[8]

Wichita, Kansas, with a population over 300,000, lies in the heart of the "Bible belt." Formerly dominated by Protestant Christianity, the city now has a great variety of Christians as well as members of several major world religions. Wichita's population includes a large number of Roman Catholic and Eastern Orthodox believers, as well as adherents to more recent American religious groups like the Seventh-Day Adventists, Jehovah's Witnesses, Church of Jesus Christ of Latter Day Saints, and Christian Scientists. Wichita also has two Jewish synagogues (Conservative and Reform). Muslim believers gather regularly for prayer in a former restaurant turned mosque. A group gathers regularly for Zen meditation and there are four Buddhist communities: Laotian, Thai, Cambodian, and a large Vietnamese population. The Vietnamese group meets in a former Protestant church, where they have erected a large shrine with an image of the Buddha and have removed all the pews so that persons can sit on the floor for meditation. Not only do I have easy access to the people of these faiths, I can go to several bookstores in Wichita and purchase the Scriptures, histories, and interpretations of these religions by believers in these faiths.

This growing awareness of pluralism has generated several responses. One is the growth of religious "fundamentalism"—a worldwide phenomenon expressed in almost all religious traditions.[9] *Fundamentalism* refers to a worldview that brings together four elements. The first is a belief in the infallibility of one's own scriptures or dogma. We see parallels, for example, between some Christian views of the inerrancy of the Bible and Muslim attitudes to the Qur'an as literally God's word communicated in Arabic to Mohammed.

Second, fundamentalists desire to create a disciplined community that is unified around a set of beliefs and values. Most are organized patriarchally and hierarchically in order to ensure orthodoxy and unity of belief and practice.

A third characteristic is the will either to convert all other people in the world to their own belief system because it alone is believed to be true, or to live their own belief and value system within a certain territory without interference or competition from any other religion. Some fundamentalists have a strong missionary impetus. Others are more inclined simply to protect community values and beliefs from competition within a particular territorial setting. The attempt to establish the territorial supremacy of one religion has created conflict and violence in contexts where adherents of several religions live together.

The fourth characteristic is resistance to modernization and lack of tolerance for religious diversity within a particular community or nation. Groups vary in how selective they are in adapting to modernity. Christian fundamentalists make much use of modern media technology and are comfortable in adapting to modern capitalism. At the same time, they resist the use of historical and scientific tools of critical analysis when applied to the Bible. They find it difficult to tolerate diversity within public institutions like the public schools, where they support prayer and the celebration of Christian holidays.

Fundamentalists react to pluralism and modernization by asserting the absolute validity and authority of their own tradition. They tend to resist any change that would deviate from a traditional interpretation of the faith. When fundamentalists seek to impose their own vision within a particular territory that is itself pluralistic, serious human conflict, including violence, is likely. Fundamentalist attitudes have resulted in ethnic and religious violence in the break-up of the former Soviet Empire, among Christian groups and between Christian groups and Muslims in Lebanon and the former Yugoslavia, within Islamic countries like Iran, where Muslim believers have attempted to apply strict Islamic law to social and political institutions with almost no tolerance for believers of other religions, in India between Hindus and Sikhs, and between Islamic traditionalists and the most extreme orthodox Jews (such as the Gush Emunim) in the occupied territories of the West Bank and Gaza Strip.

In the United States, some right-wing religious and political groups are aggressively attempting to make the United States more "Christian," thus, implicitly if not explicitly, denying equal status within the body politic to those of other religions. On specific issues like abortion, some have justified the use of civil disobedience and even violence against those who practice abortion.

A number of factors have contributed to the opposite tendency: relativism. One factor is the sociology of knowledge. Modern critical analysts of religion, such as Feuerbach, Freud, Marx, and Durkheim tend to "explain" religion in the light of psychological, social, or economic forces. Critical analyses of religion have in common an account of religion in terms of its function in human life, as a factor in solving psychological needs or providing a legitimation for society or the social order. The issue of the "truth" of a text is reduced to the question of how the text functions within a community or within people's lives.

Another factor that contributes to relativism is the modern value of tolerance of diversity. Though a positive alternative to intolerance and violence, tolerance can also lead to complete subjectivism and relativism. Religion is relegated to the private sphere of life. Belief and values are regarded as a matter of personal preference. Persons who hold this point of view believe that religion should be kept out of the public arena.

In the United States, people appeal to the Supreme Court rulings on separation of church and state as grounds for relegating religion to the private sphere.[10] Many Christians have challenged this so-called "value-neutral" position by arguing that this secularizing of society is in fact not a value-neutral or belief-neutral position. To hold that religion is private is itself a worldview, contrary to the universal significance of commitment to a God of the whole cosmos. "To each his own," so long as the beliefs one holds do not infringe on the rights of anyone else, is itself a powerful value system. As a result, religion has come to be regarded as a purely individual and private matter, having nothing to do with public spheres of life. This privatization of religion contradicts the fundamental beliefs and claims of most religious traditions.

Paradoxically, authoritarian fundamentalism and relativism are similar in many ways. Both essentially reject the use of reason or human wisdom in matters of faith. Authoritarianism refuses to make discriminating judgments about the validity of the way of life recommended in other traditions. Authoritarianism simply asserts the truth of one's own faith and the falsity of all other faiths. Relativism, too, refuses to make judgments about why something might be valid, not just for oneself but for others as well. In their reaction against Enlightenment reason, postmodern philosophies, with their emphasis upon the fluidity of the self and the resistance to boundary definitions of the self, also contribute to relativism.[11]

Both authoritarianism and relativism create serious practical problems. Authoritarianism hides insecurity and can lead to fanaticism and intolerance. Relativism does not take human interaction seriously. Instead, it provides a convenient escape from taking seriously alternative worldviews and ways of life. Relativism is an escape from freedom. Relativism refuses to recognize that not all positions can be equally valid in a world of choices that significantly affect people's lives. Persons must make choices about the validity of positions once options present themselves. On what grounds does one make choices? One cannot remain forever free and open to new possibilities of self-identity. In the real world, some ways of life are destructive. We must make judgments. And personal preference is a shaky basis for judgment, since it is subject to manipulation by others and is inadequate in the face of adversity.

Christ as Light and the Wisdom of Other Faiths

What is an appropriate response to this polarization? How can and should Christians avoid the fanaticism and violence of fundamentalism and the subjectivism and relativism of modern secularism?[12] How should we understand the relationship of Christ to the wisdom within other religious traditions? What process should the church follow in discerning the truth in its encounter with people of other faiths?

Wisdom entails relationships with persons of other faiths. We should not view our relationship to other religions abstractly. The key relationship is not between two religions as a composite set of truths, beliefs, or dogmas. Christians do not relate to religions as intellectual *constructs* or symbolic *systems*, but to *people*—people who adhere to a particular faith and way of life. A Christian response develops out of the particular issues and contexts in which Christians meet persons of other faiths. Truth grows out of a relational process between people. A healthy relationship to the other respects the mystery of the other. We should respect difference and not attempt to absorb the other into our own perspective. Such an approach involves mutual sharing and listening. Out of such a relational process, we may find common ground and a common wisdom to lead us to act in concert for the sake of the peace of the city where we dwell.

I distinguish my position from Karl Rahner's "anonymous Christianity" because I do not believe Rahner adequately respects the other. I believe we can learn from and respect others as others without absorbing them into our own system by naming them "Christian." Rather than naming another people's religious and cultural wisdom after our own, the church will recognize that the light of Christ "lights up" ways of life that are valid wherever they are found. This demands a discriminating wisdom born of humility, without the need to name the other "Christian" in order to legitimate a moral practice or belief.

Affirmation of the particularity of our own identity and those to whom we relate. A healthy relationship to people of other faiths depends upon the acceptance and affirmation of one's own particularity, not a denial of it. Genuine faith entails commitment to that which is regarded as ultimate. The ultimate is that to which persons give themselves above all, that to which they are loyal above all.[13] For Christians that commitment is to love God with heart, soul, and mind. It means to see in Jesus Christ the root metaphor for understanding who God is and what God requires of humans. The universal claims of Christianity are reflected in a variety of New Testament texts:

> I am the way, and the truth, and the life. No one comes to the Father except through me. (John 14:6)

> Therefore God also highly exalted him
>   and gave him the name
>   that is above every name,
> so that at the name of Jesus
>   every knee should bend,
>   in heaven and on earth and under the earth,
> and every tongue should confess
>   that Jesus Christ is Lord,
>   to the glory of God the Father. (Phil. 2:9-11)

At the end of the Gospel of Matthew, Jesus says, "Go therefore and make disciples of all nations, baptizing them in the name of the Father and of the Son and of the Holy Spirit" (Matt. 28:19). The Pauline writings make no sense apart from Paul's conviction that he was called by God to take the good news to the whole Gentile world. The two volumes of Luke and Acts show how the good news of the gospel begun in the life, teachings, death, and resurrection of Jesus, spread from Judea through Samaria to the "ends of the earth" (Acts 1:8). That spread of the good news is symbolized by the fact that Paul ends his ministry in Rome, the symbol of the civilized world.[14]

The mission of the church is a holistic vision, one that seeks the well-being of the whole person, including the spiritual, physical, psychological, and social dimensions. To be made whole by the good news of the gospel is to live a life as God intended it. Restoration to wholeness touches everything from a meaningful life of work to adequate food and shelter to the practice of justice and the nourishing of loving relationships. The good news is that God has entered the human condition in Jesus Christ to be in solidarity with his people and to restore the created order to the wholeness God intended. To confess Christ is to live in gratitude for the gift of that love to us. Thus, in following the model of Jesus in word and deed, Christians give their lives in service to others.

Christian mission is not primarily a matter of convincing people that they are spiritually lost and need to confess Jesus in order to be saved for eternal life. Christian mission is not simply a process of getting people to believe a set of doctrines, or to assent to a series of propositions that will "get them to heaven." People become Christians when they become inwardly convinced by the truthfulness and significance of the story of God's restoration of life in all its dimensions. People become Christians when they identify their lives with the story of God's action in Christ, when they see in that story the key to their own and the world's restoration to wholeness. It is not the task of the church to convert others. When the church thinks it does the converting, it tends to distort the gospel by watering down the good news to make it palatable, by turning the gospel into the acceptance of easy dogmatic formulas, by manipulating others through fear by pressure tactics not born out of love, or by substituting successful results for the good news of the gospel. The task of the church is simply to be faithful—to witness through word and deed in the service of others. Its task is simply to sow the seeds and then hope for transformation. The sprouting and emergence of the seed from the soil is the work of God's spirit.

This approach is to be distinguished from that of Hans Küng, who drafted the recent 1993 "Declaration of the Parliament of the World's

Religions."[15] The values identified in this document can bridge the differences between the world's religions, and I see no harm in seeking to identify common values. Such values work well in the context of mutual tolerance and respect present in the Parliament of the World's Religions. The problem is that we need an ethic especially for those contexts and situations when people who hold different worldviews conflict with each other (e.g., in Bosnia, Rwanda, or Israel/Palestine). The problem is that these values, which unite religions, are so general that they lack the richness, specificity, and resources necessary to guide persons in actual situations of tension and conflict.

Miroslav Volf highlights how the commitment to nonviolence is phrased in the document. "Persons who hold political power must work within the framework of a just order and commit themselves to the most nonviolent, peaceful solutions possible." He argues that "the most nonviolent peaceful solutions possible" is vague and ambiguous. It leaves the door open to violence where one needs nonviolence the most. In the encounter with people of other faiths, Christians cannot leave their own special commitment to a nonviolent Christ at the door for the sake of a more general and vague view on which all can agree. As Volf puts it, "How can you resist making your gods, your symbols of ultimate meaning, fight for you when the life of your family or your country is at stake? You cannot—unless your god refuses to fight."[16]

The scandal of the Christian faith is that the meaning of all of human history lies in the particular events surrounding Jesus of Nazareth. What does this mean for the church's relationships to other faiths that make universal claims? How is the church to understand other religions? Are they simply "false" in the light of a salvation to be found in Jesus and Jesus alone? How does the church avoid the triumphal arrogance that has led to bitter relationships historically to people of other faiths? Is there any wisdom in these faiths? If so, how is that to be interpreted?

Repentance as a beginning: accepting the scandal of particularity. The church confesses to others through word and deed the way of life it knows and experiences in Jesus Christ. But the church must begin its relationship to persons of other faiths with repentance. If the church's life is to be consistent with the good news of the gospel, it will not operate in a spirit of triumphal arrogance. Rather, it will acknowledge its own sinfulness. It will confess its own faults and failures in the light of the concrete, embodied Jesus, whose way we are called to follow.

The church's relationship to Muslims must begin with repentance for the way in which it turned the good news of the gospel into a message of arrogance and violence. The church must repent for its complicity in the destruction of Native American life and culture, for its insensitivity to the insights of Native Americans about a proper relationship to the earth and nonhuman life. The church must also confess its anti-Judaism, recognizing that its own Scriptures have contributed to the hatred of Jews.

We must begin with the disavowal of "Constantine." "Constantine" is the symbol of the church's imposition of its own universal territorial vision on people of other faiths. Christendom turned Jesus, the nonviolent servant who took the way of the cross, into the Imperial Christ. This had disastrous consequences for pagans, Jews, Muslims, and for dissenting Christians who did not accept the prevailing orthodoxy of a particular territory. We must in our time rediscover the Christ who made himself vulnerable to others in the cross. We must rediscover the "vulnerable" Christ who made his way known to others through servant love. We must recover a gospel whose authenticity can be expressed only through mutual listening and exchange, not through power over others.

The disavowal of Constantine leads to a greater variety of approaches to people of other faiths than presupposed by post-Enlightenment theologians who ground Christian faith in "religion." This approach searches for common ground by diminishing difference. It begins with the general and seeks to place particular Christianity within a universal Constantinian framework. But Christian mission does not search for some objective rational basis for cooperation. Rather, the church should begin with a simple confession of its own particularity. The church's vision for the world is grounded in Jesus of Nazareth. Paradoxically, this confession of particularity can undergird a less arrogant and triumphalist position. It is when the church thinks it has found an objective or rational ground for a relationship independent from its particularity that it imposes universality on others. Like everyone else, Christians have no privileged position. All they can do is confess their own particularity. When Christians accept this, they can enter into relationships with others in a spirit of love and not coercion.

Friedrich Schleiermacher defined religion as the "feeling of absolute dependence." Christianity was seen as a particular instance of this universal religious phenomenon. In his early thought, Ernst Troeltsch argued for a "religious *a priori*." Rudolph Otto saw Christianity as a particular instance of the experience of the holy. More recently, John Hick began with the universal concept of "the Real," and then viewed all faiths as partial manifestations or expressions of the Real.[17]

Behind these approaches is a foundationalist or neo-Kantian position that general categories of religion or morality are available to and understandable by all human beings. The problem with these positions is that they do not recognize sufficiently the contextual nature of our thinking and our categories of thought. There is no objective position from which to make a claim about God—no foundational religious experience, no religious *a priori* that is essentially independent from our context.

The discipline of religious studies has made us aware of how our categories are closely related to our basic views of life and the world. Are definitions of religion or God as universal as proponents claim? Is Rudolph Otto's experience of the holy as "mysterium tremendum" appropriate for all religious traditions, or does it describe primarily a theistic context? Is John Hick's concept of "the Real" universal? How does "the Real" relate to Buddhism's lack of metaphysical notions? Hick replies:

> I have tried to use [the term *God*] in such a way that it is proper to ask whether God is personal. But I accept that this usage can easily be misunderstood. I therefore prefer to speak of "the Real," and to distinguish between human experience of the Real as personal (taking such concrete forms as Yahweh, Shiva, Vishnu, the Heavenly Father, etc.) and of the Real as nonpersonal (taking such forms as Brahman, the Tao, the Dharma, Nirvana, Runyata, etc.).[18]

To encompass all expressions of faith as a manifestation of the One (or "the Real"), one must move to such a level of abstraction that the content of the word *God* becomes almost vacuous and thus loses the meaning we usually associate with the term *God*.

We can illustrate the problems of beginning with a general "religious" category by looking at the changes in Troeltsch's approach over his lifetime.[19] Troeltsch's comparative and evolutionary scheme combined both a description of the religions and an evaluation of them. In his early thought, he struggled with how to define religion in general so that he could incorporate every religion in his definition and analysis. At the same time, he asked how one could evaluate these religions. How does one make normative judgments within the context of religious plurality? In one of his earliest works, *Die Absolutheit des Christentums*, Troeltsch put Christianity within this comparative and evolutionary framework that recognized various degrees of truth and value in the religions. He lined up all the religions on an evolutionary scale, identifying the degree of truth and value in each of the religions. Christianity came out at the top of this scale of evaluation. Troeltsch raised questions in his later work about the objectivity of such an approach. The very categories of evaluation were dependent upon a particular Christian worldview.

Thus, by the time Troeltsch had reached the end of his life, he had abandoned this method. He was convinced that our knowledge and categories of thought are so deeply immersed in our own historical-cultural context that it is impossible to step outside that context to judge from some objective point of view. The most that Troeltsch would say by the end of his life is that Christianity is true for "us," referring in his case to European culture.

The result of Troeltsch's work was cultural relativism. Beginning with the universal, Troeltsch ended up with particularity. He was no longer able to claim that the particular confession of the Christian faith contained a universal norm for judging all the religions. Nevertheless, he presupposed a "Constantinian" view for European culture, the possibility that Christianity could provide the normative framework for Europe. In this respect, Troeltsch did not go far enough in recognizing the growing pluralism of Western European culture. Despite his skepticism about our ability to make normative judgments for all religions, Troeltsch believed in an ultimate unity that underlies all particularity.

> [World religions] all are tending in the same direction, and ... all seem impelled by an inner force to strive upward towards some unknown final height, where alone the ultimate unity and the final objective validity can lie. And, as all religion has thus a common goal in the Unknown, the Future, perchance in the Beyond, so too it has a common ground in the Divine Spirit ever pressing the finite mind onward towards further light and fuller consciousness, a Spirit which indwells the finite spirit, and Whose ultimate union with it is the purpose of the whole many-sided process. ... Between these two poles, however—the divine Source and the divine Goal—lie all the individual differentiations of race and civilization, and, with them also, the individual differences of the great, comprehensive religions.[20]

Karl Barth's neo-orthodox theology was an attempt to develop an alternative to Schleiermacher and Troeltsch through the affirmation of the radical particularity of God's revelation in Christ. But Barth also tried to sidestep the vulnerabilities of historical particularity. Barth did this by distinguishing between religion and Christian revelation. He argued that religion is indeed a human phenomenon and that it can be studied and analyzed with all the tools developed by the humanist and scientific disciplines. He did not reject the application of historical-critical method to the study of the biblical text. But he distinguished its findings from Christian revelation and faith, which is, he maintained, the proper object of theological reflection. Since revelation has its source in God, Barth believed he could establish a base for theology on grounds that would not be undermined by the quicksand of Enlightenment historical-critical thought.[21]

Barth's move seemed ingenuous. Scholars could seek to understand and interpret religious phenomena, including the Christian faith, with all the intellectual tools of the Enlightenment while continuing to affirm the central tenets of the Christian faith based on revelation. Barth's approach raised two problems, however. To protect revelation from the critique of the Enlightenment, revelation is grounded outside of space and time. Since revelation is from God, it belongs to the realm of faith or *Geschichte* (believed history), not *Historie* (actual lived history). The "object" of theology is God—an otherworldly norm. This "object" can easily evaporate into a vacuous nothing, which is exactly what happened in the forms of "God is Dead" theology that presupposed Barth's starting point.

However, God's revelation occurred within space and time. Jesus appeared as an historical event and certain texts are our access to that event. Thus, we cannot avoid the questions that arise from the application of historical and scientific inquiry. So Barth's critique of liberalism was not as radical as it seemed. Barth accepted one of the fundamental premises of liberalism by seeking to ground theology in something outside of space/time considerations. And insofar as revelation is not fully present within historical particularity, it is another instance of the reluctance to accept a radical particularity. He too shied away from a fully embodied Jesus, which would make us vulnerable as we relate to people of other faiths.

Listening to and seeing God in the other. The mission of the church in the world must begin with listening to others. Through listening we connect our own particular vision of life to the vision and practice of others. We will see analogies between our own practices and those of other people. To express love to others, which is the essence of the good news of the gospel, is not simply to speak and act. It is to listen to the other, to respect the other, and to learn from the other. In the process of listening, the church can discover how the good news of the gospel can enter into a positive relationship with other cultures. In seeking the peace of the city where it dwells, the church will discover where it can support, affirm, or cooperate with people of other faiths. The church will discover, if it genuinely listens, the presence of God in the person of another faith.

We see this capacity to recognize the truth in the "other" in several New Testament texts. In each of these cases, identification with the other is not abstract and general, but particular. One concrete example is the description in Acts of Paul's encounter with the Athenians at the Areopagus. Paul notes how religious they are, having even built an altar with the inscription, "To an unknown God." He then proceeds to proclaim the God revealed in Jesus of Nazareth as this unknown God, a God that is not far from them. Rather than condemning their faith, Paul quotes their own poets, suggesting that they had some knowledge of the God Paul was proclaiming. "For 'In him we live and move and have our being'; as even some of your own poets have said, 'For we too are his offspring'" (Acts 17:28).

Paul's approach in Athens suggests the metaphor we used previously. To be a Christian means to confess Jesus Christ as the light. As light, Christ illuminates the entire world. Rather than excluding truth in other religions, Christ illuminates truth wherever it is. In this metaphor of light, the paradoxical relationship of particularity and universality is made evident. We begin as Christians with a particular confession. But that confession "lights up" the entire universe, so that we can acknowledge God's intention for the cosmos within the faiths of other people, even as Paul did in Athens.

This perspective is presupposed in the Good Samaritan story of Luke 10. We often use the story to legitimate our own goodness when we reach out to people who are different from ourselves. However, this story is much more radical when we recognize that it is the *other*, a person of another religious tradition who best embodies the love of the neighbor. The other serves as a revelation of what we are called to be.[22]

This story also suggests a way of relating to others. Rather than assuming that our faith alone possesses the truth, we expect to learn from others in the process of mutual dialogue and interaction. This openness to the truthfulness in the other is also reflected in the text of Matthew 25, where people are surprised by God's judgment. Eternal life belongs not to those with the right beliefs, but to those who have welcomed the stranger, visited the sick and those in prison, and given the cup of water to the "least of these." In 1 John, love is the test of whether one really knows God. "Whoever does not love does not know God, for God is love" (1 John 4:8).

Deeds of solidarity and love. The church will find ways to share the gospel through authentic love modeling an alternative cultural vision of the Christian faith. Alain Epp Weaver shares a wonderful example from the practice of Coptic Orthodox Christians in Egypt, who have been subject to persecution and harassment by Islamic revivalists in recent years. In settings where civil dialogue between religious faiths is difficult or even impossible, how do Christians relate to others without resorting to sectarian defensiveness or acts of counterviolence?

> In this climate of hardship and suffering, some Coptic churches have adopted an interesting practice. During Ramadan, the Muslim month of fasting, some Coptic Orthodox Christians have taken to hosting evening meals, or *iftars,* for their Muslim neighbors to mark the end of their day's fast. For a religious minority to adopt the practice of the majority is a potentially risky act. Christians might legitimately fear that by appropriating a Muslim practice such as hosting Ramadan break-fasts, they are contributing to the Muslim view of Christianity as a partial, incomplete version of the true religion, and thus relativizing their own claims to ultimacy. Copts, who as a persecuted minority are understandably concerned with strengthening their religious identity, might also worry that the adoption of an Islamic practice could blur their communal self-understanding.
>
> Despite these risks, Coptic Christians have continued the practice of hosting *iftars* for Muslim neighbors, for the good, to my mind. First the practice demonstrates an ability on the part of the church to discern positive values at play in the camp of the oppressor. By hosting *iftars,* Christians at least implicitly recognize the value of Ramadan as a practice of consciously abstaining from evil and directing oneself to God. Second, the act of a persecuted minority reaching out to its "enemies," ministering to their physical need (hunger) by extending its tables manifests the truth that the kingdom of God surpasses religious boundaries, as well as demonstrates the powerful example of love of enemy. One is also reminded of the most fundamental Christian act of sharing bread, the Eucharist, in which the suffering nature of the kingdom is made real. The Syrian Orthodox patriarch, in a communion service, once observed that bread smells sweeter and becomes nourishing only when it is broken. In the same way, he continued, the church can become nourishing, a bearer of the kingdom, when it is broken as well. Christian *iftars* for Muslim neighbors in the Middle East show God's love pouring forth from a broken church.[23]

This Coptic Christian practice models an alternative to the Christian practice of crusade, Western imperialism, or the Persian Gulf War. The deed communicates far more about the Christian gospel than preaching or verbal dialogue could accomplish, though these modes of communication may also be appropriate under certain conditions.

Christian Confessionalism and Discriminating Reason

If we accept a radical particularity by grounding theology in a historical faith story, how can we avoid the dangers of subjectivism and relativism? If we appeal only to the truth of their own story, with no grounds for saying that a story is true outside itself, do we not simply legitimate relativism? Can we say any more than Stanley Hauerwas?

> The fact that we come to know God through the recounting of the story of Israel and the life of Jesus is decisive for our truthful understanding of the kind of God we worship as well as the world in which we exist. ... Because the Christian story is an enacted story, liturgy is ... a much more important resource than are doctrines or creeds for helping us to hear, tell, and live the story of God.[24]

Hauerwas makes us wonder whether the Christian story is truer than another story. His answer is that we cannot answer such a question, for the very truth of the story is internal to the story. In Hauerwas's view, then, a story is true if we believe it is true. Of course someone else can make the same claim.[25] While the position for which I am arguing has much in common with the call to confess faithfully the story the church has received, how can we avoid the kind of relativism that position seems to imply? We must think more carefully about how, out of this particularity, the church can employ reason in the service of faith.

The relationship of paradigm and data. A first step in thinking properly about the relationship of Christians to people of other religions is to understand the role of models or paradigms in our understanding of the world. We cannot know, understand, interpret, or evaluate the religious life of various communities and traditions from a completely objective or value-neutral position. We come to our understanding of the religious views of other people with our own paradigms or models of how we interpret the world. Our views of life and our conceptual frameworks of understanding will inevitably shape our view and understanding of the data as the Christ paradigm illuminates or "lights up" the data we observe in other religious faiths. The relationship between a model and the data is dynamic. The data we experience and observe shapes and changes our conceptual models, and our models and theories give shape to our understanding and interpretation of the data. Christians begin with a view of the world: their confession of Jesus Christ. From that perspective they interpret the data of other religious faiths they encounter or experience.

This interaction of model and data suggests an understanding of how normative judgments function. For example, people work from a particular paradigm, whether Christian, Jewish, or secular, which has interpretive power in helping them understand the world. If a paradigm did not have interpretive power, people would not continue to hold onto it. Nevertheless, paradigms are under constant challenge. They change as we seek to interpret the world, including the data of other people's religious views and alternative paradigms.

Christians who study or encounter other religious traditions should be engaged in a dialogical process in which they explore their own paradigms, testing them against the data and the paradigms of others. In other words, Christians use a limited "inductive" approach. This is not a strict inductive process, as it is usually understood. Naïve empiricism is impossible. We do not come to know through a purely inductive process. Knowing is a constantly interactive process involving the critical activity of the mind, with its paradigms or mental construction of the world, together with the observation and experience of the world. In an inductive process we are continually assessing our paradigms in the light of observation, experience, and the encounter with alternative paradigms.[26]

When Christians engage other religious traditions from their own confessional framework, they should employ reason to interpret and evaluate what they observe. In chapter three I named four criteria we can use in interpreting other religious traditions: adequacy, interpretive power, coherence, and the practical implications for personal and social life. These are not unusual or extraordinary categories, but ones we implicitly use in evaluation all the time. We do not blindly accept our story based on authority, but because it rings true in our lives.

> Narrative is true if it does two things. First it must empower us to make sense of our existence. We must ask whether it provides a framework of interpretation that can illuminate life, that can help us give an account of the nature of reality as we experience it. ... Second, a narrative can be said to be true only if it is fruitful, if it can empower us to live in the world in a creative and appropriate way.[27]

There is more than one powerful competing paradigm that can illuminate life. For example, both the Greek tragic view of human existence as well as a Hebraic prophetic view possess explanatory power. Though we have no final "objective" position from which to evaluate such competing paradigms, our choice of paradigms is not arbitrary, uninformed by reason. We can know some of the implications of various worldviews and some of the choices available to us. We do not simply live within one narrative framework. While we are "chosen" by a paradigm and can never completely escape our own presuppositions, we can also become aware of alternative possibilities. In that sense, our choice is not simply an arbitrary "leap of faith."

In assessing what view of life best sustains those values that are central to the well-being of the cosmos, we are caught in a process of circular reasoning. The very values we deem important are given to us in and through our narrative. However, because we live in a pluralistic world, we can become aware of alternative value systems, and we can, to some degree, choose among available alternatives rather than simply operate deterministically from the values a narrative has given to us.

The above method does not answer the normative question by a simple appeal to the authority of a particular tradition. Rather it puts our own paradigm and the paradigms of others under scrutiny to see how they hold up against a set of criteria that can be applied to all. While we cannot claim a neutral standpoint of complete objectivity, we can refuse to capitulate entirely to cultural relativism. We are prepared to work at the normative issues in an ongoing dialogical process that uses discriminating reason in the light of Christ.

Outcomes of a dialogical process. The outcome of this dialogical process will vary. And this indeed makes Christian mission a learning and growing process in which one does not know in advance what the outcome will be. From a theological standpoint, this makes the Christian encounter with the religions a venture of faith. The encounter is not unlike the call of Abraham, who "went out, not knowing where he was to go." Many outcomes of this type of dialogical process are possible, depending upon who or what is being brought into dialogue with which version of the Christian faith.

1. Complementary views. Two views may be able to complement each other.[28] One of the more compelling views of the complex relationship of Judaism and Christianity is that God relates to these two peoples through two complementary covenants. Two peoples have entered into relationship to Yahweh, one on the basis of the Torah, another in Christ. Two very different religious worldviews and ways of life have developed through the centuries. The issue is whether these two worldviews must compete and argue with each other or whether they can respectfully learn from and enrich each other.

Viewing the "Old Testament" in the light of Christ does not exclude Torah as the way to God. In the light of Christ, Christians can approach Torah as understood by Jews in a discerning way. Jewish wisdom about Torah can be affirmed positively within a Christian worldview without absorbing the Jewish people or religion into a Christian worldview. In certain respects, Torah can be seen by Christians as an authentic and valid understanding of what it might mean for Christians to love God with heart, soul, and mind, and one's neighbor as oneself. Christians can learn a great deal about the meaning of the commandments in the Hebrew Scriptures by studying the Jewish Talmud. A respectful and honest reading of the Talmud can contribute to a Christian understanding of what it means to be faithful to God and to serve the neighbor.[29]

I am not searching here for some commonality underlying both Judaism and Christianity. Rather, I wish to call both Jews and Christians to respect difference. Each tradition has its own religious system of meaning. The question is whether, given the particularity of these two religious systems, they can meet in a dialogue of mutual respect and learning.[30]

2. Paths to the same goal. Certain forms of Hinduism see different religions as paths to the same goal. Thus it has been one of the more syncretistic religions. It is able, for example, to view the Buddha as an avatar of Brahman. Because Christians begin with particularity, with Jesus of Nazareth, instead of the One or Brahman, as in some forms of Hinduism, Christianity is not syncretistic in this sense. That does not mean that the insights of a particular religion cannot contribute to the same goal. For example, Christians could say that one of the purposes of Jesus Christ is to restore worship of the One God, Allah, creator and sustainer of the universe. In that sense, Muslim and Christian worship has a common goal. That certainly is not all that Christians confess, nor does it make the Muslim worship of God identical to Christian worship. But in the light of Christ, Christians can recognize that Muslims worship God authentically when they pray to Allah as the Lord of the universe.

3. Conversion. One may also be converted from one perspective to another. In a real encounter of love marked by equality rather than by an expression of power from the superior position, Christians make themselves vulnerable by listening to the other, just as they expect to be heard. So conversion is a possibility both ways. To be converted means to adopt the central paradigm of a particular faith as the basis for orientation to life. To become a Christian is to make the story of God's dealing with people through Christ the master story of one's own life and the world. People of other faiths may choose, on the basis of what they see or hear, to become Christians. As we said earlier, it is not the task of the church to "convert" others. The Spirit of God does that as it touches people's lives. The task of the church is simply to be a faithful witness and to learn from others in the context of faithfulness to one's own vision of life.

Adopting the central paradigm of another faith is not to abandon the truth of the cultural and religious tradition that one held before the conversion. A person who has become a Christian may continue to pray to God in some of the ways they did before adopting the Christian story as their central paradigm. They may continue to practice deeds of kindness and mercy, as a Buddhist or Muslim would.

Conversion entails a creative process of discernment about what changes and what remains the same, similar to the interesting discussions we see occurring in the New Testament between Paul and new churches in the Hellenistic world. One of the questions was whether a person could eat meat sacrificed to idols. Should one remain married to unbelievers? The question of what it means for a person who was a Buddhist or Muslim to become a Christian is not, in principle, different from the self-reflection of a Christian who is a citizen in the United States. What can I affirm in my citizenship that is authentic and does not contradict my Christian identity?

4. *Appropriating other religious practices into one's own worldview.* It is possible to appropriate aspects of one religious perspective within another. For example, Christians should affirm insights of Buddhist meditative practices to help overcome anxiety and ego-centeredness and develop inner peace and calm. Eastern ideas and practices can enrich the Western tradition. Buddhism can contribute insights where the West has blind spots. One does not become a Buddhist by adopting certain insights or practices of Buddhism.[31] Many people fear that to practice meditation at all implies that one has "bought into" an interpretation of the world. To return to the metaphor we have been using, Christ "lights up" the world so that the insights of others can be incorporated into a Christian vision of life. Gandhi's insights into nonviolent resistance had an impact on the Christian vision of Martin L. King Jr. Gandhi was influenced by Jesus, and King in turn by Gandhi, so Gandhi helped King see Jesus in a new light.

5. Change after encountering the other. A fifth possibility is the alteration of one's own religious perspective after an encounter with the "other." One is struck by how frequently anthropologically sensitive Christian missionaries modify their own self-understanding of the Christian faith after an encounter with the other. I recall hearing several persons who spent time in Africa refer to how their encounter with African culture and spirituality sensitized them to the issue of spiritual powers and healing in the New Testament—aspects they had overlooked in their one-dimensional "scientific" Western culture.

6. Judgment. Finally, one may conclude that one's own or another religious perspective is fundamentally flawed. I have tended to give examples of positive interaction, partly to correct the tendency to view other religions in terms of their failures. We tend to compare the best of our own faith with the worst of others. But a Christian vision also provides a standard of judgment about what is valid or authentic. A Christian standard will also appropriately provide a basis for criticism and judgment.

Other religions will criticize appropriately what they believe are the failures of Christianity. The most fruitful encounters between religious traditions at this level will address the issue of what holding a certain perspective entails in living within the cosmos. Rather than engaging others about speculative truths concerned with metaphysical claims about the universe, the key issue is what a particular view entails about how one lives.[32] For example, the concept of the law of karma and doctrine of reincarnation in the Hindu tradition tend to a kind of determinism and legitimation of a stagnant social structure, such as the caste system, that is detrimental to life as God intended it. But the criticism must go both ways. Christians need to do some real soul-searching of their own tradition for how it has stereotyped and treated "the Jew."[33] Humility and respectful listening to another point of view does not entail a "wishy-washy" tolerance of everything.

7. Mission. Is this Christian mission? Is the center of the Christian faith the conviction that a way of life must appear concretely in historical time and space? If so, this truth must be expressed in its encounter with the actualities of history. Christ appeared in a world of clashing and competing understandings of life. It is no different for us. We too must engage the Christ of history as interpreted by a contemporary living community with the great plurality of worldviews as they are embodied in the people and communities we meet. Insofar as that contact is a genuine encounter of love, that contact will involve both speaking and listening. A contact of love is one that shares its own vision of life *and* that allows itself to be vulnerable in its contact with another. Genuine love both speaks and listens. It listens in a way that is so vulnerable that it must entertain the possibility of being changed in its contact with the other. To make an advance determination of truth based upon authority is fundamentally contrary to the nature of God as persuasive love. To be "in Christ" is to enter into a relationship of love with another in which both parties are open to the possibility of being changed by one's engagement with the other.[34]

Christianity appropriately varies in form as it interacts with the wisdom from cultures around the world over time. Most of the time, Christians have historically confused the wisdom of a particular cultural pattern with the gospel. In the colonial era, Christian missionaries often carried with them a mix of the gospel and the cultural patterns integral to Western Europe. This mix was often both alien to the cultures of Asia or Africa and sociologically lethal. Students of missiology now recognize the importance of contextualization. The Christian faith must be expressed in the symbols, stories, myths, rituals, aesthetic forms, and types of social organization where the church dwells.

To seek the peace of the city is to relate to the cultural wisdom where it lives, not to impose alien cultural forms from outside that culture. Cultural "outsiders" best serve the church as a catalyst to aid in the discernment of the people who are part of the culture. The people who are immersed in and sensitive to the nuances of the cultural wisdom where the church lives must do a careful and faithful reading of the gospel. The "outsider" can be an important catalyst to help those within a culture see what might be missed because it is too familiar to recognize.

This movement back and forth between cultures should not have North America and Europe as the primary reference. Such interaction should also come from Asia, Africa, and other nonindustrialized nations. Christians in the West have often integrated the church with industrial capitalism and other dimensions of Western culture. It would be good to have missionaries from Asia and Africa to help the church in the West discern what is truly wisdom in the West and how it can be integrated faithfully with the gospel.

I have experienced a paradox in my dialogue with other faiths. The more I understand my own Christian faith, the more I am able to appreciate and learn from others outside my own faith tradition. Our particularity is crucial. As we embrace rather than deny or dilute who we are, we are better able to relate to others. We relate to others most authentically not by absorbing them into ourselves but by respecting the differences. This respect allows us to learn from each other.

God as mystery, as ground of all being, transcends every limited conception of God known through a particular tradition. The Muslim scholar Riffat Hassan puts it this way:

> There comes a moment in our spiritual evolution when we come to the end of the road and we still have not found God, because God is beyond our tradition. ... We have to follow our traditions as far as they can take us, but recognize that any tradition and every tradition ends where God has not yet begun.[35]

THE SCIENTIFIC PARADIGM IN CHRISTIAN THEOLOGICAL PERSPECTIVE

Christians must seek to incorporate "scientific" knowledge wisely in their vision of life. The scientific paradigm of knowledge (and its application in modern technology) has been powerful and has shaped our culture in profound ways. A Christian theology of culture can respond to this paradigm in a discerning way.[36]

Our relationship to science is similar to our relationship to other religious traditions. In the first place, we can affirm wisdom gleaned from scientific inquiry. There need be no ultimate tension between discoveries of science and of Christian faith. Second, as we will see, there are significant parallels between science and religion. Both involve the creative interaction of models or paradigms and the interpretation of our experience of the world. Assessing other religions requires a dialectical process. We come to our encounter with others from the perspective of our commitment to Jesus Christ, which shapes our encounter with them. At the same time, we are shaped by our experience as we engage in a genuine dialogue with persons of other faiths, which has an impact on how we conceive our own faith paradigm.

This same dialectic is operative in scientific inquiry itself, as well as in our encounter with science. We view the insights of science from the perspective of our Trinitarian understanding of God. At the same time, this Trinitarian structure and paradigm is modified and changed by what we learn from modern science.

Starting with an Adequate Understanding of Science

The starting point for a proper relationship with modern science is an accurate assessment of what science is. Too many responses to science are based on outmoded positivist and reductionist models of science that many scientists and philosophers of science no longer hold. Science entails the careful observation of how society and the universe work. According to Ian Barbour, the "fundamental components of modern science are: (1) particular observations and experimental data, and (2) general concepts and theories."[37]

Based on careful observation, scientists describe laws and develop theories that seek to account for what is known or observed about the world of nature and society. Theory and observation are dialectically related. Data undergirds theory and theory affects the way in which data is selected for study and interpretation. Scientific description is inductive. It attempts to develop theories based on observation. But the observation of the world also is integrally connected with the thinking processes scientists use in defining a problem as they mark off territory for study and interpret the data they observe. In other words, as Barbour puts it, "all data are theory-laden."[38]

Theories are judged in terms of four basic criteria, according to Barbour. First, do they agree with the data? Second, are they consistent with other accepted theories? Third, are they broad enough in scope to unify previously disparate domains? And fourth, do they hold promise in providing a framework for further research by generating new hypotheses and suggesting new experiments?

Barbour draws on the tradition of Thomas Kuhn. He argues that scientific knowledge is paradigm-dependent.[39] A scientific paradigm is a set of comprehensive theories or laws (such as the Copernican vs. the Ptolemaic view of the universe) that embodies the conceptual and methodological assumptions of a research community. Scientists may agree about data they observe, but when they hold to two different paradigms, they will not agree about how to interpret the same data. Paradigms resist falsification by data, but if a particular paradigm is increasingly unable to account for anomalies, it may eventually fall. Scientists share criteria for evaluating paradigms, but there are no rules as such for paradigm selection.[40]

Nancey Murphy and George F. R. Ellis have pointed out how Imre Lakatos sought to provide a broader picture of scientific rationality in response to Kuhn. The issue Kuhn raised was whether objective, rational standards exist for evaluating competing scientific paradigms. Lakatos answered these problems with his "methodology of scientific research programs." A research program has a core theory, an ultimate explanatory principle. Surrounding that theory are auxiliary hypotheses that take into account potentially falsifying data and relate that data to the core theory. So "a research program is a temporal series of networks of theory, along with supporting data, since the core theory stays the same but the belt of auxiliary hypotheses changes over time to account for new data."[41]

Thus, the choice between competing paradigms is not simply circular. It can be tested by how well the auxiliary hypotheses can account not only for the anomalies, but also for the "prediction and corroboration of a 'novel fact,' that is, one not to be expected in light of the previous version of the research program."[42] While the core theories of paradigms are resistant to falsification by data, the accumulative affect of data that cannot adequately be accounted for by auxiliary hypotheses can affect the viability of a particular paradigm. The community of scientists choose paradigms on the basis of shared judgments on the adequacy of paradigms to account for the data, their comprehensiveness, and their simplicity.

Scientists use language to describe a limited sphere of the world. Scientists deliberately limit their sphere of inquiry in order to describe a domain they believe is supported by observation. Scientific descriptions are contingent. They are always subject to change as new data becomes available and scientists think of new ways to interpret the data. Though scientists base their theories on careful observation of data, scientific description is never an exact replica of the world as it is. Scientists understand data by means of a paradigm, an overarching set of conceptual, methodological, and metaphysical assumptions.

Scientific description is therefore always a more-or-less true description of the world. Barbour describes this understanding of scientific knowledge as critical realism. A critical realist believes that there is a connection, but not a literal correspondence, between the model and the real world. Scientific knowledge depends on models, structures of thinking that organize and interpret the data. Such models are not literal descriptions of the world. Barbour calls such a view naïve realism. But neither are they simply useful fictions. The critical realist goes beyond scientific description as useful fiction. It seeks a description that "works" for us, even though we do not know whether it describes the world as it really is.

Barbour also contrasts his position with the naïve realist, who believes there is a direct correspondence between scientific description and the real world. The critical realist recognizes that no description directly corresponds the way the world is. Our descriptions of the world are more or less "like" the world.

Analogies and Differences between Science and Religious Faith

Scientific knowledge, then, is dependent upon analogies between what is believed already to be known and what is being researched. Ian Barbour suggests that science is a form of language that uses metaphor and models in developing a view of the universe.[43] This reveals some significant analogies to theology. The old dichotomies between science and theology were based in part upon inadequate views of science. The old mechanistic model of causal determinism assumed by Kant and many who followed him required that one posit human freedom in a realm separate from "nature" or the phenomenal world. Today we recognize that the image of the universe as a "machine" is itself a metaphor or model that may account for some data, but is inadequate to describe much of what we know or see. For example, a mechanistic model cannot account for the behavior of particular particles at any particular moment, or for genetic mutation or the process of evolutionary development.

Unfortunately Christians often dichotomize science and religion because they base their view of science on an outmoded positivism and reductionism. It is important that Christians be aware of the multiple ways in which we claim to know something and use language to describe what we know. Ludwig Wittgenstein's work in the philosophy of language has contributed a great deal to an adequate view of the multiple uses of language. The positivists sought to reduce all knowledge to empirical facts or logical reasoning. Their philosophy led to a sharp dichotomizing of knowledge and belief and the false association of science with "knowledge" and religious faith with "belief."

However, the philosophy of science represented by Barbour and others recognizes the role of analogy in scientific knowledge and the interplay of thinking and data in the construction of all knowledge. Such a view of science does not accept the sharp dichotomy between "subjective" imagination and "objective" data. While "objective" data do exist, the interpretation and meaning of such data are always dependent upon the subject who is developing the theory of the data.

Reductionism "reduces" all knowledge to elementary physics. The assumption behind reductionism is that one defines reality best by breaking it down into its most elementary particles. In *God and the New Biology*, Arthur Peacocke describes the limitations of this reductionism by arguing that in order to understand organisms in biology, one must look at them as total systems. The reduction of understanding to the component parts does not in fact enable us to understand the emergence of activity, which is possible only if one looks at the system or the whole.[44]

A more adequate understanding of science enables us to understand better how science is similar to and different from religious faith. Religious faith also involves a claim to know something about the nature of reality; it is also a claim to describe things as they are. Religious statements reflect attempts by human beings to interpret the data of human experience. Religious beliefs are not simply, as Freud put it, subjective illusions that meet psychological needs.[45] Science is not strictly objective, but depends on the development of analogies or models for its understanding of data. Metaphor and models play significant roles in religious faith. Critical realism may thus appropriately describe the nature of both religious and scientific knowledge.

There are also critical differences between religious statements and scientific language. Scientists deliberately limit their sphere of inquiry to a particular sphere of finite reality. Religious statements attempt to be more comprehensive. They make statements about the nature of reality as a whole. If science and religion were placed on a spectrum, science would more likely be closer to an objective description of reality, particularly when it limits its sphere of inquiry instead of developing comprehensive paradigms. Religious knowledge is more dependent upon faith, which goes beyond what we can know in an objective sense, since religious knowledge involves a view of the whole. While faith integrates what we know, it is also beyond our finite capacities as humans. Such views of reality are more dependent upon the judgments of a particular community of people. Scientists confirm what they know within a community of inquiry, but scientists have a more recognized universal method that cuts across religious, ethnic, and cultural boundaries when they judge whether something is true, more or less. Judgments of truth in matters of religious faith are more dependent upon what is plausible to a particular faith community.

So while scientific and religious ways of knowing are expressed in different languages that serve different functions, they are also similar in many respects. It is important, therefore, in interpreting religious texts like the Genesis accounts of creation that we not confuse the different functions of science and religious faith. The religious language of Genesis is not scientific language. It does not purport to give a scientific account of *how* the universe functions. Rather it makes certain claims about the meaning and value of the universe in the light of the ultimate reality of God. Genesis is more concerned about questions of *why* than *how*, with questions about *purpose* rather than the processes of how things came to be. Two of these *purposive* claims, among others, are that nothing lies outside God's sovereign power and ordering process and that what God has ordered is fundamentally good.

The first creation story (Gen. 1:1–2:4a) assumes the ancient Near Eastern view of cosmology, in which a half-sphere firmament separates waters above it from the heavens under it. This view of the cosmos is bound up with Ancient Near Eastern culture. In interpreting Genesis for our time, Christians can affirm the theological claims of the text while integrating those theological claims with modern scientific notions of astronomy and evolution. Modern theories of astronomy and evolution conflict with religious faith only when they go beyond their limits as science to make metaphysical claims about the nature of reality, as, for example, in the social Darwinism of Herbert Spencer.

However, scientific theories should not be insulated in some sphere of life separate from religious faith. They do affect Christian faith. In chapter four I attempted to develop a concept of God as persuasive love that takes account of a dynamic, evolving universe billions of years old. Process theology seeks to interpret the nature and activity of God in relationship to the evolutionary process.[46] Arthur Peacocke has shown how a particular understanding of nature influences theology. Peacocke develops the scientific concept of the emergence of systems in the evolutionary process, which results in a hierarchy of interconnected systems. Consequently, when he speaks theologically, his theology is integrated with this view of nature.

> When human beings are exercising themselves in their God-directed and worshiping activities they are operating at a level in the hierarchy of complexity which is more intricate and cross-related than any of those that arise in the natural and social sciences which are in the province of the humanities. ... No higher level or dimension of integration in the hierarchy of natural systems could be envisaged than that between the human person (whose brain-in-body constitutes the most complex organization of matter in the known universe), the whole natural nonhuman order, and God the ultimate ground of all being and source of all-that-is. Theology is concerned with the conceptual and theoretical articulation of the process and characteristics of this subtle unity-in-diversity and diversity-in-unity which we call "religion."[47]

The boundaries of science do pose religious questions. For example, at the boundaries of physics and astronomy we ponder the connections of God to the big bang theory of the universe.[48] We ponder the theological implications of the anthropic principle. How is it that we live in a universe that has evolved in such a way as to produce an environment favorable to life? Even the slightest change in the way in which the universe expanded would have produced a universe very different from the one we know. This leads Nancey Murphy and George F. R. Ellis to propose the following thesis:

The (apparent) fine-tuning of the cosmological constants to produce a life-bearing universe (the anthropic issue) seems to call for explanation. A theistic explanation allows for a more coherent account of reality—as we know it from the perspective of both natural and human sciences, and from other spheres of experience such as the moral sphere—than does a non-theistic account.[49]

This mystery prompts the poetic words of Václav Havel, a statesman reflecting as a philosopher and theologian, on the occasion of the Liberty Medal ceremony in Philadelphia, on July 4, 1994. He draws upon this anthropic cosmological principle to direct our thoughts beyond the anthropocentric self-interests of humans to the cosmos and the miracle of being.

We are not at all just an accidental anomaly, the microscopic caprice of a tiny particle whirling in the endless depths of the universe. Instead, we are mysteriously connected to the entire universe; we are mirrored in it, just as the entire evolution of the universe is mirrored in us. Until recently it might have seemed that we were an unhappy bit of mildew on a heavenly body whirling in space among many that have no mildew on them at all. This was something that classical science could explain. Yet the moment it begins to appear that we are deeply connected to the entire universe, science reaches the outer limits of its powers [and finds itself] between formula and story, science and myth. In that, however, science has paradoxically returned, in a roundabout way, to man, and offers him—in new clothing—his lost integrity. It does so by anchoring him once more in the cosmos.

This cosmic orientation, says Havel, is ultimately grounded in transcendence, a "God" that can save us.

In today's multicultural world, the truly reliable path to coexistence, to peaceful coexistence and creative cooperation, must start from what is at the root of all culture and what lies infinitely deeper in human hearts and minds than political opinion, convictions, antipathies, or sympathies: it must be rooted in self-transcendence. Transcendence as a hand reached out to those close to us, to foreigners, to the human community, to all living creatures, to nature, to the universe; transcendence as a deeply and joyously experienced need to be in harmony even with what we ourselves are not, what we do not understand, what seems distant from us in time and space, but with which we are nevertheless mysteriously linked because, together with us, all this constitutes a single world. Transcendence is the only real alternative to extinction.

> The Declaration of Independence, adopted ... years ago in this building, states that the Creator gave man the right to liberty. It seems man can realize that liberty only if he does not forget the One who endowed him with it.[50]

In citing Havel, we are not proposing a natural theology, as if we could move from scientific knowledge of the universe to a comprehensive view of God. The data and theories of science are ambiguous. Scientific theories do not logically entail any particular theological view. Theological claims are always a matter of faith. What we can claim, however, is the desirability of a theology of nature. In the light of a Christian conception of God, we can make sense theologically of the anthropic principle—that we live in a purposive universe shaped by a loving God.

ETHICAL DISCERNMENT AND EMPIRICAL WISDOM

If such theoretical questions are interesting and important for Christian theological reflection, the intersection of Christian faith and science is a concrete and practical question. In discerning how Christians should engage the culture so as to contribute to shalom, we must weigh empirical knowledge in our discernment. Every ethical decision involves the intersection of theological, ethical, and empirical wisdom.

We have seen throughout this book how knowledge from nontheological disciplines intersects with Christian theological reflection. I use James Gustafson's word *intersection* to reflect the dialectical nature of discernment in a Christian theology of culture. We live on the boundary as Christians. We engage our culture from a particular standpoint in the light of the particular identity we have in Christ. At the same time our understanding of the world, of ourselves, and of God in Christ is shaped by and modified by knowledge we learn through our culture. As Gustafson puts it, the traffic flows both ways.[51] We bring to the discerning process an alternative cultural vision even as we approach human wisdom "with the open possibility that theology and ethical theory will be informed and even altered by concepts, information, and theories that they meet at particular intersections."[52]

We can see how these intersections work when we make ethical judgments on complex issues in areas like bioethics. An ethical judgment on death and dying, for example, involves a complex relationship of factual, ethical, and philosophical/theological factors, as well as assumptions about the roles that the doctors, nurses, patients, family members are playing.

A deductive model of the relationship of empirical knowledge and theology is inadequate. In this view, ethics consists of eternal principles or truths embedded in a handed-down tradition—in a church tradition, in the Bible, or embedded in natural law or the legal system. These absolutely valid norms are true for all time and place, for all varieties of human cultures, and though our scientific knowledge or technology may change, morality never really changes.

In this deduction model, we should apply the same eternally valid moral principles to specific cases in a way that does not change the morality. For example, the Roman Catholic Church has always held that one of the central purposes of marriage is procreation. In reinforcing this central value, it has prohibited the use of contraceptives, any artificial means to prevent the birth of children. Therefore, despite population pressures and the wishes of some parents not to have more children because of the inability to support more children, the church has held fast to its opposition to birth control. We could identify many other cases where Catholic and Protestant churches have taken and continue to take primarily deductive positions. No matter what is known about homosexuality, or the role of women, or the appropriateness of slavery, churches stand firmly in their traditional point of view, unwilling to change in the light of new knowledge.

Also inadequate is the opposite end of the spectrum—the contextual or inductive model. Persons who hold this view believe that ethical viewpoints are fundamentally shaped by the cultural context—that we form our moral judgments not in terms of eternally, absolutely valid moral principles, but in the light of the social community and the cultural context into which we have been socialized. They argue that we should recognize this fact and adapt to the changing circumstances and situations in our world. We should allow our moral thinking to be shaped by the circumstances within which we find ourselves. In this view, morality is always under construction by humans. Morality is a human institution, not an eternally valid God-given set of principles valid for all time and place.

A third model, the interactive model, seeks to draw from both of the two previous models while avoiding the problems of both. The strength of the deductive model is that it recognizes certain valid theological and ethical principles that we as Christians continue to affirm despite changing circumstances. For example, God has revealed Godself in Christ, whom we are called to follow by giving ourselves in love and service to our fellow human beings. That does not change. But what that expression of Christian love means as we apply it to new knowledge must involve us in ongoing interpretation and change. This applies to new knowledge about homosexuality or human genetics and to powerful new technologies that can fundamentally alter the processes of life and death. Scientific knowledge and technology do affect—and should affect—our ethical thinking. Ethical decisions involve a dynamic interaction between theological and ethical principles on the one hand and new scientific knowledge or awareness of social change on the other.

These are not primarily issues of academia. Pastors and laypersons in the church are constantly faced with the intersection between areas of knowledge and their identity as Christians. Unfortunately, the church often does not provide a structure for a process of critical discernment. Persons bring to their participation in the church assumptions about the world and about humans that are not critically assessed. In the church, people often receive the Word passively without exploring the intersection between Christian theology and ethics and the assumptions people bring with them from their professional involvements.

We must foster a genuine give-and-take, exploring not simply how the traffic moves in one direction, but how it goes both ways. Teachers in public schools, for example, presuppose an anthropological understanding of children and how they learn. They ask questions like, Are behavior modification models compatible with a Christian understanding of humans as relational beings with the capacity for creative interaction with their environment? What does learning theory tell us about humans? How do we assess the competing paradigms of how people learn and how they should be taught? As economic actors we need to ask questions like, Are we governed primarily by egoistic self-interest? Are there alternative ways to understand economic behavior? How do we assess competing models of economic theory and practice?

What is difficult to convey in a book such as this, which is more general in its approach, is that these intersections are always specific and rich in detail when it comes to discerning how we should think and act. For example, peacemaking necessarily incorporates analysis of social structures if it is to speak to issues of social justice. Peacemaking depends on understanding the psychological and sociological processes of conflict resolution. It must draw on the insights of human psychology and anthropology if it is to deal with the anger and hatred in ethnic violence that centuries of violence and oppression have fostered.

This general knowledge, if it is to be relevant, must be brought to bear on specific conflicts in specific settings. General theory, while helpful, is not a substitute for the rich, detailed knowledge we need if we are to be effective peacemakers. Even with this detail, Christians of good will can disagree about how to respond to a particular conflict. In other words, there is no clear theological or ethical response to a concrete issue in a particular context. We need the discerning process in the church to serve as a kind of "check and balance" so we can avoid serious mistakes. We must also realize that people of good will do not always agree what is to be done, so we have to learn to live with ambiguity.

Depending upon the issues the church is facing, the relevant disciplines and data will vary. For example, in responding to ecological issues, the natural sciences become more prominent. In this case, we cannot easily make a sharp separation between empirical analysis (the "is") and ethical prescription ("the ought"). A proper relationship to the earth is shaped significantly by how we understand the workings of a healthy ecosystem and how humans must respond if the health of that ecosystem is to be preserved. As we pointed out earlier, nature served as a guide for human moral behavior in the wisdom literature of the Bible.

To illustrate the complexity of the relationship between "is" and "ought" questions and the ambiguity about how to relate biblical insights and modern knowledge, we can look briefly at the dispute about abortion. In the ancient Hebrew view, life was identified with breath. For example, in Genesis we read that God breathed into Adam and Adam became a living being (Gen. 2:7).[53] In the Jewish tradition, the tendency has been to identify human life with birth. Persons valued life in the womb because it was to become a human being at birth. From a theological standpoint, human life did not really begin until birth. That explains why in Exodus 21:22-25 human life after birth seems to be valued more highly than life before birth.[54]

Rather than placing the emphasis upon breath as the mark of human life, contemporary biology emphasizes the presence of the fundamental building blocks of life given by our genetic inheritance, which we receive at the moment of conception. Contemporary biological approaches to the moral issue of abortion tend to sensitize us to the taking of human life after the moment of conception. We recognize a fundamentally continuous process from conception through birth to infant development. The crucial biological event is not necessarily the emergence of life from the womb, though it has great symbolic meaning, but the joining of sperm and egg, which lays the groundwork for what the human being is to become. But as Lewis B. Smedes says, the genetic alphabet tucked into the DNA is not yet a short story. Building blocks are not a building; even if you have a pile of lumber, the tools of the builder's trade, and a carpenter standing by, you do not yet have a cottage. What finally goes into the making of an individual person includes a lot more than his genetic building blocks.[55]

Modern science has made us aware that the emergence of human life is a process, during which it is impossible to mark the magic moment when there is a human being. All people can agree that from the moment of conception, we have a developing human life. But where should we identify the life as a "person," such that taking life is murder? Modern biological science cannot answer the question of when human life becomes a person. Although our awareness of the potential that resides in the genetic code from conception leads many to object to taking that life, the presumption against abortion does not, however, mean that abortion is never justified.

Daniel Callahan explains how changing scientific and technological factors affect the legal issues surrounding abortion.[56] In the Supreme Court decision *Roe v. Wade*, the court stated, "With respect to the State's important and legitimate interest in potential life, the 'compelling' point is viability. This is so because the ... capability of meaningful life outside the mother's womb, usually placed at about seven months (28 weeks) ... may occur earlier, even at 24 weeks." Since that decision in 1973, the line has gradually shifted even earlier, perhaps now even 22 weeks (and this was written in 1986!). Callahan says,

> This change calls into question the continuing utility of "viability" as a concept useful for drawing legal and policy lines. The Supreme Court said that its dividing lines had "logical and biological justifications." But perhaps "viability" will no longer provide either kind of justification. As a "logical" justification it is a double-edged sword: if it is to bear great moral and legal weight, then that same weight will inexorably work against late abortions as the time of viability is pushed back even more. Even now, it is beginning to touch that point at which abortions are performed for genetic indications after amniocentesis (19–20 weeks but sometimes, because of delays, up to 24 weeks). As a "biological" justification, it is clearly a shifting one, a function of the present state-of-the-art of neonatal medicine.[57]

Society and the church are being torn apart by complex issues like abortion and homosexuality. It is critical that we Christians model a respectful conversational process, listening to each other as we seek to discern what it means to be faithful. Critical to genuine discernment is a Trinitarian view of God. The transcendence of God can correct our yearning for certainty and our idolatrous commitment to our own policies and programs as if they were ultimate. The call to be followers of Christ can correct our tendency to evade our responsibility to be faithful and can challenge us to courageously take a stand on issues even if unpopular or contrary to the views of those in the dominant culture around us.

We live in the tension between "transcendence" and "faithfulness." This tension can be embraced within the reconciling wholeness of God's Spirit, which can liberate us to live a life of joy and abandon. The coming of God's kingdom does not depend ultimately on us. We can be empowered to see that we are not in control. We can be surprised by the creative power and love of God as we continue the pilgrimage of Abraham and Sarah, who set out without knowing where they were going (Heb. 11:8).

Postscript

I COME TO THE END OF MY PILGRIMAGE in writing this book, profoundly aware of the limits of my own thoughts and of language to
convey those thoughts. More than ever this process has made me conscious again of the multilayered network of tensions that Christians
live with in being faithful to the gospel:

- citizens whose fundamental identity is shaped by the dominant
  culture around them, but who also live as aliens with an alternative cultural vision;
- called to "be" the church and be "separate" from the world,
  while engaging the wider culture in seeking the peace of the
  city where we dwell;
- living between the times in the light of the cross and the resurrection, longing for the gift of God's reign throughout the cosmos, yet living in the midst of brokenness and pain;
- recipients of the serendipity of God's grace to become who we
  are—not by our own doing, yet motivated to act and take responsibility for what we do and to participate in God's work
  of bringing healing to the nations;
- called to follow the way revealed in the concrete, particular,
  embodied Jesus of history, who is at the same time Lord of the
  nations and the light of the cosmos;
- profoundly humbled by our own particularity and the limits of
  our own knowledge and faithfulness, yet called to be witnesses
  to a "way" that transcends our limits;
- knowing at the deepest level our oneness as Christians in the
  Body of Christ, yet divided by our own partial insights and the
  diversity of ways we experience the good news;
- conscious that every expression of the Christian faith is culturally particular to a given context, yet knowing that the good
  news of the gospel transcends every cultural form;

291

- knowing both the presence of God's spirit in our work and throughout the cosmos and the "absence" of God who transcends every human project;
- compelled to live out a vision of life within the boundaries of our own time and space, yet drawn beyond ourselves in a process that is open to the future and invites us to imagine new possibilities;
- lured toward that future by the One God who transcends us, who became flesh and dwelt among us, and whose Spirit abides with us.

Appendix

ARTISTS: A TRINITARIAN MODEL

	God the Creator	God in Christ	God the Holy Spirit
Trans-cendent Power	*Transcendence: Godness of God* Artists: Transcendence through play, metaphor Alternative vision, break boundaries & limits of thought Confront idolatry	*Kingdom of God: Justice/Righteousness* Artists: Prophetic imagination Disturb & challenge Help us to see/know brokenness and pain	*Power/Empowerment Liberation* Artists: Moving people to feel/act Giving voice to the Powerless (i.e. in civil rights struggle, or in disappeared in Latin America)
Loving Power	*Persuasive Love of God* Artists: Evoke consent by expressing beauty, attraction of the gospel Portray the anguish, lament, and mourning of God (the price of human freedom)	*Cross: Sacrificial Love/ Servanthood* Artists: Simplicity/honesty (unpretentious) Costly nature of Discipleship Pain/suffering of love	*Grace: Giftedness of Existence; Gratitude* Artists: Renewing of Spirit Gift of creativity to challenge one-dimensional &mundane Spiriting the ordinary with new reality & meaning
Creative Power	*Creativity/Presence of God in all reality* Artists: Open our eyes to see/know the richness & intensity of reality To delight Evoke joy and wonder	*Church: New Creation/ New Humanity* Artists: Unifying function of arts to transcend difference Role in worship, liturgy Build solidarity & community	*Shalom: Wholeness Reconciling Presence* Artists: Integration Helping to see Holistically Totality of vision Overcoming of Fragmentation & split of reason and feeling

CITIZENS: A TRINITARIAN MODEL

	God the Creator	God in Christ	God the Holy Spirit
Trans-cendent Power	*Transcendence: Godness of God* Citizens: Humility. Critique of penultimate loyalties: Nationalism American way of life ethnic identity/race religious identity classism/ideology as basis of exclusion and violence	*Kingdom of God: Righteousness/Justice* Citizens: Repentance. Justice based on needs. Earth is the Lord's. Social solidarity. Criticism of individual self-interest, merit, market, utility, as basis of social justice	*Power/Empowerment/ Liberation* Citizens: Transformation Naming, unmasking, and engaging powers Liberation from racism, sexism, militarism, violence People power Courage overcoming fear and timidity
Loving Power	*Persuasive Love of God Respect for Freedom; Consent/Nonviolence.* Citizens: Protection of religious liberty Consent of governed Limits of government, dangers of civil religion Critique of repressive, controlling societies	*Cross: Sacrificial love and Servanthood.* Citizens: Nonviolent social transformation (King) Peacemaking/conflict-resolution strategies. Restorative justice Critique of myth of redemptive violence	*Grace: Giftedness of Existence; Gratitude.* Citizens: Restorative justice Alternatives to punishment Forgiveness to break retribution cycle Thankful stewardship to benefit earth Dignity/gift of work
Creative Power	*Creativity/Presence of God in all of reality* Citizens: Pluralism & multicultural diversity Foster creativity/diversity of language, arts, culture Criticism of culture of homogenization and conformism	*Church: New Creation/ New Humanity* Citizens: Practices derived by analogy of new society Participatory association Balance of dignity of individual and solidarity Inclusion of marginal Hospitality to stranger and alien	*Shalom: Wholeness. Reconciling Presence.* Citizens: Community work aimed at healing, wholeness. Networks and linkages Overcome dangers of specialization Ecological vision Relationship of people and earth

PHILOSOPHERS: A TRINITARIAN MODEL

	God the Creator	God in Christ	God the Holy Spirit
Trans-cendent Power	*Transcendence: Godness of God* Philosophers: Awareness of relativity/ particularity Recognition of limit/ finitude and hubris Limits of foundational-ism and various forms of universalism	*Kingdom of God: Justice/Righteousness* Philosophers: Critical social/political Analysis Identify alternative models of political and economic organization Signs of hope; positive transformation	*Power/Empowerment Liberation* Philosophers: Analysis of systems/ power. How does change occur? Naming/unmasking legitimization of systems of domination Conscientization
Loving Power	*Persuasive Love of God Respect for Freedom Consent/Nonviolence* Philosophers: Reality as process Openness to future vs. closed deterministic systems With creative freedom also comes potential for evil; Recognition of suffering, pain	*Cross: Sacrificial Love/ Servanthood* Philosophers: Evidence (historical and concrete) of nonviolent transformation Critique/unmasking of myth of redemptive violence Study/development of peacemaking practices Living with tragedy	*Grace: Giftedness of existence; Gratitude* Philosophers: Stories, testimonies, autobiography, historical memory Processes of restoration Identification of dependency on others for flourishing of life Dynamic of brokenness violation/alienation
Creative Power	*Creativity/Presence of God in all of reality* Philosophers: Knowing as relational Resist dualism and reductionism Knowing/attention to both rich diversity and ecological wholeness	*Church: New Creation/ New Humanity* Philosophers: Pathology and health of organizations/systems Ecology of systems (i.e. cities/families/schools) Dynamic balance of individual & social	*Shalom: Wholeness Reconciling Presence* Philosophers: Healing Arts Spiritual ministry, social work, education, psychotherapy, etc. Spiritualities: resources of world religions

Notes

AUTHOR'S PREFACE

1. J. Lawrence Burkholder, "The Peace Churches as Communities of Discernment," *Christian Century* (Sept. 4, 1963): 1072–1075.

2. See Karl Barth and Johannes Hamel, *How to Serve God in a Marxist Land* (New York: Association Press, 1959).

3. See the description of this position in the chapter by Loren Friesen, "Culturally Engaged Pacifism," in *Mennonite Peace Theology: A Panorama of Types* (Akron, Pa.: Mennonite Central Committee, 1991).

4. See James Juhnke, *Dialogue with a Heritage* (N. Newton, Kan.: Bethel College, 1987), and his article, "Mennonite History and Self-Understanding: North American Mennonitism as a Bipolar Mosaic," in *Mennonite Identity: Historical and Contemporary Perspectives*, ed. Calvin Redekop and Samuel J. Steiner (Lanham, Md.: University Press of America, 1988), 83–100.

5. See, for example, Epp's writings on the Middle East conflict: *Whose Land is Palestine?* (Grand Rapids: William B. Eerdmans, 1970); *The Palestinians: Portrait of a People in Conflict* (Scottdale, Pa.: Herald Press, 1976; *The Israelis: Portrait of People in Conflict* (Scottdale, Pa.: Herald Press, 1980).

6. Glen Stassen, ed. *Just Peacemaking: Ten Practices for Abolishing War* (Cleveland: Pilgrim Press, 1998).

CHAPTER ONE

1. See especially their book *Resident Aliens: A Provocative Christian Assessment of Culture and Ministry for People Who Know That Something Is Wrong* (Nashville: Abingdon, 1989); see also *Hauerwas, After Christendom? How the Church is to Behave if Freedom, Justice, and a Christian Nature Are Bad Ideas* (Nashville: Abingdon, 1991).

2. George Lindbeck, *The Nature of Doctrine: Religion and Theology in a Postliberal Age* (Philadelphia: Westminster, 1984).

3. James Gustafson, "The Sectarian Temptation: Reflections on Theology, the Church and the University," *Proceedings of the Catholic Theological Society* 40 (1988): 83–94.

4. James Gustafson, *Intersections* (Cleveland: Pilgrim Press, 1996), xi.

5. David Tracy, *The Analogical Imagination: Christian Theology and the Culture of Pluralism* (New York: Crossroad, 1981).

6. Gordon Kaufman, *In Face of Mystery: A Constructive Theology* (Cambridge: Harvard University Press, 1993).

7. Larry Rasmussen, *Moral Fragments and Moral Community: A Proposal for Church in Society* (Minneapolis: Fortress, 1993); *Earth Community, Earth Ethics* (Maryknoll, N.Y.: Orbis Books, 1996); Glen Stassen, *Just Peacemaking: Transforming Initiatives for Justice and Peace* (Louisville: Westminster, 1992); Glen Stassen, D. M. Yeager, and John Howard Yoder, *Authentic Transformation: A New Vision of Christ and Culture* (Nashville: Abingdon, 1996); John Howard Yoder, *For the Nations: Essays Public and Evangelical* (Grand Rapids: Eerdmans, 1997).

8. John H. Yoder supports the point I am making here: "A soft pluralism, when consistent, provides the most livable cultural space for Jews and Anabaptists, as well as for Jehovah's Witnesses and followers of Rev. Moon. As a civil arrangement, pluralism is better than any of the hitherto known alternatives. As an ecclesiastical arrangement, it is better than the monarchical episcopate. As a marketplace of ideas, it is better than a politically correct campus or a media empire homogenized by salesmanship. For such reason, Stanley Hauerwas's characterization of English-speaking justice as a set of 'bad ideas' [cf. Hauerwas, *After Christendom*] strikes me as too simple" (John H. Yoder, "Meaning After Babel: With Jeffrey Stout beyond Relativism," *Journal of Religious Ethics* [Spring 1996]: 135n).

9. See especially chapter 7, from which I am quoting, Walter Brueggeman, "Rethinking Church Models through Scripture," *Cadences of Home: Preaching Among Exiles* (Louisville: Westminster John Knox, 1997), 102–103.

10. "Rethinking Church Models," 100-101.

11. "Rethinking Church Models," 105, 107.

12. "Rethinking Church Models," 107-108.

13. Rasmussen, *Moral Fragments and Moral Community,* 140. In his book *For the Nations*, John H. Yoder shows how recovery of the Hebrew Scriptures and the Jewish experience is integrally related to a right understanding of our relationship of the church to culture. One example of Yoder's emphasis can be seen in the following statement. "The rootage of Jesus in Hebrew history gives to his ministry a depth in dialogue with community experience which was missing in the Jesus of Tolstoy and of Rauschenbusch, who became by a simple reversal of signs also the Jesus of Reinhold Niebuhr. That depth of social substance is missing as well in the Jesus of American fundamentalism. When we see Jesus in the perspective of the Hebrew heritage, his themes of judgment and fulfillment take on far more substance" (141).

14. In an earlier draft of this chapter, I had written that the "separation of church and state" was a sign of the secularization process. I am grateful to Glen Stassen for suggesting this different language. He argues that Luther's split between the secular public world and private church world—later altered and cemented in by the Enlightenment—has been a crucial cause of secularization. Separation of church and state, on the other hand, originated by Anabaptists and Baptists, was meant to free pastors from control by the state so they could speak concretely about public questions without state censorship, as did Menno Simons, and the Baptists, Richard Overton, and Roger Williams. In other words, separation of church and state in the Anabaptist and Baptist sense was never intended to suggest that the church should not speak on public issues in the public sphere. Thus, religion is not reserved for

the personal and private sphere of life. Rather, followers of the God of Jesus who "hunger and thirst for justice" (Matt. 5:6) are publically involved in seeking the shalom of the cities where they live.

15. For an analysis of the process of secularization, see Peter Berger, *The Sacred Canopy* (Garden City: N.Y.: Anchor Books, 1969) and *The Heretical Imperative* (Garden City, N.Y.: Anchor Books, 1980).

16. For Troeltsch's definition of *church* and *sect*, see chapter 2 below.

17. For a complete analysis of Troeltsch's position, see my dissertation: "The Relationship Between Ernst Troeltsch's Theory of Religion and His Typology of Religious Association" (Ph.D. diss., Harvard University, 1972). The basic argument of this dissertation is stated in my essay "A Critical Analysis of Troeltsch's Typology of Religious Association" in *Studies in the Theological Ethics of Ernst Troeltsch* (Lewiston, N.Y.: Edwin Mellen Press, 1991), 73–118.

18. John H. Yoder, *The Priestly Kingdom: Social Ethics as Gospel* (Notre Dame, Ind.: University of Notre Dame Press, 1984). George Williams uses the term *radical reformation* to describe the variety of groups in the sixteenth-century continental Reformation that sought to implement the Reformation more thoroughly than the magisterial reformers, particularly in their challenge to the medieval concept of a corpus Christianum. Franklin Littell uses the term *free church* in his book, *The Free Church* (Boston: Starr King Press, 1957). Donald Durnbaugh uses the term *believers church* in his book, *The Believers' Church* (1968; reprint, Scottdale, Pa.: Herald Press, 1986).

19. James McClendon, *Systematic Theology: Ethics* (Nashville: Abingdon, 1986), 19–20, 31–34.

20. James Davison Hunter, *Culture Wars: The Struggle to Define America* (New York: Basic Books, 1991).

21. See Karl Barth and Johannes Hamel, *How to Serve God in a Marxist Land* (New York: Association Press, 1959).

22. For a full discussion of the biblical concept of shalom, see Perry Yoder's *Shalom: The Bible's Word for Salvation, Justice and Peace* (Newton, Kans.: Faith and Life Press, 1987). See esp. 45, where Yoder shows that shalom in the Bible links salvation with justice.

23. Stanley Hauerwas and William H. Willimon, *Resident Aliens* (Nashville: Abingdon, 1989), 38, emphasis mine. The authors work with false dualisms throughout the book. They state, for example, "We do not argue that the bomb is the worst thing humanity can do to itself. We have already done the worst thing we could do when we hung God's Son on a cross. We do not argue that we must do something about the bomb or else we shall obliterate our civilization, because God has already obliterated our civilization in the life, teaching, death, and resurrection of Jesus" (89). This is a confusing statement. What does "the bomb" symbolize if not our commitment to an idol rather than Christ, an idol that we have put our trust in to preserve life? The bomb is a symbol of (not separate from) our continued crucifixion of Christ. Perhaps more than any other modern symbol, it expresses the paradox that our society hopes for life through a symbol of death.

The above statement is confusing also because the authors use the word *obliterate* in two quite different senses. On the one hand they say God "obliterates" our civilization in the sense that the gospel is a critique of the way of death symbolized by the bomb. The other meaning of *obliterate* is that the bomb destroys that which is valued by God—not just "our" civilization, but flora and fauna, the very created order which makes life possible. This obliteration is unalterably opposed by the good news of the gospel. Thus to oppose the bomb is not something other than doing God's work in the world. It is because we are people of God that we must oppose the bomb.

I agree when they say that Christian hope cannot be dependent upon the achievement of political peace. But here again they have created a false dichotomy. Christians who are attuned to the good news of the gospel will work passionately for peace because of the hope that is in them. Yet they undermine this passionate commitment to peace by legitimating perpetual violence in the world. "The world of nations has no means of being at peace other than means that are always violent, or at least potentially violent" (89). To believe that the "lamb who was slain is ultimately the most powerful reality in the universe" is not limited to the church. The problem is that Hauerwas and Willimon limit the power and hope of the kingdom of God to the church, rather than seeing the potential of God's power and rule throughout the entire universe.

24. Hauerwas and Willimon, *Resident Aliens*, 51.

25. Douglass John Hall, "Ecclesia Crucis: The Theologic of Christian Awkwardness," in *The Church Between Gospel and Culture: The Emerging Mission in North America*, ed. George R. Hunsberger and Craig Van Gelder. (Grand Rapids: Eerdmans, 1996).

26. Stanley Hauerwas, *Against the Nations* (Notre Dame, Ind.: University of Notre Dame Press, 1992); John H. Yoder, *For the Nations: Essays Public and Evangelical* (Grand Rapids: Eerdmans, 1997).

27. It is a mistake to equate Yoder's position with Stanley Hauerwas's views. This is often done because Hauerwas attributes such importance to Yoder in shaping his ideas. Yoder is much more ready to see connections between what the church stands for and movements in the culture at large. In some of his recent writings, for example, he has distinguished his approach from Hauerwas. (See footnote 8 above.)

28. Although I first began to think about the significance of Jeremiah's advice to the exiles while in East Germany during the cold war, another stimulus to my thinking were John H. Yoder's Menno Simons Lectures at Bethel College in 1982, entitled "The Jewish-Christian Division: A Reassessment from a Radical Reformation Perspective." I now see many of the seeds evident in those lectures bearing fruit in Yoder's recent book, *For the Nations*. See especially his essay, "See How They Go with Their Face to the Sun," 51–78.

CHAPTER TWO

1. Ernst Troeltsch, *The Social Teaching of the Christian Churches*, trans. Olive Wyon, first published in English in 1931, two vols. (New York: Harper Torchbooks, 1960), 999–1000.

2. For a more complete analysis of the connection between Troeltsch's theory of religion and his typology of religious association, see "The Relationship Between Ernst Troeltsch's Theory of Religion and his Typology of Religious Association," Ph.D. diss., Harvard University, 1972. See a shorter analysis of this issue in my article, "Normative Factors in Troeltsch's Typology of

Religious Association," *Journal of Religious Ethics* 3/2 (1975): 271–283. For an analysis of Troeltsch's dualism, a description of the antinomies, and an explanation of how they affect his evaluation of the types, see Duane K. Friesen, "A Critical Assessment of Troeltsch's Typology of Religious Association," in *Studies in the Theological Ethics of Ernst Troeltsch*, ed. Max A. Myers and Michael R. LaChat (Toronto Studies in Theology; Lewiston, N.Y.: Edwin Mellen Press, 1991), 73-118.

3. Max Weber influenced Troeltsch in important ways, but Troeltsch was not a descriptive sociologist like Weber. Troeltsch was more concerned with the normative question: What can we learn from the past in order to address the social crisis of the modern world? See my dissertation for a thorough analysis of the relationship of Weber and Troeltsch.

4. Troeltsch, *Social Teaching*, 1010.

5. Troeltsch, *Social Teaching*, 1012.

6. Troeltsch, *Social Teaching*, 1002.

7. Troeltsch, *Social Teaching*, 61.

8. For a more thorough description and analysis of Niebuhr's work than I can give here, see the book by Glen H. Stassen, Diane Yeager, and John Howard Yoder, *Authentic Transformation: A New Vision of Christ and Culture* (Nashville: Abingdon, 1996).

9. H. Richard Niebuhr, *Christ and Culture* (New York: Harper and Brothers, 1951), 32.

10. Niebuhr, *Christ and Culture,* 12–13.

11. Niebuhr, *Christ and Culture,* 24.

12. Niebuhr, *Christ and Culture,* 16.

13. Niebuhr, *Christ and Culture,* 21.

14. Niebuhr, *Christ and Culture,* 27–28.

15. Charles Scriven, *The Transformation of Culture* (Scottdale, Pa.: Herald Press, 1988), 41.

16. Niebuhr, *Christ and Culture,* 27.

17. Niebuhr, *Christ and Culture,* 44.

18. Stassen, *Authentic Transformation,* 52.

19. See above, p. 30.

20. See above, p. 31.

21. A more detailed analysis could show how this duality in Troeltsch and H. Richard Niebuhr arises out of the influence of Kant, who made a sharp distinction between the phenomenal and the noumenal world. This duality, which places religion in the arena of the noumenal and other reality in the phenomenal world, has had an enormous influence on theology since Kant. Many have been influenced by this Kantian duality, including Kierkegaard, neo-orthodox theologians like Barth, liberal theologians like Schleiermacher, and Albrecht Ritschl. In all these cases, theology sought a foundation in a reality that is more secure than the phenomenal realm of history. Such a theology contributes to a kind of "Gnostic" Christology in which Christ is abstracted from his actual, historical, cultural, phenomenal world.

It has also had disastrous implications for relationships between Christians and Jews. The rediscovery of the Jewishness of Jesus in recent biblical scholarship is another implication of an attempt to overcome this Kantian residue. For a more complete analysis of Niebuhr's thought, see Glen Stassen, "Concrete Christological Norms for Transformation," in *Authentic Transformation,* esp. 147–150). Stassen argues that during the period of Niebuhr's life when he wrote *Christ and Culture,* Niebuhr turned away from a more concrete, embodied Christology because of the Kantian residue in his thought and in reaction to Karl Barth's exclusive Christocentrism (174–196). I fully agree with Stassen, who corrects Niebuhr with an embodied Christology from which we can derive concrete norms for how to act *within* history. Stassen argues one can find this emphasized elsewhere in Niebuhr, if not in *Christ and Culture.*

22. For a more comprehensive study of the term, see Kathryn Tanner, *Theories of Culture: A New Agenda for Theology* (Minneapolis: Fortress, 1997).

23. Niebuhr, *Christ and Culture,* 32.

24. Clifford Geertz, "Religion as a Cultural System," in *The Religious Situation 1968,* ed. Donald Cutler (Boston: Beacon Press, 1968), 641.

25. Clifford Geertz, *The Interpretation of Cultures* (New York: Basic Books, 1973), 50.

26. Geertz, *Interpretation of Cultures.* See chapter 1, "Thick Description: Toward an Interpretive Theology of Culture," esp. 6-30.

27. I do not deny that some animal species may display some rudiments of what we call "culture." I am only claiming that for human beings, culture is of such power and significance that this degree of difference makes the significance of human culture unique among animals.

28. Clifford Geertz has a series of essays on different aspects of culture. He refers to religion, ideology, common sense, and art as "cultural systems." For example, what we usually call "common sense," as if it were based upon obvious facts, is itself an *interpretation* of life. As Geertz puts it, "Common sense is as much an interpretation of the immediacies of experience, a gloss on them, as are myth, painting, epistemology, or whatever; ... like them, [it is] historically constructed and, like them, subjected to historically defined standards of judgment" (*Local Knowledge* [New York: Basic Books, 1983], 76). Similarly, he argues that art is an element of our symbolic system of meaning, not just an aesthetic object expressing "pure form." Geertz quotes Matisse, who says, "The purpose of a painter must not be conceived as separate from his pictorial means, and these pictorial means must be more complete (I do not mean more complicated) the deeper his thought. I am unable to distinguish between the feeling I have for life and my way of expressing it" (*Local Knowledge,* 96).

29. Larry L. Rasmussen, *Earth Community, Earth Ethics* (Maryknoll, N.Y.: Orbis Books, 1996), 7.

30. Rasmussen, *Earth Community, Earth Ethics,* 32.

31. Tanner, *Theories of Culture,* 44. See especially Tanner's chapter 3, "Criticism and Reconstruction," where she critiques previous views of culture that are too static or assume that culture is a self-contained aesthetic whole. She argues for a corrective to our understandings of culture from a post-modern perspective. Such an approach would attend more to historical process, fluidity, change, conflict, and the limits of consensus models of culture. She also argues against the idea of a "Christian" culture. I agree with her in one sense, that there is no one cultural form that Christianity must take. On the other hand, she emphasizes so strongly the way in which Christian identity interacts with elements of the larger culture that she does not sufficiently recognize the importance of distinctive marks of Christian identity that need to

be discerned in each historical period and context in the life of the church. Her position is based on the Word of God theology of Barth, which provides leverage for her critique of all idolatries—that all cultural forms are subject to critique and thus there can be no Christian culture. This position is overemphasized however, at the expense of our need also to have a clear norm as we make choices about how to relate to culture. According to Gordon Kaufman (*In Face of Mystery*), a God concept serves two functions: to relativize all human standpoints and to serve as a standard of humanization, which I ground in an embodied Christology.

32. Niebuhr, *Christ and Culture*, 69.

33. Niebuhr, *Christ and Culture*, 32.

34. Walter Wink, *Engaging the Powers* (Minneapolis: Fortress, 1992), 51.

35. Jaroslav Pelikan, *Jesus through the Centuries* (New Haven: Yale University Press, 1985).

36. Stassen, *Authentic Transformation*, 56.

37. See Yoder's discussion of the use of typological method in "How H. Richard Niebuhr Reasoned: A Critique of Christ and Culture" in *Authentic Transformation*, 31–90; see esp. 43–52.

38. Stassen, *Authentic Transformation*, 247.

39. Stassen, *Authentic Transformation*, 246–265.

CHAPTER THREE

1. Clifford Geertz, *The Interpretation of Cultures* (New York: Basic Books, 1973), 50.

2. Gordon Kaufman, *In Face of Mystery* (Cambridge, Mass.: Harvard University Press, 1993), 10.

3. See Kaufman's autobiographical statement in *Religious Studies Review* 20/3 (July 1994): 177.

4. Lydia Neufeld Harder, *Obedience, Suspicion and the Gospel of Mark: A Mennonite-Feminist Exploration of Biblical Authority* (Waterloo, Ont.: Wilfrid Laurier University Press, 1998), 38.

5. Kaufman, *In Face of Mystery,* ix. There are a number of continuities in Gordon Kaufman's career as a theologian, beginning with his book, *Relativism, Knowledge and Faith* (1960) and culminating in his recent systematic theology, *In Face of Mystery: A Constructive Theology* (1993). Kaufman made a major shift in direction with his book, *An Essay in Theological Method* (1975). This shift to "imaginative construction" and away from theology as "hermeneutical" (the interpretation of an authoritative tradition) is reflected in the quotation from Kaufman's 1975 essay.

6. Kaufman, *In Face of Mystery*, 61.

7. Kaufman, *In Face of Mystery*, 8.

8. Clifford Geertz, "Religion as a Cultural System," in *Reader in Comparative Religion,* ed. William A. Lessa and Evon Z. Vogt (New York: Harper & Row, 1965) 204–216; reprinted in *Religion: North American Style*, 3d ed., ed. Thomas E. Dowdy and Patrick H. McNamara (New Brunswick, N.J.: Rutgers University Press, 1997), 11–19.

9. See John K. Sheriff, *The Fate of Meaning* (Princeton, N.J.: Princeton University Press, 1989). I do not intend to defend meaning over against deconstruction or to argue for a particular theory of language. I do share the

"'linguistic turn' in twentieth century thought that sees language as the medium of all human experience and knowledge" (Sheriff, *Fate of Meaning*, xiii). Rather than argue for a particular theory of meaning, I simply begin with the notion that meaning is essential to our lives—that we cannot live without it—and language is integral to knowing and expressing that meaning. When human beings use signs, those signs represent something *to them*. Signs involve the sign itself, the referent of the sign, and the meaning of the sign for a community of persons. Though based on the theory of Charles Peirce, John K. Sheriff, my colleague, has made the case for this triadic understanding of language. Sheriff argues that the dyadic theory of signs of Ferdinand de Saussure, carried forward by Jacques Derrida, cannot establish a basis for meaning. In a dyadic system of sign/object, meaning is separate from language. Therefore, meaning must always be "deconstructed" or deferred. Sheriff argues that a sign is always triadic. It consists of the sign, its referent, and the interpreter who uses the sign. Meaning is inherent in or inseparable from language because signs are always *for us*. Signs have meaning only in relationship, in a context, and thus humans can never establish what something is in itself, only what it means in relation to us.

The truth of meaning systems cannot be established with certainty, for symbol systems are always open-ended, subject to further interpretation. We can never step outside of language into some "objective" frame of reference. The "choice" of the system of symbols human beings use is integrally tied to the quest for and definition of meaning. I put *choice* in quotes because the systems of symbols human beings use are social—learned through practice among a community of persons. I follow here Ludwig Wittgenstein, who says we learn to use language in a variety of ways appropriate to a particular social use or frame of reference. For example, the arts "express" meaning and follow different rules than are used in scientific description. Humans "choose" these languages because they serve a variety of human purposes and interests. The meaning is dependent upon the choices humans make to use different languages for varied purposes and interests.

10. Kaufman provides a model of how this is done. Kaufman argues for the plausibility of a metaphysical rather than a strictly phenomenalistic account of humanity and the world. Second, he argues for the world as cosmic evolution rather than an eternal structure. Third, he argues for the presence of serendipitous creativity in the bio-historical process. *All three of these require steps of faith.* By "serendipitous creativity" Kaufman means we live in a universe that is open to the future, that in the course of evolution new events produce consequences (both good and evil) that are quite surprising and unpredictable. Fourth, Kaufman argues that as we look back at the cumulative evolutionary and historical development, we can see a series of creative advances in this cosmic process that, from our point of view as humans, is "good." Though we have no firm objective, scientific basis to view the process as more than a chance or random occurrence, we can choose to take a step of faith to see in this process a tendency in the nature of things toward purposeful development. As Kaufman puts it, "The trajectory eventuating in the creation of human historical existence could be seen ... as a significant expression of the serendipitous creativity manifest in the cosmos as a whole; and thus the appearance of human modes of being in the world would be properly regarded not as a metaphysical surd but rather as grounded in the

ultimate nature of things, in the ultimate mystery" (Kaufman, *In Face of Mystery*, 284).

11. See Paul Tillich's *Dynamics of Faith* (New York: Harper Torchbooks, 1957).

12. Dietrich Bonhoeffer, *Letters and Papers from Prison*, ed. Eberhard Bethge (New York: MacMillan, 1972). "Tillich set out to interpret the evolution of the world (against its will) in a religious sense—to give it its shape through religion. That was very brave of him, but the world unseated him and went on by itself; he, too, sought to understand the world better than it understood itself; but it felt that it was completely misunderstood, and rejected the imputation" (Bonhoeffer, *Letters and Papers*, 327–328).

13. See Alasdair MacIntyre's books *After Virtue: A Study in Moral Theory* (Notre Dame, Ind.: University of Notre Dame Press, 1981); and *Three Rival Versions of Moral Inquiry: Encyclopedia, Genealogy and Tradition* (Notre Dame, Ind.: University of Notre Dame Press, 1990).

14. Sallie McFague, *Metaphorical Theology* (Philadelphia: Fortress, 1982), 42.

15. Personal metaphors for God—for example, that God makes covenants or is just and loving—does not suggest that God is *a* person. When we refer to God as *Father*, such language does not suggest that God is masculine. It is necessary, therefore, to use a great variety of personal metaphors—both masculine and feminine—in order to correct the view that God *is* a patriarch.

16. Tillich, *Dynamics of Faith*, 46.

17. Though there is not agreement about what the word *postmodern* means, we can identify three general characteristics. James McClendon Jr. and Nancey Murphy attempt to define postmodern theology in their article "Distinguishing Modern and Postmodern Theologies," *Modern Theology 5* (April 1989): 191–214. They isolate the following characteristics: "holism in epistemology, the relation of meaning to use in philosophy of language, and the discovery of an organic (yet not premodern) view of community in ethics and epistemology—a corporate metaphysics" (199). Postmodernism moves away from a Cartesian epistemology, which assumes that our sensations can give us objective knowledge of the world. Postmodern theology recognizes that human beings do not have a raw or objective experience of the world, but that all experience is interpreted within a symbolic system of meaning. Thus all knowledge is paradigm-dependent, interpreted within a framework or worldview sometimes referred to as "holism in epistemology."

Ludwig Wittgenstein recognized that we learn these worldviews in a context, within a community of discourse and practice. In these communities we learn to use language in a particular way. The appropriate use of language is defined by standards of internal coherence rather than by an external referent. The language we use does not refer to a world "out there." Rather, it serves to orient our lives in a meaningful way within a particular community or cultural context. Third, postmodernism moves away from the attempt to define external or objective standards according to which we can judge truth or moral validity. Postmodernism rejects any kind of foundationalism, any attempt to base morality in some objective moral law built into the nature of God or the universe. Theology must begin with the recognition of the situatedness of our lives within our own bio-historical consciousness. We cannot

escape our symbolic systems, our worldview, or our framework of interpretation. The sociology of knowledge has made us profoundly aware of the way
in which our theology is a reflection of our social location.

Third-world theologies of liberation, feminist theory, and black theologies
make us even more aware of how historically and socially conditioned our
thinking is. It is impossible to secure a universally persuasive foundation for
theology by appeal to the authority of the Bible, of church tradition, of natural law, or of some universal religious experience. It is also impossible for a
secular perspective to claim it has some universal, detached truth perspective
from which to reject Christian faith. We are all in the same boat in that we
have no choice but to seek understanding from the particular perspective of
our communities. Some perspectives make better sense and lead to better
ways of life than others. We may unapologetically believe and act from without our faith communities and test them by their fruits.

18. See Gordon Kaufman's "Two Models of Transcendence" in *God the
Problem* (Cambridge, Mass.: Harvard University Press, 1972). In this essay,
Kaufman argues that interpersonal relations serve as the most appropriate
model for thinking about transcendence or God.

19. See John Sheriff, *The Fate of Meaning*.

20. See Ian Barbour's *Religion in an Age of Science* (New York: Harper &
Row, 1990) and Sallie McFague's *Models of God* (Philadelphia: Fortress,
1987).

21. See Gordon Kaufman's concept of theological imagination, developed
in his *The Theological Imagination*.

22. Kaufman, *In Face of Mystery*, 395.

23. Augustine reflected on these issues in Books XI–XIII in the *Confessions,* where he discusses the relationship between the eternal and the temporal. In and through the particularity of Augustine's own individual struggle of
faith, he found intimations of God—the universal. Augustine's insight into
the connections between his own particularity and the nature of God is in-
structive. The confessions are specific and concrete. They are rooted in time.
But that leads Augustine to ask what time is, and how time is related to the
eternal. How is the limitless eternal related to the temporal, bounded by the
limits of time? He posed the problem in Book XI: "In eternity nothing moves
into the past: all is present. Time, on the other hand, is never all present at
once. The past is always driven on by the future, the future always follows on
the heels of the past, and both the past and the future have their beginning
and their end in the eternal present. If only man's minds could be seized and
held still" (*Confessions* [Baltimore: Penguin Books, 1961], 261–262).

After an extensive discussion of time, Augustine arrives at an interesting
description of the triadic nature of time: "The present of past things is the
memory; the present of present things is direct perception; and the present of
future things is expectation" (*Confessions*, 269). In an unusually imaginative
and creative way, Augustine interprets his own rootedness in time as a reflection of the Trinity. Since time is not three separate units—past, present and
future—but rather memory, perception, and expectation within in the present, time is really a reflection of or intimation of the eternal in the present.
So time as past, present, and future and the self as being, knowledge, and will
reflect the very image of God.

24. Gayle Gerber Koontz put it well when she said, "The Bible is authori-

tative because it freely evokes consent, offers insight which can be seen to be 'of God.' A functional view of authority asks less for a 'submission of will than for an opening of the imagination, the mind and heart.' It recognizes that on an important level the Bible cannot be believed unless it rings true to our deepest capacity for truth and goodness" ("The Trajectory of Scripture and Feminist Conviction," *Conrad Grebel Review 5* [Fall 1987], 214).

25. For a more complete statement of my position on biblical authority, see "Biblical Authority: The Contemporary Theological Debate," *Mennonite Life* (Sept. 1989): 26–33.

26. H. Richard Niebuhr, *The Meaning of Revelation* (New York: MacMillan, 1941).

27. Glen Stassen, *Authentic Transformation*, 162–167.

28. See Stassen's description of how these norms are validated both from outside and inside the community, *Authentic Transformation*, 157–162.

29. See Ian Barbour, *Myths Models and Paradigms* (New York: Harper & Row, 1974), for an analysis of how paradigms and the data of experience interact with each other.

30. George A. Lindbeck distinguishes between "intratextual" and "extratextual" methods. "The latter locates religious meaning outside the text or semiotic system either in the objective realities to which it refers or in the experiences it symbolizes." He holds to an "intratextual" method, which locates meaning not outside the text, for "meaning is constituted by the uses of a specific language rather than being distinguishable from it. Thus the proper way to determine what 'God' signifies, for example, is by examining how the word operates within a religion and thereby shapes reality and experience rather than by first establishing its propositional or experiential meaning and reinterpreting or reformulating its uses accordingly. It is in this sense that theological description in the cultural-linguistic mode is intrasemiotic or intratextual" (*The Nature of Doctrine: Religion and Theology in a Postliberal Age* [Philadelphia: Westminster, 1984], 114).

31. Stanley Hauerwas, *After Christendom?* (Nashville: Abingdon, 1991), 107.

32. There is a significant difference here between Hauerwas and John H. Yoder. See chapter 1, notes 8 and 27.

33. Martin Luther King Jr. *Why We Can't Wait* (New York: Signet Books, 1964), 86.

34. James Cone makes this point strongly in his book *Martin and Malcolm and America* (Maryknoll, N.Y.: Orbis Books, 1991). In his introduction to *A Testament of Hope: The Essential Writings and Speeches of Martin L. King, Jr.*, editor James Washington says, "King's roots are indeed in the religion of his black slave forebears" ([New York: Harper, 1986] xii). I recommend highly Cornell West's essay, "Martin Luther King, Jr.: Prophetic Christian as Organic Intellectual" in *Prophetic Fragments: Illuminations of the Crisis in American Religion and Culture* (Grand Rapids: Eerdmans, 1988). West says, "And let us ... never forget that the great American prophetic figure of our time, Martin Luther King Jr., was a child of the black church—an individual product of the major institutional product of black people in this country" (4).

35. Martin L. King Jr., *Stride Toward Freedom* (New York: Ballantine Books, 1958), 86.

36. King said this in a sermon he preached at the National Cathedral, Washington, D.C., March 31, 1968. *Testament of Hope: The Essential Writings of Martin Luther King* (San Francisco: Harper & Row, 1986), 269.

37. King, *Testament of Hope,* 269–270.

38. Many Christians believe that human sin did not extinguish completely all knowledge of God or of the moral law (cf. Rom. 2:15). God relates to the entire cosmos and to all human beings. Thus all can in some sense know God and the moral law. However, Paul believed that Jesus Christ is the basis of authentic knowledge of God. But because God is in relationship to all peoples, we can gain insight into the nature of God through other religions, a knowledge that may supplement or add to (though not contradict) the knowledge of God we have through Jesus. This insight into God's nature is similar to the way our understanding of God is enlarged as we come to know the nature of the physical universe.

CHAPTER FOUR

1. Augustine, *City of God* 11.24 (New York: Image Books, 1958), 233.

2. Trinitarian ways of thinking have had a profound impact on philosophical thought in persons like Hegel and Whitehead. Much is owed to Karl Barth for his contribution to the revival of the importance of the Trinity in contemporary Christian theology. See Ted Peters, *God as Trinity: Relationality and Temporality in Divine Life* (Louisville: Westminster/John Knox, 1993), for a helpful description of theological positions, especially in recent theology.

3. Kaufman, *In Face of Mystery,* 412.

4. See John H. Yoder's essay in *Authentic Transformation,* esp. 61–65.

5. For a helpful discussion of this issue, see "The Idea of Relativity and the Idea of God," in Gordon Kaufman's *The Theological Imagination: Constructing the Concept of God* (Philadelphia: Westminster, 1981), 80–95.

6. See Paul Tillich's *Dynamics of Faith* and *Courage to Be.*

7. God is one, yet human parenthood usually involves two parents, a mother and father. Here we see the limitations of metaphors. Just as metaphors are both like and unlike that to which they point, so God is both like and unlike a parent. I find it useful to think about God with both feminine and masculine images and thus appropriate to refer to God as Loving Parent or as Father and Mother of the Universe. But in that duality, God is one, unlike human parents. The metaphor of *parent* with both its masculine and feminine components is clearly preferable to the one-sidedly masculine images of God that have been so prevalent in Christian theology. There are many critiques of patriarchal language for God. See especially Sallie McFague's critique of the monarchical model of God as a king ruling over the universe (*Models of God: Theology for an Ecological, Nuclear Age* (Philadelphia: Fortress, 1987), 63–69; and Dorothee Soelle's *Theology for Skeptics* (Minneapolis: Fortress, 1995), 19–35. Soelle says, "The relativizing of symbols for God used as an absolute, as represented by 'father' is a minimal demand. ... There are other symbols for God: keeping within the use of familial language, we can say 'mother' or 'sister' to her. To me symbols from the natural world, with their non-authoritarian qualities, are clearer yet. To be free of images of dominance, theological language can go back to the mystical tra-

dition. 'Wellspring of all good things,' 'living wind,' 'water of life,' are symbols of God without authority or power and without a chauvinistic flavor" (28).

8. See the essay by Charles Birch, "Chance, Purpose and the Order of Nature," in *Liberating Life: Contemporary Approaches to Ecological Theology,* ed. Charles Birch, William Eakin, and Jay B. McDaniel (Maryknoll, N.Y.: Orbis Books, 1990).

9. E. Frank Tupper, *Scandalous Providence: The Jesus Story of the Compassion of God* (Macon, Ga.: Mercer University Press, 1995).

10. Miroslav Volf, *Exclusion and Embrace: A Theological Exploration of Identity, Otherness, and Reconciliation* (Nashville: Abingdon, 1996). See especially the last chapter, "Violence and Peace," 275–306.

11. See Walter Wink's interpretation of Revelation in the light of Christ's "domination-free order." *Engaging the Powers* (Minneapolis: Fortress, 1992), 99.

12. See Dorothee Soelle, *Suffering* (Philadelphia: Fortress, 1975); Dorothy Soelle, *Theology for Skeptics: Reflections on God* (Minneapolis: Fortress, 1995); Dietrich Bonhoeffer, *Letters and Papers from Prison* (New York: Macmillan, 1972); Martin Luther King Jr., *A Testament of Hope: The Essential Writings of Martin Luther King, Jr.,* ed. James M. Washington (San Francisco: Harper & Row, 1984); Akio Hashimoto, "Theology of the Pain of God: An Analysis and Evaluation of Kazor Kitamori's [1916–] Work in Japanese Protestantism," Th.D. diss., Concordia Seminary, 1992; Keosuke Koyama, *Mount Fuji and Mount Sinai: A Critique of Idols* (Maryknoll, N.Y.: Orbis Books, 1984); Jon Sobrino, *Christology at the Crossroads* (Maryknoll, N.Y.: Orbis Books, 1978); Larry Rasmussen, *Dietrich Bonhoeffer: His Significance for North Americans* (Minneapolis: Fortress, 1990); and "The Cross of Reality," in Larry Rasmussen, *Earth Community Earth Ethics* (Maryknoll, N.Y.: Orbis Books, 1996).

13. Charles Birch, "Chance, Purpose and the Order of Nature," in *Liberating Life: Contemporary Approaches to Ecological Theology* (Maryknoll, N.Y.: Orbis Books, 1990), 195.

14. A number of authors develop this point of view. One of the more helpful summaries of this point is by the Australian biologist, Charles Birch, who develops the view of God as persuasive love and explains how that perspective illuminates evolutionary theory. See "Chance, Purpose and the Order of Nature," 182–200.

15. Elizabeth A. Johnson, *Women, Earth, and Creator Spirit* (New York: Paulist Press, 1993), 52. See also *She Who Is: The Mystery of God in Feminist Theological Discourse* (New York: Crossroad, 1992); and Elizabeth Schüssler Fiorenza, *In Memory of Her: A Feminist Theological Reconstruction of Christian Origins* (New York: Crossroad, 1983).

16. Johnson, *Women, Earth, and Creator Spirit,* 44.

17. Johnson, *Women, Earth, and Creator Spirit;* Rasmussen, *Earth Community Earth Ethics;* McFague, *Models of God;* James A. Nash, *Loving Nature: Ecological Integrity and Christian Responsibility* (Nashville: Abingdon, 1991); Charles Birch, "Chance, Purpose and the Order of Nature"; Jay B. McDaniel, "Revisioning God and the Self," in *Liberating Life.* Rasmussen quotes Luther, who he says is "boldly pan-en-theistic" (273). "For how can reason tolerate it that the Divine majesty is so small that it can be substan-

tially present in a grain, on a grain, over a grain, through a grain, within and without, and that although it is a single Majesty, it nevertheless is entirely in each grain separately, no matter how immeasurably numerous these grains may be?" *Martin Luther's Werke: Kritische Gesamtausgabe (Weimarer Ausgabe)* (Weimar: H. Böhlaus Nachfolger, 1912–1921), 32.134–136.36.

18. Nash, *Loving Nature*, 115.

19. Rasmussen, *Earth Community Earth Ethics*, 272–273. The quote from Bonhoeffer is from "Auftrage der Bruderräte" (December 1939) in *Gesammelte Schriften*, ed. Eberhard Bethge (Munich: C. Kaiser, 1966), 3:388.

20. See John H. Yoder's essay, "The Hermeneutics of Peoplehood," in *Priestly Kingdom*, 15–45.

21. See the development of an alternative theology of atonement for a non-Constantinian church by J. Denny Weaver, "Atonement for the Nonconstantinian Church," *Modern Theology* 6 (July 1990): 307–323.

22. Letha Scanzoni and Nancy Hardesty, *All We're Meant to Be: A Biblical Approach to Women's Liberation* (Waco, Tex.: Word Books, 1974), 56, 59.

23. Walter Wink, *Engaging the Powers* (Minneapolis: Fortress, 1992), 114.

24. See Wink's chart, where he contrasts the domination system and God's domination free order: *Engaging the Powers*, 46–47.

25. Glen Stassen, *Just Peacemaking: Transforming Initiatives for Justice and Peace* (Louisville, Ky.: Westminster/John Knox, 1992), 41.

26. Stassen, *Just Peacemaking: Transforming Initiatives*, 41.

27. For a more thorough statement of this understanding of Jesus, see John H. Yoder, *Politics of Jesus* (Grand Rapids: Eerdmans, 1972).

28. Stassen, *Just Peacemaking: Transforming Initiatives*, 46.

29. For a more complete description of this new model, see chapter 4 in my *Christian Peacemaking and International Conflict* (Scottdale, Pa.: Herald Press, 1986).

30. Wink, *Engaging the Powers*, 149. See the work of René Girard, *Violence and the Sacred*, trans. Patrick Gregory (Baltimore: Johns Hopkins University Press, 1977).

31. For a fuller description of narrative ethics, see my analysis of Stanley Hauerwas's views in "A Critical Analysis of Narrative Ethics," in *The Church as Theological Community: Essays in Honor of David Schroeder* (Winnipeg: Canadian Mennonite Bible College, 1990). In that essay I contrast narrative ethics with two competing paradigms of ethics: natural law ethics and liberal democratic ethics. Both natural law ethics and democratic liberalism are ethical paradigms that seek to develop a standard of the "good" independent of the story of Jesus. Natural law claims that universal moral law can be known by all rational beings capable of transcending their particular cultural or historical conditions. Democratic liberalism is a form of natural law theory that grounds ethics in the centrality of the individual who has certain rights. Both paradigms legitimate coercive force in the exceptional case. The failure by some human beings to accept reason or to violate what is regarded as rational thus becomes the occasion for those who hold to a strictly rational system of ethics to "violate" rational argument and persuasion and to impose standards upon others by force. This contradiction lies at the heart of "rational" systems of ethics.

32. C. Norman Kraus, *The Community of the Spirit* (Grand Rapids: Eerdmans, 1974), 15.

33. Kraus, *Community of the Spirit*, 20.

34. Some interpreters believe that Matthew has "spiritualized" Luke by having Jesus say, "Blessed are the poor in spirit for theirs is the kingdom of heaven" (Matt. 5:3). This text creates a double difficulty for interpreters. Based on our modern understanding of the word, *heaven* suggests a realm beyond this life. We know, however, that Matthew used the word *heaven* as a substitute for the name *God* out of respect for Jewish piety, which refused to use the name of God because of its holiness. The virtue of humility, suggested by being "poor in spirit" should not lead us to assume that Matthew is indifferent to actual and real poverty. See Luise Schottroff on this point:

> The beatitude of the poor (Luke 6:20f.) is addressed in both versions to the *ptochoi*, the utterly destitute. It is repeatedly assumed that the beatitude of the poor in spirit (*ptochoi to pneumati*; Matt. 5:3) is a spiritualized version of a macarism addressed originally to the poor in an economic sense. Depending on people's theological interests, the spiritualized version has been praised or condemned. Yet the assumption that Matthew's Gospel presents a spiritualized version is based in a false conception that itself presupposes a dualistic distinction /137/ between bodiliness/material existence on the one hand and spiritual poverty on the other. Such a distinction fails to do justice to the language of the Hebrew Bible and the New Testament. In the context of the theological tradition of Judaism, poverty is in every instance a theological and holistic term. Whoever is poor in the material sense cannot praise God; whoever experiences hunger also experiences the destruction of the relationship with God. That is why poverty is a scandal before God and humankind, a transgression against the likeness of God. "Poor in spirit" says explicitly what Luke 6:20 says implicitly: the poor are poor right down to the marrow of their bones; even their very *pneuma*, their capacity for the dignity and power God bestows, is threatened." Luise Schottroff, *Lydia's Impatient Sisters*, trans. Barbara and Martin Rumscheidt, foreword by Dorothee Soelle (Louisville, Ky.: Westminster John Knox, 1995), 136–137.

35. Robert Bellah, Richard Madsen, William M. Sullivan, Ann Swidler, and Steven M. Tipton, *Habits of the Heart: Individualism and Commitment in American Life* (Berkeley: University of California Press, 1985), 153.

36. For a deeper analysis, see the trilogy of books by Walter Wink: *Naming the Powers: The Language of Power in the New Testament* (Minneapolis: Fortress, 1984); *Unmasking the Powers: The Invisible Forces that Determine Human Existence* (Minneapolis: Fortress, 1986); *Engaging the Powers* (Minneapolis: Fortress, 1992).

CHAPTER FIVE

1. See Paul Ramsey's "Liturgy and Ethics" in *The Journal of Religious Ethics* 7/2 (Fall 1979), which shows the connections between believing, ethical living, and worship.

2. I am not using the term *liturgy* to mark a formal style of worship. As Paul Ramsey puts it, "In family prayer, there the church is worshipping.

When Evangelicals lustily sing, 'There is power, there is power, in the blood; there is power in the blood of the Lamb,' ... that is liturgy, and faith confessed and Christian life formed. ... When members of the Society of Friends meet in silence, that is liturgy. Even without the external signs of the 'quaking' that used to go on, we ought to suppose ... that the Friends are not just communing with their better natures but are rather engaging in a liturgical action designed to ... allow 'opening' to come, the inner supernatural light to enkindle." *The Journal of Religious Ethics* 7/2 (Fall 1979): 142.

3. Quoted by Larry L. Rasmussen, *Moral Fragments and Moral Community* (Minneapolis: Fortress, 1993), 145.

4. John H. Yoder, *The Politics of Jesus* (Grand Rapids: Eerdmans, 1972), 40.

5. Daniel Smith, *The Religion of the Landless: The Social Context of the Babylonian Exile* (Bloomington, Ind.: Meyer-Stone Books, 1989).

6. For documentation and analysis of this variety, see Raymond E. Brown, *The Churches the Apostles Left Behind* (Maryknoll: N.Y.: Paulist Press, 1984).

7. I do not share the view of Franklin Littell, who described the Anabaptists as "restitutionists" who sought to restore the one normative vision of the New Testament church, a position that came to be referred to as "primitivism." See Franklin Littell, *The Anabaptist View of the Church: An Introduction to Sectarian Protestantism* (Hartford, Conn.: American Society of Church History, 1952), later revised as *The Origins of Sectarian Protestantism* (New York: Macmillan, 1964). Scholars dispute Littell's description of the Anabaptists. See the summary of this discussion in John H. Yoder's chapter, "Anabaptism and History," in *Priestly Kingdom* (Notre Dame: University of Notre Dame Press, 1984, 123–134). Not all Anabaptists specified one particular vision, though they did share a common critique of Constantinianism. In this sense, they sought to "go back" to the general form of the church as a believing, minority community prior to Constantine.

8. I cite John H. Yoder extensively because *The Priestly Kingdom* states so well what I believe should be the approach of all Christians who acknowledge their particularity, yet hope to contribute to the church universal. "If it be the case that Judaism and Christianity by the nature of things cannot be but particular historical communities, it will follow that the specific form of Christian commitment any given author espouses will be best understood by taking into account, rather than abstracting away, the particularity of the author's time and place" (8). Yoder explains why he draws on the historical traditions of the Radical Reformation. He objects to those who treat this confessional approach with a condescending tone, who label it as "sectarian" and marginalize it. While reflecting his own Radical Reformation perspective, he did not write *Priestly Kingdom* for an ethnic Mennonite subculture within American society. As he puts it, "These pages do not describe a Mennonite vision. They describe a biblically rooted call to faith, addressed to Mennonites or Zwinglians, to Lutherans or Catholics, to unbelievers or other believers" (8).

9. Rasmussen, *Moral Fragments*, 142.

10. Sallie McFague exhibits the kind of rethinking and imagining we must do with respect to our view of God in her book *Models of God: Theology for an Ecological, Nuclear Age* (Philadelphia: Fortress, 1987).

11. See Nicholas Wolterstorff, "Justice as a Condition of Authentic Liturgy," and the responses to that essay in a series of essays under the title,

"Symposium: The Revisioning of Worship" in *Theology Today* 48/1 (April 1991): 6–21.

12. See the development of this thesis in a new edition of the book by James Cone, *The Spirituals and the Blues* (Maryknoll, N.Y.: Orbis Books, 1991).

13. Rasmussen, *Moral Fragments*, 48.

14. Rasmussen *(Moral Fragments,* 73) quotes from Alan Wolfe, *Whole Keeper? Social Science and Moral Obligation* (Berkeley: University of California Press, 1989), 122, who is citing H. Geoffrey Brennan and James M. Buchanan, *The Reason of Rules: Constitutional Political Economy* (Cambridge: Cambridge University Press, 1985), 150.

15. Rasmussen, *Moral Fragments*, 73–74.

16. Miroslav Volf, *Exclusion and Embrace: A Theological Exploration of Identity, Otherness and Reconciliation* (Nashville: Abingdon, 1996), 20.

17. Rasmussen, *Moral Fragments,* 129–130. Rasmussen draws heavily on the work of Philip Selznick, *The Moral Commonwealth: Social Theory and the Promise of Community* (Berkeley: University of California Press, 1992). He also cites Michael Walzer, *Spheres of Justice* (New York: Basic Books, 1983).

18. Kathryn Tanner, *Theories of Culture: A New Agenda for Theology* (Minneapolis: Fortress, 1997), 116.

19. Tanner, *Theories of Culture*, 101.

20. Tanner, *Theories of Culture*, 155.

21. Rasmussen, *Moral Fragments and Moral Community,* 154–155. For an account of a theory of virtue, which draws especially on Aristotle, see Alaisdair MacIntyre, *After Virtue,* 2d ed. (Notre Dame, Ind.: University of Notre Dame Press, 1984). MacIntyre argues that a theory of virtue has three essential components: "practices," a narrative order to one's life, and a moral tradition to which one belongs. See especially 187, where MacIntyre defines a practice as follows: "By a 'practice' I am going to mean any coherent and complex form of socially established cooperative human activity through which goods internal to that form of activity are realized in the course of trying to achieve those standards of excellence which are appropriate to, and partially definitive of, that form of activity, with the result that human powers to achieve excellence, and human conceptions of the ends and good involved are systematically extended. Tic-tac-toe is not an example of a practice in this sense, nor is throwing a football with skill; but the game of football is, and so is chess."

22. Phil Stoltzfus, "How to Stop Constructing Things: Kaufman, Wittgenstein, and the Pragmatic End of Constructivism," *Mennonite Life* (March 1997): 37–43.

23. See the book edited by Dorothy C. Bass, *Practicing Our Faith: A Way of Life for a Searching People* (San Francisco: Jossey-Bass Publishers, 1997), for an example of a list of practices (many of which overlap with my list) developed by a group of persons, each of whom contributed an essay to describe one particular practice.

24. See the discussion of Geertz's definition of religion in chapter 3.

25. Roger Schmidt, *Exploring Religion*, 2d ed. (Belmont, Cal.: Wadsworth Publishing, 1988), 392. Clifford Geertz's discussion of ritual can be found in his essay, "Religion as a Cultural System."

26. For many people, sports events are ritual activities that orient their lives and become an all-consuming reality that distorts priorities. Identification with local high school teams or even children's softball games sometimes take on enormous importance for parents. The same is true of identification with a state university team, such as the "Big Red" football team in Nebraska or a national soccer team whose victory or defeat can lead to violence. Large groups of people participate ritually in the world of sports, either directly in the event itself or by indirect identification through television and newspaper coverage of high school state tournaments, bowl games, Super Bowls, quests for national championships, the World Series, the Stanley Cup, the World Cup in soccer, or the Olympic Games.

National symbols and rituals, such as July 4, Memorial Day, the playing of the National Anthem, or the ceremony surrounding a flag, can also take on great significance. The Memorial Day parade had great significance for Armenian immigrants in Watertown, Massachusetts. It showed that now they were Americans, that they had sacrificed for their new country in World War II. In his presidential address to the American Academy of Religion ("The Rituals of Jesus, the Anti-Ritualist," *Journal of the American Academy of Religion* [1971]), James Burtchael vividly described several rituals surrounding the Vietnam War. Protesters and counter-protesters at the University of Notre Dame and in central Kansas attempted to express their identity and values. The response of Americans to the Persian Gulf War through rallies, parades, and the display of yellow ribbons is another recent example of the prominence of ritual in people's lives. Wearing or displaying yellow nearly became a test of patriotism. Yellow legitimated war against Iraq and support for American troops. School children and teachers were pressured to support rituals like tying yellow ribbons on fences of schoolyards. There was no space for a dissenting child or teacher in some schools. The pervasiveness of yellow symbolized the pressure either to support the war or to remain silent in voicing dissent.

As a Christian who confesses ultimate loyalty to Jesus Christ in the rituals of Christian worship, I do not feel quite at home in a group who recites the pledge of allegiance to the United States of America. Allegiances to Christ and to the USA sometimes clash with each other. I remember feeling this unease already as a boy in elementary school in American Falls, Idaho, as one of only three Mennonites of pacifist conviction in the entire school. Somehow I learned at an early age that the ritual of confession in Christian worship and the ritual of the pledge of allegiance mark off two identities that sometimes do not harmonize with each other.

27. Hans Denck, "Whether God is the Cause of Evil," written in 1526. This quotation from Denck is taken from the first page of the interpretation and translation of key texts by Clarence Bauman, *The Spiritual Legacy of Hans Denck* (New York: E. J. Brill, 1991).

28. Yoder, *Priestly Kingdom*, 24.

29. Volf, *Exclusion and Embrace*, 48.

30. Rasmussen, *Moral Fragments and Moral Community*, 157–159.

31. My discussion here is consonant with Paul Tillich's discussion of symbols in his book, *Dynamics of Faith* (New York: Harper Torchbooks, 1957), 41–54.

32. Bronislaw Malinowski distinguishes between magic and religion. In

magic, the aim of a rite or ceremony is to produce a particular or practical end. Through proper exercise of the rite, one insures a particular end. The assumption behind magic is that the performance of the rite so participates in the holy that proper behavior can itself control the gods. In religious ceremony, one does not have necessarily do the performance of a particular rite in order to secure a subsequent event. See *Magic, Science and Religion* (Garden City, N.Y.: Doubleday, 1954), 37–38.

33. Anthony Ulgonik, *The Illuminating Icon* (Grand Rapids: Eerdmans, 1989), 45.

34. For an insightful theological interpretation of the significance of the Sabbath, see Karl Barth's *Church Dogmatics*, III/4, The Doctrine of Creation (Edinburgh: T. and T. Clark, 1961), 47–72.

35. Abraham Heschel, *The Sabbath*, 13.

36. Rasmussen, *Earth Community, Earth Ethics* (Maryknoll, N.Y.: Orbis Books, 1996), 224–225.

37. The quotations are from Stassen's essay in *Authentic Transformation*, 167.

38. Martin Luther King Jr., *Stride Toward Freedom*, 86.

39. Wink, *Engaging the Powers*, 298.

40. Wink, *Engaging the Powers*, 298–299.

41. Wink, *Engaging the Powers*, 304.

42. Henri Nouwen, *Seeds of Hope* (Elgin, Ill.: Brethren Press, 1989), 172–173.

43. Jean Janzen's text is hymn number 482 and Brian Wren's text is hymn number 233 in *Hymnal: A Worship Book* (Elgin, Il.: Brethren Press; Newton, Kan.: Faith & Life Press; Scottdale, Pa.: Mennonite Publishing House, 1992).

44. Irene Jackson Brown, "Tradition, Transformation, Empowerment: Dynamics of Music in the African-American Worship Event," an address given at "A Symposium on the Arts and Prophetic Imagination: Expressions of Anguish and Hope," Jan. 11–13, 1991, Bethel College, N. Newton, Kansas. In her analysis of African-American worship, Brown referred to the work of anthropologist Edward T. Hall, who analyzed how cultures organize space.

45. See his essay, "Sacrament as Social Process: Christ the Transformer of Culture," in the volume of essays on worship in *Theology Today*, 48/1 (April 1991): 33–44. See also his more recent reflections especially in "The Hermeneutics of Peoplehood: A Protestant Perspective," in *Priestly Kingdom* (15–45).

46. Yoder, *Priestly Kingdom*, 25.

47. In our time, the ritual of "confirmation" in the churches that practice infant baptism can have meanings similar to what adult baptism meant for believers churches. Confirmation involves an intentional choice to *remain* in the church, to be a disciple, and to commit oneself to hear the counsel of one's fellow disciples. William Everett describes confirmation as a public commitment to take responsibility within a particular community. Such an act transcends our natural memberships of family, race, and nation. Within this community of faith one participates in prayer and dialogue with the Word. To be confirmed in the church is to *con*fess as well to *pro*fess to live out a certain way of life in the world. Though Everett discusses the church in very general categories and does not explain what a process of "dialogue with the Word"

would mean, I think he could accept the substance of Yoder's position. See William Everett, *Journal of Religious Ethics* 7/2 (Fall 1979), 203–214.

48. Yoder, *Priestly Kingdom*, 15.

49. Yoder, *Priestly Kingdom*, 25.

50. John H. Yoder, *Body Politics: Five Practices of the Christian Community Before the Watching World* (Nashville: Discipleship Resources, 1994), 1–3.

51. Yoder, *Body Politics*, 12.

52. See William Klassen's description and analysis of the biblical concept of forgiveness in his book *The Forgiving Community* (Philadelphia: Westminster, 1966).

53. Hannah Arendt, *The Human Condition* (The University of Chicago Press, 1958), 237.

54. Donald Shriver, *An Ethic for Enemies: Forgiveness in Politics* (New York: Oxford University Press, 1995). Alan Geyer has been a participant with a group of scholars in developing a set of ten criteria for just peacemaking. One of the processes that can contribute to peace is "to acknowledge responsibility for conflict and injustice, and seek repentance and forgiveness." Glen Stassen, ed., *Just Peacemaking: Ten Practices for Abolishing War* (Cleveland, Oh.: Pilgrim Press, 1998), 77-89. See also Desmond Tutu, *No Future without Forgiveness* (New York: Doubleday, 1999).

55. Yoder, The Priestly Kingdom, 33.

56. Yoder, The Priestly Kingdom, 33.

57. Rasmussen, *Moral Fragments and Moral Community*, 163

58. Rasmussen, *Moral Fragments and Moral Community*, 163–164.

59. Some of my ideas are drawn from lectures on Christian hospitality that Christine Pohl gave at Associated Mennonite Biblical Seminary, Feb. 18–19, 1998. See Christine D. Pohl, *Making Room: Recovering Hospitality As a Christian Tradition* (Grand Rapids: Eerdmans, 1999).

60. Leo Tolstoy, *What Men Live By: Russian Stories and Legends* (New York: Pantheon Books, 1960), 79–96.

61. Fyodor Dostoyevsky, *The Brothers Karamazov* (New York: Modern Library), 62–65.

62. Philip Hallie, *Lest Innocent Blood Be Shed* (New York: Harper and Row, 1979).

CHAPTER SIX

1. James Luther Adams, *Taking Time Seriously* (Washington, D.C.: University Press of America, 1978), 15.

2. See the appendix for an outline of how a Trinitarian vision is reflected in the Christian's role as artist.

3. Alice Walker, *The Color Purple* (New York: Washington Square Press, 1982), 174–179.

4. Walker, *Color Purple*, 175–178.

5. Walker, *Color Purple*, 249.

6. See Karl Barth's *Wolfgang Amadeus Mozart*. My reference is from Frank Burch Brown, *Religious Aesthetics* (Princeton, N.J.: Princeton University Press, 1989), 30.

7. Nicholas Wolterstorff, *Art in Action* (Grand Rapids: Eerdmans, 1980), 84.

8. Rudolf Arnheim's book, *Art and Visual Perception: A Psychology of the Creative Eye* (Berkeley: University of California Press, 1974), elaborates in depth the visual language used by the artist and describes the impact on the viewer of the way this language is employed.

9. I highly recommend the journal, *Arts: The Arts in Religious and Theological Studies*, which seeks to advance the place of the arts in theological education. The address is *Arts*, 3000 Fifth St NW, New Brighton, MN 55112.

10. Margaret Miles, *Image as Insight* (Boston: Beacon Press, 1985). See "Image and Language in Contemporary Culture" for an analysis of the powerful role of visual image in our culture (127–137), and "Language and Images: A Theory," where she analyzes the connections between language and visual image (139–154).

11. Surprisingly, Miles urges us to return to Plato to get our bearings. I use the word *surprising* because of Plato's ambivalence to the arts. Plato was concerned that we clarify concepts through careful reflection. In Plato's dialogues, Socrates' role is to help students who were confused because they misrepresented reality with concepts. By identifying their linguistic flaw, Socrates helped students clarify their thinking and overcome their conceptual disorientation. Miles says it was not accidental that Plato, fascinated by the power of language, banished artists from his republic. Rather than banishing artists, we need to learn to understand them, to clarify how they use visual language, just as Socrates helped students clarify concepts.

In Plato's description of physical vision as the foundation of abstract thought in the *Symposium* (210a–212b) we see the foundation for an understanding of the role of images in culture. This view was influential later (mediated through Plotinus) in the medieval idea of vision. In the *Symposium*, Plato describes how students, attracted to the sight of a beautiful body, notice other beautiful bodies and eventually are moved to contemplate beauty in its abstract form. Miles notes that in the contemplation of the beautiful, the visual experience of physical beauty is not eliminated, but "remains as a permanent connection between ideal beauty and the sensible world" (Miles, *Image as Insight*, 139–40). So visible beauty in the sensible world becomes the means for expressing the ideal of beauty. Plotinus, a third century philosopher, carried on this notion, believing himself to be a faithful interpreter of Plato: "Now beauty, as we have said, shone bright amidst these visions, and in this world below we apprehend it through the clearest of our senses, clear and resplendent. For sight is the clearest mode of perception vouchsafed to us through the body" (Miles, *Image as Insight*, 142).

12. Susanne Langer, *Feeling and Form* (New York: Scribner, 1953), 26.

13. Langer, *Feeling and Form*, 27.

14. See the section entitled, "The aesthetic and the religious: theory at an impasse," in Brown, *Religious Aesthetics,* 24–30.

15. Brown, *Religious Aesthetics,* 25.

16. Brown, *Religious Aesthetics,* 28–29.

17. John M. Janzen and Reinhild Kauenhoven Janzen, *Mennonite Furniture: A Migrant Tradition (1766–1910)* (Intercourse, Pa.: Good Books, 1991), 201.

18. Brown, *Religious Aesthetics,* 136.

19. Thomas Aquinas, *Summa Theologica* I, Q. 39, art. 8. *Basic Writings of Saint Thomas Aquinas*, ed. Anton C. Pegis (New York: Random House, 1945), 378.

20. Quoted by Wilson Yates in "The Arts, Spirituality and Prophetic Imagination," an address given at Bethel College, N. Newton, Kan., Jan. 11, 1991.

21. Richard Cartwright Austin, "Beauty: A Foundation for Environmental Ethics," *Environmental Ethics* 7 (Fall 1985): 197–208.

22. Robert Regier, "Aesthetic Values in Environmental Decision-making," unpublished lecture given at Bethel College, N. Newton, Kan., Feb. 28, 1992.

23. Merrill Kraybill, "Thoughts About Art," *A Drink from the Stream*, vol. 2, ed. John J. Sheriff and Heather Esau (N. Newton, Kan.: Bethel College, 1996), 98.

24. Quoted by Wolterstorff, *Art in Action*, 97.

25. Brian Wren, "Poet in the Congregation," *Arts: The Arts in Religious and Theological Studies* 2/1 (Fall 1989): 10.

26. Coherence does not necessarily mean symmetry. See the discussion of the value of the aesthetic tension between symmetry and asymmetry in Soetsu Yanagi's *The Unknown Craftsman: A Japanese Insight into Beauty* (Tokyo: Kodansha International, 1972). For more discussion of these ideas see note 35.

27. See Wolterstorff's discussion of aesthetic excellence, *Art in Action*, 156–174.

28. From the song, "Little Boxes," words and music by Malvina Reynolds. ©1962 Schroder Music Co. (ASCAP) Renewed 1990. Used by permission. All rights reserved.

29. I am grateful to Robert Regier for suggesting these examples of postmodern architecture that raise questions of integrity.

30. Sylvia Shaw Judson, *The Quiet Eye: A Way of Looking at Pictures* (Chicago: Regnery Gateway, 1982).

31. Wolterstorff, *Art in Action*, 181–182.

32. Robert Regier, "Learning from the Gesture," in *A Drink from the Stream*, vol. 2, ed. John J. Sheriff and Heather Esau (N. Newton, Kan.: Bethel College, 1996), 181.

33. Regier, "Learning from the Gesture," 183.

34. Quotation from the brochure handed out at the exhibit.

35. Quotation from the brochure handed out at the exhibit.

36. Wendell Berry, "Song (4)" in *Collected Poems* (New York: North Point Press, 1984).

37. My appreciation for this visual language of symmetry/asymmetry depends on the work by Soetsu Yanagi, *The Unknown Craftsman*. Beauty for Yanagi involves the tension between pattern and irregularity. To see nature as beautiful is to see the pattern in it. This pattern, however, is not simply what lies *in* nature, but is the result of the freedom of the imagination we bring to it. "A beautiful pattern is always receptive to the spirit of the viewer. One never tires of looking at it. Through pattern, the world and our own hearts are made beautiful. A country without pattern is an ugly country, a country that does not care for beauty. Beauty is the transformation of the world into pattern" (115). But beauty and pattern do not require complete symmetry. In a chapter entitled, "The Beauty of Irregularity," the perfect is symbolized by the symmetrical, as in the Greek vision of the human body. Yanagi says, "The precise and perfect carries no overtones, admits of no freedom; the perfect is static and regulated, cold and hard. We in our own human imperfections are repelled by the perfect, since everything is apparent from the start and there

is no suggestion of the infinite. Beauty must have some room, must be associated with freedom. Freedom, indeed, is beauty. The love of the irregular is a sign of the basic quest for freedom" (120–121). Thus the bowl used in a Japanese tea ceremony does not have the "perfection" of a machine-produced object, which is indeed not a living but a dead object. The spirit or beauty of a bowl lies in the blending of pattern and irregularity. For an introduction to Paul Soldner's work, see *Paul Soldner: A Retrospective*, ed. Mary Davis Mac-Naughton (Seattle: University of Washington Press, 1991).

38. See Wolterstorff, *Art in Action*, esp. 21-63.

39. Most of Paul Tillich's writings assume an expressionist theory of art—that art expresses religious depth or ultimate concern. This is an exaggerated claim for art and too narrow a view. Later in life, Tillich began to modify his expressionist theory as he encountered art that did not fit. We noted earlier in this chapter Susanne Langer's too-restrictive romantic view of art as that which expresses feelings. Hans-Georg Gadamer absorbed aesthetics into hermeneutics (Brown, *Religious Aesthetics*, 11) by stressing that art communicates or reveals truth. This, says Brown, is a corrective to pure aestheticism, but it also is too restrictive in reducing art to one thing. With Mozart as his ideal, Karl Barth thought of art primarily in terms of a Platonic ideal.

Much contemporary art reveals something quite other than a Platonic ideal by confronting us with the brokenness and alienation in our world. Hans von Balthasar is one of the few theologians who has a fully developed theological aesthetic. In his major three-volume work, *Herrlichkeit: The Glory of the Lord*, he argues that Christian revelation reveals all truth and beauty. This too is an exaggerated claim. It is no more true in aesthetics than it is to claim that all scientific and mathematical truth is revealed in Christian revelation. Aesthetic value should be consistent with Christian revelation, but not all beauty is revealed by Christian revelation. See Brown, *Religious Aesthetics*, for a more thorough review of these aesthetic theories.

40. Richard R. Niebuhr, *Experiential Religion* (New York: Harper & Row, 1972), 44.

41. Claus Westermann, *The Living Psalms* (Grand Rapids: Eerdmans, 1984), 10.

42. Westermann, *Living Psalms*, 17, gives three examples of this parallelism: (1) In synonymous parallelism, one phrase repeats the other, as in Psalm 103:1: "Bless the Lord, O my soul; and all that is within me, bless his holy name!" (2) In synthetic parallelism, one sentence supplements the other, as in Psalm 103:2: "Bless the Lord, O my soul, and forget not all his benefits." (3) In antithetic parallelism one sentence opposes the other, as in Psalm 91:7: "A thousand may fall at your side, but it will not come near you."

43. Westermann, *Living Psalms*, 17.

44. Duane Friesen, *Christian Peacemaking and International Conflict: A Realist Pacifist Perspective* (Scottdale, Pa.: Herald Press, 1986), 238–239.

45. Wolterstorff, *Art in Action*, 69.

46. St. Augustine, *The City of God*, 14.26 (Garden City, N.Y.: Image Books, 1958), 318.

47. Wolterstorff, *Art in Action*, 69–70.

48. Derek Walcott, as interviewed by Bill Moyers, *A World of Ideas* (New York: Doubleday, 1989), 429.

49. Langer, *Feeling and Form*, 52.

50. *Black Elk Speaks*, ed. John Neihardt (Lincoln, Neb.: University of Nebraska Press, 1979).

51. See Paul Tillich, *On Art and Architecture,* ed. John and Jane Dillenberger (New York: Crossroad, 1987), 247.

52. Tillich, *Art and Architecture,* 235.

53. Václav Havel, *Letters to Olga* (New York: Henry Holt, 1983), 258–259.

54. Peter Berger, *A Rumor of Angels* (New York: Doubleday, 1970).

55. See the book introducing the exhibit by John S. Oyer and Robert S. Kreider, *Mirror of the Martyrs* (Intercourse, Pa.: Good Books, 1990).

56. Walter Brueggemann, *The Prophetic Imagination* (Philadelphia: Fortress, 1978).

57. Wilson Yates, "The Arts, Spirituality and Prophetic Imagination," address given to the Symposium on the Arts, Bethel College, Jan. 11–13, 1991, 9.

58. Abraham Heschel, *The Prophets*, two vols. (New York: Harper & Row, 1962). See esp. chapter 6 on Jeremiah, 1:103–139.

59. Brueggemann, *Prophetic Imagination*, 66.

60. In developing these ideas, Hyde draws upon the work of the French anthropologist, Marcel Mauss, whose seminal work on gift-giving in primitive and archaic societies is foundational for work by anthropologists on gift rituals. Hyde reflects on the connections of these rituals to religious systems of meaning, the social structure of these societies, and the connection of these societies to their physical environment. Hyde is himself not an anthropologist, but his particular interest is in the place of creativity and the role of the artist in a market-oriented society. See Lewis Hyde, *The Gift* (New York: Vintage Books, 1979).

61. I am not suggesting that it is inappropriate for an artist to be compensated for their work, any more than it is inappropriate for any other professional like a social worker, minister, or teacher to be compensated. My point is that my primary motivation as a teacher, like the artist, is not to make money through my teaching, but the purpose of my work is the gift I pass on to those I teach.

62. Hyde provides insight into his concept of gift by citing examples of gift-giving in many societies and by referring to the folklore, myths, and rituals that serve to foster the spirit of giving. When European settlers came to this country, they often did not understand the giving function in Native American societies. The purpose of gift-giving is to circulate gifts in an ongoing way. Someone gives to me and I in turn give to others. Gift-giving is violated when a gift is appropriated as accumulated capital. Thus when Native Americans gave gifts to settlers, they expected the gift to continue to circulate. European settlers did not understand this, so they labeled this expectation "Indian giving," a pejorative connotation we maintain in our language to this day. Native American societies also bartered for and traded objects that did not circulate within the gift sphere. The key for Native Americans was to maintain that the priorities and proper relationships between the two spheres. Hyde does not reduce these societies to "gift" societies, but rather wants us to understand the relationship of the "gift" and "commodity" spheres.

Hyde describes the rituals of the Indian tribes of the Pacific Northwest, who depended upon the salmon for their sustenance. Thus when the salmon reached the season to return from the ocean and entered the mouths of the rivers to spawn, an elaborate greeting ceremonial took place. A symbolic first fish was caught, the flesh eaten in a communal ceremony, and the bones of the salmon returned to the ocean. The return to the sea was seen as a gift back to the gods, who were responsible for the gifts that sustained life. Giving is thus part of the religious system of meaning, since the gift of life itself does not arise from human effort. We are familiar with these notions and their attending rituals in the Old Testament. When the Israelites entered the Promised Land and reaped an abundant harvest, they were reminded to return the first fruits back to God as a reminder of the gifted nature of human existence. Hyde points out abundant salmon existed for centuries in the Pacific Northwest. However, once the salmon were seen simply as a natural resource to be exploited for market purposes, the ecological balance was threatened, and the life on which human beings depended was threatened.

63. Hyde's concept of "gift" also applies to the role of scientific inquiry in society. We can contrast scientific research whose aim is the production of knowledge for the sake of the "market" with "pure" science, whose interest is simply to know. Science for the market aims to gain a competitive edge in the development of a product. Such research is not readily shared. In fact, efforts may be made to keep such research secret, as in the Manhattan Project's development of the atomic bomb. Science in this sense is like a commodity that is appropriated to gain a competitive edge. Hyde contrasts such science with scientific research in the gift sphere—the search for truth for its own sake, and the sense of satisfaction and joy in discovery of the "secrets" of nature. Such scientific work is not unlike the experience of artists who have a sense that they have received the gift of knowledge, that something has happened to them as the "secrets" of nature unfold to them. Most importantly, the spirit of this kind of science is to share knowledge, not keep it secret. Such knowledge does not "belong" to a corporation, to be used for personal gain; it belongs to the community. In community, that knowledge is tested by other scientists. Sharing the gift of knowledge in turn creates and fosters the community of scientists. Again we have the threefold nature of gifts—a gift given to the scientist, the gift of knowledge itself, and the sharing of the gift in the scientific community.

CHAPTER SEVEN

1. I acknowledge the tension between Luke's apologetic and theological interests and historicity. The point here is not what "really happened," but what the story in Acts reflects about the theological interpretation of dual citizenship.

2. Glen H. Stassen, D. M. Yeager, and John Howard Yoder, *Authentic Transformation: A New Vision of Christ and Culture* (Nashville: Abingdon Press, 1996), 51–52.

3. Walter Wink, *Engaging the Powers* (Minneapolis: Fortress, 1992). See especially the two chapters: "The Myth of the Domination System," (13–31); and "Unmasking the Domination System," (87–104). See also my own book, where I argue that belief in the "necessity" or "inevitability" of war is one of the most pervasive ideas in our culture that needs to be delegitimated and replaced with an alternative belief system. Duane Friesen, *Christian Peacemak-*

ing and International Conflict: A Realist Pacifist Perspective (Scottdale, Pa.: Herald Press, 1986).

4. Many young Mennonite conscientious objectors in World War II worked in mental health institutions. Partly out of this experience of seeing how mental patients were cared for and treated, Mennonites developed a number of mental hospitals, introducing some of the more innovative mental health care facilities in the country. See Vernon H. Neufeld, *If We Can Love: The Mennonite Mental Health Story* (Newton, Kan.: Faith and Life Press, 1983).

5. Howard Zehr, *Changing Lenses: A New Focus for Crime and Justice* (Scottdale, Pa.: Herald Press, 1990).

6. Portions of this material are taken from my chapter, "Encourage Grassroots Peacemaking Groups and Other Voluntary Organizations," which is one of the criteria of a just peacemaking paradigm, elaborated in the book, *Just Peacemaking*, ed. Glen Stassen (Cleveland, Oh.: Pilgrim Press, 1998).

7. Michelle Tooley, *Voices of the Voiceless: Women, Justice and Human Rights in Guatemala* (Scottdale, Pa.: Herald Press, 1997), 177.

8. See the documentation of this case in Daniel L. Buttry, *Christian Peacemaking: From Heritage to Hope* (Valley Forge, Pa.: Judson Press, 1994), 132–135.

9. Buttry, *Christian Peacemaking*, 182–185.

10. Robert D. Putnam, "Diplomacy and Domestic Politics: The Logic of Two-Level Games," in *Double-Edged Diplomacy: International Bargaining and Domestic Politics*, ed. Peter B. Evans, Harold K. Jacobson, and Robert D. Putnam (University of California Press, 1993), 436.

11. David Cortwright, *Peace Works: The Citizen's Role in Ending the Cold War* (Boulder: Westview Press, 1993), 248.

12. Gene Sharp, *The Politics of Nonviolent Action* (Boston: Porter Sargent, 1973), 8.

13. Barth, *Church Dogmatics*, III-IV:639–641.

14. James Luther Adams, "Our Responsibility in Society," in *The Prophethood of All Believers*, ed. George K. Beach (Boston: Beacon Press, 1986), 151–152.

15. Robert Bellah, Richard Madsen, William M. Sullivan, Ann Swidler, and Steven M. Tipton, *Habits of the Heart: Individualism and Commitment in American Life* (Berkeley: University of California Press, 1985).

16. Quoted by Stanley Hauerwas in *Truthfulness and Tragedy* (Notre Dame, Ind.: University of Notre Dame Press, 1977), 90–92.

17. Herbert Deane makes it clear that Augustine defines the church "spiritually." "The City of God, the true Jerusalem, is the whole assembly of the saints; it is identical with the Church of which Christ is the Head and all the citizens are members, that is, the *invisible* church. ... Even the visible Church, which contains many of the reprobate along with the elect, is not an earthly division of the City of God, although, having been established by Christ Himself as the vehicle through which the elect are to be gathered together out of the world during the period from the Incarnation to the Last Judgment, it is more closely related to that City than any earthly state or society can ever be" (Herbert Deane, *The Political and Social Ideas of St. Augustine* [New York: Columbia University Press, 1963], 28–29, emphasis mine).

18. Luther's position is developed in many of his writings. See esp. "Secu-

lar Authority: To What Extent It Should Be Obeyed," written in 1523, in *Martin Luther: Selections from his Writings*, ed. John Dillenberger (Garden City, N.Y.: Doubleday, 1961), 363–402.

19. H. Richard Niebuhr, *The Kingdom of God in America* (New York: Harper and Brothers, 1937), 39–40.

20. Bellah, *Habits of the Heart*, 29.

21. Karl Barth, "Christian Community and Civil Community," in *Community, State and Church* (New York: Doubleday, 1960), 168–171. The implications of this approach are developed by Philip LeMasters in a paper presented at the meetings of the Society of Christian Ethics, Jan. 8–10, 1993, in Savannah, Georgia.

22. Stephen Charles Mott, *A Christian Perspective on Political Thought* (New York: Oxford University Press, 1993), 200.

23. Christians need the equivalent of a Jewish *Talmud* which on any given page gives a cross section of interpretation reflecting hundreds of years of thinking of what it has meant to be faithful to the Torah in the light of changing contexts.

24. *The Challenge of Peace: God's Promise and Our Response* (Washington, D.C.: United States Catholic Conference, 1983), 4.

25. Thomas Aquinas, *The Summa Theologica*, ed. Anton Pegis (New York: Random House, 1945), 2:746.

26. *The Challenge of Peace,* §17,7.

27. John Calvin, *Institutes of the Christian Religion* (Philadelphia: Westminster, 1960). Vol. II, ch. 2, 270. See also II/13 and II/17.

28. Stephen Charles Mott, *A Christian Perspective on Political Thought* (New York: Oxford University Press, 1993), 131.

29. Mott, *A Christian Perspective*, 136.

30. Bellah, *Habits of the Heart*.

31. John Rawls, *A Theory of Justice* (Cambridge, Mass.: Harvard University Press, 1971), 60.

32. Rawls, *Theory of Justice*, 83.

33. Friesen, *Christian Peacemaking*, 110–111.

34. See the insightful analysis of Miroslav Volf of how a Trinitarian perspective provides resources for an ethic that can both protect the individual from exclusion by embracing the "other" within community, while at the same time protecting space for the individual to be without absorption into community (*Exclusion and Embrace*, 125–131). See also his book, *After Our Likeness: The Church as the Image of the Trinity* (Grand Rapids, Mich.: William B. Eerdmans, 1998). See as well the appendix, where I show how a trinitarian structure impacts how we view the role of citizen.

35. Mott, *A Christian Perspective*, 141.

36. Herbert A. Deane, *The Political and Social Ideas of St. Augustine* (New York: Columbia University Press, 1963), 117.

37. Martin Luther, "Secular Authority, To What Extent It Should be Obeyed," in *Martin Luther: Selections from his Writings*, ed. John Dillenberger (New York: Doubleday, 1961), 367.

38. Luther, "Secular Authority," 371.

39. Though the Anabaptists were deeply influenced by the Augustinian/Lutheran view of the state, scholars of Anabaptism are increasingly recognizing that there was not one unified view of civil government. (See J. Denny

Weaver, *Becoming Anabaptist* [Scottdale, Pa.: Herald Press, 1987] and James Stayer, *Anabaptists and the Sword*, rev. ed. [Lawrence, Kan.: Coronado Press, 1975].) The pacifist Anabaptist viewpoints (some Anabaptists, such as Belthasar Hubmaier, were not pacifists) range in perspective from dualist views to more monist perspectives. By *dualism* I mean those Anabaptists who believed there was one ethical standard for the church (Jesus Christ) and another standard mandated by God for government (the sword). Many Mennonites have understood the Anabaptist tradition this way. Many regard the Schleitheim Confession of Faith of 1527 as the locus classicus for such a dualism. For the authors of Schleitheim, participation in government is questionable: particularly holding government office, since the essence of government is the sword. Other Anabaptists inclined to monism. *Monism* refers to the position that there is one ethical standard for both church and society. Taking Jesus Christ as the revelation of God, monists believe that God has one standard, not two. The God revealed in Christ is a God who seeks to redeem the world through the persuasive power of love. Hans Denck held this position, and it is close to the position of Menno Simons. Menno Simons' monist position is evident particularly in the statement where he calls Christians in government to follow the standard of Christ on the matter of capital punishment. For Denck's view of God as persuasive love, see his treatise, "Whether God is the Cause of Evil," in *Spiritual and Anabaptist Writers*, ed. George Williams (Philadelphia: Westminster, 1957), 88–111. Menno Simons says, "It would *hardly become a true Christ rule to shed blood.*" He goes on to argue against capital punishment. For a complete statement of his position, see *The Complete Writings*, ed. J. C. Wenger (Scottdale, Pa.: Herald Press, 1965), 920–921.

40. For a more thorough analysis of Romans 13:1–7, see John H. Yoder's *Politics of Jesus* (Grand Rapids: Eerdmans, 1972), 193–214.

41. Stassen, *Just Peacemaking: Ten Practices for Abolishing War*.

42. Mott, *A Christian Perspective*, 195.

43. The fourfold dimension of a Christian view of politics is developed more thoroughly in my book, *Christian Peacemaking*. See esp. chapters 3 and 4.

44. *Christian Peacemaking* spells out more completely the position I have outlined here.

45. For example, in 1980 the General Conference Mennonite Church passed a statement on abortion that included the following sentences: "We believe that the demands of discipleship are to be accepted voluntarily, not imposed legally upon everyone regardless of conviction. The New Testament church, as well as the church the three centuries before Constantine, was interested in working out what is morally responsible behavior *for Christians.* ... We do not believe that this [the church's position on abortion] position should be imposed upon the society in general. Because of the diversity of moral conviction in the civil community, we realize that what the law permits is not necessarily Christian moral behavior. We believe, however, that the church should witness to society concerning the sanctity of the fetus. We also believe that the church should be concerned that legislation not coerce people to act against their convictions and that it conform to standards of justice."

The concern for justice in the above statement refers to the fairness of laws with respect to how the law affects the poor (who under restrictive laws have less options) and the affluent (who have access to abortion in other states or countries with less restrictive laws). The entire statement on abortion is available from the General Conference Mennonite Church, Commission on Education, 722 Main St., Newton, Kan. 67114.

46. See "The Christian Origin of Human Rights" in Glen H. Stassen, *Just Peacemaking: Transforming Initiatives for Justice and Peace* (Louisville, Ky.: Westminster/John Knox, 1992).

47. Stanley Hauerwas, *After Christendom?* (Nashville: Abingdon Press, 1991).

48. Stassen, *Just Peacemaking: Transforming Initiatives*, 158.

49. Socialism has taken many forms other than Marxism. Socialism is a venerable tradition with deep roots in biblical ideas. We see these ideas expressed in the seventeenth-century left-wing Puritans. Christian socialism has influenced theologians as diverse as Karl Barth, Paul Tillich, and Reinhold Niebuhr. Michael Harrington has long been an advocate of democratic socialism. Its root value is an emphasis on community, which it translates structurally into cooperative forms of the control and ownership of production. The idea has been institutionalized in the Israeli kibbutz movement. It has inspired ideas and practices that have been integrated into such institutions as rural cooperatives, customer-owned cooperatives, and worker-owned cooperatives.

50. I am following Stephen Mott's description of Marxist socialism and other forms of socialism in his *A Christian Perspective on Political Thought*, 183–218.

51. Mott, *A Christian Perspective*, 187.

52. Mott, *A Christian Perspective*, 186.

53. Mott, *A Christian Perspective*, 193.

54. Hannah Arendt, *The Human Condition* (Chicago: University of Chicago Press, 1958), 237.

55. Volf, *Exclusion and Embrace*, 124–125, emphasis mine.

56. Fyodor Dostoyevsky, *The Brothers Karamazov*, trans. Constance Garnett (New York: The Modern Library, 1929), 362.

57. Dostoyevsky, *Brothers Karamazov*, 363.

58. Dostoyevsky, *Brothers Karamazov*, 384.

59. Toni Morrison, *Beloved* (New York: New American Library, 1987).

60. Dostoyevsky, *Brothers Karamazov*, 436–437.

61. See Friesen, *Christian Peacemaking*, 109–121, for a more thorough analysis of the Christian concept of justice. See also Philip LeMasters' analysis of how practical moral reasoning works in the church, *Discipleship for All Believers: Christian Ethics and the Kingdom of God* (Scottdale, Pa.: Herald Press, 1992), 89–101.

62. See Duane K. Friesen, *Mennonite Witness on Peace and Social Concerns: 1900–1980* (Akron, Pa.: Mennonite Central Committee, 1982).

63. Stassen, *Just Peacemaking: Transforming Initiatives*, 139.

64. John H. Yoder, "Sacrament as Social Process: Christ the Transformer of Culture," *Theology Today* 48/1 (1991): 38.

65. "Every member of the body as a 'gift' is an immediate alternative to vertical 'business' models of management. Paul's solidarity models of deliber-

ation correlate with the reason that the Japanese can make better cars than Detroit. It is not by accident or whim that I could use as labels the modern secular handles of 'egalitarianism,' 'democracy,' and 'socialism,' although each of these terms needs to be taken in a way different from their secularistic and individualistic usages" (Yoder, "Sacrament as Social Process: Christ the Transformer of Culture," 41). Yoder points out that he does not agree with Stanley Hauerwas, who warns Christians not even to use parallel secular terms like *equality* or *justice* because these are terms of the liberal establishment. Yoder agrees that we must be careful not to be co-opted by the secular use of terms, but we cannot avoid using terms in our culture, any of which can be co-opted, including those that Stanley Hauerwas uses, like *narrative* and *virtue*. Our job, Yoder says, is to use the language of our culture creatively by redefining it in the light of the vision of the church and the story of Jesus. The New Testament does this throughout. Paul uses military metaphors to convey the meaning of the Christian message without condoning militarism thereby. The Gospel of John uses the Greek concept of "logos," but the writer gives it his own special meaning.

66. For a description of this position on capital punishment, see Howard Zehr, *Death as a Penalty: A Moral, Practical and Theological Discussion* (Elkhart, Ind.: Mennonite Central Committee, 1983).

67. Howard Zehr, *Changing Lenses: A New Focus for Crime and Justice* (Scottdale, Pa.: Herald Press, 1990); Arthur P. Boers, *Justice That Heals: A Biblical Vision for Victims and Offenders* (Newton, Kan.: Faith and Life Press, 1992).

68. See Friesen, *Christian Peacemaking*. Four other works that make the case for Christian nonviolence are Martin L. King Jr., "Pilgrimage to Nonviolence," in *Stride Toward Freedom: The Montgomery Story* (New York: Harper & Row, 1958); John H. Yoder, *Politics of Jesus*; Stanley Hauerwas, *The Peaceable Kingdom* (Notre Dame, Ind.: University of Notre Dame Press, 1983); and Walter Wink, *Engaging the Powers*.

69. Stassen, *Just Peacemaking: Transforming Initiatives*, 33–51.

70. Walter Wink, *Engaging the Powers*.

71. Stassen, *Just Peacemaking: Transforming Initiatives*, 94.

72. See Stassen, "How Just Peacemaking Got Rid of the Missiles in Europe," *Just Peacemaking: Transforming Initiatives*, 114–134.

73. Elise Boulding, *Building a Global Civic Culture: Education for an Interdependent World* (New York: Columbia University, 1988).

74. Several paragraphs in this section are also in Duane Friesen, "Encourage Grassroots Peacemaking Groups and Voluntary Associations, in Stassen, *Just Peacemaking: Ten Practices for Abolishing War*, 176-188. An example of the persistence of an ecumenical organization of churches that made an impact on public policy is given in Renate Pratt's book, *In Good Faith: The Canadian Churches Against Apartheid* (Waterloo, Ont.: Wilfrid Laurier University Press, 1997). The persistence and competence of the Task Force on the Churches and Corporate Responsibility proved effective (1975–1990) as they engaged the corporate culture of economic organizations and kept in focus their moral vision of the church's commitment to justice.

75. John Richard Burkholder, "Mennonites in Ecumenical Dialogue on Peace and Justice," *MCC Occasional Paper* 7 (1988):15–16. Ideas from this section of the chapter are developed more thoroughly in Duane K. Friesen,

"The Anabaptist View of the Church," in *A Drink from the Stream*, ed. John K. Sheriff and Alain Epp Weaver (N. Newton, Kan.: Bethel College, 1991).

76. Reinhold Niebuhr, *The Children of Light and the Children of Darkness* (New York: Scribner), xi.

77. John H. Yoder, "The Christian Case for Democracy," in *The Priestly Kingdom* (University of Notre Dame Press, 1984), 166.

78. See Larry Rasmussen, *Earth Community, Earth Ethics* (Maryknoll, N.Y.: Orbis Books, 1996).

79. See the trilogy of books by Walter Wink: *Naming the Powers* (1984), *Unmasking the Powers* (1986), and *Engaging the Powers* (1992) (Philadelphia: Fortress).

CHAPTER EIGHT

1. See the appendix for a chart of the underlying Trinitarian structure of the Christian's role as philosopher, a lover of wisdom.

2. The revival of the study of this material was stimulated particularly by Gerhard von Rad, *Wisdom in Israel* (Nashville: Abingdon Press, 1972). See also James L. Crenshaw, *Old Testament Wisdom: An Introduction* (Atlanta: John Knox Press, 1981); the helpful summary of scholarship by Dianne Bergant, *What Are They Saying about Wisdom Literature?* (New York: Paulist Press, 1984); and the study by Roland E. Murphy, *The Tree of Life: An Exploration of Biblical Wisdom Literature* (Anchor Bible Reference Library; New York: Doubleday, 1990).

3. Murphy, *The Tree of Life*, 126.

4. Murphy, *The Tree of Life*, 147.

5. Murphy, *The Tree of Life*, 113.

6. Murphy, *The Tree of Life*, 113. The reference is to von Rad's *Wisdom in Israel*, 301.

7. William Orr and James Arthur Walther, *1 Corinthians* (Anchor Bible; Garden City, N.Y.: Doubleday, 1976). See 159, where the commentators make this point. They go on to state what I do not believe is warranted by the text. "Paul declares that this has been in the wisdom of God: the inability of the human mind to discover God has been part of God's wise plan" (160). They then appropriately add that "Paul does not develop this idea here." Indeed that is not Paul's view. The authors have injected their own assumptions about the qualitative difference between God's wisdom and human wisdom that render the human mind impotent to know God. I do not think that is Paul's view.

8. For an excellent account of how the major world religions have dealt with pluralism, both historically and among contemporary thinkers within these traditions, see the book by Harold Coward, *Pluralism: Challenge to World Religions* (Maryknoll, N.Y.: Orbis Books, 1985).

9. The word *fundamentalism* is a difficult term to define and perhaps we should not use it. It is often used pejoratively rather than descriptively—usually by an outsider to describe something with which they disagree. Almost no one uses the word *fundamentalism* to describe himself or herself. See the four volumes of the fundamentalism project of the American Academy of Arts and Sciences edited by Martin E. Marty and R. Scott Appleby (University of Chicago Press, 1991–1994). For a good analysis of the issues involved in

defining and describing fundamentalism, see the review of the project by Robert Wuthnow, *The Christian Century* (April 22, 1992): 426–429; and (April 29, 1992): 456–458.

10. See Stephen Carter, *The Culture of Disbelief* (New York: Basic Books, 1993), who seeks to defend the traditional idea of the separation of church and state in America without privatizing or trivializing religion.

11. See Miroslav Volf's critique of the relativism of various forms of post-modernism in *Exclusion and Embrace* (Nashville: Abingdon, 1996), particularly his critique of Lyotard (105–110), Derrida (202–203), Foucault (244–250), and Deleuze (286–290).

12. See James Davison Hunter, *Culture Wars: The Struggle to Define America* (New York: Basic Books, 1991), for an analysis of the conflict about how to define America. My description of the two extremes corresponds in part to what Hunter defines as different understandings of culture and of the relation of the public and private sectors of life in America today. My intention is not to define a Christian theology of culture in terms of either the orthodox or progressive position, as Hunter names these worldviews. My effort is to define a Christian alternative cultural model as a third way, an alternative to either of the two worldviews Hunter identifies as the basis of America's culture wars.

13. See Paul Tillich's *Dynamics of Faith* (New York: Harper Torchbooks, 1957).

14. For a description of the correlation between the structure of Luke/Acts and the message of the universal significance of the gospel, see Norman Perrin, *The New Testament: An Introduction* (New York: Harcourt Brace Jovanovich, 1974). See especially the outline at the end of chapter 9, 205–206.

15. Hans Küng and Karl-Josef Kuschel, ed. *A Global Ethic: The Declaration of the Parliament of the World's Religions* (New York: Continuum, 1993).

16. Volf, *Exclusion and Embrace*, 284–285.

17. John Hick, *An Interpretation of Religion: Human Responses to the Transcendent* (London: Macmillan, 1989).

18. Quoted by Harold Coward in his helpful analysis of a range of points of view in his book, *Pluralism: Challenge to World Religions*, 30.

19. See my analysis of the "religious" category in Troeltsch in Duane Friesen, "The Relationship Between Ernst Troeltsch's Theory of Religion and His Typology of Religious Association," Ph.D. diss, Harvard University, 1972. See especially chapter 2.

20. Ernst Troeltsch, "Christianity Among World Religions," in *Christian Thought: Its History and Application*, ed. Baron von Hugel (New York: Meridian Books, 1957), 61. Troeltsch died before he was able to deliver this lecture in London in March 1923.

21. Karl Barth, "The Revelation of God as the Abolition of Religion," in *Christianity and Other Religions*, ed. John Hick and Brian Hebblethwaite (Philadelphia: Fortress, 1980), 32–51.

22. See Alain Epp Weaver's analysis of the story of the Good Samaritan as a framework for understanding the relationship of the Christian faith to other religious traditions in "We All Drink from the Same Stream," *Mennonite Life* (March 1997): 10–18.

23. Epp Weaver, "We All Drink from the Same Stream," 25–26. In one of

his endnotes, Epp Weaver notes the political dimensions of the practice of the Lord's Supper, which we also noted in our discussion of the focal practices of the church. See also John H. Yoder's, *Body Politics* (Nashville: Discipleship Resources, 1992). "What is significant about Christian *iftars* is that, unlike Muslim *iftars* or communion, this bread-sharing takes place across religious boundaries. Middle Eastern Christians engaging in this practice are acting in accordance to Yoder's observation about interfaith relations that it is 'one's solidarity (civil, social, economic) with [one's interlocutor] as neighbor [that] is what must and can be defined' before evaluating the 'truth content or validity of the ideas or experiences of another religion as system or performance.' The question of truth certainly has its place, but Christians should first of all be concerned with discerning how to manifest God's nonviolent love by standing together with the marginalized and the oppressed, including those persons of other faiths" (28). Epp Weaver's quotation of Yoder comes from his essay, "The Disavowal of Constantine," in Michael G. Cartwright, ed. *The Royal Priesthood: Essays Ecclesiological and Ecumenical* (Grand Rapids: Eerdmans, 1995), 256.

24. Stanley Hauerwas, *The Peaceable Kingdom* (Notre Dame, Ind.: University of Notre Dame Press, 1983), 25–26.

25. See my critique of narrative ethics in *The Church as Theological Community: Essays in Honor of David Schroeder*, ed. Harry Huebner (Winnipeg: Canadian Mennonite Bible College, 1990), 234–241.

26. See Ian Barbour's approach, described in chapter 8. Particularly helpful are *Myths, Models and Paradigms* (New York: Harper & Row, 1974); and *Religion in an Age of Science* (San Francisco: Harper & Row, 1990).

27. Huebner, *The Church as Theological Community*, 235.

28. See how Peter Berger views the complementary relationship of Eastern and Western religious traditions in his book, *The Heretical Imperative* (New York: Anchor Books, 1979).

29. A vast literature has developed in the last several decades around the dialogue between Jews and Christians. This scholarly arena is one of the richest and most exciting areas of scholarly research.

30. If I understand Jacob Neusner accurately, the position I am arguing here is similar to his. He does not believe that there is a common Judaic-Christian tradition, but that Judaism and Christianity are two separate religious systems of meaning. He begins his book, "While these days Christians and Judaists undertake religious dialogue, there is not now and there never has been a dialogue between the religions, Judaism and Christianity. The conception of a Judeo-Christian tradition that Judaism and Christianity share is simply a myth in the bad old sense: a lie. ... Each of the two religious traditions pursues its own interests in its own way, addressing its own adherents with self-evidently valid answers to urgent and ineluctable questions" (ix). Dialogue begins on the basis of mutual respect and understanding. Jacob Neusner, *Jews and Christians: The Myth of a Common Tradition* (Philadelphia: Trinity Press International, 1991).

31. See the writings of the Vietnamese Buddhist monk, Thich Nhat Hanh, whose insights I have found helpful in my own life, esp. those in his earlier work, *The Miracle of Mindfulness* (Boston: Beacon Press, 1976). His writings can contribute to a richer understanding of Christian peace theology.

32. For an elaboration or defense of the pragmatic or ethical test as op-

posed to speculative metaphysical debates about truth, see Gordon Kaufman, "Christian Theology and the Modernization of the Religions," *Bangalore Theological Forum* 8/2 (1976): 81-118. This essay is reproduced in Kaufman's book, *The Theological Imagination: Constructing the Concept of God* (Philadelphia: Westminster, 1981) 172–206.

33. An excellent model of this soul-searching can be found in Rosemary Radford Ruether's book, *Faith and Fratricide: The Theological Roots of Anti-Semitism* (New York: Seabury Press, 1974).

34. For a fuller development of the idea of Christian mission as dialogical, see the article by John H. Yoder, "The Disavowal of Constantine: An Alternative Perspective on Interfaith Dialogue," *Tantur Year Book 1975/76* (Jerusalem: Ecumenical Institute for Advanced Theological Studies): 47–68.

35. Riffat Hassan, Muslim scholar from Pakistan and professor of religious studies at the University of Louisville, presented these ideas at a Middle East Symposium at Bethel College, N. Newton, Kan., April 9–11, 1989.

36. I have found a variety of recent works helpful. One of the more recent and thorough accounts is the jointly authored book by Nancey Murphy and George F. R. Ellis, *On the Moral Nature of the Universe: Theology, Cosmology, and Ethics* (Minneapolis: Fortress, 1996). Another by Nancey Murphy is *Theology in the Age of Scientific Reasoning* (Ithaca: Cornell University Press, 1990). A number of books by Ian Barbour are helpful: *Myths, Models and Paradigms* (New York: Harper & Row, 1974); *Issues in Science and Religion* (Englewood Cliffs, N.J.: Prentice Hall, 1966); *Religion in an Age of Science* (1990); and *Ethics in an Age of Technology* (1993), vols. 1 and 2 (Gifford Lectures 1989–1991; San Francisco: Harper & Row). See also John Cobb and Charles Birch, *The Liberation of Life: From the Cell to the Community* (New York: Cambridge University Press, 1981); and Arthur Peacocke, *God and the New Biology* (San Francisco: Harper & Row, 1986).

37. Barbour, *Religion in an Age of Science*, 31.

38. Barbour, *Religion in an Age of Science*, 33.

39. See Thomas Kuhn's significant book, *The Structure of Scientific Revolutions* (Chicago: University of Chicago Press, 1962).

40. Kuhn, *Structure of Scientific Revolutions*, 53–54.

41. Murphy and Ellis, *On the Moral Nature of the Universe*, 11.

42. Murphy and Ellis, *On the Moral Nature of the Universe*, 13.

43. See the following books by Ian Barbour, noted above: *Issues in Science and Religion*; *Myths, Models, and Paradigms*; and *Religion in an Age of Science*.

44. Peacocke, *God and the New Biology*. See the first two chapters, "The Sciences and Reductionism," and "Is Biology Nothing but Physics and Chemistry?"

45. Freud's argument in *The Future of an Illusion* (Garden City, N.Y.: Anchor Books, 1964) is a particularly good example of a reductionist approach.

46. See especially the work of John Cobb. One of the more comprehensive efforts to work out the connections between modern evolutionary biology and Christian theology is the book by Charles Birch and Cobb, *The Liberation of Life*.

47. Peacocke, *God and the New Biology*, 30. Another book that works with the notion of an interconnected set of hierarchical systems in understanding the universe is Kenneth Boulding's book, *The Image* (Ann Arbor,

Mich.: University of Michigan Press, 1956). Boulding helpfully discusses the levels of organization that build upon each other, from the biological level to human consciousness.

48. See the interesting theological questions posed by Stephen Hawking's book, *A Brief History of Time: From the Big Bang to Black Holes* (New York: Bantam Books, 1988).

49. Murphy and Ellis, *On the Moral Nature of the Universe*, xv.

50. Václav Havel, "Address of the President of the Czech Republic, His Excellency Václav Havel, on the Occasion of the Liberty Medal Ceremony," Philadelphia, July 4, 1994.

51. James M. Gustafson, *Intersections: Science, Theology Ethics* (Cleveland: Pilgrim Press, 1996), xvii.

52. Gustafson, *Intersections*, 4.

53. See Phyllis Trible, *God and the Rhetoric of Sexuality* (Philadelphia: Fortress, 1978). Trible argues that the reference to *adam* or *adamah* in the text may appropriately be translated "humankind," and that the text does not give a gender-specific identity to Adam as a man (15–21).

54. The Bible says practically nothing directly about the issue of abortion. Though persons support an anti-abortion stance with passages like Ps. 139:13-14, "thou it was who didst fashion my inward parts; thou didst knit me together in my mother's womb," this passage does not speak as such to the value of fetal life in relation to life that is already born. There is no doubt that life in the womb was highly valued, because it led to the birth of a child. We get more indirect guidance about *when* the Hebrews believed life began from Exodus 21:22-25: "When in the course of a brawl, a man knocks against a pregnant woman so that she has a miscarriage but suffers no further hurt, then the offender must pay whatever fine the woman's husband demands after assessment. Wherever hurt is done, you shall give life for life, eye for eye, tooth for tooth, hand for hand, foot for foot, burn for burn, bruise for bruise, wound for wound."

In this passage a miscarriage is an unintended result of a blow that is struck by another person in the course of a brawl. It does not speak directly to the issue of abortion where terminating a pregnancy is an intended action by the pregnant mother herself. The passage does, however, give an idea of the value attached to the fetus, which is of prime importance to the abortion issue. Some interpreters of this passage emphasize the high value attached to the fetus. Because killing the fetus is of concern to the community, recompense for injury must be paid to the woman's husband. However, the value seems not to be placed on the fetus as such, but on the property value of the fetus to the husband, who is to be compensated for its loss in the context of the covenant code of Exodus 20:22–23:19. The fetus is treated in the same way as other property, which must be compensated when it is damaged or destroyed.

A second line of interpretation of this passage emphasizes the higher value placed on the mother than on the fetus. For the death of the fetus, the husband is to be compensated with money, but where the wife suffers hurt or death, there shall be "life for life, eye for eye." This line of interpretation is reflected in the Jewish Talmud, a collection of Jewish rabbinical literature built up around the law. There it states explicitly that the fetus is not a separate entity, but part of the mother until it is born. Jewish law gives it a status inferior to a person already born, thus explaining why causing a miscarriage is a lesser crime than causing the death of the mother. The Talmud therefore justifies abortion: "If a woman has difficulty in childbirth, one dismembers the embryo within her limb for limb because her life takes precedence over its life. Once its head (or the greater part) has emerged, it may not be touched, for we do not set aside one life for another" *Mishnah* (Oholet 7, 6).

Once the head emerges, it become a human person and cannot be sacrificed for another person even if the mother's life is at stake. This seems to reflect the general view of the Hebrew Scriptures—that human personhood is associated with breath, which in the creation story is the life given by God.

This endnote comes from a statement on the biblical perspectives on abortion I prepared for an abortion study packet for the General Conference Mennonite Church in the late 1970s. John Connery discusses the interpretation of the Talmud in his book, *Abortion: The Development of the Roman Catholic Perspective* (Chicago: Loyola University Press, 1977), 15.

55. Lewis B. Smedes, *Mere Morality* (Grand Rapids: Eerdmans, 1983), 129.

56. See Daniel Callahan, "How Technology is Reframing the Abortion Debate," *Hastings Center Report* (Feb. 1986): 33–42.

57. Callahan, "How Technology is Reframing the Abortion Debate," 34.

Subject Index

Names and Places Index

Scripture Index

The Author

DUANE K. FRIESEN GREW UP on a farm in southeast Idaho. He received his B.A. degree from Bethel College, N. Newton, Kansas; his B.D. from Mennonite Biblical Seminary, Elkhart, Indiana; and his Th.D. in Christian social ethics from Harvard Divinity School, Cambridge, Massachusetts. He is currently Professor of Bible and Religion at Bethel College.

Friesen's work is informed by his deep involvement in the life of the church and in public policy issues. Among his goals is to communicate with the larger lay church community as well as the scholars. His interest in the arts has developed over a lifetime as a result of his training in piano as a youth, relationships with family members who are artists, and interactions with Bethel College colleagues. He intends *Artists, Citizens, Philosophers* to be informed by and in dialogue with the best scholarship even as it communicates with the lay reader interested in how church and culture should interrelate.

Among his many other books and writings, Friesen is author of *Christian Peacemaking and International Conflict: A Realistic Pacifist Perspective* (Herald Press, 1989). He serves on the Peace Committee of Mennonite Central Committee and is on the board of the Great Plains Seminary Education Program. He is a member of the Bethel College Mennonite Church and of the Society of Christian Ethics and the American Academy of Religion.

He is married to Elizabeth Friesen, and they have two daughters.